D1593805

STORM OF STEEL

A volume in the series *Cornell Studies in Security Affairs*

edited by Robert J. Art, Robert Jervis, and Stephen M. Walt

A full list of titles in the series appears at the end of the book.

STORM OF STEEL

Mary R. Habeck

The Development of Armor
Doctrine in Germany and the
Soviet Union, 1919–1939

CORNELL UNIVERSITY PRESS : ITHACA AND LONDON

First published 2003 by Cornell University Press

Printed in the United States of America

Library of Congress Cataloging-in-Publication Data

Habeck, Mary R.

    Storm of steel : the development of armor doctrine in Germany and the Soviet Union, 1919–1939 / Mary R. Habeck.

        p. cm — (Cornell studies in security affairs)

Includes bibliographical references and index.

    ISBN 0-8014-4074-2 (cloth : alk. paper)

    1. Tank warfare.   2. Military doctrine—Germany—History—20th century.   3. Military doctrine—Soviet Union—History—20th century.   I. Title.   II. Series.

    UE159 .H33   2003

    358'.18'094309041—dc   2002012501

Cloth printing   10 9 8 7 6 5 4 3 2 1

To every gray hair on my mother's head caused by this book.

And to my father, who never had the chance to read it.

Contents

Introduction

ON 22 JUNE 1941 Germany began a conflict with the Soviet Union that was the ultimate test of both countries' prewar planning. The German and Soviet militaries had spent the previous twenty years imagining future conflicts and arming their nations to win the coming war of technology. The results of the first few months of fighting seemed to show that the German army, after two decades of debate about armor doctrine, more correctly understood the nature of modern warfare than the Red Army. Yet, just five years before the outbreak of war, it was the Soviet army that had had the most advanced armor doctrine and organization in the world. Even more surprisingly, these ideas were similar to the concept, known as "blitzkrieg," that the Wehrmacht would use to overwhelm the Red Army during that desperate summer of 1941. Why the Germans, forbidden by the Versailles Treaty to own even a single tank, embraced an innovative and effective technique for using their mechanized forces, while the Soviet army adopted and then rejected a similar theory, is the central question in the development of armor doctrine in these two countries.

Most answers to this question emphasize internal factors. Bruce Gudmundsson, for instance, has persuasively argued that changes in German infantry tactics just before and during the First World War were the essential prerequisites for the later development of blitzkrieg.[1] Robert Citino tries to show that blitzkrieg was developed primarily in response to the threat from Poland. While surely an overstatement of the influence that the Polish state and army had on Reichswehr doctrine, his thesis does highlight the power that the perceived danger from the East had on the German army.[2] Another study by Citino argues that Hans von Seeckt laid the theoretical basis for blitzkrieg that later innovators would transform into a practical doctrine.[3] James Corum agrees with this interpretation of doctrinal develop-

---

1. Bruce I. Gudmundsson, *Stormtroop Tactics: Innovation in the German Army, 1914–1918* (New York: Praeger, 1989).

2. Robert M. Citino, *The Evolution of Blitzkrieg Tactics: Germany Defends Itself Against Poland, 1918–1933* (Westport, Conn.: Greenwood, 1987).

3. Robert M. Citino, *The Path to Blitzkrieg: Doctrine and Training in the Germany Army, 1920–1939* (Boulder, Colo.: Lynne Rienner, 1999).

ment in his closer study of Seeckt.[4] On the Soviet side, the earliest influence on doctrine was a desire to create a purely proletarian way of fighting, different from anything accepted by the capitalist world.[5] There is too the undeniable effect that certain extraordinary individuals, most especially Heinz Guderian, Mikhail Tukhachevskii, and Vladimir Triandafillov, had on doctrine in both countries.

Barry Posen's more general study of doctrinal development argues that a combination of factors such as defeat, external pressures, and institutional desires for expansion can push militaries to innovate.[6] Defeat would seem to help in understanding why Germany rethought doctrine, but does little for explicating processes within the Red Army. On the other hand, external pressure (the "capitalist encirclement") pushed the Soviet Union to consider changes in military theories, and may also have been a significant factor in Germany, which always saw itself as surrounded by hostile nations. But, while both the Soviet and the German militaries sought to expand during the interwar period, neither was able to do so until quite late. Stephen Rosen disputes the idea that defeat is a sufficient explanation for changes in doctrine, or that outsiders ("mavericks") can push militaries to innovate. He argues instead that the development of doctrine must be understood as an ideological struggle, generally between senior officers and younger inventive officers, who must be promoted for their ideas to succeed.[7] As we shall see, this analysis does help to understand at least some, but not all, of the dynamics in the disputes within both the German and Soviet armies.

The principal difficulty is that none of these explanations accounts for the adoption by the Red Army and the Wehrmacht of the very same doctrine. The easy answer, copying each other's ideas, can be discarded for a number of reasons.[8] In the first place, the two high commands came to their conclusions on doctrine almost simultaneously and in the case of the Germans, did not widely discuss this view of warfare which was in any case not accepted by everyone within the high command. In addition, the main conduit for sharing ideas on armor affairs, the military collaboration at Kazan, did not get under way until 1929, after most innovation on doctrine had already taken place. The other source of information about doctrine associated with the collaboration, the officer exchanges, also did not encourage

4. James S. Corum, *The Roots of Blitzkrieg: Hans von Seeckt and German Military Reform* (Lawrence: University of Kansas Press, 1992).

5. The first discussion of the doctrine is in M. V. Frunze, "Edinaia voennaia doktrina i Krasnaia armiia," *Armiia i Revoliutsiia*, no. 1 (1921): 13–29.

6. Barry Posen, *The Sources of Military Doctrine: France, Britain, and Germany between the World Wars* (Ithaca: Cornell University Press, 1984), 47, 54–55, 190.

7. Stephen Peter Rosen, *Winning the Next War: Innovation and the Modern Military* (Ithaca: Cornell University Press, 1991), 8–14, 20–21.

8. The Seatons argue that Soviet armor organization, technology, and doctrine was based on the German example and that they slavishly followed even minor changes in force structure. Albert Seaton and Joan Seaton, *The Soviet Army. 1918 to the Present* (New York: New American Library, 1986), 82–88, 90–92.

imitation. Most commanders in both armies were disdainful of the "primitive" ideas, technology, and attempts at implementation associated with the other military's armor forces. Rather than promoting a desire to copy ideas, the exchanges generally bolstered feelings of superiority in German and Soviet officers alike.[9]

A comparative study of the path that the two armies took during the interwar period offers another compelling explanation for the similarities in armor doctrine: shared influences and assumptions about war. The single most important element shared by both countries was an admiration for British concepts of tank warfare. Thanks to J. F. C. Fuller, the British army until 1929 had the most advanced ideas on armor use anywhere in the world, and British exercises and manuals profoundly affected German and Soviet thought.[10] Scholars have long recognized the effect that British thought had on German doctrine, although they disagree on its significance. Some, such as Charles Messenger, argue that blitzkrieg originated in Fuller's earliest explication of armor use, "Plan 1919," while Kenneth Macksey wrote that German armor doctrine was no more than British thought, modified slightly.[11] B. H. Liddell Hart believed that his own writing had played a major role in the development of blitzkrieg, and some German officers supported this claim.[12] Other scholars have sought to minimize the impact of British thought on German doctrine, preferring to stress internal factors.[13] As Dermot Bradley cautions, Guderian's enthusiasm for Liddell Hart's thought, which the German general described in his memoirs as existing even during the twenties, was in fact almost certainly the result of the friendship that the two men enjoyed after the Second World War.[14] Yet a comparison of sources in Germany and Russia shows that British ideas were a significant factor in armor doctrine development in both countries. Officers in the two armies urged their respective militaries to use British ideas and carefully followed maneuvers and publications in that country. Other sources of innovative thinking that affected both armies, such as the writings of a former Austrian officer named Fritz Heigl, were in many cases reinterpretations of British thought. By the late twenties, too, many specific characteristics of tank tactics and operational art in the two armies resembled British manuals and practice too closely for this to be mere coincidence. The logical explanation is that the Reichs-

9. The exception was German educational and training methods, which the Soviets did indeed imitate.

10. First described in J. F. C. Fuller, *The Reformation of War* (London: Hutchinson, 1922).

11. Charles Messenger, *The Art of Blitzkrieg* (London: Ian Allan, 1991), 29; Kenneth Macksey, *Tank Warfare: A History of Tanks in Battle* (London: Rupert Hart-Davis, 1971), 86, 92.

12. B. H. Liddell Hart, *The Memoirs of Liddell Hart.* vol. 1 (London: Cassell, 1965), 235; Erich von Manstein, *Aus einem Soldatenleben 1887–1939* (Bonn: Athenäum, 1958), 240–43.

13. Corum, for example, writes that Germany's armor doctrine did not come straight from the works of British theorists and especially not from the works of Liddell Hart. *Roots of Blitzkrieg*, 136–43.

14. Dermot Bradley, *Generaloberst Heinz Guderian und die Entstehungsgeschichte des modernen Blitzkrieges* (Osnabrück: Biblio, 1978), 152.

wehr and the Red Army did in fact use British experience and thought to aid the evolution of their own doctrine.[15]

Armor doctrine in both countries was, however, more than just a direct copy of
British thought. Immediately after the First World War, officers in the Reichswehr
and Red Army ignored Fuller and other British thinkers for cultural, ideological,
and technical reasons. The result was that until 1926 doctrine in Germany and the
Soviet Union had not changed much from the limited concepts of tank use pro-
mulgated during the war. Skeptical attitudes toward a more extensive employment
of armor were transformed by the second conditioning factor for a shared development of doctrine: radical improvements in tank technology. Once Britain produced the light, fast Vickers tank, many German and Soviet military thinkers began
to discard their prejudices against a war of machines. The question of how exactly
the new tanks would fight was another issue altogether. Some wanted to use armor
forces as more efficient infantry support, while others agreed with Fuller and his
British supporters that tanks should fight in independent operative formations far
from the foot soldiers, and preferably on the flanks and rear of the opponent.

It was at this point that a third factor, the contributions of certain key individuals, came into play. True, it would be misleading to conclude that these men, and
in particular Heinz Guderian, Mikhail Tukhachevskii and Vladimir Triandafillov,
were solely responsible for the elegant theories of war later known as "blitzkrieg"
and "deep battle." But there can be no doubt that all three, impressed by the new
tank and British ideas about its use, made major contributions to thought on armor. A lively controversy persists over how much credit should be assigned to these
"innovators," with historians especially divided over the part played by Guderian.
Some authorities conclude that the German general almost single-handedly invented blitzkrieg, or at least first proposed the concept of independent armor
units.[16] Others have argued that Guderian was not the sole author and founder of
either armor doctrine or the armor forces.[17] As one historian put it, tactical innovations do not "spring forth full-blown from the heads of certain consecrated individuals."[18] Erich von Manstein, who himself had a hand in the evolution of
German thought on tanks, more fairly wrote that the Wehrmacht would not have

15. In 1936 Guderian admitted as much in his seminal work on armor tactics, writing that German doctrine was largely based on British ideas, and specifically on the *Provisional Instructions on
Tank and Armoured Car Training, Part II, 1927*, although he cautioned that there were a number of
purely German features. Major-General Heinz Guderian, *Achtung – Panzer!* tr. Christopher Duffy
(London: Arms and Armour Press, 1992), 168.

16. General Nehring, *Die Geschichte der deutschen Panzerwaffe 1916 bis 1945* (Berlin: Propyläen Verlag, 1969), 56–59; Larry H. Addington, *The Blitzkrieg Era and the German General Staff, 1865–1941* (New
Brunswick, N.J.: Rutgers University Press, 1971), 33–36.

17. Corum, *Roots of Blitzkrieg*, 136–43.

18. S. J. Lewis, *Forgotten Legions: German Army Infantry Policy 1918–1941* (New York: Praeger, 1985),
xiv.

gotten their armor force without the tenacity and "fighting spirit" of Guderian. Yet he agreed that the General Staff as a whole had already thought about the use of large independent armor units long before Guderian came to power.[19] As we shall see, the development of German armor doctrine was a collective effort, involving beside Guderian such men as Ernst Volckheim, Alfred von Vollard-Bockelberg, Otto von Stülpnagel, and Oswald Lutz. Guderian would prove indispensable for the later implementation of the new ideas, but the record shows that he did not even become interested in armor until around 1929, that is, after the basic concepts were proposed and refined by other officers.

How much resistance Guderian and others ran into from the rest of the staff in their quest to have the army adopt the new ideas on tank doctrine and organization also remains controversial. In his later years Guderian would complain bitterly about the "conservative" attitude of Beck and other officers, which kept the German army from adopting blitzkrieg and from gathering all its tanks into the armor divisions. Other writers, including Guderian's close ally Walther Nehring, and some historians, agree with this interpretation of Beck's influence on the armor forces.[20] Herbert Schottelius and Gustav-Adolf Caspar put a slightly different spin on Beck's "opposition," contending that this stemmed not from a conservative attitude toward mechanization, but rather from a concern with preventing the creation of an army within the army.[21] At the other end of the spectrum are those scholars who argue that Beck favored mechanization, independent armor divisions, and the other elements of blitzkrieg, but felt compelled as well to raise the offensive power of the entire army by giving armor to the infantry.[22] Few take as reasonable a view of the debate as does Heinemann, who emphasizes Guderian's influence, while taking into account the role played by Beck.[23] As for opposition from the rest of the officer corps, scholars are evenly divided between supporters of Guderian's contentions and those who downplay any negative attitude of the

19. Manstein, *Aus einem Soldatenleben*, 240–43.

20. Heinz Guderian, *Erinnerungen eines Soldaten* (Heidelberg: Kurt Vowinckel, 1951), 26–27; Kenneth Macksey, *Guderian. Creator of the Blitzkrieg* (New York: Stein and Day, 1975), 61, 63–64; Kurt J. Walde, *Guderian* (Frankfurt: Ullstein, 1976), 44–45; Nehring, *Geschichte der deutschen Panzerwaffe*, 71, 73–74.

21. Herbert Schottelius and Gustav-Adolf Caspar, "Die Organisation des Heeres 1933–1939" in *Handbuch zur deutschen Militärgeschichte 1648–1939*, vol. 8: *Wehrmacht und Nationalsozialismus (1933–1939)*, ed. Hans Meier-Welcker and Wolfgang von Groote (Munich: Bernard & Graefe, 1978), 343.

22. See Klaus-Jürgen Müller, *Armee, Politik und Gesellschaft in Deutschland 1933–1945* (Paderborn: Ferdinand Schöningh, 1979), 88–91; Robert J. O'Neill, "Fritsch, Beck and the Führer," in *Hitler's Generals*, ed. Corelli Barnett (London: Weidenfeld and Nicolson, 1989), 28; Wilhelm Deist, *The Wehrmacht and German Rearmament* (Toronto: University of Toronto Press, 1981), 42–43; Hubertus Senff, *Die Entwicklung der Panzerwaffe im deutschen Heer zwischen den beiden Weltkriegen* (Frankfurt am Main: E. S. Mittler, 1969), 20, 29; Manstein, *Aus einem Soldatenleben*, 240–41.

23. W. Heinemann, "The Development of German Armoured Forces 1918–40," in *Armoured Warfare*, ed. J. P. Harris and F. H. Toase (London: Batsford, 1990), 51–69.

staff to blitzkrieg. S. J. Lewis and Corum, for instance, argue that the staff as a whole had already accepted the idea of large armor units by the time Guderian was in position to push for more emphasis on tanks, and that he did not have to struggle against a reactionary military establishment.[24] Yet as others have pointed out, there is ample documentation of resistance from certain quarters to the new ideas of mobile armor warfare.[25] The balance of the evidence suggests that Beck and the majority of the high command did indeed support ideas similar to those of Guderian, Lutz and other innovators, but that there were strong currents within the officer corps which tried to "moderate" what was seen as a radical and impractical view of warfare.

If scholars are divided over how much credit to give Guderian, they also disagree about the exact part played by Tukhachevskii, Triandafillov, and other military thinkers in Soviet armor doctrine development. Scholars like Isserson, Stoecker, and Simpkin attribute the majority of the work in creating and implementing deep battle to Tukhachevskii.[26] As with German doctrine, however, the creation of deep battle was the work of more than just one man: Vladimir Triandafillov, Konstantin Kalinovskii, Aleksandr Egorov, and Aleksandr Sediakin all profoundly affected Soviet thought on the subject. Tukhachevskii of course added vital touches to the deep battle/deep operations concept, yet the records show that Kalinovskii and Triandafillov also proposed ideas that later writers, including Tukhachevskii and Sediakin, would transform into a well-explicated theory of combat. Isserson's impassioned defense of Tukhachevskii's unique role in the development of deep battle probably has more to do with the time at which he was writing (not long after the Soviet government rehabilitated the purged marshal), and his personal friendship with Tukhachevskii, than with a balanced presentation of that officer's contributions.

Regardless of the support of Tukhachevskii, Guderian, and the others, the new tank doctrines would not have been adopted by the Germans or Soviets if their leaders had not agreed with and supported the ideas. Both Hitler and Stalin were interested in military technology, kept themselves informed of the latest developments in armor affairs, and generally supported the "radical" proposals of the tank advo-

24. Lewis, *Forgotten Legions*, 50–52; Corum. *Roots of Blitzkrieg*, 136–143. See also Manstein, *Aus einem Soldatenleben*, 240–41.

25. Posen, *Sources of Military Doctrine*, 209–10; B. H. Liddell Hart, *The Other Side of the Hill* (London: Macmillan, 1993), 65, 122. Gordon shows that even before the development of blitzkrieg, there was ample room for discontent on the part of junior against senior officers, caused, in his opinion, by the subordination of the younger men who had however commanded large units in the Freikorps. Harold J. Gordon, Jr., *The Reichswehr and the German Republic 1919–1926* (Princeton, N.J.: Princeton University Press, 1957), 86–87.

26. G. Isserson, "Zapiski sovremennika o M. N. Tukhachevskom," *VIZh*, no. 4 (April 1963): 64–78; Sally Stoecker, *Forging Stalin's Army: Marshal Tukhachevsky and the Politics of Military Innovation* (Boulder, Colo.: Westview, 1998); Richard Simpkin, *Deep Battle. The Brainchild of Marshal Tukhachevskii* (London: Brassey, 1987). Simpkin recognizes the part played by Triandafillov, although he gives Tukhachevskii the lion's share of credit (32).

cates. Manstein and Guderian commented on Hitler's attention to technical details, and the German leader's direct intervention placed Guderian in a position to push more forcefully for the armor division idea.[27] Posen is certainly overstating the case, however, when he argues that German doctrine was largely the creation of Hitler.[28] The Führer influenced doctrine only in the broadest outlines, by favoring an offensive technological type of combat, and had little or no say in the details of the German way of war. In the Soviet Union, Stalin took a personal interest in armaments and technology, including tanks, and had at least some input into the selection of models, but again did not determine doctrine.[29] The coincidence of the two leaders' enthusiasm for modern weaponry meant, however, that before 1936 in the Soviet Union, and after 1933 in Germany, the more revolutionary armor innovators such as Tukhachevskii and Guderian were able to implement their ideas.

In addition to the support of their nations' leaders, the adoption of the nearly identical doctrines suggested by armor innovators was aided by the fact that the German and Soviet officer corps held similar views on the basic principles of combat. Solely for internal reasons, each was committed to an offensive, mobile way of fighting that used technology, but did not neglect the infantry, in a combined-arms battle deep in the enemy's positions. Although some historians contend that the Germans developed these ideas by completely rethinking their views of war after defeat in the world war, the balance of the evidence suggests that Posen is right in this regard: both the Reichswehr and the Red Army simply grafted new pieces of technology onto old doctrines.[30] Unlike the French army, which decided that the basic principles of combat no longer held for modern conflicts, the Germans concluded that defeat had been a purely technical matter and not the result of doctrinal failure. As scholars have pointed out, the innovative use of tanks, airplanes, and motorized units on the battlefields of the next war resulted then from an accommodation of traditional doctrine to new technology.[31] Using different reasoning, the Soviets decided that an offensive, mobile style of combined-arms combat that exploited technology but gave equal weight to a mass army best fit the world's first proletarian state, and thus adopted principles of warfare that coincidentally matched those of the German army.[32]

27. Guderian, *Erinnerungen eines Soldaten*, 53–55; Manstein, *Aus einem Soldatenleben*, 216.

28. Posen, *Sources of Military Doctrine*, 179, 210–13.

29. See e.g. Albert Seaton, *Stalin As Warlord* (London: Batsford, 1976), 86–89.

30. Posen, *Sources of Military Doctrine*, 55; also Citino, *Evolution of Blitzkrieg Tactics*, 196.

31. Addington, *Blitzkrieg Era*, 29; Lewis, *Forgotten Legions*, 45. Posen argues that the German military needed stability and certainty in everything, including doctrine, in order to rebuild. Other factors that added to their desire for an offensive doctrine may have been the type of army imposed on Germany and Germany's international situation, surrounded by states that the army perceived as hostile. Posen, *Sources of Military Doctrine*, 184–88.

32. David M. Glantz analyzes the proletarian military doctrine in *Soviet Military Operational Art: In Pursuit of Deep Battle* (London: Frank Cass, 1991), 65.

Finally, the Red Army faced a challenge that the Germans did not: the need to create a military-industrial complex before considering the mechanization and motorization of the army. The successes of tank and automobile production after 1928 encouraged the Soviets toward ever more radical visions of the machine in warfare. This was a common phenomenon of the first Five Year Plan. As Peter Rutland has shown, there were two basic justifications for growth given during the debates over industrialization, the so-called "genetic" and "teleological" arguments. The genetic argument said that planning should use available resources to determine policy, while those who favored a teleological approach thought that growth should be based on where policymakers wanted to go.[33] In the case of armor affairs, there is evidence to suggest that a genetic argument shaped thought on doctrine and organizational structures in the late twenties and early thirties.[34] This interpretation is challenged by other scholars, who believe that industrialization followed military planning rather than preceded it.[35] The archival evidence shows that even before the industrialization push, Tukhachevskii and others in the high command did recognize the need to modernize the Red Army both technically and tactically. As one Soviet author pointed out, however, Tukhachevskii's most important memorandum on this point discussed airplanes, artillery, and strategic cavalry, but failed to mention armor forces.[36] Only after the Five Year Plan had begun to create an industrial base that could produce thousands of tanks annually did he realize that his old ideas of armor warfare had perforce become obsolete. Other commanders had already suggested the theoretical groundwork for deep battle, but as the Plan progressed, Tukhachevskii's (and others') schemes for using armor in battle became even more ambitious. The most radical idea of all, deep battle/ deep operations, was a result of the underlying factors discussed above coupled with the vision of huge tank armies that the successes of industrialization encouraged.

If the Second World War had begun in 1936, then, the Soviet Union and Germany would have entered the conflict with nearly identical armor doctrines. Instead the Soviet army decided in that crucial juncture to undo all that Tukhachevskii, Triandafillov, Sediakin, and the others had worked so long to achieve. The reasons for this decision were threefold: a failure to implement the deep battle idea, the discrediting of those who supported the concept, and the lessons of small wars.

33. Peter Rutland, *The Myth of the Plan: Lessons of Soviet Planning Experience* (London: Hutchinson, 1985), 78–79.

34. Bayer argues that the Red Army tailored its doctrine to suit the new weapons of industrialization. Philip A. Bayer, *The Evolution of the Soviet General Staff, 1917–1941* (New York: Garland, 1987), 182.

35. Harriet Fast Scott and William F. Scott, *Soviet Military Doctrine: Continuity, Formulation, and Dissemination* (Boulder, Colo.: Westview, 1988), 13.

36. A. Ryzhakov, "K voprosu o stroitel'stve bronetankovykh voisk krasnoi armii v 30-e gody," *VIZh*, no. 8 (August 1968): 105.

Throughout the thirties, the Red Army held numerous exercises designed to test and perfect deep battle. Almost without exception, the maneuvers were dismal failures, and by 1935 many in the high command were not certain that it would ever be possible to use the concept in actual combat. When Tukhachevskii was executed for treason in 1937, the idea, already under attack, was thoroughly discredited. Soon many of the officers who had helped to oversee the development of deep battle were under suspicion and would shortly vanish into the maelstrom of the purges as well. Added to these two elements were the lessons from the small wars fought by Red Army forces during this period: the conflicts with Japan in the Far Eastern borderlands, the Spanish Civil War, the invasion of Poland, and the winter war with Finland. With the exception of Zhukov's use of tanks at Khalkhin-gol, the armor forces performed poorly in these campaigns, leading the new high command to conclude that they had been correct to jettison deep battle. Only after the swift defeat of France in 1940 did the officer corps rethink this conclusion, and by June 1941 it had begun to reintroduce the organizational and theoretical structures of deep battle.

Yet it would be wrong to conclude that the Germans had worked out their own concepts perfectly by 1941. Although able to overwhelm the Polish, French and British armies, and to do the same in the early part of the war to the Soviet Union, the Wehrmacht ran into trouble in late summer 1941. The Germans penetrated Soviet defenses deeply, but had difficulty completing encirclements before Red Army forces retreated. This was due to a seminal weakness with the blitzkrieg idea, which became apparent only in the depths of the Soviet Union: the failure to solve long-standing problems with logistics and armor-infantry cooperation. German difficulty in supplying its mechanized forces across the vast plains of Ukraine and Belarus has already been recognized as one reason that the Wehrmacht failed to defeat the Red Army that first year.[37] The other obstacle to the conquest of the Soviet Union is less well known, yet ever since the creation of the first fast tanks, the German military had realized that it would be difficult to coordinate the action of the new machines with the slower foot soldiers. The correct answer was armored personnel carriers for the infantry, but the Wehrmacht high command was slow to recognize this and German industry was even slower to produce them. For the wars in Poland and France, the differential in speed did not much matter, since the distances to be crossed by soldiers on foot were not that great. But in the expanses of the Soviet Union, the failure to find an answer to the dilemma of armor-infantry cooperation, added to severe problems with logistics and weather, would be fatal.

37. Rudolf Steiger, *Panzertaktik im Spiegel deutscher Kriegstagebücher, 1939–1941* (Freiburg: Rombach, 1973), 145–162; see Kenneth Macksey, "The Smolensk Operation 7 July–7 August 1941," in *The Initial Period of War on the Eastern Front, 22 June–August 1941*, ed. David M. Glantz (London: Frank Cass, 1993), 346–47, for a discussion of the first appearance of this problem.

STORM OF STEEL

CHAPTER ONE

The Unfinished Machine, 1919–1923

HE TANK appeared on the battlefield in 1916, as large as an elephant and just as frightening to ordinary German soldiers as Pyrrhus's "secret weapon" had been to the Romans. Somewhat to their own surprise the British and French created a phenomenon new to the war: outright panic among the best infantrymen in the world. The Germans had to invent a new word, "tank horror," to describe the panic inspired by the first use of these "monsters,"[1] and there was some hope among the Allies that they had found, at last, an answer to the stalemate of the Western Front. In battles at Cambrai and Amiens the ungainly machines seemed to live up to this expectation, first shocking the Germans and then pushing through the front to create the largest breakthroughs of the war. The British, who had invented the tank, were particularly heartened by the successes of their armor forces and officers like J. F. C. Fuller were soon dreaming of the day when the machines would end the useless bloodshed of modern industrial war.[2]

Unfortunately for these early hopes, while the early tank could and did frighten unprepared soldiers, its defining characteristic was an imperfect technical design. It was first suggested by Winston Churchill in 1915 as the "land ship" that would break through the trench system on the Western Front, and engineers had only one year to create and test a completely new piece of technology. The result was obvious from the first time the British deployed the machines in the autumn of 1916. The small number of tanks available for use terrified the German troops, but they were also clumsy and noisy, and broke down frequently on the battlefield. The heavy tanks used in this battle, the British Mark series, were also incredibly slow, moving at no more than two to three miles per hour on the crater-filled battlefield. As soon as the German infantry stopped running, they also saw that the lumbering machines could be rather easily picked off by artillery fire. Later models developed by both the French and British were lighter and somewhat faster, but had only thin

---

1. The German words were "Tankschrecken" and "Ungeheuer" or "Ungetüm" all of which were frequently used in the early German literature on the machines.

2. One of the best descriptions of the early use of tanks in the War is still J. F. C. Fuller, *Tanks in the Great War, 1914–1918* (London: Murray, 1920). Fuller's first full analysis of the coming war of machines is in J. F. C. Fuller, *The Reformation of War* (London: Hutchinson, 1922).

armor and machine guns, making them even more vulnerable to artillery and infantry fire. The frightening vehicles made an impressive entrance on the Western Front, but European armies were divided between officers who focused on the successes of early armor warfare and those who saw only the tank's limited technical capabilities.

The German military establishment, once past their initial surprise at the successes of the early tanks, generally chose to emphasize, even overemphasize, their failings. This attitude had nothing to do with a natural disinclination to use new technology, a charge later leveled at the high command by its critics. In fact the Reichswehr had earlier found and used quite effectively technical answers to trench warfare (most especially gas, mortars, flamethrowers, and massive artillery pieces) that nearly broke the Allied lines. The British and the French adapted quickly, however, and soon were producing their own "frightful" weapons to answer German inventiveness. Realizing that the homeland could not afford to produce ever more expensive technology, by 1916 the German army became more interested in a tactical innovation known as "stormtroop tactics" that promised to create a strategic breakthrough without any manufacturing costs. Stormtroop tactics were predicated on a new conceptualization of the battlefield; one in which taking the entire front was no longer the goal of the army. Instead, picked forces would probe the line ahead of the main body of troops, seeking to push through any weak spots and creating gaps in the enemy line that reserves could exploit opportunistically.[3] Stormtroop tactics caught the attention of the Reichswehr high command because they were based on three concepts that were seminal to German thinking about warfare: first, that the infantry had to be the core of any offensive; second, that to succeed the infantry had to cooperate closely with the other forces (in this case the artillery) in a combined-arms battle; and third, that local initiative (Auftragstaktik, or mission-based tactics) – giving low-ranking commanders in the field leeway to take advantage of favorable conditions and act as they saw fit – was absolutely vital for victory.

Just as the German high command was considering the new tactics, the sudden appearance of huge and noisy machines able to crush the strongest defensive placements shocked even the most battle-hardened of troops. Given that tanks had broken through in areas that normally would have repulsed the strongest infantry and artillery assaults, the immediate response by part of the officer corps was to call for the development of a German tank that would be able to imitate the success of the Allies.[4] Other officers were not convinced that the new weapon had any value at all.

---

3. Bruce I. Gudmundsson, *Stormtrooper Tactics: Innovation in the German Army, 1914–1918* (New York: Praeger, 1989); Timothy Lupfer, *The Dynamics of Doctrine: The Changes in German Tactical Doctrine during the First World War*, Leavenworth papers, no. 4 (Fort Leavenworth, Kansas: Combat Studies Institute, 1981).

4. Ernst Volckheim, *Die deutschen Kampfwagen im Weltkriege* (Berlin: Mittler, 1923), 18.

Analyses of battles in which tanks had taken part showed that even in those clashes in which they had been most successful, German troops had been able to blunt the assault, bring artillery to bear, and retake lost ground.[5] The fear caused by tanks persisted among the ordinary soldiers, but if one could stop this initial reaction, then the technical failings of the machines made tank attacks easy to repulse. In November 1917, Ludendorff distributed a memorandum on defensive measures against tanks in which he warned against this denigration of tanks, while acknowledging that it was, for the most part, justified.[6]

The strict discipline of the German army, along with a growing conviction that tanks were not the omnipotent weapon soldiers had first thought them, thus combined to dissipate the fear of the tank.[7] In a short while notable triumphs in defeating tank attacks considerably lessened the first enthusiasm in the General Staff for developing a native version of the weapon.[8] The lower priority given to tanks, together with the new enthusiasm for stormtrooper tactics, helped to delay the deployment of the tank by almost two years. Yet the high command was forced by the limited successes of Allied tanks in 1916 and 1917 to acknowledge that the machines might have some use in positional warfare, and they requested the construction of a German version. The vehicle turned out by industry, the A7V, was even more technically flawed than the British or French tanks, which only added to the high command's reluctance to depend on armor.[9] By the beginning of 1918, German industry had managed to build only fifteen A7Vs, plus another five for a reserve. Added to the thirty British and French tanks that the army had captured in earlier clashes, there was a grand total of forty-five German tanks set to oppose the hundreds of the Allies.[10]

In January 1918, as these tanks prepared to take part in the coming spring offensive, Ludendorff issued a handbook entitled *Guide for the Deployment of Armored Vehicle Assault Units* that set out the official views of the General Staff on tank usage. The guide dealt with concrete problems of command, control, and terrain reconnaissance, as well as tank tactics, reflecting the German army's practical experi-

---

5. A fact which was later acknowledged even by the tank enthusiasts. See B. H. Liddell Hart, *The Real War, 1914–1918* (London: Faber & Faber, 1930), 369–80.

6. "Abwehrmaßnahmen gegen Tanks," 24 November 1917, BA-MA, PH 3/294.

7. For interesting descriptions by ordinary German soldiers of how they felt once the horror of the "flame-spewing monsters" had faded, see Hauptmann Wegner, "Panzerwagen und Kampfwagen (Tanks)" in *Die Militärischen Lehren des Großen Krieges*, ed. M. Schwarte (Berlin: Mittler, 1920), 176–77.

8. For example, the recapture of the territory lost during the famous tank battle of Cambrai, as described by Liddell Hart, *The Real War*, 369–80.

9. The designer of the A7V was a German engineer named Vollmer, who would later design a tank for the Soviet army. See below, chapter 3. Barton Whaley, *Covert German Rearmament, 1919–1939: Deception and Misperception* (Frederick, Md.: University Publications of America, 1984), 31, 32.

10. Guderian, "Kraftfahrkampftruppen," *Militär-Wissenschaftliche Rundschau*, no. 1, 1936, p. 56.

ence in the war. Interestingly enough, rather than placing tanks at the disposal of the infantry or cavalry, the General Staff chose to separate them bureaucratically from the main army branches, subordinating them directly to the Army High Command or, when assigned to an army, to the Commander of Motor Vehicle Troops. This would become significant when the German army began rearming with modern weaponry during the thirties, since it created a precedent for a separate organization for tank forces that could serve as a model for the Wehrmacht. The tank doctrine that the booklet suggested was, not surprisingly, similar to that of the Allies. The main mission of tanks was "by offensive action, to support the advance of the infantry through (a) rolling over and destroying enemy obstacles, (b) the suppression of enemy troops, in particular those occupying bases and machine gun nests, (c) the repulsion of enemy counterstrikes."[11] Like the stormtroopers, tanks were not to attack the strongest point of the enemy but rather to push through a weakly occupied front, exploiting their surprise appearance to clear the way for an infantry breakthrough. The description in the handbook of an actual tank attack, in line with accepted German practice, gave only general principles and left the particulars to local commanders. Tanks were to fight in several waves, for instance, but there were no guidelines on how many of these there should be or what types of tanks would fight in each. Other details of the battle were similarly vague, left to the discretion of the officers on the spot and to the special conditions of each battle.

The one exception to this general rule was the infantry's role, which the handbook took care to describe in detail. Constant, very close contact with the infantry was of vital importance for a tank attack and should always be maintained. While tanks could create a tactical breakthrough, they were unable to hold any territory gained, and therefore they would require infantry to follow them closely. Tank crews themselves were to take part in the infantry battle, either to act as shock troops or to man machine gun bases for defense against counterthrusts. The concepts that tanks should stay in very close contract with infantry and that tanks were unable to hold territory constituted the core of German armor doctrine for the next ten years. Together they implied that tanks, and thus the entire tempo of an attack, had to remain tied to the speed of the infantry. This conception of the role of the infantry vis-à-vis tanks was prompted both by the German army's commitment to the infantry as the heart of the army and by the common image of the tank as a delicate machine that could not be trusted to function throughout the entire battle. Only in the twenties, when the tank became faster and technically more perfected, would some military thinkers begin to question the idea of tying the armor forces so closely to the infantry.

Equipped with the General Staff's guide, the new German "Assault Armored Vehicle Units," consisting of five tanks each, saw action more than ten times between

---

11. This and the discussion following are from "Anleitung für die Verwendung von Sturm-Panzerkarftwagen-Abteilungen," 18 January 1918. BA-MA, PH 3/355, pp. 1–3.

March and November 1918.[12] In the spring Hindenburg launched what he hoped would be the final offensive of the war using troops from the now quiet Eastern Front to reinforce the army in the West. The offensive was at first successful, pushing back the exhausted British and French units almost at will. But for those officers who had hoped that the new weapon would prove worthwhile, tank combat during the offensive was a disappointment. The small number of the vehicles available for deployment during any single battle was the source of one major problem, since Allied use of tanks had been most successful when they had massed for a single effort.[13] In the attack by the German army on Villers-Bretonneux, the largest clash of the war in which both the Allies and the Germans fielded tanks, only three German tank units, fifteen A7V's in all, took part.[14]

The technical shortcomings of the German tanks, and the ease with which the Allies could destroy them, created more serious problems. The A7V was a heavy tank, with thick armor and a large number of machine guns and main guns which ought to have provided protection against its natural enemy, the artillery. It was, however, even slower on the battlefield than the British Mark series, with a newly designed engine and tread parts that engineers had not completely perfected. In addition, due to the way in which the caterpillar treads were fitted onto the vehicle, it was unable to maneuver on rough terrain as well as other tanks.[15] All this made the vehicles vulnerable to artillery fire and to mishaps in the deep trenches and bomb craters that covered First World War battlefields. It was no wonder that the main impression their own tank made on the German officer corps was of a weapon useful for terrorizing ill-trained troops, but unsuited for more complex missions.

This lukewarm feeling for tanks changed completely during the Allied counteroffensive, where armor played an important role in several key battles. As soon as the German advance had exhausted itself, the Allies began an offensive that would end only in November with the defeat of the Kaiser's army. On 8 August 1918, which Ludendorff would later bemoan as the "black day of the German Army," the Allies pushed back German troops from Amiens, gains made possible only because tanks were able to create the initial breakthrough.[16] The British used their tanks in waves, divided according to weight and armament, to punch through the German trenches and lead the infantry, who followed closely, into the enemy's deep rear. The German high command, belatedly conscious that the machines could make a difference, formulated ambitious plans to expand their tank and armored car corps for the 1919 campaign. Then came the devastating, and for some in the officer

---

12. Wegner, "Panzerwagen und Kampfwagen," 178–80.

13. In their most successful tank battle of the war, 415 British and French tanks attacked at one time. Fuller, *Tanks in the Great War*, 223.

14. Wegner, "Panzerwagen und Kampfwagen," 179.

15. Volckheim, *Die deutschen Kampfwagen im Weltkriege*, 5, 7–11, 30.

16. Erich von Ludendorff, *My War Memories, 1914–1918*, 2 vols. (London: Hutchinson, 1919), 2:679–80.

corps, unexpected declaration of a cease-fire on 11 November. The German soldier had, however, seen enough war, and as soon as the Armistice came into effect, whole units melted away. Yet there were officers who believed that this was nothing more than a pause to reach terms with the enemy rather than a surrender, and they did not give up hope that some day soon plans for an armor force might be fulfilled.[17] During the months between the end of fighting and the signing of the peace treaty, official planning for the future of the German military was thus only in a state of suspension, not outright cancellation, while the army waited for the final terms from Versailles. Unofficial evaluations of the war and plans to rebuild the army began almost immediately, as high-ranking officers in both the War Ministry and the Great General Staff expressed their opinions about the tactics and organization appropriate for the new army that would emerge from the peace negotiations.

In April 1919 a series of articles entitled "Contributions to the Reconstruction of Our Army" showed how the German army was thinking about its future. None of the articles dealt directly with the question of tanks, but two of them, subtitled "Do We Still Need Cavalry?" and written by General Max von Poseck, the head of the German cavalry, showed how the high command felt about machine warfare. Poseck wrote to answer those officers who argued that Western Front–type warfare had ended forever the usefulness of the cavalry, and that some sort of machine should replace the horse. He examined the uses of the cavalry during the war, especially on the Eastern Front, and concluded that the horse had been, and still was, indispensable for both reconnaissance and combat. Although the overwhelming firepower of machine guns and heavy artillery had limited the usefulness of the cavalry on the Western Front, the mobile warfare in the East, where the cavalry had appeared in a much better light, might prove to be more typical of future conflicts. The General Staff could not, therefore, neglect training men for battle on horseback when rebuilding the army.[18]

Other members of the officer corps, generally young men who had served on the Western Front, disagreed with this attitude and suggested that the reconstructed Reichswehr pay more attention to technical developments than had the old Prussian-dominated army. They thought that the military establishment had responded too slowly to new technology in general and tanks in particular. One representative of this faction wrote a memorandum to Wilhelm Groener, the new Quartermaster General, to contend that a lack of understanding of and training and interest in technology in the General Staff, the exclusion of civilian engineers from the technical equipping of the army, and limited intelligence about the enemy's technological progress had retarded the development of a German tank. He recom-

17. Guderian, "Kraftfahrkampftruppen," 56.
18. Generalmajor v. Poseck, "Beitrag zum Wiederaufbau unseres Heeres: Brauchen wir noch Kavallerie?," Militär-Wochenblatt, nos. 118 (1919): 2151–58; 119 (1919): 2177–86.

mended that the new army include technical training for officers to foster an interest in the subject among the leading ranks of the army.[19]

There was a middle ground between these two ways of viewing machine warfare, although it is uncertain how many officers chose to occupy it. Writing several days after Poseck's piece appeared, a young cavalry officer concluded that it was the use of cavalry *in cooperation with* tanks that had allowed the Allies to push back the German army during the terrible August offensives, and eventually, to achieve victory. The army had "considerably undervalued" the tank, while the British, French, and Americans had found a way to combine machines and horses in order to return to the cavalry their old combat capabilities. The Allies had also been able to stop some of the infantry bloodletting during their offensives by allowing men to advance behind tanks, while German soldiers had broken and run in those final months when confronted by tanks and bold infantry in their front and cavalry in their rear.[20]

The positions that these three officers articulated – one pro-armor, one procavalry (and infantry) and a third trying to find some middle ground – were forerunners of later arguments about the lessons of the world war and the use of machines in warfare that would dominate discussions in the German military throughout the twenties.

In the meantime, Germany was still awaiting notification of the terms of the peace treaty. There was some hope in the high command that these would be lenient, since the army had, after all, asked for a cease-fire while still in possession of at least part of the field. There were also Wilson's Fourteen Points, the ostensible basis for the Armistice, which renounced the annexation of land; and, more pragmatically, the Allies' need to have a buffer state to block the westward expansion of a new threat from the east – Soviet Russia.[21] The disclosure of the treaty's harsh conditions created a shock wave throughout the nation and the officer corps.[22] The forced limitation of the army to only one hundred thousand men, the huge reparations, the "war guilt" clause, the elimination of the Great General Staff, and the occupation of the best industrial areas of their country were difficult enough to swallow, but just as galling were the uncompromising provisions that governed the modern weapons produced during the war. The Allies would oversee

19. Muths, "Denkschrift über die Technik im deutschen Heere," BA-MA, N 46/132, pp. 21–28. Groener responded that the tank had arisen out of trench warfare, which no one could have foreseen. The army thus could not be blamed for its slow response to the appearance of the tank. Ibid., marginalia.

20. Major v. Troschke, "Kavallerie und Tanks," *Militär-Wochenblatt*, no. 127 (1919): 2339–42.

21. Seeckt hoped that the latter consideration would sway Allied opinion even after the signing of the treaty. "Zur Eingabe der Landeskammer der Provinz Schlesien vom 14.2.20," BA-MA, N 247/89.

22. See Erfurth for a look at the fight over the Versailles Treaty and the strong opposition of the Reichswehr to signing. Waldemar Erfurth, *Die Geschichte des deutschen Generalstabes von 1918 bis 1945* (Göttingen: Musterschmidt, 1960), 41–48.

the collection and destruction of all airplanes, submarines, heavy artillery pieces, and tanks and their use, production or importation by the Reichswehr was forbidden in perpetuity.[23] At one stroke, the Entente powers had reduced the German military from a world-class fighting machine to the ranks of the most primitive of armies. Further developments in the field of tank doctrine would henceforth depend on a more abstract working out of the problem.

At precisely this moment the new Soviet regime was facing similar problems with its armor forces. The Bolsheviks inherited a collapsed economy and prostrate country, one just as incapable of producing any complicated military technology as Germany after the Versailles Treaty. The war against Austria-Hungary and the German empire had pushed Russian industry, in 1914 just beginning to develop fully, to its limits. The stresses placed upon the economy, and upon the workers who had to produce for the war, along with defeats at the front, had allowed the Bolsheviks to seize power. Once in control they had more important matters on their minds than tanks. The tsar's supporters – the Whites – almost immediately began an uprising against the new socialist government. The desperate civil war that now developed meant that Lenin, Trotsky, and the other rulers of Soviet Russia had to concentrate on simply surviving. There was in addition the fact that the tsarist empire had never built any tanks and the Germans had not used the few tanks that they possessed against the Russians, so that the new Red Army inherited neither experience with, nor examples of, the new weapons.[24] The Soviets thus started at a distinct disadvantage when attempting to evaluate how tanks would affect the future of warfare, and depended on a second-hand analysis of Allied deployment of the new technology. The earliest Soviet conceptions of armor doctrine were, in fact, little more than borrowings from Allied and German war experiences.

Two short Red Army handbooks, *Armored Cars (Tanks) – A New Type of Combat Artillery* (1918), and *What Tanks Are and How to Combat Them* (1919), demonstrated this fact clearly. The starting point for the examination of tank tactics in both booklets was the positional war of the Western Front, and they assumed that commanders would use tanks in wars of the same type in the future. Both authors visualized tanks inserted into battle to create panic among the enemy through their sudden and frightening appearance. The battle of Amiens of August 1918 was the primary

23. The terms governing tanks and other weapons are in articles 165–71, 181, and 198–202 of the treaty. *Conditions of Peace of the Allied and Associated Powers* (Berlin: Engelmann, 1919), 77–78, 84, 89–90. Seeckt, who was the leading military expert in the German delegation at Versailles, had hoped for an army of at least three hundred thousand and general conscription. F. L. Carsten, *The Reichswehr and Politics 1918 to 1933* (Oxford: Clarendon, 1966), 37.

24. Although the Soviets did manage to produce a few copies of the French Renault tank in 1920, the first true Soviet tanks were made long after the end of the Russian Civil War. Report to Deputy Chairman, RVS SSSR, from Kuibyshev, Temporary Commander, Moscow military district, and Bulin, Member of District RVS, 3 June 1928. RGVA, f. 27, op. 1, d. 344, ll. 143–56.

model for the rest of their tank tactics. As during this battle, the vehicles would advance en masse and in echelons to provide close support for infantry in breaking through strongly fortified fronts. When describing in more detail exactly how tanks would do this, they followed British armor tactics closely. As in First World War battles, a line of light tanks would crush wire entanglements and other obstacles on their way to the enemy's rear.[25] This would open a path that the infantry could follow through the enemy front line. A second wave, made up of heavier tanks, would support the first by directing its fire against more stubborn points of resistance. Working with the infantry, who would follow them closely, the tanks would clear trenches and destroy machine gun nests before moving deeper behind enemy lines.[26]

Only in their final statements on the worth of tanks did the two analyses diverge significantly. The writer of the earlier booklet, while acknowledging that the new technology still had many shortcomings, believed that tanks had changed forever the future of warfare. On the Western Front

> innumerable numbers of steel monsters more than once smashed the stubbornness and fortitude of the German forces' first-class military training and education! Henceforth the war, having lasted more than four years, had entered a new phase of struggle – a war of machines! The time of the old, neat battle picture, a time of complete poetry, had passed forever – a soulless machine had replaced everything, technology would dominate in every aspect, and the victor would be he who was more richly and more completely supplied with technology![27]

The war of machines that this author greeted with such enthusiasm evoked a very different response from the author of the later booklet. Writing at the beginning of the Civil War and Allied intervention, he emphasized the weaknesses and failures of tanks and concluded that "the tank is a machine, and like any machine, easily susceptible to damage."[28] The two opinions reflected in these accounts would find expression in later years in a split between Soviet thinkers who believed that the tank had revolutionized warfare, and those who saw themselves as realistically evaluating the new weapon.

While the reliance by early Soviet military thinkers on Western ideas may seem out of place in the context of a society that explicitly defined itself as revolutionary and anti-Western, it had the support of the new War Commissar, Leon Trotsky. During the Revolution Trotsky played a major role by rousing worker support for the

---

25. For a complete description of tank tactics see Fuller, *Tanks in the Great War.*

26. Odobreno Voenno-Tekhnicheskoi Redaktsiei, *Bronevye avtomobili (tanki) – novoe boevoe sredstvo artillerii,* (Moscow: Izdatel'stvo Vserossiiskogo Tsentral'nogo Ispolnitel'nogo Komiteta, Voennyi Otdel, 1918), 6–7; *Chto takoe tanki i kak s nimi borot'sia* (Moscow: Izdatel'stvo Vserossiiskogo Tsentral'nogo Ispolnitel'nogo Komiteta, Voennyi Otdel, 1919), 6–8.

27. *Bronevye avtomobili (tanki),* 12.

28. *Chto takoe tanki i kak s nimi borot'sia,* 9–15.

Bolshevik platform and by planning and helping to execute the actual seizure of power. In recognition of his contribution, Trotsky was made head of the new Red Army and a key member of the leadership circle. He also quickly became one of the main ideologues of the party, and as such was able to influence the direction that the Soviet army would take over the first few critical years of its life.

Trotsky's military philosophy reflected his general belief (and that of Lenin) in a pragmatic reaction to events. He argued forcefully that the young army could not afford to ignore the collective wisdom of the ages by labeling it "bourgeois." In speeches and articles he insisted that science (and military science in particular) was outside the bounds of any ideology, containing its own logic that had to be followed by capitalist and proletarian alike. This attitude would inform his decision to permit "military specialists," a euphemism for former tsarist officials – including members of the old officer corps – to hold their old positions and work for the new Soviet regime. Trotsky also argued as early as March 1918 that the Russian proletariat was not yet mature enough to take on all the various functions that former officers had performed. While it was imperative for communists to control the military administration, the Red Army needed these highly trained men, as long as they remained loyal, to fulfill the technical and operational/strategic side of military work.[29] One month later, he again answered critics of his support for tsarist officers by saying that, although this was not the ideal policy, "[i]n questions of a purely military, operational, and even more so in questions that are purely combat oriented, military specialists in every institution have the decisive word." The proletariat was simply not capable of producing instantly the new officers and technical leaders that the army desperately needed.[30] As long as Trotsky was War Commissar, the specialists, and thus the ideas on tactics and doctrine that they proposed, had the grudging support of the Soviet government.

The intervention by the Allies in the Civil War then transformed the purely theoretical nature of early Soviet tank doctrine into a more practical evaluation of the machines' capabilities. From the first, the term "Whites" gave both the Bolsheviks and outside observers a false image of unity within the anti-Soviet resistance. In fact the leadership of the widely separated opposition armies was split among a number of former tsarist officers, each of whom refused to cooperate with the others. The result was that the Civil War took place as a series of disjointed attacks on Bolshevik-controlled territory which lasted until after 1920 and included a separate war with Poland. The Soviets were able to beat back the separate assaults, moving their forces from one part of the country to the next in time to face another offensive before any of the White armies could overrun either Petrograd or Moscow. The entire

29. Leon Trotskii, "'Novaia Armiia': Rech' v Alekseevskom Narodnom Dome 22 marta 1918g. (v den' Krasnoi Armii)," in KVR, 3:99–100.

30. Leon Trotskii, "'Krasnaia Armiia': Rech' na zasedenii V.Ts.I.K. 22 aprelia 1918g.," ibid., 1:102–3.

character of the war changed when the Allied nations decided to intervene in the conflict to help defeat the Bolsheviks. None of the assistance provided to the various White commanders was enough to determine the outcome of the war, but it was sufficient to convince the Bolsheviks that the entire capitalist world had combined with their internal enemies to destroy them – the beginning of the Communist belief in a "capitalist encirclement" that would not fade until the new Soviet state was no more. After the end of hostilities with Germany, the British supplied tanks and crews as part of their aid to the Whites. In March 1919, the first shipment of twelve tanks arrived in southern Russia where Anton Denikin, the head of one White army, used them to support his offensives. Nikolai Yudenich, commander of the White Russian Northwestern Army, also received a few of the weapons.[31] By the fall of 1919, tanks had taken part in several engagements and shown considerable promise, particularly in their ability to frighten the largely peasant Red Army.[32]

There was a natural tendency to exaggerate the abilities of these "steel monsters" – Red soldiers who faced the machines in fact reported that it was useless to fight them, since tanks could crush not only men and trees but whole cities as well.[33] Matters deteriorated so quickly that Trotsky felt compelled to issue a special appeal in October to Bolshevik troops "to stop the shameful panic in our ranks which takes place when Tanks appear."[34] Trotsky's plea, along with tough enforcement of an earlier order to shoot deserters, seemed to have some effect.[35] At the battle of Detskoe Selo later in October, the Red infantry was able to fight successfully a small number of tanks.[36] One month later the British reported that in Yudenich's attack on Petrograd there were particularly heavy casualties inflicted on the enemy "as he made some attempt to stand in contrast to his usual tactics of retiring as soon as Tanks were known to be in the vicinity."[37]

The surprise appearance on the Bolshevik side of a few vehicles that they called "tanks" may also have bolstered Red Army morale during the battle for Petrograd. Built in that city, the car-like machines had armor and caterpillar treads, but were so unlike the British idea of a true tank that the latter ridiculed the pretension of the Reds.[38] Trotsky, present in the city to direct its defense personally, thought that the

---

31. WO106/377, Weekly Tank Notes no. 54 (23 August 1919) and Weekly Tank Notes no. 59 (27 September 1919).

32. WO 106/377, Weekly Tank Notes no. 62 (18 October 1919), and "Operation Reports of 1st Division of Russian Tank Corps" for 18 May–3 August 1919.

33. *Chto takoe tanki*, 3.

34. Quoted in WO 106/377, Weekly Tank Notes no. 64 (1 November 1919).

35. Trotskii, "Prikaz Predsedatelia Revvoensoveta Respubliki i Narkomvoenmora ot 6 iiunia 1919g, No. 107, st. Balakleia," KVR, 2a:200.

36. P. Gladkov, *Taktika bronevykh chastei: Kurs voennoi akademii* (Moscow: Vysshii Voennii Redaktsionnyi Sovet, 1924), 23.

37. WO 106/377, Weekly Tank Notes no. 66 (15 November 1919).

38. Ibid.

"tanks" took part in battle with some success, lukewarm praise that suggests they did very little to help the Bolsheviks.[39] To encourage any men still frightened by enemy tank attacks, he drafted an article on the vehicles in which he also gave some insight into how he viewed them. After stating that there was no need to fear a machine that succeeded only by frightening the unprepared, he wrote that "tanks play a large role in positional warfare. Where on a certain sector soldiers sit unmoving in trenches, tanks, able to crawl across trenches, can cause a great deal of damage. It is only necessary for them to act with surprise, in a large mass, by the tens and hundreds. But in our field war, two-three tanks cannot play a serious role." We are making our own tanks, he continued, and these have done as well as the enemy's, "but in and of themselves, tanks – either the English or ours – cannot decide the issue. Everything depends on the living people, on their bravery, consciousness, resoluteness, and dedication to the cause of the working class."[40] If it came to a choice between machines and morale, Trotsky threw in his lot with the human spirit.[41]

The capture of a considerable number of the British tanks did much to strengthen the morale of Bolshevik troops. The Reds had taken no more than four tanks before the end of 1919. Since it was very probable that their crews managed to damage these before abandoning them, they were of little use to the Reds.[42] In 1920, however, the White positions that had received British weapons suffered their first serious defeats and the number of tank captures increased dramatically. The fall of Taganrog, where the British army had set up a "mechanical school" in early 1919, delivered twenty-five of the machines to the Reds in January.[43] Later that same month, another fifteen tanks fell into Bolshevik hands after battles near Rostov and Novocherkassk.[44] Throughout the year, the Whites received replacement tanks from both the French and the British and just as quickly lost them to the Bolsheviks. Although many of the captured vehicles were certainly damaged beyond repair, the Red Army for the first time had enough to use them in battle against the very enemy who had built them.[45]

Commanders in the field, too impatient to wait for the central authorities to tell

39. Trotskii, "Perelom," KVR, 2:406.

40. Trotskii, "Tanki," ibid., 411–12.

41. To encourage bravery in the ranks of Petrograd's defenders, he also ordered the arrest of families of traitors and the immediate shooting of anyone who tried to cause panic. Trotskii, "Prikaz Predsedatelia Revvoensoveta Respubliki i Narkomvoenmora po 7-i armii ot 2 noiabria 1919g, No. 163, gor. Petrograd," ibid., 430.

42. "Svedeniia o broneotriadakh, nakhodiashchikhsia na Iuzhnom Fronte," 27 May 1919. RGVA, f. 27 (Upravlenie Bronevykh Sil RKKA), op. 1, d. 145, ll. 191; information on number of vehicles taken, 27 June 1919. RGVA, f. 27, op. 1, d. 145, ll. 298–303; WO 106/377, Weekly Tank Notes no. 69, 6 December 1919.

43. WO 106/377, Weekly Tank Notes no. 59, 27 September 1919; Weekly Tank Notes no. 78, 14 February 1920.

44. WO 106/377, Weekly Tank Notes no.o. 74, 17 January 1920.

45. See RGVA, f. 101, op. 1, d. 95, ll. 127–30; reprinted in T. F. Kariaeva, ed., M. V. Frunze na iuzhnom fronte: Sbornik dokumentov (Frunze: Kyrgyzstan, 1988), 107–9.

them how to use their new prizes, threw together their own tank units on the spot.[46] In April, the new Inspector of Armor Units, Kotovskii, had to circulate instructions to ad hoc armor units ordering them to send captured tanks to the rear for formation into regular detachments.[47] A month later the Revolutionary Military Council (RVS), the central command for the Soviet military, felt that the Red Army possessed enough tanks to warrant formulating the first official battle order for an "Auto-Tank Detachment." The battle order called for only three tanks in each unit, evidence both for the small number of tanks that the Red Army had captured and for their intention not to use the weapons en masse. It also provided for a mixture of one heavy, one medium, and one light tank in a detachment, an indication that the Reds continued to foresee different battle missions for the three types of tanks.[48]

The first engagements involving the new tank units took place that summer. The young Red Army, exhausted by almost two years of constant fighting, turned from the destruction of Denikin to face an invasion of the thinly held western territories by Poland. Under the leadership of Mikhail Tukhachevskii, the Red Army managed to halt Pilsudski's offensive in June. Tukhachevskii was a former tsarist officer, a lieutenant who had become convinced that Communist ideology, and the Bolsheviks, were correct. Throughout the Civil War he had shown a certain professionalism, if not brilliance, in his command of various units. His actions during the war with Poland would, however, both make his reputation as a military genius and provide the ammunition for his later downfall. By early July Tukhachevskii had gathered enough forces to launch his own attack and, pushing the overstretched Polish army back through Belorussia in less than a month, began to move towards the border with Poland. The First Cavalry Army, led by Semën Budënnyi and Iosif Stalin, and already famous for its actions across the southern Russian plains, handled much of the fighting.[49] On the occasions when the Poles were able to dig in before the arrival of the cavalry, however, the Reds called for tanks to force them out of their trenches. A small clash at Ziabka, a town near the Polish border, was typical of early use of the new machines. The 2nd Tank Detachment and the 14th Armored Car Detachment, working together with an armored train and the 15th Army, created a breakthrough in a fortified position. The battle began with the use of the train to distract attention from a short artillery barrage on the Polish positions. This diversion permitted the surprise appearance of the tanks on the battlefield and their successful breakthrough. The 14th Armored Car Detachment and

46. A not uncommon problem. See Sbornik sekretnykh prikazov RVSR 1919, no. 57, 4 January 1919. RGVA, f. 4, op. 3, d. 30, l. 15; and Sbornik sekretnykh prikazov RVSR 1919, no. 1213/230, 31 June 1919, RGVA, f. 4, op. 3, d. 31, l. 122.

47. Circular Memorandum from Kotovskii to the heads of armor units of fronts and armies, 13 April 1920, RGVA, f. 27, op. 1, d. 89, l. 60.

48. Sbornik sekretnykh prikazov RVSR 1920, no. 905/160, 28 May 1920. RGVA, f. 4, op. 3, d. 34, l. 288.

49. See S. Budënnyi, *Proidënnyi put'*, 3 vols. (Moscow: Voennoe Izdatel'stvo Ministerstva Oborony SSSR, 1958–1965), 2:26–68.

the cavalry then exploited the success.[50] Some of the tactics employed in this battle, including the use of a short artillery barrage rather than a protracted one and cooperation with other types of mobile forces, would appear later in textbooks as standard armor doctrine.

Despite the successes won in minor battles such as this, the Soviet military establishment had little time to spare for a minor weapon like the tank. This was evident in the way that they handled training and staffing for new armor units. In the first place, the high command did not overly concern itself with the problem of finding men who knew how to use tanks in battle or who had the training necessary to repair their complex machinery. A series of requests by the Armor Department, a section of the Main Military Engineering Directorate (GVIU), were ignored by the General Staff, which decided that bourgeois specialists were too valuable a commodity to spare on tank units.[51] They instead suggested training Red Army men to replace specialists, although at that point the new country had no way to train them owing to the "complete absence of appropriate equipment."[52] To remedy the situation Kotovskii and the head of GVIU proposed the creation of a special unit to prepare Red specialists for service in tank detachments.[53] The RVS did not issue the order authorizing this to proceed, however, until the end of September.[54] The Soviet military thus took more than six months, from the capture of the first significant numbers of tanks until the establishment of the training unit, to create the basic support system necessary for deploying tanks in battle – and this during a time of war, when an army is likely to make decisions about militarily important matters most quickly. The organization of the new training unit did not mean that enough men were available to use tanks properly. In October the RVS noted that armor units were still employing women, a sign that they had not yet prepared enough men to replace them.[55]

The neglect of the tank stemmed not only from the technical failings of the machine, but also from the fact that the highly fluid warfare of both the Civil War and the war with Poland favored forces able to move and attack quickly, not those designed for slow, systematic trench battles. Fronts shifted radically throughout the years of combat, and the cavalry, viewed by some Western authorities as having out-

50. S. Keler, Kratkii uchebnik po bronevomu delu (Moscow: Vysshii Voennyi Redaktsionnyi Sovet, 1922), 34–36.

51. Memorandum to the Field Staff of the RVS from Korostashev, Chief of GVIU, and Kotovskii, 26 August 1920. RGVA, f. 27, op. 1, d. 167, l. 9.

52. Ibid., and Letter to the Inspector of Armor Units, from Fleisner, May 1920. RGVA, f. 27, op. 1, d. 89, l. 151.

53. "Polozheniia ob otdel'nom zapasnom divizione formirovanii i popolnenii tankovykh otriadov," Kotovskii and Korostashev, 14 July 1920. RGVA, f. 27, op. 1, d. 167, ll. 10–11.

54. Sbornik sekretnykh prikazov RVSR 1920, no. 1961/368, 28 September 1920, RGVA, f. 4, op. 3, d. 34, ll. 536–38.

55. Sbornik sekretnykh prikazov RVSR 1920, no. 2058/395, 6 October 1920, RGVA, f. 4, op. 3, d. 34, l. 568.

lived its usefulness on the modern battlefield, could still fulfill its old functions on the Russian plains. Many Reds thus preferred horses above the cumbersome machines captured from the Whites, even before the war with Poland. In September 1919 Trotsky had already issued an article entitled "Proletariat, to Horse!" which called for the Red Army to take the old tsarist cavalry, that most reactionary of forces, and use it in the name of the workers. He argued that, while in the world war the cavalry had only played a minor role, in the very mobile conditions of the Civil War the significance of the horse had increased. The Reds would use cavalry to effect breakthroughs and deep encirclements, and to cut through to the rear of the enemy, all missions that the early Soviet writers had visualized the tank performing.[56] Another commander, fighting on the southwestern front, agreed with this and in fact argued that the progress of technology could not make cavalry obsolete, because the more technology advanced, the more cavalry could be perfected.[57] In the later debates over the relative merits of the horse and the machine, the fact that the Red cavalry had performed well throughout both conflicts would lend a great deal of credibility to its claim to relevance in modern warfare.

Once the Soviet high command had decided to proceed with training men in the mechanical operation of tanks, however reluctantly, the next step was to instill in the new specialists a knowledge of the tactics necessary to use the machines in larger-scale combat. In earlier battles, such as that at Ziabka, Red commanders had employed tanks as little more than terror weapons. After the tanks had frightened the enemy out of their trenches, they stood back while other mobile forces, including cavalry and armored cars, finished them off. Attempting to make Soviet tank usage more sophisticated, Inspector Kotovskii prepared a short guide entitled *Instructions for the Employment of Tanks in the Worker-Peasant Red Army*. The guide was most remarkable for its slavish adherence to Western Front tactics, although Kotovskii added minor adjustments to reflect lessons learned from the Civil War. Again emphasizing the importance of the technical capabilities of the new weapons, the instructions began with the positive and negative characteristics of tanks. Kotovskii noted their ability to operate in most sorts of terrain, their great maneuverability, thick armor, and damaging effect on the morale of the enemy. but he devoted more space to their numerous drawbacks: their low speed, small radius of action, constant need for oil and other supplies, vulnerability to breakdowns, and the high temperatures and poor ventilation inside them. Tanks were, in short, fit for use as auxiliary weapons but not meant for independent action. They would assist the primary force, the infantry, by delivering short and crushing blows on an enemy in fortified positions, as they had done during the world war.[58]

56. Trotskii, "Proletarii, na konia!" KVR, 2:287–88.

57. Grigorov, "Znachenie konnitsy v sovremennykh voinakh," *Revoliutsionnyi front*, no. 8 (1920): 28–29.

58. "Instruktsiia po primeneiiu tankov v Raboche-Krest'ianskoi Krasnoi Armii," RGVA, f. 27, op. 1, d. 167, l. 17.

When describing the missions that tanks should perform the instructions again differed in only minor respects from world war experience and earlier Soviet conceptions. As before, tanks would help to create breakthroughs, destroy barricades and wire entanglements, and sow panic among the enemy infantry, although Kotovskii also recommended that tanks act like mobile artillery, directing flanking fire on enemy positions, or, like cavalry, destroy lines of communication in the enemy's rear.[59] Near the end of the instructions, he detailed how exactly tanks would fulfill these missions, departing only slightly from the familiar tactics of the Western Front. In a normal offensive, he thought, the tank detachment should divide into two echelons. One wave would advance through defensive positions without firing until it had reached their rear, and only then open fire on the enemy's reserves. The second echelon would clear approaches of obstacles and then concentrate on helping the artillery by focusing flanking fire on the opponent's infantry hiding in trenches. The cavalry and infantry would follow immediately behind the vehicles, using the approaches that the second group of tanks had cleared to allow them to occupy the enemy's positions.[60] The concepts outlined by Kotovskii and other armor experts, including the distribution of tank units into different echelons determined by mission and the vision of the other forces working together to support the armor attack, would shortly become standard Soviet doctrine.[61]

Thus, although the Russian Civil War and the war with Poland in their sweeping advances and retreats were completely unlike the trench warfare that had produced the tank and early ideas of how to use the machine, the Soviet concept of an armor battle remained basically unaltered. Influenced above all by the faulty technology of existing tanks, Soviet officers concluded that a more significant use of them was simply impossible. The power of the available engines combined with the difficult terrain over which they fought dictated the slow speed of tanks in battle. Limited fuel supplies and the effects on the crew of the heat, noise, and bad air kept advances to no more than twenty miles before rest and refueling became necessary. Tanks shook severely when their engines were running, effectively preventing accurate fire even if they were stationary, and thus making more understandable the decision by tacticians to concentrate on the shock effect of tanks, rather than their firepower. Less reasonably, but consistent with their conviction about the relative unimportance of tanks, Soviet commanders expected them to remain near the infantry throughout the battle. Though some of the vehicles were capable of fighting far from the lines of advancing foot soldiers, armor theorists envisaged tanks acting as little more than moving shields for the infantry.

It is instructive to compare Soviet tank doctrine with their ideas for the other mo-

59. Ibid., ll. 18–19.

60. Ibid., ll. 19–20.

61. See also S. Mikheev, *Tanki i boevoe ikh primenenie* (Moscow: Izdanie Literaturno-Izdatel'skogo Otdela Politicheskogo Upravleniia Revoensoveta Respubliki, 1920).

bile land forces, cavalry and armored cars, as this illuminates the question of how they might have used the tank, absent its logistical and technological problems. In June 1920 Kotovskii prepared a draft handbook, *Short Instructions for Commanders of Front and Army Armor Units on Battle Command/Control and Employment of Armor Units.* The handbook applied to all types of armor units, including tanks, but contained separate instructions for armored cars. Unlike the battle for positions in which he and other writers envisaged the use of tanks, his tactics for armored car units called for "(a) a short battle, relying on the surprise and speed of [their] appearance, the invulnerability of the units, strength of firepower and moral effect, (b) avoiding the use of armor units for prolonged battle missions of a positional character."[62] Cars were to exploit fully their quickness and maneuverability to speed through the enemy's front lines and fortified positions, disrupting supply lines, creating confusion in the rear, and aiding in the pursuit. The tactics that Kotovskii expected from armored cars were, in fact, the familiar ones of the other force that combined mobility and firepower, the cavalry. The Red cavalry was famous for its speed of maneuver, quick attacks on the flanks and rear of the enemy, use in pursuits, and exploitation of tactical successes.[63] Although tanks too could maneuver and possessed even greater firepower, Red commanders realized that technological weaknesses prevented any more sophisticated use of the machines, and thus assigned them limited missions compared to those of the other mobile forces. It is significant, however, for later developments that Kotovskii and others hoped to imitate some traditional cavalry tactics by having tanks drive through enemy positions to attack the rear or to exploit successes together with the other mobile forces.

The RVS adopted Kotovskii's guide for tank use, with some minor changes, in September 1920.[64] A few days later the RVS also issued the final draft of the *Short Instructions* for armor units, extensively modified.[65] Kotovskii's first draft had stated that the General Staff should permit officers in armor units to take part in decisions about concentrations of armor.[66] In his comments on this point, the Inspector for Infantry argued that armor units were auxiliary weapons, no more able than the artillery or engineering troops to operate independently. Armor units should take their orders from the combined-arms commander, who was responsible for coordinating the action of the different types of forces on the battlefield.[67] Like the Ger-

62. "Kratkaia Instruktsiia Nachal'nikom Bronechastei Frontov i Armii dlia Boevogo Upravlenia i Primeneniia Bronevykh Chastei" (June 1920), RGVA, f. 27, op. 1, d. 89, l. 359.

63. See Budënnyi, *Proidënnyi put'.*

64. Sbornik sekretnykh prikazov RVSR 1920, no. 1741/331 6 (September 1920), RGVA, f. 4, op. 3, d. 34, ll. 496–503.

65. Ibid., l. 503.

66. "Kratkaia Instruktsiia Nachal'nikom Bronechastei Frontov i Armii dlia Boevogo Upravlenia i Primeneniia Bronevykh Chastei" (June 1920), RGVA, f. 27, op. 1, d. 89, l. 359.

67. "Zakliuchenie k Kratkoi Instruktsii 'Nachal'nikam Bronechastei Frontov i Armii dlia Boevogo Upravleniia i Primeneiia Bronesil'" from Temporary Infantry Inspector of the Field Staff of the RVSR, 27 June 1920, RGVA, f. 27, op. 1, d. 89, l. 417.

mans before them, the Soviets visualized tanks with a force structure separate from the infantry and cavalry, but firmly under the control of one overall commander. The Infantry Inspector's argument prevailed, reflecting a desire by the Soviet high command to have all forces cooperate closely on the battlefield, and the final version of the instructions gave control of armor unit deployment to the combined-arms commanders.[68]

Unfortunately for Soviet attempts to put their new tactics into effect, the technical imperfections of the early tanks intervened. By early October 1920, the Bolsheviks had eleven tank units, consisting of some thirty machines altogether, ready for battle.[69] Although GVIU was able to deploy four of the eleven tank units on the southwestern and Caucasian fronts, they had to send the remainder of the vehicles to reserve armies at Kazan and Moscow for "organization and repair in the rear."[70] This problem plagued the Reds throughout both the Civil and the Polish wars. From June through December 1920 alone, the Sormov and Kharkov factories worked on at least forty-one tanks; in just fifteen days during August, the Sormov factory had to repair fifteen small tanks.[71] Throughout the rest of the year, no more than five tank units, consisting of about eighteen tanks in all, were able to take the field at any one time.[72]

The technical failings of the tanks greatly limited the ways that the Red Army could deploy them, but Soviet armor experts were not discouraged. They believed that tanks would one day prove themselves, and they even became more innovative in their ideas on the possibilities for using the vehicles in battle. One description imagined them not only demoralizing the enemy and breaking through fortified positions when necessary, but also carrying out reconnaissance, employing poison gas, and transporting infantry detachments.[73] Lame and halting as the machines were, the very existence and promise of the tank was creating a cadre of men who believed in mechanized warfare, and who would fight to keep the tank from sinking into the obscurity that the rest of the army felt it deserved.

A similar indifference threatened the development of armor in post-Versailles Germany. Never very impressed by its few tanks during the war, the new Reichswehr

68. Another draft version of "Kratkaia Instruktsiia Nachal'nikom Bronechastei Frontov i Armii dlia Boevogo Upravlenia i Primeneniia Bronevykh Chastei," RGVA, f. 27, op. 1, d. 89, l. 479.

69. "Tablitsa Kolichistva Bronechastei FSFSR za vremia 1918–1922 gody," RGVA, f. 27, op. 1, d. 430, l. 54.

70. A list of armor units in the Republic from Kotovskii to the Operational Directorate of the Field Staff, 5 September 1920, RGVA, f. 7, op. 2, d. 24, ll. 2–3.

71. Report on tanks worked on at Sormov Factory, RGVA, f. 27, op. 1, d. 386, l. 50; repairs at Kharkov Locomotive Factory, RGVA, f. 27, op. 1, d. 410, ll. 23–27.

72. List of armor units in the Republic from Gladkov, Inspector of Armor Units, 8 October 1920, RGVA, f. 7, op. 2, d. 24, ll. 19–21. List of armor units in the Republic, 6 December 1920, RGVA, f. 7, op. 2, d. 24, 1. 34.

73. Gladkov, *Taktika bronevykh chastei*, 68–69.

faced a variety of problems afterwards, all of which were more important than the question of what to do with the new weapon. The treaty and the formulation of the army's response to it – most especially finding ways to violate its terms even before the ink was dry; the need to create a reason for hope among the demoralized ranks of the officer corps; and as with all defeated armies, the endless evaluations and reevaluations of the lessons learned from defeat – absorbed the attention of the high command. In addition the Reichswehr, thanks to Versailles, no longer possessed even those few tanks that it had owned during the war. There was, apparently, little reason for the German military to concern itself with the question of the tank.

In the first few months after the peace treaty was signed Hans von Seeckt, the new head of the Truppenamt (literally "Personnel Office," as the army decided to call a disguised General Staff), and soon to be named head of the Army Command, focused his considerable energy on reorganizing the army and reviving the morale of the officer corps, rather than on armaments.[74] Seeckt had performed heroically during the world war, helping to bring about one of the major breakthroughs on the Eastern Front. He also took part in the Versailles negotiations, so that he was well aware of the hostility of Germany's neighbors and determined to support a strong military. He argued not long after the treaty was signed that only a revitalized Reichswehr could save the country from her internal and external enemies.[75] The primary stumbling blocks in his attempts to create a new fighting force were the unsettled condition of the young Weimar Republic and the treaty restrictions, which allotted him an army too small and too ill-armed either for quelling disturbances inside the country or for guarding Germany's borders.[76] Seeckt responded by molding an officer corps equipped with belief in itself and its mission, if not with modern weaponry, and by seeking to remain outside the political debates that embroiled much of the rest of the country.[77] He also began the formulation of a military doctrine that would best suit a small, extremely mobile army. Only after completing this fundamental task did he turn to the no less vital one of covertly supplying the Reichswehr with modern weaponry and doctrines to fit them.

But Seeckt was not alone in his quest to find a doctrine that would suit the new German army. The officer corps as a whole provided vital input, so that the final product of his first two years as head of the army, new field regulations that ap-

---

74. See for example memorandum from Seeckt to all General Staff officers, 7 July 1919 and memorandum from Seeckt, 18 October 1919, BA-MA. N 5/18, pp. 12–13 and 41–42.

75. Friedrich von Rabenau, *Seeckt: Aus seinem Leben, 1918–1936* (Leipzig: Hase & Koehler, 1940), 159–202.

76. According to the law of 6 March 1919, which created a temporary Reichswehr, these were to be the tasks of the new army. Erfurth, *Geschichte des deutschen Generalstabes*, 26–27. The final law was signed 23 March 1921. Ibid., 87.

77. He also expected political leaders not to interfere with his army. Hans von Seeckt, *Thoughts of a Soldier* (London: Benn, 1930), 33–45 and 68–80.

peared in 1921, reflected both the debates among the high command as well as his own views. These early discussions show that after the signing of the Versailles treaty German officers looked to the past to draw lasting tactical and doctrinal lessons from the world war. The most surprising aspect of their conclusions was how little the experiences of combat changed their fundamental understanding of what constituted the correct way to fight. Significantly, they decided that there was nothing wrong with German doctrine; it was only the special nature of the Western Front, the combined strength of the Allies, and certain key mistakes by the German military leadership that had led to defeat. One judgment about the war was, for instance, that conducting a war offensively remained the only way to win. Thoughtful military men in other nations decided from their four-year experience of suicidal frontal assaults that the overwhelming defensive firepower demonstrated in the war had made the offensive obsolete. The army that was able to retire behind heavily fortified positions and wait until the attacker had exhausted his resources would win future conflicts.[78] The German officer corps argued to a man that they would still have to wage future wars offensively since a purely defensive stance led inevitably to defeat.[79] The Reichswehr would need to do everything possible to preserve the offensive spirit of the infantry, building it up wherever the positional nature of the war had damaged it.[80] The army also refused to acknowledge that the retreat to the trenches during the world war had proved that all other conflicts would eventually bog down in the same sort of stalemated warfare.[81] It concluded instead that this had been an aberration that it could not, and would not, allow to reoccur. A war of maneuver with great offensive battles was the only form of warfare that brought decision, and the German army would therefore strive to regain the freedom of movement that had characterized the short wars of the previous century.[82] True, in fighting such a war, German military thinkers now favored flanking movements or encirclements rather than frontal assaults, but this, too, was fundamentally a conservative view. German military authorities from Clausewitz to Schlieffen had praised attacks on the rear and flanks of the enemy as more efficacious than simple offensives on the sector where he was most heavily concentrated, his forward positions.[83] Finally the officer corps concluded that the war had

78. The lessons that the French learned are ably discussed in Judith M. Hughes, *To the Maginot Line: The Politics of French Military Preparation in the 1920s* (Cambridge, Mass.: Harvard University Press, 1971). See in particular pp. 68–81 on "The Legacy of the First World War."

79. See for example Friedrich von Bernhardi, *Vom Kriege der Zukunft: Nach dem Erfahrungen des Weltkrieges* (Berlin: Mittler, 1920), 235; General der Infanterie v. Kuhl, "Vom Kriege der Zukunft," *Militär-Wochenblatt*, no. 116 (1920): 2138.

80. "Verwendung der Infanterie mit ihren Hilfswaffen im Angriff im Bewegungskriege," ibid., no. 121 (1920): 2240.

81. Among many others, Kuhl, "Vom Kriege der Zukunft," 2137.

82. E.g. Major Rohrbeck, *Taktik: Ein Handbuch auf Grund der Erfahrungen des Weltkrieges* (Berlin: Mittler, 1919), 1.

83. Ibid., 3–5. See also Carl von Clausewitz, *On War* (Princeton, N.J.: Princeton University Press,

demonstrated that the infantry remained the most important of the armed forces, while the other forces – the cavalry and artillery – were to support their every move.[84] The Reichswehr had decided in fact, as Friedrich von Bernhardi so aptly put it, that the form of war changes, but the basic laws of war do not.[85]

Despite a commitment to these traditional principles of warfare, German officers recognized that they needed a response to the increased strength of the defensive. They might have chosen, as the British did, to find the answer in new technology like tanks, but their experience with the flawed machines, and the provisions of Versailles, prevented any serious consideration of this solution. A potential alternative had already been found during the war: "stormtroop" tactics. Seeckt, and the German officer corps as a whole, concluded that the new concept answered the problem of modern warfare and that, therefore, the Reichswehr did not need to find a technical solution to strong defenses. Only after the midtwenties would the high command realize that they could have their cake and eat it too, integrating technology and the new tactics into a unified whole.

The result was that the German army at first relegated tanks, and the study of armor doctrine, to relative but not absolute neglect. Seeckt oversaw the creation of "Motor-Transport Battalions," a cover name for tank units that were attached directly to infantry divisions. Lacking real vehicles with which to work, the units were given the task of building wooden mock-ups of tanks and training foot soldiers in antiarmor defense.[86] The handful of officers who chose to assess the impact of tanks on warfare were generally as conservative as the rest of the officer corps, suggesting an armor doctrine very like the one propounded by the General Staff during the war. While there were slight differences in emphasis, they had decided that this was as sound as the other accepted principles of warfare. The most important mission that tanks could perform, for example, was still the creation of confusion in the rear of the opponent and panic among the infantry.[87] One author explicitly compared the tank to the elephants used against the Romans by Pyrrhus – useful for surprising and frightening an unprepared enemy, but not for much else.[88]

As for the course of an actual tank attack, some preferred to leave the details of battle as vague as had the General Staff, while others thought that certain elements of the attack should be more fixed. One description of a tank attack is particularly interesting as it shows just how close German tactics were to Soviet concepts. The

---

1984), 530–31; Alfred von Schlieffen, *Cannae* (Fort Leavenworth, Kansas: The Command and General Staff School Press, 1931). Argued throughout the book but especially pp. 297–306.

84. Rohrbeck, *Taktik*, 22, 81.

85. Bernhardi, *Vom Kriege der Zukunft*, 1.

86. "Ausbildung der jüngeren Hauptleute des Reichswehrministeriums, Winter 1923/24: Kriegsgliederung der 3. Div.," BA-MA. RH 2/73, p. 58.

87. Ibid., 59–60; Rohrbeck, *Taktik*, 198.

88. Bernhardi, *Vom Kriege der Zukunft*, 37. This was actually a quite common comparison at the time.

anonymous author proposed a combined-arms approach to combat, in which all forces – armor, air, infantry, and artillery – would work together closely to defeat the enemy. Specifically, he foresaw tanks advancing in two or more echelons, accompanied by "numerous" airplanes and exploiting smoke cover to hide their progress. Like the Soviets, the officer recommended that fast tanks attack in the first wave, pushing far forward to cause confusion and keep the defender from using his defensive measures. The heavy tanks would bear the brunt of the battle, crossing back and forth over the battlefield to suppress the enemy's artillery and machine gun fire and create a safe passage for the following infantry.[89] There is no evidence to suggest that the Soviet and German authors knew each other's work; the coincidence in ideas stemmed instead from the world war, in which the British had used tanks in this way, and from similar notions of what tanks were capable of.

In July 1921, Colonel Friedrich von Taysen (wartime commander of an infantry regiment) published a short pamphlet on mobile warfare that was, in many ways, a summary of the lessons from the world war that the Reichswehr thought it had learned up to that time. Taysen concluded, as had Bernhardi, that the conditions of modern warfare demanded serious modifications in tactics, but that the basic principles of war on which German doctrine was based would always be the same. The offensive, for instance, "obviously" was and would remain the stronger form of battle, while mobile warfare, which allowed full play for the "German" ideals of speed, surprise, and broad maneuver, should be the rule in future wars rather than the exception as in the last one.[90] He argued too that the Moltkean envelopment strategy, which had ruled German military thought before the war, was essentially correct. Even in the positional warfare of the world war, frontal assaults had been useless, and only flanking and enveloping movements had allowed the capture of the deep defensive zones of the enemy.[91] He agreed that, in some ways, the advent of new technologies had changed warfare, shifting the main emphasis from man to materiel, but went on to say that the German army must not allow this to happen, as if sheer willpower were enough to change the inevitable. The human factor was and must remain decisive in war, he wrote, for all machines were useless and dead without human energy to animate them.[92] Two years later he would become

89. Rohrbeck, Taktik, 197–98.

90. Oberst v. Taysen, "Ueber die Formen des angelehnten Angriffs und die Verteidigung im Bewegungskriege," Wissen und Wehr, special issue, Juli 1921 (Berlin: E.S. Mittler & Sohn, 1921), 1–3. It is interesting to note that Taysen (and others') maxim about the offensive was a direct contradiction of Clausewitz's thought. See Clausewitz, On War, book 6. Wallach has pointed out that many German military thinkers, convinced of the innate superiority of the offensive, consciously chose to reject this idea of the writer whom they otherwise treated as an infallible genius. Jehuda Lothar Wallach, The Dogma of the Battle of Annihilation: The Theories of Clausewitz and Schlieffen and Their Impact on the German Conduct of Two World Wars (Westport, Conn.: Greenwood, 1986), 23–25.

91. Taysen, "Ueber die Formen des angelehnten Angriffs," 21–23.

92. Ibid., 1–3.

embroiled in a furious debate over these very ideas with officers who supported the supremacy of materiel.[93] With these principles as background, he also examined the impact of the tank and contended that the experiences of the last year of war had shown that it could achieve no more than limited success against a determined defender. Like many other German officers he was unwilling, however, to exclude altogether the possibility that technical advances might make the tank a more useful offensive weapon in the future. The early success of both gas and the tank was proof enough for him that the surprise appearance of a new technology, or new way of fighting, could be enough to swing the balance of a battle, if not a war.[94]

Later in the year the new field regulations appeared, systematizing the lessons of the world war learned by the German officer corps. *Command and Combat with Combined Arms*, or F.u.G, as the regulations were called, generally reflected the opinions of Seeckt, and showed the direction that his evolving concepts would take. F.u.G. was interesting not only because Seeckt used it to endorse officially the changes in tactics made during and after the war, but also because he treated the weapons banned by the Versailles treaty rather routinely, as if it were obvious that the German army would one day be using them in battle. He in fact dedicated the second part of F.u.G. solely to an examination of how the army would use tanks, airplanes, and gas once it possessed these weapons. In his introduction Seeckt stated rather defiantly that the doctrines in the manual were based on the strength, armament, and equipment of the army of a modern military great power, and not just on the hundred-thousand-man force permitted by the peace treaty.[95]

The limited nature of the alterations that Seeckt, and the German army as a whole, were willing to make in their basic ideas of how to fight a war was unmistakable in the first half of F.u.G., which dealt with general principles of battle. While Seeckt recognized here officially that the Reichswehr would have to alter many of the specifics of infantry and cavalry tactics in order to adjust to conditions on the modern battlefield, he also reaffirmed the general German belief that the principles of war which formed the basis for all doctrines remained sound. The regulations endorsed, for instance, the use of infiltration tactics and stormtroopers, but reiterated that the offensive was the sole means for achieving victory; the army was to resort to defensive action only to allow an attack in another place or at a later time. Envelopments and attacks on the flanks and rear were best, as the war had shown, but this was not to imply that German troops should shy away from frontal assaults. The basis for battle was a combined-arms approach, with cavalry, infantry, and artillery working closely together to achieve success – again an idea central to German military thought even before the war. On cavalry specifically, F.u.G. called for smaller detachments, reflecting the German army's recognition that the in-

93. See below, pp. 52–70.
94. Taysen, "Ueber die Formen des angelehnten Angriffs," 50–52, 3.
95. F.u.G., 3–4.

creased fire on battlefields excluded battle on horseback in large units, but also its belief that this did not change the basic tasks of the arm. Horse troops were still the main means of close reconnaissance, and the cavalry was also to continue performing combat missions, exploiting its mobility and firepower to envelop the enemy's wings or attack his rear lines of communication.[96]

This conservative understanding of the lessons of the war makes more understandable the treatment of the tank in F.u.G. The tactics that Seeckt prescribed in the manual were extremely cautious, precluding a full exploitation of the few good qualities that the early tanks possessed. Tanks were to attack in great quantities, with surprise and en masse, for instance, but they were also bound to the speed of the slowest foot soldier since they were supposed to maintain the "tightest contact" with the infantry. In another section, Seeckt stipulated the usual two tank echelons but, rather than allowing the light tanks to exploit their greater speed and mobility, he called for the heavy tanks to lead them into battle.[97] This further lowered the speed of tank attacks, since heavy tanks were naturally much slower than light ones. Where the earlier German doctrine, like that of the Soviets, sought to have tanks move as quickly as possible across the battlefield and into the enemy's rear, offensives based on the new regulations could proceed at a pace no greater than the three to five miles per hour that was the maximum speed that heavy tanks could achieve. Finally, the second half of F.u.G., which went into tank usage in greater depth, gave a negative assessment of both the tank's physical properties and the possibilities for using it on a modern battlefield.[98]

Over the next two years the reading by Seeckt and the German army of the tank's technical capabilities, and thus of the possibilities for using it in battle, slowly began to change. The principal reason for this seems to have been a general recognition that the pace of technological innovation, rather than leveling off as some officers expected, had actually accelerated. Engineers found solutions for the most egregious of the technical problems that had plagued early tank design, and the internal combustion engine became more efficient and better designed. One of the first signs of the change in attitude toward the tank appeared in the new *Infantry Training Manual* (A.B.I.), issued by Seeckt in October 1922. In A.B.I. Seeckt – with the input of the German command as a whole – delineated more precisely than he had in F.u.G. his evolving ideas on how foot soldiers would interact with new military technology. The manual also shed light on how Seeckt believed the infantry would be able to overcome superior defensive firepower. In a very traditional manner, A.B.I. began with the premise that the infantry decided the battle and that it was the mission of all other types of forces, cooperating together, to facilitate the success of the foot soldier. As for battle itself, Seeckt noted that only the offensive, and

96. Ibid., 9–11, 44–47, 139–40.
97. Ibid., 185–86.
98. F.u.G., pt. 2, paras. 728–39.

the offensive spirit that should permeate every action of the German soldier, would make victory possible. This was so vital that although success in battle depended on the cooperation of all arms, the infantry should not allow waiting on the help of its "sister forces," including tanks, to damage its offensive spirit, but should instead be able to depend on superior training, courage, and cunning to carry it to victory.[99]

Naturally enough, A.B.I. visualized tank tactics in almost exactly the same way as did F.u.G., but with a few important additions that reflected Seeckt's recognition that technological improvements could transform the way that tanks would fight. The newer manual recognized, for instance, that only the fact that tanks offered a large target, and that they could not fire accurately while moving, limited their use; they could find employment against any objective, and could attack in many different formations.[100] A.B.I. was thus predicated on the principle that the technological failings of the machines were not an eternal given, that nations such as France and Britain were remedying the tank's problems, and that this would entail a rethinking of armor doctrine. It is interesting for later developments that A.B.I. did not examine the effects that greater firepower or thicker armor would have on tactics, but chose instead to highlight the possibilities offered by higher speed and a wider radius of action – an emphasis entirely consistent with Seeckt's overriding commitment to mobile warfare.[101] Other German military authorities, writing at about the same time as the issue of A.B.I., agreed with its basic reading of the changes taking place in tank technology and tank tactics, showing that Seeckt's understanding of the importance of technical innovation was shared by at least some of the officer corps.[102]

Over the next three years the writings of Ernst Volckheim, a lieutenant in a Prussian motor transport battalion, worked through the implications of this rethinking of tank tactics. Volckheim had served in the young German armor forces during the war, an experience which convinced him of the worth and bright future of the ungainly machines. Yet unlike others who had worked with tanks during the war (such as Fuller or Liddell Hart), he did not allow his enthusiasm for the weapons to rule out a very pragmatic reading of their prospects. His theories about tank usage were thus rather modest, based on the assumption that technology would be able to engineer a machine that was somewhat better than the one currently available, but not the "super tank" of men such as Fuller.

Volckheim's first publication, in 1923, was a study of the German tank during the world war. His main purpose seems to have been to rescue the tank from the

---

99. *Ausbildungsvorschrift für die Infanterie. (A.B.I.)* Heft I. (H. Dv. Nr. 130) (Berlin: Verlag der Reichsdruckerei, 1922), 18, 25.

100. Ibid., 91–92, 97. The term used was "abschnitts- oder wellenweise."

101. Ibid., 89, 97.

102. See, for example, "Die gegenwärtigen französischen Ansichten über die Verwertung der Kampfwagen," *Militär-Wochenblatt*, no. 22 (1922): 448–50.

obscurity into which it had fallen since the war and to predict its further technological and tactical evolution. He described first the limited success of the A7V, and
blamed this on the technical failings of the vehicle and the lack of attention ac-
corded tanks by the German high command.[103] This was then contrasted with the
much greater possibilities for what he termed "the tank of the future." Reflecting
the still prevalent skepticism about tanks, he began by asking whether a more technically perfected tank would be able to play a significant role in future wars. He answered this affirmatively for three reasons. First, Germany's former enemies were
assuming this to be true and preparing for tanks to participate fully in the next war.
In addition, Versailles had forbidden the Reichswehr to own tanks, surely a good
argument for their importance. Finally, the technological progress which tanks
were experiencing, beginning during the war itself, showed that they would have a
significant future.[104]

Unlike the tank of the world war, which was fit only for a war of position, Volckheim predicted that future tanks would find employment primarily in the mobile
warfare favored by Seeckt and the rest of the German high command. Here the
heavy tank, faster than its predecessor, able to travel further and overcome obstacles of every kind, would fight in independent units although assisting the infantry
closely. Light tanks, armed with machine guns and able to travel at fifty to sixty kilometers per hour, would remain tied to infantry and cavalry formations and would
be used for tactical reconnaissance. In the battle itself the army would deploy heavy
tanks in three echelons, each with a specific mission. The first would break through
enemy lines and destroy strong points, the second would fight the opponent's artillery and machine guns that threatened the first echelon, while the last wave
would cooperate closely with the infantry. Like Seeckt and other officers, Volckheim repeatedly stressed that only a faster tank and one able to go long distances
without refueling or breaking down would be able to fight in this way; the need for
greater firepower and other improvements was not as important as this requirement.[105]

The growing awareness of Seeckt and officers like Volckheim that tank technology was progressing very quickly should not, however, be taken to mean that the
German army viewed armor units as anything more than auxiliary forces, on a par
with the artillery or engineer branches. The infantry was the center of all German
thinking about future war, and would remain so for the entire interwar period. Von
Altrock, a former major general and chief editor of the *Militär-Wochenblatt*, the principal journal of the German military, recognized this when he reviewed Volckheim's book favorably in his paper. He agreed that the German army had
underestimated armor during the world war, and called Volckheim's arguments for

103. Volckheim, *Die deutschen Kampfwagen im Weltkriege*, 30–35.
104. Ibid., 35–36.
105. Ibid., 37–42.

the tank, and in particular his views of the "tank of the future," especially significant. At the end of his review Altrock acknowledged that tanks were not central to German thinking about warfare by expressing his hope that Volckheim's work would "rescue the achievements of the German tank from oblivion."[106]

The Soviet army faced, in some ways, a brighter future at the beginning of 1921 than did the Reichswehr, and yet it also began to share at least one problem with the German army; a severe reduction in size and political power. After Tukhachevskii drove the Polish army to the very edge of Warsaw, Pilsudski managed to rally his troops and begin an offensive that would push the Red Army back behind its borders. The Soviet commanders, who included Stalin, Budënnyi, and Voroshilov in addition to Tukhachevskii, blamed each other for the debacle, and Voroshilov and Budënnyi would use Tukhachevskii's "failure" at the gates of Warsaw as ammunition in their later struggle with him. But the defeat was probably inevitable. The new country had already stretched its resources to their limit, and the failed push into Poland marked the high-water mark for pre-Stalinist expansion of revolutionary socialism. Even before the setback near Warsaw, the attention of the leadership had shifted to the more mundane problems of the country, such as food production and distribution, which the pressure of Civil War had forced them to neglect. The economy had in fact simply collapsed, and once it became clear that Poland was unable to continue its fight with Soviet Russia, the Red Army found that it could no longer command the instant budgetary respect to which it had become accustomed. The official recognition of this lack of respect came at the end of 1920, when Bolshevik leaders ordered a massive demobilization, reducing the army's size from 5.3 million men to less than 600,000 by mid-1924.[107]

The one bright spot during this time of relative neglect was that the high command had the leisure to make more permanent decisions about the tactics, strategy, and organization most suitable for a communist army. In all these debates, the development of armor affairs was not a high priority. Trotsky and the rest of the RVS agreed to appoint a commission to study how to construct tanks in January, and a month later urged armor unit staff officers to work on the technical side of the armor question, but did little to help them.[108] The more ardent supporters of armor affairs refused to allow this disregard to affect the units under their supervision. In late January, Inspector Kotovskii and Liubyshskii, the new Chief of the Armor Inspectorate, wrote a letter to Trotsky in which they argued that armor units needed more attention, not less, as open warfare with the imperialists ended. Up to that

106. v. Altrock, "Die deutschen Kampfwagen im Weltkriege," *Militär-Wochenblatt*, no. 28 (1923): 592–93.

107. Number of men in armed forces, 1 July [1924]. RGVA, f. 4, op. 2, d. 26, l. 163.

108. Protokol no. 131, Zasedaniia RVS Respubliki, 28 February 1921. RGVA, f. 4, op. 1, d. 13, l. 173; Sbornik sekretnykh prikazov RVSR 1921, no. 111/20 (13 January 1921). RGVA, f. 4, op. 3, d. 1674, l. 26.

point the military had shown little appreciation for the value of tanks and armored cars, even allowing responsibility for them to become split among the departments of four different branches of the army. This was wrong, the two men wrote, because "[a]s a type of weapon, by their combat characteristics and tactics, armor units are highly distinctive and may not be fully likened to any one of the types of weapons that currently exist."[109] This was an important point since the Soviet military had attempted to treat tanks and other armor vehicles as if they were hybrids of different existing weapons, rather than a distinct new force. In some ways armor units were like engineering units, useful for furthering the advance of the infantry, and therefore assigned to GVIU. They also had guns like artillery and thus the Artillery Directorate (AU) was responsible for tank weaponry. One military expert even thought that the tank was a "land battleship," and might need the tactics and organization of a naval force.[110] Kotovskii and Liubyshskii argued that armor vehicles were nothing like these other branches of the military and suggested that the War Commissar set up a new directorate, separate from GVIU and directly subordinated to the RVS, to manage armor affairs.[111] They also included an estimate of the number of armor units that the republic needed in order to be ready for the next war; for tanks alone, they suggested fifty detachments, rather than the current fourteen, with nearly seven thousand men.[112]

The head of GVIU responded to the armor expert's outline, which threatened to take away his control of the armor forces, by producing an alternative plan. He accepted as a given that tanks and armored cars were not distinctive types of weaponry, deserving their own organization and support system. They were specialized engineering weapons created, like bridging equipment or mine-clearing devices, to help foot soldiers in their advance on enemy positions. Arguing that the Civil War had demonstrated the need for centralized command and control in the organization of all the forces, he called for the unification of all the various engineering technologies under GVIU.[113] In March Kolesov, the Assistant for Frontline [Armor] Units, countered with a report in which he emphasized that armored cars and tanks were indeed distinctive and entirely new types of weapons. Yet since armor units had appeared during the war, "the structure of armor unit administration has changed radically seven times and in defiance of the unsuccessful protests

109. Report from Kotovskii to Trotsky on armor directorate organization, 27 January 1921, RGVA, f. 7, op. 1, d. 181, ll. 44–45.

110. Ibid., l. 44; *Chto takoe tanki*, 3.

111. Report from Kotovskii to Trotsky on armor directorate organization, 27 January 1921. RGVA, f. 7, op. 1, d. 181, ll. 44–45, 48.

112. Ibid., l. 50. The figure of fourteen tank detachments was a slight exaggeration. The official numbering of units for the four-year period 1918–22 showed only ten tank detachments at the beginning of 1921, although the number rose to thirteen by October 1921. "Tablitsa Kolichistva Bronechastei FSFSR za vremia 1918–1922 gody," RGVA, f. 27, op. 1, d. 430, l. 54.

113. Letter from Chief of GVIU, RGVA, f. 7, op. 1, d. 181, ll. 63–64.

of the armor specialists who are guiding armor affairs." This had led to a great waste of time and effort, which only the foundation of an independent Armor Directorate could rectify.[114]

In the end, the argument of the armor experts prevailed, although the debate over the two conceptions of armor units continued over the next few months. In May, the RVS finally ordered the establishment of a directorate of the chief of armor forces of the RKKA, which was to answer directly to the chief of staff.[115] It is symptomatic of the continuing neglect of armor affairs that the directorate was not actually set up until July.[116] The wide range of duties that the RVS assigned to Kotovskii as the new head of armor forces shows, however, that the creation of a separate directorate was meant to give him real power over the future of the tank within the Red Army.[117] Kotovskii set to work immediately to make Soviet armor forces more battle-ready, although worsening economic conditions complicated his efforts. In a report submitted to him in June, for instance, one of the engineers in charge of tank repairs noted that there was a backlog at the factory because workers were out searching for food rather than repairing tanks.[118] With this in mind, and remembering the earlier problems involving bourgeois specialists, one of Kotovskii's first actions was to ask the RVS to create a "Detached Training Auto-Tank Armor Brigade." The brigade was to consist of a very large number of men, but only four armored cars and four tanks, with its main duty listed as the preparation of "Specialist Red Army Men" and lower command staff for service in all armor units.[119] Once again, the RVS was occupied with more important matters and the order authorizing the formation of the brigade was not issued until September.[120]

Kotovskii's next step was to ask the first assistant to the chief of staff to send him information about armor affairs in the West.[121] It was vital for the new directorate to be completely up-to-date on progress made by Great Britain, France, and the United States which were, after all, potential enemies of the new socialist republic.

114. Report from Kolesov, March 1921, RGVA, f. 27, op. 1, d. 206, ll. 207–8.

115. Sbornik sekretnykh prikazov RVSR 1921, no. 974/168 (6 May 1921), RGVA, f. 4, op. 3, d. 1674, l. 336; Prikaz RVS Respubliki, no. 974/168 (6 May 1921), RGVA, f. 27, op. 1, d. 126, ll. 4–15.

116. "Otchet k 5-ti letiiu Oktiabr'skoi Revoliutsii," prepared by the Directorate of Armor Forces RKKA. RGVA, f. 27, op. 1, d. 430, l. 70.

117. "Polozhenie ob Upravleniia Nachal'nika Bronesil RKKA" 1921, RGVA, f. 27, op. 1, d. 206, l. 24.

118. Report from Senior Supervising Engineer for the Repair of Tanks in GVIU, June 1921, RGVA, f. 27, op. 1, d. 147, l. 78.

119. "Shtat Otdel'noi Uchebnoi Avto-Tankovoi Bronevoi Brigady," RGVA, f. 27, op. 1, d. 206, ll. 45–46.

120. Sbornik sekretnykh prikazov RVSR, no. 1914/325 (2 September 1921), RGVA, f. 4, op. 3, d. 1677, ll. 200–206.

121. Memo from Kotovskii to First Assistant Chief of Staff RKKA, 15 July 1921, RGVA, f. 27, op. 1, d. 214, l. 84.

Just as importantly Soviet Russia lacked the industrial infrastructure to build its own tanks and therefore might have to depend on the West, either directly by buying tanks, or indirectly through borrowing ideas on tank construction. Up to that point the only tanks that the Red Army had managed to manufacture were the so-called "Russian Renaults," copies of the light French tank built at the Sormov factory.[122] All the other tanks in the Soviet arsenal had been captured from the British and French during the Civil War. As Kotovskii's memorandum shows, the lack of native engineers and the availability of superior vehicles from capitalist countries was already fostering a dependence on Western technological progress that would last until the first Five Year Plan – and beyond.[123]

The economic crisis affected armor affairs in other ways as well. In March 1922 the government mobilized tanks to help improve the desperate conditions in agriculture, and about six of the vehicles were sent to Ukraine "to cultivate the land."[124] That summer Soviet tanks plowed fields and sowed grain – fighting, as one newspaper article put it, "on the economic front."[125] A more serious consequence of the economic crisis was a reduction in the size of the Armor Directorate and a corresponding decrease in armor units.[126] Tanks were especially hard hit by the slowing economy as they required constant repairs and replacement parts. During 1922 alone there was a 50 percent reduction in tank detachments while the number of tanks in fighting condition began a steep decline that would not end until the start of the first Five Year Plan.[127]

The cutbacks did not alter thought on armor doctrine, which had changed little from earlier conceptions. In a short guide to the use of tanks and armored cars in battle, Kotovskii reiterated his earlier points about the technical shortcomings of tanks. He again argued that tanks were not able to perform even the limited missions assigned to armored cars, and were designed only to assist other arms.[128] The comments of an anonymous commander, made during the fighting against the

122. Report from Kuibyshev, Temp. Commander of District Forces (MVO), and Bulin, Member of District RVS, to Deputy Chairman. RVS SSSR, 3 June 1928, RGVA, f. 4, op. 1, d. 344, l. 147.

123. Soviet commanders became so concerned about developments abroad that they considered copying Western ideas even when the reasons for doing so were not clear. See e.g. Report from Deputy Head of RKKA Armor Forces to Chief of Staff RKKA, 23 August 1921. RGVA. f. 27, op. 1, d. 214, l. 100.

124. Report on placement of tanks, March 1922, RGVA, f. 7, op. 8, d. 438, ll. 14–20.

125. N. N. Sokolikhin, "Rabota tankov na khoziaistvennom fronte," *Tekhnika i Snabzhenie Krasnoi Armii*, no. 15 (1922): 43–45.

126. Report on size of Directorate of Chief of Armor Forces, RGVA, f. 27, op. 1, d. 115, ll. 21–22; "Tablitsa kolichestva bronechastei FSFSR za vremia 1918–1922 gody," RGVA, f. 27, op. 1, d. 430, l. 54.

127. "Otchet k 5-ti letiiu Oktiabr'skoi Revoliutsii," prepared by the Directorate of Armor Forces RKKA, RGVA, f. 27, op. 1, d. 430, l. 72.

128. Kotovskii, "Kratkoe rukovodstvo boevogo primeneniia bronevykh avtomobilei, tankov i bor'ba s nimi," RGVA, f. 27, op. 1, d. 217, l. 6.

remnants of anti-Soviet forces, favored using tanks to support slow, deliberate advances through fortified areas in positional warfare or, at the very most, for the defense of stationary positions.[129] The Soviets were not, however, completely adverse to experimenting with new tactics, especially if this would mean an expansion in the role of armor during the next conflict. At an August meeting of the commanders of military districts, for instance, Kotovskii and Kolesov suggested that the army could use armor units, including tanks, for "the protection of the borders of the Republic during the first period of the commencement of military actions." As for the rest of the armor units, they could be "distributed across the territory of the Republic for the protection of those railroads which ought to be protected in agreement with a decree of the Council of Labor and Defense (STO) and, in case of the commencement of military actions, these units would be a front reserve."[130]

But the range of opinions held by the experts is best illustrated by two tank manuals, one designed for training purposes and the other written for internal purposes to glorify the tank's past and future. The first was a short text on armor prepared by an officer in the Armor Forces Directorate. The manual repeated the prevailing wisdom, detailing, for instance, well-known positive and negative aspects of tank construction and the limits on tank usage that these implied, although admitting that the technology was still evolving. Throughout the book, the emphasis was on the auxiliary role which armor would play, helping other types of forces to achieve success while sacrificing itself.[131] The other book, an official account of the development of armor prepared by the Armor Forces Directorate for the fifth anniversary of the October Revolution, was more positive. It argued that it was Allied technology – most notably tanks – which had allowed them to triumph over Germany, and that the tank's future uses were limitless.[132] Once again, the emphasis was on the technological changes that the tank had already experienced, combined with a firm belief that these would continue and lead to a bright future.

Unfortunately for these hopes, that same year there was a serious decline in the limited influence of the armor forces, which would culminate in the elimination of the Armor Forces Directorate in 1924 and the reassignment of tanks and other armored vehicles to the AU. It is ironic that this occurred just as tanks were over-

129. Ibid.; report from commander of auto-armor unit in Dondivizii, 20 June 1921, RGVA, f. 27, op. 1, d. 214, l. 83; Sorokin-Razhev, "Bronevye voiska i v chastnosti ikh ispol'zovaniia v bor'be s banditizmom," 30 June 1921, RGVA, f. 27, op. 1, d. 224, l. 82.

130. Kotovskii and Kolesov, "Konspekt doklada na s"ezde Komanduiushchikh," 13 August 1921, RGVA, f. 27, op. 1, d. 206, l. 225.

131. Keler, *Kratkii uchebnik po bronevomu delu*, 22–24, 27, 61.

132. "Otchet K 5-ti letiiu Oktiabr'skoi Revoliutsii," prepared by the Directorate of Armor Forces RKKA, RGVA, f. 27, op. 1, d. 430, ll. 67–69. See also Skif, "Po povodu diskussii 'Problemy bronevogo dela': Avtomobil' ili tank?" *Tekhnika i Snabzhenie Krasnoi Armii, Bronevoe Delo*, no. 15 (1 September 1922); 2–3. For a further look at Skif's ideas see Skif, "Po povodu diskussii 'Problemy bronevogo dela': (Prodolzhenie)," ibid., no. 19 (1 October 1922): 1–2.

coming the technological problems that had limited their tactical usage, and thus, as in Germany, should have enjoyed greater, not less, popularity. The main reason for the decline was a lack of money for expensive weapons which, however improved, were still secondary to the main types of forces.[133] The Soviet economy, particularly the agricultural sector, had failed to recover when the Civil War ended. Faced with the prospect of widespread famine, the leadership disagreed about how to end the crisis. Trotsky argued that production in both factories and the countryside would improve only through iron discipline and a revolution without end. Other Bolsheviks, including Lenin and Bukharin, were not certain that the country could survive a continuation of this "War Communism." Stalin had already decided that the War Commissar would be his main rival in any struggle for power, and thus gave his support to the majority within the Politburo. The result was the rejection of Trotsky's permanent revolution and the implementation instead of the strategic retreat from socialism known as the New Economic Policy (NEP). The decision for NEP signaled the beginning of the end of Trotsky's influence. After Lenin's death in 1924 he lost his position as head of the army and shortly thereafter found himself fighting for his political life. For the military, the straitened economic conditions of the country suggested that the Red Army should concentrate on buying new equipment for the infantry, cavalry, artillery, or even the air forces. Rather than expanding the size of the armor forces, the army focused on better organization for the few tanks and cars that it already possessed.

The men who oversaw the armor forces did not agree with this decision and fought throughout 1923 to expand the role of the tank in the military. Antonovskii, who temporarily replaced Kotovskii as chief of the armor forces, asked in January to add another 109 tanks to the 40 that the Red Army had.[134] Sergei Kamenev, commander in chief of the army, countered with a war plan that foresaw only the already existing ten tank detachments deployed in the next conflict.[135] In late April, the new permanent Chief of Armor Forces, Baranov, decided to be more realistic and requested only twenty million rubles for his directorate over the next five years.[136] Two days later, during a debate on this issue and the rest of the military budget, Chief of Staff Lebedev supported the twenty million ruble figure, but added that "[t]he armor forces had to give up extensive development." By comparison the figure for the development of the aviation program was two hundred million rubles

133. The expense of tanks and other armor forces was continually brought into the discussion when there were debates on the budget. See Sbornik sekretnykh prikazov RVSR 1922, no. 457/78 (25 February 1922), RGVA, f. 4, op. 3, d. 41, l. 154.

134. Report by Antonovskii (Temp. Chief of Armor Forces), "SMETA na raskhody po zagotovleniiu material'noi chasti pri razvertyvanii bronechastei," 27 January 1923, RGVA, f. 4, op. 1, d. 31, ll. 123–24.

135. Disposition of troops in case of war, S. Kamenev, Supreme Commander, to Supreme Head of Supply, 2 February 1923, RGVA, f. 4, op. 1, d. 31, ll. 41–42.

136. Report from Baranov, 25 April 1923, RGVA, f. 7, op. 1, d. 160, ll. 89–90.

over the course of the next five years, ten times that for the armor forces.[137] With military expenditures for the entire five-year period estimated at 2.8 to 2.9 billion rubles, the amount set aside for armor forces was truly insignificant.[138]

A radical organizational scheme for tank forces, proposed by supporters of armor, showed that there were commanders who were not willing to accept the reduced role for tanks that the financial figures suggested. Sometime at the end of 1922 or beginning of 1923 a Commission for the Revision of Red Army Organization of Armor Units was set up, probably under the auspices of the STO.[139] Kotovskii, although he had left the armor forces to lead the Communications Directorate by January 1923, continued to be interested in the progress, or lack thereof, in armor affairs. He and the director of the Armor Military Technology Council presented a report in which they proposed to the commission a sweeping reorganization of tank forces.[140] This foresaw the widespread use of tanks in the next war and envisaged the fighting potential of the vehicles in a very different way from earlier theories. Kotovskii began by noting that all the Western countries were acquiring large numbers of tanks and organizing them in huge independent units. France for instance, although claiming to have only 2,600 tanks, in reality had either 5,000 or 6,000, while Britain had more than 6,000. In view of the immense importance that potential enemies placed on tanks, Kotovskii requested that the Soviet Union build up from the current force of 79 tanks to a much larger tank army with 1,580 tanks and 36,500 men. He also suggested that the Red Army reorganize the tanks into an independent branch of the army, which would consist of "batteries" of four to six tanks, "flotillas" of three or four batteries, "divisions" of five flotillas, and "squadrons" of four divisions. The mix of terminology here is obviously deliberate, and says something very interesting about the way in which Kotovskii, and others, thought about tanks. The term "battery" (*divizion*), for instance, was usually reserved for artillery, a reminder that, as Kotovskii stated in his report, some thought of tanks and especially heavy tanks as mobile armored cannon, pounding the defenses of an entrenched enemy so that the infantry could advance. "Flotilla" (*flotiliia*) and "squadron" (*eskadra*), on the other hand, were naval terms; the "squadron" discussed here was, significantly, different from the word for a cavalry "squadron" (*eskadron*). While

137. Protokol no. 169, Zasedanie RVSR (27 April 1923), RGVA, f. 4, op. 1, d. 31, ll. 3, 5. The twenty million ruble figure was confirmed in a letter to the chief of the armor forces later in the year. See letter to Chief of Armor Forces confirming budget, RGVA, f. 7, op. 1, d. 161, l. 24.

138. Reports by Chief of Staff, RGVA, f. 7, op. 1, d. 161, ll. 1, 17.

139. See for example "Ob'iasnitel'noi zapiski k khodataistvu pered Sovetom Truda i Oborony o provedenii v zhizn' proekta tankovoi organizatsii," RGVA f. 27, op. 1, d. 700, l. 45; "Dokladnaia zapiska v Komissiiu po peresmotru organizatsii bronechastei RKKA: 'Osnovnye Polozheniia dlia organizatsii sushchestvuiushchikh tankov,'" RGVA, f. 27, op. 1, d. 700, l. 56.

140. See report from Khalepskii as Chief of Communications Directorate, RGVA, f. 4, op. 1, d. 31, l. 138, for his switch to the Communications Directorate; the rest of this discussion is taken from his report in the report by Kotovskii and "Directorate of Affairs of the Technical Council," RGVA, f. 27, op. 1, d. 206, ll. 235–37.

ships may seem a counterintuitive metaphor for tanks, this comparison was common in the early days. Other military thinkers, both German and British, also saw them as the armored cruisers of the land that would "sail" the plains, as invulnerable to the fire of their enemies as were the earliest metal ships.[141]

A more polished version of this proposal, circulated in February 1923, explained further how tanks were the land battleships of the future, and presented an organizational plan that reflected this belief.[142] The proposal also had a new command structure with an independent Chief of Armor Forces, who would control all aspects of the tank forces except for operational use. The author provided the precise costs of implementing the scheme, which included the production of tanks in Soviet factories beginning in 1925 and before that the purchase of parts abroad. The final figure of 62,785,200 rubles was far more than the Soviet high command could afford.[143] It is significant that the new version of the proposal stressed recent steps forward in tank technology, and the contrast with German discussions of this issue is illuminating. Where Reichswehr officers talked about the speed and radius of action of the new tank as its most significant technical advance, the Soviets looked at the tank's thicker armor and its ability to surmount larger obstacles, wade through deeper water, and carry more men and more powerful weaponry.[144] The Germans thought that the tank of the future would be a small, light vehicle that could strike quickly and move on to the next target, while the Soviet organizational proposals focused on heavy and medium tanks for use as shock weapons, with light tanks performing reconnaissance. Germans were, in other words, excited about the new possibilities for using tanks in mobile fighting while Soviets still thought of the improved tank primarily in terms of positional and trench warfare. This is not to say that there were not other Red commanders who looked at the new tanks and saw much the same thing as did German armor experts.[145] The majority of those Soviet military thinkers who wrote about armor affairs, however, still thought of the tank, even in improved form, as best suited for positional warfare.

141. In fact Winston Churchill, who could arguably be viewed as the true intellectual father of the tank, was probably the first to think of tanks as a land fleet. The first official British commission set up by Churchill to study the feasibility of the tank, in February 1915, was called the "Land Ship Committee." Martin Gilbert, *Winston S. Churchill*, vol. 3: *The Challenge of War, 1914–1916* (Boston: Houghton Mifflin, 1971), 536–37. Fuller, too, saw them as ships. Fuller, *Reformation of War*, 154–167. For earlier Russian ideas on this subject, see RGVA, f. 192, op. 6, d. 31, l. 138; and *Chto takoe tanki*, 3.

142. "O razvertyvanii tankovykh sil v techenie 5 let," 10 February 1923, RGVA, f. 27, op. 1, d. 701, l. 2.

143. Ibid., ll. 2–3, 6–8.

144. Ibid., l. 1; "Ob'iasnitel'noi zapiski k khodataistvu pered Sovetom Truda i Oborony o provedenii v zhizn' proekta tankovoi organizatsii," RGVA, f. 27, op. 1, d. 700, l. 46.

145. "Dokladnaia zapiska v Komissiiu po peresmotru organizatsii bronechastei RKKA: 'Osnovnye Polozheniia dlia organizatsii sushchestvuiushchikh tankov,'" RGVA, f. 27, op. 1, d. 700, ll. 56–57.

In late 1923 and early 1924 the Red Army adopted the new organizational structure for the Soviet armor forces, if not the expensive production scheme, but it was in place only a few months before being dismantled completely.[146] The idea of tanks as land battleships fired the imagination of at least some within the Soviet military, yet the costs involved in setting up the rather grandiose plan ensured its early demise.[147] By late 1924 the armor forces would be assigned to the care of the AU and almost completely ignored for the next three years. In their worst condition since the foundation of the Armor Forces Directorate, and with no prospects for future restoration, Soviet tanks were apparently doomed to slip into obscurity. Only external developments, and the internal support of a few tank enthusiasts, would cause this to change.

146. The new structure was finally adopted in March 1924. Sbornik Sekretnykh Prikazov RVS SSSR 1924, no. 407/79 (21 March 1924), RGVA, f. 4, op. 3, d. 2156, ll. 204–6, 209–10. The tanks were re-formed into regular regiments by September 1924. Sbornik Sekretnykh Prikazov RVS SSSR 1924. no. 1161/184 (17 September 1924), RGVA. f. 4, op. 3, d. 2155, ll. 39, 79–81.

147. See an article of August 1923 discussing the need to have a "land fleet." The author of this article would later become a defender of mechanization and tanks. K. Kalinovskii, "Vnemanie sukhoputnomu flotu – tankam," *Tekhnika i snabzhenie Krasnoi Armii, Bronevoe Delo*, no. 7 (1923): 1–3.

CHAPTER TWO

Materiel or Morale?

The Debate over the Mechanization of Warfare, 1923–1927

VEN AS the German high command relegated tanks to a subordinate fighting role and the Red Army in effect dismantled such armor forces as it possessed, officers in Germany and the Soviet Union became embroiled in a philosophical debate about the significance of the tank that showed both the depth of skepticism about machine warfare and the growing strength of those who supported the tank. This sort of discussion was not new. In France and Great Britain armor enthusiasts had argued since the world war that the tank would transform the face of warfare and that machines would soon replace men on the battlefield. German and Soviet officers, even those who had served in armor units, had dismissed this idea as a fantasy, not even worth serious refutation. They had focused on pragmatic discussion of armor doctrine given the current technological development of the machines and had left theorizing about the future of warfare to armchair warriors.

From 1923 onwards, various events and processes changed this attitude in the two countries. As we have seen, the Soviet high command, pressured by a worsening economy and the need to reform their military as a whole, neglected expensive technological weapons like tanks to concentrate their limited resources on the "principal types of forces," the infantry and artillery. The few tanks in the Red Army arsenal rusted away in the near oblivion of the AU, as the Soviet Union in effect voluntarily matched Germany's forced lack of tanks. During the summer of 1924, the dissolution of the independent Armor Directorate and the subordination of tanks to the artillery forces was set for the first of October. This reorganization would soon be caught up in the more general military reform begun by the new head of the army, Mikhail Frunze, who had earlier advocated replacing the army with a mixed system of a large territorial militia and a small regular army. Frunze had successfully attacked Trotsky and his military specialists, arguing that the first socialist state had to have an army that matched its ideological convictions, in other words a militia of all workers and peasants rather than a professional standing army. He also made the indisputable argument that a militia would be less expensive than a regular army. The reorganization of the tanks, seen by Frunze as necessary to simplify and centralize control over armor affairs, had the unintended effect of ending as well the innovative organizational ideas that had treated armor forces like a "land navy," and guaranteed that they were almost forgotten by the Red Army high command. The final figure for men in armor forces was placed at forty-five hundred, but by June 1926 the numbers had fallen to less than three thousand.[1] In a complete misreading of the complications involved in staffing the technological forces of a modern army, Frunze declared at a meeting of the RVS in late November 1924 that the shrinking of armor units would not cause much damage since they were only material units and the Red Army could therefore reestablish their trained cadres in a very short time.[2]

The number of tanks in the Soviet arsenal also declined precipitously. A 1924 report from the AU, surveying the tank units newly placed under its command, found only forty-six of the vehicles.[3] In December 1925 the AU issued a list of prices for various weapons which showed that the army had ordered no tanks at all during the period 1923–25. Although the report added that the army was in the process of producing a new tank, it gave the current stage of readiness of the single prototype at only 3 percent.[4] In February 1926 Tukhachevskii asked the head of the Organization-Mobilization Directorate to produce a comparison of Soviet military strength with that of the other countries of Europe and the United States. This showed that the Soviet Union had fewer tanks than any other potential enemy except Japan.[5] Nor did the official war plans for 1924/25 and 1926, which called for the Soviet army to deploy only a few more tanks than were already in their arsenal, foresee a mass use of tanks during the next war.[6] The lack of actual tanks with which to experiment combined with the need to react to the claims of foreign mechanizers encouraged Soviet officers to spend more time considering the philosophical implications of the new weapons of war rather than their practical use.

1. "Otchetnyi Doklad (sek.) Tsentral'nykh Upravleniy RKKA za Period s Aprelia po Oktiabr' m-ts 1924g.," RGVA, f. 4, op. 2, d. 16, ll. 140–64; Report of meeting of the RVS SSSR, 8 June 1926, RGVA, f. 4, op. 1, d. 327, l. 25.

2. "Stenograficheskii Otchet Plenuma RVS SSSR," 24 November–1 December 1924, RGVA, f. 4, op. 18, d. 35, l. 50. Frunze was involved in planning for his comprehensive reform of the Soviet military and may have not wanted to be distracted by expensive weapon systems. For a discussion of the Frunze military reforms, see Raymond J. Swider, Jr., *Soviet Military Reform in the Twentieth Century. Three Case Studies* (Westport, Conn.: Greenwood, 1992), 34–69. Von Hagen discusses the political and social implications of the reforms. Mark von Hagen, *Soldiers in the Proletarian Dictatorship: The Red Army and the Soviet Socialist State, 1917–1930* (Ithaca: Cornell University Press, 1990), 183–267.

3. Report prepared by Sadlutskii, Chief of the AU, listing all tank units in the RKKA, by type and condition, dated 22 December 1924, RGVA, f. 20, op. 21, d. 1, ll. 41–48. The types of tanks were the Ricardo, Taylor, French Renault, and Russian Renault-Fiat.

4. Memo from Chief of the AU on equipment prices, December 1925, RGVA, f. 33987, op. 3, d. 93, l. 2.

5. Memo from Tukhachevskii to Bentsov requesting list of potential enemy tank strength, with list, RGVA, f. 7, op. 10, d. 205, ll. 341 and 342.

6. Report from Chief of the II Directorate RKKA, "Skhema razvertyvaniia brone-tankov. chastei RKKA po variantu 5-ie 1926g.," 30 November 1926, RGVA, f. 7, op. 10, d. 161, ll. 1–6.

The second impetus toward a reconsideration of machine warfare in the Soviet Union was the highly paradoxical result of the ouster of Trotsky from his position in the Red Army. As head of the army, Trotsky had fought a temporarily successful battle against Frunze and others who argued that the Red Army needed to have a specifically proletarian military doctrine as well as a proletarian militia. Based on "objective" scientific principles, this unified military doctrine would be completely different from capitalist concepts and would ensure that any war which the Soviet republic fought would end in the victory of the proletariat.[7] Trotsky had disagreed furiously with this concept of warfare, arguing as he had during the Civil War that war was an art, not a fixed science.[8] Although the art of war included certain enduring basics, such as those dealing with training and logistics, doctrine had to adapt to the shifting conditions of the real world. The young Red Army thus needed to learn the basics of warfare from its more experienced bourgeois neighbors rather than simply denigrating them, while remaining flexible enough to adjust to new technological or political situations.[9] Stalin, Frunze, and other detractors of Trotsky made certain that the debate over a unified military doctrine became entangled with the larger question of the war commissar's fitness to lead the army. Through careful maneuvering, and aided by organizational confusion within the military, Trotsky's authority was undermined throughout 1924. By 1925 he had no alternative but to resign and was immediately replaced by his deputy, Frunze. Trotsky's fall from power meant that men like Frunze, who sought an ideological rather than a strictly pragmatic basis for the conduct of war, were now free to push for the adoption of their ideas. The search for a proletarian way of fighting was on and would deeply affect the debate over machine warfare which early in the Soviet Union became one that involved, above all else, philosophical and ideological concepts about man and his worth.

Meanwhile, further improvements in tank technology also helped to change the

---

7. The authors of the doctrine contrasted the workers' style of warfare with the old capitalist style: they claimed, for instance, that the Russian Civil War had shown that the offensive and maneuver were specifically proletarian ways of fighting, while the capitalist way of war was defensive and positional in character, as the world war had demonstrated. M. V. Frunze, "Edinaia voennaia doktrina i Krasnaia armiia," Armiia i Revoliutsiia, no. 1 (1921): 13–29. See David M. Glantz, Soviet Military Operational Art. In Pursuit of Deep Battle (London: Frank Cass, 1991), 65. The Soviet idea of a unified military doctrine, unlike the earlier tsarist concept of the same name, was ideologically based. Although it too brought together the officer corps under a single accepted concept of battle, the main emphasis was on finding a specifically proletarian doctrine. Bruce W. Menning, Bayonets before Bullets: The Imperial Russian Army, 1861–1914 (Bloomington: Indiana University Press, 1992), 215–17.

8. During the main debate over the unified military doctrine at the meeting of the military delegates to the 11th Party Congress, Tukhachevskii agreed with this part of Trotsky's argument, denying that anything like a "proletarian" concept of war existed. Francesco Benvenuti, The Bolsheviks and the Red Army, 1918–1922 (Cambridge: Cambridge University Press, 1988), 199.

9. Leon Trotsky, Military Writings (New York: Pathfinder Press, 1971).

attitudes of some German and Soviet military thinkers toward the arguments of Allied armor enthusiasts. During and immediately after the world war vocal supporters of the tank, most notably Fuller, Liddell Hart, and the French theorist George Soldan, had called for the mechanization of war.[10] Fuller's name in particular became associated with the idea of a war of machines and the creation of huge "tank armies" that would not need ordinary foot soldiers at all. Although their ideas at first provoked ridicule in both Germany and the Soviet Union, much of this early scorn disappeared as tanks became steadily faster, more maneuverable and less susceptible to breakdowns in the field.

The result of all these factors working together, but especially the improvements in technology, was an increase in the number of Soviet and German military thinkers who agreed with the Soviet writer who in 1918 had proclaimed the advent of "a war of machines" that would change future conflict forever.[11] By the mid-twenties German and Soviet officers had stopped ignoring Fuller's "fantastic" ideas and instead followed closely the debate over machine warfare in France and Britain, some agreeing with the ideas of the mechanizers and others vehemently disagreeing.

The result was a series of disputes that to some extent followed the lines of the perennial argument between the advocates of "materiel" and "morale" as the deciding factor in warfare. Those who argued against mechanization saw it as the logical extension of the sort of impersonal machine warfare that had characterized the First World War and resisted bitterly a continuation of a process that had already made war too automated and inhuman. Tank supporters, on the other hand, thought that machine warfare would return mobility to the battlefield, shorten wars, and save lives. The majority of the officers in the Soviet Union and Germany probably supported neither of these extremes, trying instead to find a happy medium between complete mechanization and total neglect of armor forces.

It would, in fact, be a mistake to view either the "morale" or the "materiel" supporters as unified groups. There was a wide variety of basic philosophies that determined how German and Soviet officers reacted to the idea of mechanization, including, but not limited to, socialist and Marxist ideologies, readings of national character, and views about the inevitability of technological progress. Depending on the writer a Soviet military thinker could base his support for materiel on an underlying Bolshevik commitment to mechanize all life, discussed so well by Fülöp-Miller, or conversely his support for morale and the human spirit on Trotsky's pronouncements on the subject.[12] Many German writers, as well as a few Soviets,

---

10. See for example J. F. C. Fuller, *The Reformation of War* (London: Hutchinson, 1923); Georges Soldan, *Der Mensch und die Schlacht der Zukunft* (Oldenburg: Stalling, 1925); and B. H. Liddell Hart, *The Remaking of Modern Armies* (London: Murray, 1927).

11. See above, chapter 1.

12. René Fülöp-Miller, *The Mind and Face of Bolshevism: An Examination of Cultural Life in Soviet Russia* (New York: Harper & Row), esp. pp. 18–25.

argued in terms of supposed racial, national, or social characteristics which "proved" that a truly German (or socialist) army must rely on morale. Other writers could point to the constant evolution of military hardware and tactics as an argument for more dependence on the machine. One interesting result was that regardless of the justifications for their beliefs, morale and materiel supporters in both countries came to the same conclusions about the need to either mechanize or refrain from mechanization. Morale supporters in both Germany and the Soviet Union denigrated the possibilities for using materiel, and tanks in particular, while glorifying the human spirit, just as supporters of machine war in both countries thought that they were simply giving a more realistic appraisal of the future of warfare than their "old-fashioned" morale-advocating opponents.

It is not surprising then that the image of machine warfare that officers in both countries held was very much alike. For supporters of morale, mechanization meant that men would lose control over the action on the battlefield and ultimately over war itself. Machines would no longer obey the orders of the men who had made them, and instead would dominate their supposed masters. In time, men would "suffocate in the mechanism," as one German officer put it; become no more than cogs in a faceless, impersonal war machine that would grind up the strong and brave as easily as the weak. The courage, manliness, and will to conquer of the individual soldier would no longer make a difference in battle – only the overwhelming weight of the machines as they moved over the battlefield, inexorable, unfeeling, and unthinking. If machines began to dominate battle, Soviet theorists also saw that one of their sources of superiority over the capitalist countries, the ability to foment revolution within the ranks of their enemy's armies, would no longer exist. The imperialists could simply replace potentially rebellious workers with silent, obedient machines.

Materiel and tank supporters had an entirely different image of mechanized warfare. They saw the new machines as the cavalry of the future, restoring to battle all those glories that the world war had taken away: movement, speed, decision, and individual achievement. Wars would no longer bog down in hopeless stalemates; machines would allow quick, decisive attacks and encirclements – the broad maneuvers of earlier wars, but at even greater speed. At last individual soldiers, riding their tanks and automobiles as the knights had ridden their horses, would be able to perform the heroic deeds that the last war had made impossible. This school of thought also argued that machine warfare was the future; progress in technology was, in the final analysis, inevitable. However much some officers wanted to return to the past – and materiel supporters did not understand why they would want to do that – there was no going back. Stated in such stark terms, these differences in how war was imagined made a clash over machine warfare as inevitable as the technical progress that tank supporters celebrated.

In the early twenties there was a rough balance between the economic, political, and technological arguments each side employed that seemed to give as much credibility to the morale way of thinking as it did to those who favored mechanization. The one area where advocates of morale in both Germany and the Soviet Union clearly triumphed over their opponents was in their philosophy of warfare, a victory demonstrated by the fact that the mechanizers felt obliged to adopt or adapt these philosophical foundations to their own arguments. By the mid-twenties the supporters of morale had in fact established several interlocking arguments against mechanization based on their belief in the primacy of man, the overwhelming strength of man's fighting spirit, and the need for other forces besides tanks. These arguments became the foundation not only for their antimachine diatribes, but were generally accepted by German and Soviet armies alike.

On the Soviet side, the initiative in the debate over mechanization quite clearly belonged to morale advocates. Trotsky gave his support early on, arguing during the Civil War that tanks could not replace men on the battlefield, that everything depended on the training, spirit, and dedication to the revolution of the ordinary soldier.[13] His philosophy of war was more complex than that, since he also thought that technology was necessary for achieving victory, but if it came to a choice he came down on the side of man and morale. He stated, in an often cited passage, that war was moral strength augmented by technology, and not the other way around.[14] Other morale advocates built on this foundation, holding as a central thesis that socialism required a militia, an army composed of all the people, as its armed force. It this were true, man must form the core of the army while machines and other military equipment merely provided the means for man to achieve his ends. The obvious corollary was that the infantry would therefore always retain its overwhelming significance, while the other branches of the military, including armor forces, were but aids to the infantry. A. A. Neznamov, a tsarist military specialist who adopted the cause of the revolution, stated it best when he wrote that

> [s]ocialism denies war but is forced to conduct it. Its armed force – theoretically – is a militia (*militsiia*) or an all-inclusive militia (*pogolovnoe opolchenie*). Here again, only the infantry can be, inevitably, the main type of force in terms of both numbers and preparation. . . . [T]he infantry inevitably will preserve its place among the armed forces of the state. No success of technology is able to change those conditions which determine its place. By virtue of these conditions all studies and attempts to reduce armed struggle on land between peoples to a struggle of certain machines ought to be recognized a priori as erroneous. As long as "infantry" exists, the main factor in this struggle will remain "man." Technology (the ma-

---

13. See above, chapter 1.

14. B. Fel'dman's article "Dve taktiki," *Voennyi vestnik*, no. 24 (1924): 19–22, quotes Trotsky's maxim twice.

chine) can strengthen him, can facilitate the conservation of his strength up to the moment of the decisive skirmish, but can never (on land) replace him.[15]

Neznamov argued that the world war, especially in its positional phase when machines of every sort had been used, had shattered the illusions some had held about the possibility of replacing man with machines, while the Russian Civil War "eloquently confirmed" Soviet confidence in the supremacy of the infantry.[16]

Not just any infantry could overcome the new technologies of war, however. Soviets who thought that man was more important than dead machines added that they would have to be infused with revolutionary zeal and a vital sense of unity with each other and their government's policies. The infantry *were* the people themselves, and they would most possess the spirit of warriors when "the relations between the 'people' and their government are abruptly disrupted, that is during revolutions."[17] Only a state that embodied this revolutionary spirit could direct and control it, using it to fulfill the true desires of the people because it was formed from the people themselves.[18] The Soviet Union thus did not have to fear the technology of the bourgeois because it had "that strength which is not in bourgeois armies. The Red Army is united; behind and at one with it stands the entire worker-peasant population."[19]

This unity could prove decisive in battle, B. Fel'dman argued, contrasting capitalist and socialist governments and their respective armies: "[w]here an army is drafted to protect interests foreign to it, those of a hostile ruling class, where the rulers have reason not to trust the spirit of their own soldiers who were forcibly placed under arms," and where a highly developed industrial base allows the production of large amounts of deadly machines and gases "for the service of which the necessary cadres of specialists from among their 'own' may be used, there tactics follow the path of machinization, the path of replacing unreliable man with the speechless, obedient machine, there manuals and regulations 'delicately' discuss the moral element as an appendage to the machine." On the other hand, "[w]here the army is bound by blood with the ruling class, where the army goes into battle with a full consciousness of the rightness of its cause, where the army instills complete confidence in its people," and where industry is just barely on its legs and not able to cope with the demands of tactics, "there to emphasize mechanization would be a fatal mistake, there the moral factor ought to lie at the basis of the army's education."[20] He believed in addition that the international solidarity of the

15. A. A. Neznamov, *Pekhota* (Petrograd, 1923), 5–6.

16. Ibid., 1.

17. Ibid., 4.

18. Baratov, *Budushchie voiny* (Moscow: Gosudarstvennoe Voennoe Izdatel'stvo, 1925), 37–38.

19. Litovchev, *Tekhnika na voine* (Moscow: Gosudarstvennoe Izdatel'stvo, Otdel Voennoi Literatury, 1927), 30.

20. Fel'dman, "Dve taktiki," 19–20.

proletariat was one of the psychological weapons that would bring success over superior technology. Over time, the unity of the working classes and thus their moral superiority could only grow, fueled by the deepening of class hostilities in the West. That was why Soviet tactics should not imitate those of foreigners, but find their own path.[21]

In examining these foreign tactics for machine war, some Soviet writers thought that they had found the true reason capitalists wanted to replace men with machines: their reluctance to be dependent on revolution-prone workers. Looking at technology in the next war, Vladimir Lishchintskii concluded in 1927 that machines would be important, but "this great significance of technology in modern warfare has nothing in common with what is often ascribed to it. Usually they see the whole meaning of technology in some kind of exceptional superiority in comparison to the military value of living forces (to the capabilities of man himself). From this comes the proposition about the possibility of almost completely replacing living forces with military technology. This view is radically wrong." The bourgeois countries, misled by this view of technology, were attempting to replace men with machines, "[b]ut this dream of ruling capital had in its foundation not the actual capabilities of technology, but a simple wish to depend less in the field of battle on the working masses, who form the basis of living forces." Such capitalist writers as Fuller would ideally like to have an army that consisted of one man pushing a button to defeat the enemy. But of course this was nothing but an empty daydream.[22]

Various interpretations of socialist ideology constituted only one part of the arguments of Soviet morale advocates. The tsarist emphasis on the decisiveness of the bayonet, the ideal of the unconquerable human spirit, and the negative national characteristics of materiel supporters were also evoked to explain why man would always triumph over machine.[23] Aleksandr Lignau, who as the infantry instructor at the new Frunze Military Academy had a great deal of influence on military thought during the twenties, fully supported the general understanding of the infantry as the backbone of the army. In his infantry textbook, which every officer in the Red Army read as part of his course of study at the academy, Lignau discussed in depth the decisive character of the infantry and described the tank as nothing more than an infantry weapon, without mentioning class or socialist bases for these beliefs. Instead he thought that "as a general proposition, without an attack with the bayonet, the infantry battle cannot be considered complete. Only hand-to-

---

21. Ibid., 19–22.

22. Vl. Lishchintskii, *Tekhnika v budushchei voine i oborona SSSR* (Moscow: Gosudarstvennoe Izdatel'stvo, 1927), 3–5.

23. Even after the Russo-Japanese War, the tsarist Field Regulations of 1912 still returned to the bayonet charge as the way to achieve final success in an engagement. Menning, *Bayonets before Bullets*, 141–42, 261–62, and passim.

hand combat or the real threat of a bayonet thrust can compel a staunch opponent to surrender or yield his positions."[24] Lishchintskii took this reliance on the bayonet, which had dominated tsarist readings of the centrality of the infantry, and went one step further. "What especially determines the interrelation of technology and living forces," he argued, "is the question of the bayonet." Before the world war the bayonet was rejected as defective, but now every nation recognized that this weapon "crowns the affair."[25] Man had thus not lost his great importance in battle, since only he could carry out the requisite bayonet charge.

In addition to his support of the bayonet, Lishchintskii's concept of warfare included other nonsocialist ideas about the intrinsic value of man as warrior. He pointed out that only man could fight at any time and under any conditions, while machines such as the tank made a real difference in battle only in the right terrain and at the proper time. He added that people were also capable of performing many different kinds of tasks while machines could only carry out missions for which they had been specifically designed.[26] More than that, "[w]arriors know how to fight, they know their business and are full of courage – that is the main weapon of the warrior, without which the most wonderful accomplishments of military technology lose all military value."[27] Lishchintskii even argued that rather than diminishing the number of men on the battlefield, "[t]echnology, while fortifying military action, increases the scale of struggle to an extent that will demand the participation of a multimillion-man army and the intense labor of the entire nation." Finally, he concluded, the real significance of technology lay solely in the fact that it strengthened the soldier so that he could accomplish his mission.[28] Other military writers blamed the alleged defects of foreign nations for their "excessive" interest in tanks. The French, one wrote, had to depend on the tank because of "the insufficient 'moral' fortitude of the French infantry which demands the support of powerful material means; this may be linked with the steady decline in birthrates in France, which forces everyone to an ever greater degree to replace men with mechanized fighting equipment."[29]

The economic weakness of the Soviet Union and the overwhelming industrial strength of its probable opponents gave further support to the ideological and philosophical arguments of morale supporters. Here was one area where materiel and morale supporters could agree in both Germany and the Soviet Union: the ailing economies of both countries and the huge expense involved in mechanization

24. A. Lignau, Pekhota: Opyt issledovaniia ustroistva i boevogo primeneniia v usloviia manevrennoi voiny, 2d ed. (Moscow: Voennyi Vestnik, 1927), 7–9, 400.

25. Lishchintskii, Tekhnika v budushchei voine, 6–7.

26. Ibid., 7–10.

27. Ibid., 10.

28. Ibid., 14, 23.

29. S. Vishnev, "Tanki i ikh organizatsiia," Voennyi Vestnik, no. 5 (1925): 44.

were constant themes in discussions of the tanks by both German and Red Army officers. There were, in fact, several problems that the Red Army had to take into consideration when debating the question of mechanization; a sagging economy, lack of industrial development, and severe technological backwardness. Despite some improvements during NEP, the Soviet economy was still extremely weak, suffering throughout the twenties from a variety of serious problems caused by underdevelopment and exacerbated by two wars, capital flight, and bad management. In a rare candid admission one author was forced to acknowledge that "extremely limited funds" had brought the Soviet Union down to the same level as Germany in military technology.[30]

The Soviet Union, however, also lacked the basic heavy-industry infrastructure that developed European nations could take for granted when planning for war. The mass production of any vehicles, whether tractors or cars for civilian use or tanks and armored cars for the military, was nothing more than a dream. Officers who supported the tank and materiel in general tried to ignore this problem, simply assuming that a modern industrial state would be created in the near future, and were sharply attacked for this by their opponents.[31] The third difficulty was related to this industrial underdevelopment, namely that the Soviet Union lacked the technological expertise needed to create modern weapons, especially in comparison to their Western neighbors. The Soviets did not have the engineers, the know-how, or the training to produce sophisticated weapons like tanks, but morale supporters argued that the greater spiritual power and unity of purpose of the new socialist state could make up for any deficiency in technology. After all, machines could not act without people, and the Civil War had shown that men with superior motivation and physical and mental strength could defeat the "well-armed forces of the counter-revolutionaries."[32]

Some of those who discussed the relationship between economic development and mechanization thought that the Soviet Union did need to build a military-industrial infrastructure, but in the meantime socialist morale would be decisive. Fel'dman wrote that the tactics of a country had to match its economic and spiritual development. Thus the French had adopted tactics whose leitmotif was "the opposition of matter to spirit, the hypnotic fascination with a factory-made way of conducting wars, and the pitiful remnant of a moral element." The Red Army was the exact opposite of the French army because the Soviet form of government was the opposite of imperialist France. What sort of tactics would match the economic conditions and spiritual values of the world's first socialist state? To begin with, a "machinization" of the Red Army without a corresponding development in indus-

30. Ia. Fedorov, "Pekhota i tanki (Po nemetskim istochnikam)," ibid., no. 20 (1925): 24.
31. Fel'dman, "Dve taktiki," 21.
32. Baratov, *Budushchie voiny*, 37–38.

try was impossible.[33] The Soviets could, however, count on "moral stability" in the Red Army and it would therefore be a terrible error to concentrate on an artificial mechanization of the army when the strength of the Soviet Union lay elsewhere. Fel'dman frankly admitted that the Red Army would have few machines during the next war, that their opponents would be technologically stronger. But in spite of this, he believed, the Soviet army would be more powerful than its enemies because it possessed an arsenal of psychological weapons that would overpower their superior technology. Men thus armed with high morale would be able to triumph over any amount of materiel.[34]

The residual technological, and consequent tactical, weaknesses of the tank were the other practical factor that reinforced Soviet advocacy of morale. Although the tank was a much-improved machine in 1923 compared to the clumsy vehicle that had made its first appearance in 1916, and would be even more refined by 1927, it still had a number of serious technical problems. Those who supported morale seized on these to denigrate the tank and to prove that no machine would be able to replace man in battle.[35] Tanks were supposed to be able to move on any kind of terrain, for instance, but on Soviet roads and bridges very heavy vehicles would get stuck. Officers described them as delicate machines that had to be babied so that they would not break – even brought to battle on trucks or trains – and that were "afraid" of cannons and bullets. The Soviet army thus had nothing to fear from the technology of the bourgeoisie, but could rest secure knowing that its spirit of unity would carry the day.[36]

As might be expected, the morale supporters, and in fact majority Soviet opinion on the matter, thought that Fuller, Liddell Hart and others went too far in their claims about the use of tanks and other technologies in a future war. One of the earliest critics of Fuller echoed Lishchintskii's deprecation of the ideal Fuller army, condemning the idea that tanks could replace infantry and artillery, and ending with the often repeated cliché that the infantry remained the "queen of the battlefield."[37] Another author briefly reviewed Fuller's latest work on "The Role of Tanks in Rear Guard Operations," saying that in the article "there is absolutely nothing new. As in others of his works, some sort of ideal tanks of the future are performing, tanks that do not need to be taken apart and cleaned after every action and are capable of the most complex maneuvers [using] all their striking mass in battle."[38] Conversely, those military writers who tried to take a more balanced view of ma-

33. "Machinization" was a common term in Soviet Russia during the early twenties for the use of machines in place of man.

34. Fel'dman, "Dve taktiki," 19–22.

35. Lishchintskii, Tekhnika v budushchei voine, 47–48; Lignau, Pekhota, 7–9.

36. Litovchev, Tekhnika na voine, 16–17, 30.

37. "Problema mekhanicheskogo vedeniia voiny," Tekhnika i snabzhenie Krasnoi armii, Bronevoe delo, no. 7 (1922): 29–38, esp. 36–37.

38. N. Lesevichkii, "The Journal of the Royal Artillery," Voina i Revoliutsiia, no. 6 (October 1925): 203.

chine warfare were also willing to judge Fuller's ideas less harshly. Vishnev, in reviewing Fuller's seminal work, *The Reformation of War*, was quite evenhanded in his analysis of Fuller's theses on the war and army of the future. The only serious mistake he made was to believe that the British officer corps accepted the views expressed in this work.[39]

Other Soviet officers were not so certain that sheer willpower or high morale would be victorious over the crushing weight of the capitalists' superior materiel. They believed that technology, ever progressing technology, was changing the future of war in a fundamental way. While they acknowledged that the supporters of morale had valid points to make about the human spirit and about the country's economic weaknesses, they also thought that their opponents were blind to the realities of modern warfare. In their discussions about the worth of tanks and other types of technology, materiel supporters combined a number of different arguments, generally pragmatic ones, to suggest that morale alone could never win the day. Their weakest point was ideology, for while there were various socialist ideas current about the value of technology, progress and modernity, supporters of materiel did not try to use them in the debate. They instead recognized up to a certain point the validity of their opponents' arguments for morale, and then focused their criticism on the more "objective" side of the question, that is, technological advances and developments in other nations.

One of the earliest critics of excessive admiration for morale, M. P. Kamenskii, was an exception to the general lack of philosophical arguments for materiel. Kamenskii wrote a study in 1923 on the relationship of the offensive and defensive in modern warfare throughout which he scattered in equal part criticisms of the morale supporters' positions and defenses of "machinization." He condemned early on any "dogmatism" about the infantry as the main type of force.[40] The heart of his dispute with the morale supporters, however, was that "'[r]evolutionary enthusiasm' and 'revolutionary zeal' from the viewpoint of military ideology and the scientific organization of military affairs is the same sort of foolishness as the flashy 'we'll bombard them with hats.' The apologia for spirit ought to have its limits."[41] He asserted, moreover, that the machine reeducates man, "refines the psyche," and gives him control. Not only was the tank not bad for man, it was a positive good, molding him into a new and better soldier.[42]

The most important of the arguments against morale was, however, the latest improvements in tank and other military technology. Instead of claiming – simply because the Soviet economy was unable to equal capitalist technological achieve-

39. S. Vishnev, "Fuller: *Preobrazovanie voiny*," ibid., no. 1 (January–February 1925): 283–87.

40. M. P. Kamenskii, *Nastuplenie i oborona v sovremennoi voine (etiud)* (Petrograd: Voennoe Izdatel'stvo Petrogradskogo Voennogo Okruga, 1923), 8, 32.

41. Ibid., 42.

42. Ibid., 43.

ments – that these improvements would have little significance, the materiel supporters asserted that the Soviet Union must match them. Thus critics of morale argued firstly that Soviet industry, even if currently weak, could and should try to keep up with developments in the West. A few weeks after Fel'dman published his article critiquing the Soviet economy and thereby discounting the chances for mechanizing the Red Army, another officer attacked this extremely negative attitude towards Soviet industry and technology. Although he acknowledged that moral strength was decisive in war, at the same time it would be very bad for morale if soldiers were taught that they would certainly face superior technology in the next war. Soviet technological weapons would have to work twice as well and be quickly concentrated in crucial areas of the battlefield to match the enemy's strength, but this could be done and it was this that should be emphasized when training troops. More than that, there was no guarantee that opponents of the Soviet Union would have morale inferior to that of the Red Army; instead one should believe them equal to oneself and then work on undermining their morale. Otherwise, as in the war with Japan, this overconfidence could lead to "sad results." Finally, he argued that something could be done about the poor state of Soviet technology, just as something could be done about the development of the Soviet economy. The article ended by warning that morale alone was not enough to make up for deficiencies of armament; this sort of thought would only lead to many deaths – mechanization was just as necessary as morale.[43]

As for specific technological advances, the advocates of materiel emphasized that the latest French and British tanks traveled farther and faster than ever before, that they broke down much less frequently, and that they were being improved every day. E. A. Stoliapevskii was thus optimistic in his assessment of the tank's present and future capabilities, writing that French reorganizations to include more materiel were dictated by their optimism about its possibilities. He felt, as did many other supporters of armor warfare, that the most important development in tank technology was its enhanced ability to maneuver on the battlefield, a technical revolution that would greatly affect tactics as well. Neatly reversing the principle that was basic to morale advocates' arguments, he argued that the mission of the infantry lay in consolidating and developing the successes achieved by the tanks. Rather than tanks serving man, man would be working for the tanks.[44]

Materiel and tank supporters also used the successes of other nations to "prove" that their understanding of future warfare was correct. A corollary to this was the belief that the capitalists, already more advanced than the Red Army, would pull even further ahead unless the Soviet government and high command took modern

43. A. Krenke, "Tekhnika i taktika," *Voennyi Vestnik*, no. 30 (1924): 48–50; see also Levichev, "'Mashinizirovannaia' rota i ee protivniki," ibid., no. 4 (1923) 15.

44. E. A. Stoliapevskii, "Voprosy primeneniia tankov," ibid., no. 1 (1924): 54–57; see too Ia. Fedorov, "Pekhota i tanki," ibid., no. 20 (1925): 24.

weaponry more seriously. Since the French and the British led in the production, use, and theoretical study of tanks, it was to them that materiel supporters turned when making their case. "The tank question seriously occupies the attention of [foreign] military thinkers," Stoliapevskii warned, "and with technical progress, new possibilities for using tanks are being sought. Hidden from outside view, the perfection of old systems and the invention of new ones continue." He then went on to describe the progress in technology and tactics taking place in Britain and France and to urge that Soviet principles of armor use be based on the military characteristics of the new tanks.[45] V. Kaisarov likewise discussed in great detail the English maneuvers of 1925, arguing that the accomplishments there showed the tremendous strides that technology and tactics were making. The maneuvers demonstrated that mechanization was beginning to show its worth, he wrote, and the new mobile armor units answered the demands of maneuver warfare significantly better than had older tanks.[46]

Meanwhile the German army began its own debate over the relative worth of man and technology, a debate that would deeply affect the Reichswehr's views of the tank. In a major shift from just the year before, a sizable portion of the German officer corps finally took note of the improvements in tank technology and the increased usefulness of the tank. Thus while a 1924 textbook on weapons theory planned for nothing more than world war tactics, Seeckt's revised introduction to F.u.G., issued the same year, praised the tank much more highly. Among other things, he now argued that the armor tactics in F.u.G. were already outdated, that the tank was continually being perfected and that improved tanks would be able to fight in mobile as well as positional warfare.[47] That same year Volckheim, already well known for his studies of armor, published two short books on the tank and its usage. In the first he warned against overrating the tank while at the same time stressing the ability of the tank to develop further. As in his earlier works, he stated that the tank was an auxiliary weapon subordinated to the infantry, but it would evolve beyond this stage and then tanks would have infantry assigned to them, and not the other way around.[48] The rest of the tank tactics in the book were standard for the German army, which makes all the more interesting his second book published just months later. Writing in answer to critics of the tank, Volckheim noted that current armor tactics were the same as those used in the world war, but emphasized more strongly than before that these were meant for the limited tank of

45. Stoliapevskii, "Voprosy primeneniia tankov," 54–55.

46. V. Kaisarov, "K voprosy o 'mekhanizatsii' armii," *Voennyi Vestnik*, no. 47 (1926): 37–39.

47. F. Zimmerle, *Waffenlehre: Kurzgefaßtes Lehr- und Nachschlagebuch der neuzeitlichen Bewaffnung* (Berlin: Mittler, 1924), 128–31; *Einführung und Stichwortverzeichnis zu Abschnitt I–XVII von "Führung und Gefecht der verbundenen Waffen"* (H. Dv. 487) (Berlin: Verlag "Offene Worte," 1924), 47–49.

48. Ernst Volckheim, *Betrachtungen über Kampfwagen-Organisation und -Verwendung: Zu einer Abhandlung des englischen Majors Sherbrooke* (Berlin: Mittler, 1924), 1, 5, 9.

the moment.[49] In his final chapter, he theorized about the further technical development of the tank and the improvement of its tactical capabilities. The future tank, or more precisely future tanks – since he thought that one type would be unable to perform all the necessary missions – would be faster, more mobile, yet more powerfully armed than current tanks. With their new speed and armaments, tanks would able to fight independently of infantry, artillery, and engineers, accompanied by armor vehicles built for every possible tactical need.[50]

The following year Fritz Heigl wrote his "tank pocketbook," a manual which would be influential in both German and Soviet military circles. The Frunze Academy would adopt Heigl's study as one of its standard textbooks, while both German and Soviet armor supporters would quote it as a source for their own writings. Heigl began with the view that the tank had been a decisive weapon during the last war and that its role in the next was incalculable.[51] After describing current British and French views on tank usage, he then turned to the new high-speed tanks and their enhanced capabilities. Unlike the world war machines, he wrote, the new tanks were eminently suited to maneuver warfare, able to play a role like that of the cavalry during the Napoleonic Wars by speeding toward the artillery zone so as to wreak havoc ahead of the infantry battle. How then would the two arms coordinate their actions? In a reversal of the usual answer to this question, he refused to consider slowing the tanks down (which would be "pure suicide for the tank") and instead considered how to help the infantry keep up with the tanks. Noting that here technology had progressed faster than tactics, he wrote that a possible answer was to place the infantry in high-speed "infantry tractors."[52] The army would then be able to bring to bear the full speed and firepower of the tank, united with the fighting abilities of the infantry, on any area of the enemy.

Yet Heigl, Volckheim, and even Seeckt were far ahead of other German officers in their understanding of the future of tank doctrine. A standard tactical textbook was extremely conservative in its ideas about tank usage, although acknowledging that technological progress would overcome the tank's current technical weaknesses.[53] In his examination of the tactical bases for infantry combat manuals, Lieutenant Colonel Muff also showed little confidence in the tank. He began with the old premise that the infantry was still the decisive force and that all other branches of the service needed to cooperate closely with it. The tank was nothing more than an infantry weapon, providing the steel armor that the foot soldier

49. Ernst Volckheim, Der Kampfwagen in der heutigen Kriegführung: Organisation, Verwendung und Bekämpfung: Ein Handbuch für alle Waffen (Berlin: Mittler, 1924), 1–6, 27–67.

50. Ibid., 81–90.

51. Fritz Heigl, Taschenbuch der Tanks (Munich: Lehmanns, 1926) (completed October 1925), 13.

52. Ibid., 300–305, 322–26.

53. Grundriß der Taktik, Auf Grund der Erfahrungen des Weltkrieges (Berlin: R. Eisenschmidt, 1925), 9–10, 126.

needed to carry the battle deep into the enemy's positions.[54] That same year an official assessment of what would need to be done to increase the size of the army after 1931 – when the army would (hopefully) no longer be constrained by Versailles – foresaw a rebuilt army with an armor force of only fifty-one tank companies and 765 men.[55]

After 1925, however, the tide turned decisively in favor of the tank. The reasons for this change can be directly tied to the technological improvements that made the tank faster and more reliable, as well as to British successes with armor forces in their war games. Although disagreements over armor doctrine would continue until the Second World War began, the German high command became virtually unanimous in its belief that the tank was essential for future war. As early as May 1925 the Procurement Office (Waffenamt) would secretly ask three German firms to develop two medium tanks. By 1926, the Reichswehr had expanded this to three light and two medium tank prototypes.[56] A revised infantry textbook of September 1926 showed the old heavy tanks only fighting with world war tactics and tightly linked to the infantry. New fast tanks, on the other hand, could create breakthroughs, attack the rear of the enemy, or engage in large turning maneuvers. Since the new vehicles were so much faster than the infantry, the textbook argued that the army should not tie them closely to foot soldiers, but rather allow them to fight ahead of their accompanying infantry, sometimes deep in the enemy's rear.[57] Seeckt, whose views of armor doctrine had, as we have seen, already begun to evolve in this direction, agreed that tank tactics had to depend on technological development. In his official "Remarks of the Chief of the Army Command for 1926," Seeckt concluded that armor forces now needed two separate tactics. He could only theorize about the first kind, on the basis of continuing progress with high-speed tanks, but he suggested that they attack independently followed by infantry who would exploit their success. High-speed tanks could also take part in missions against far-flung objectives either independently or in cooperation with additional fast-moving forces. The other tank tactics were of course based on the slower world war tanks, which would support the infantry attack directly.[58]

54. Oberstleutnant Muff, "Über die taktischen Grundlagen unserer infanteristischen Gefechts- und Ausbildungsvorschriften," *Das Wissen vom Kriege*, no. 4, suppl. to *Deutsches Offiziersblatt* 29 (1925), 14–15.

55. "Die organisatorische Lage für eine personelle Heeresverstärkung vom Jahre 1931 ab," Anlage 5. BA-MA, RH8/v.894a. pp. 91–125.

56. Werner Oswald, *Kraftfahrzeuge und Panzer der Reichswehr, Wehrmacht und Bundeswehr* (Stuttgart: Motorbuch Verlag, 1973), 239.

57. Rühle v. Lilienstern, *Die Gruppe: Die Ausbildung der Infanterie-Gruppe im Gefecht an Beispielen auf Grund der Kriegserfahrungen*, 4th rev. ed. (Berlin: Mittler, 1927), 11–13.

58. *Bemerkungen des Chefs der Heeresleitung, Generaloberst von Seeckt bei Besichtigungen und Manövern aus dem Jahren 1920 bis 1926* (Berlin: Reichswehrministerium, 1927), BA-MA. RHD18/294 (book). pp. 40–41. See also Captain Robert J. O'Neill, "Doctrine and Training in the German Army 1919–

The growing interest of the Reichswehr in the tank and other vehicles of war led to a strong backlash against the idea of mechanization. The underlying philosophical beliefs of the officers and military thinkers who took part in this reaction were similar to the ideas of Soviet morale advocates. The centrality of man, and especially his fighting spirit, to the conduct of war and the need to concentrate on infantry and cavalry rather than tank or other materiel forces, formed part of the German as well as the Soviet ideology of morale. Even those officers who thought that this attitude toward technology was backward found the ideas on the worth of man and his spirit compelling enough to concede them in their refutations. There were also specifically German components to the morale side of the debate, including a desire on the part of some officers to discredit French military thought, with its (supposed) support for materiel, and a belief that "hiding" behind armor ruined the martial spirit. Practical objections to reliance on materiel based, as in the Soviet Union, on the nation's terrible economic situation and on the technological weaknesses of the tank also played a role in the German debate. In this often charged atmosphere, other officers attempted to find a concept of war that would balance morale and materiel. It is interesting that most of these ended by attacking the "excessive" attachment to materiel of technicians in their own army or belittling French and British "fantasists" like Soldan and Fuller.

The first sign of opposition to materiel in Germany appeared in 1923 in a work by Friedrich von Taysen, still the Inspector of Infantry but now a major general, *Materiel or Morale? A Contribution to the Assessment of the Prevailing Principles of Battle in the French Army.* This short book started a veritable firestorm of controversy in the Reichswehr, not least because it was deliberately provocative, a well-written diatribe against the evils of "Frenchified" materiel. Among other achievements, Taysen was able to weave together three different strands of antimateriel thought in his book: the primacy of man, the importance of the fighting spirit, and the need for nontechnological forces (infantry and cavalry) in order to achieve victory. He began by describing current French views on the usefulness of technology, noting that they were limiting the number of personnel in the army while increasing artillery, tank, and air forces. He criticized each of these, concentrating especially on armor, perhaps because here the danger of replacement of humans by machines was the greatest. He described the tank as fatally flawed both technically and tactically,[59] and then proceeded to the heart of his argument against materiel. "Foot soldiers who are accustomed to the tonic of the tank," he wrote, "will always call for it and, if it is not present or is refused, will only very reluctantly attack. Above all else they will also lose their independence, the will to gain victory for themselves through

---

1939" in *The Theory and Practice of War. Essays Presented to Captain B. H. Liddell Hart*, ed. Michael Howard (London: Cassell, 1965), 146.

59. Friedrich von Taysen, *Material oder Moral? Ein Beitrag zur Beurteilung der im französischen Heere herrschenden Kampfgrundsätze* (Charlottenburg: Verlag "Offene Wort," 1923), 5–27.

superior courage, skillful leadership, and utilization of terrain. Thus habituation to the tank can lead to the death of offensive thought."[60] Dependence on materiel like the tank would, in other words, destroy the offensive military spirit that was the basis for the German ideal of war.

Taysen argued, moreover, that increasing the number of tanks and other technological weapons on the battlefield would not allow countries to create smaller armies, since more soldiers would be needed as ammunition carriers or to tend the machines. Nor would the French be able to save lives in actual battle, because the eternal competition between armor and projectile, between shield and spear, would lead to the creation of ever more powerful antiarmor weapons able to smash the toughest protection. He thought that the stationary battle of materiel, as in the world war, was the kind of war that the French wanted and would create with their emphasis on technology and machines. Finally, the real reason why materiel was so important to the French was because they were a "sterile nation" that could not count on allies for their next war with Germany. He ended by musing on the fact that just as the infantry was a reflection of the people of a nation, so the whole totality of that nation's conception of battle was a reflection of its culture, from which it sprang in the first place. Thus,

> Roman culture sees its fulfillment in Form, but Germanic culture in Limitlessness, [expressed] in our days in the systematic materiel offensive of the Gaul and in the power thrust of the German, which subordinates all resources to one goal; breaking through [any] boundaries to achieve that crucial limitless movement . . . *Therefore we shall, in accordance with our nature, further stretch the spiritual bounds and see that it is the living will that is decisive, not dead materiel – and then the Will shall find its way!*[61]

Military thinkers in both Germany and the Soviet Union responded to Taysen's controversial views either by seeking to modify what they saw as his extremist position, or by expressing their agreement with most of what he had to say. It is striking that there was about a two-year delay in these responses, showing that officers in both countries felt comfortable defending the tank only after the machine had developed technologically. The first semicritical response to the book appeared in the pages of the *Militär-Wochenblatt* in late 1925. Also entitled "Materiel or Morale?", the anonymous article first found fault with Taysen's allegations that the French were completely dependent on materiel and that the Reichswehr should in turn trust only in superior morale. He provided quotations from the French service regulations which showed that the French army also thought that "[w]illingness to make sacrifices and the will to win are still the guarantors of final success."[62] It was simply a truth of modern warfare, on the other hand, that the extraordinary rise in

60. Ibid., 27–28.
61. Ibid., 58; Taysen's emphasis.
62. "Material oder Moral?" *Militär-Wochenblatt*, no. 28 (1925): 824–25.

firepower during the last war had tipped the scales in favor of materiel. If this was an indisputable fact, it was also true that materiel was not necessarily a bad thing, as Taysen alleged. Materiel did not, for instance, destroy the morale of soldiers, but rather increased it. It was lack of materiel that would shake an army's spirit, as the example of the tanks during the world war had clearly shown.[63]

Not that the author of this article denied the overwhelming importance of morale in battle: "It would of course be wrong to fall into the opposite [error] and assert that materiel will decide the next war, that the military profession will soon no longer exist, and that in future war will be conducted by engineers." The truth was quite the contrary, since "[i]t will always be men and not machines that engage in battle and throw themselves on the opponent during decisive close combat." The relationship between materiel and morale had to be like that between the human spirit and the tools of man. After all, armaments were a powerful means for discouraging the opponent and for lifting the morale of one's own troops, but in the final analysis it was always morale which led to victory.[64] The writer concluded by saying that materiel and morale could not be separated from each other and that the title of Taysen's book should therefore be reformulated as "Materiel *and* Morale" – and woe to the nation that entered the next war without enough materiel.[65]

At about the same time a Soviet writer, Braginskii, published an article in which he critically examined Taysen's thought. Braginskii's article offers another look at the continuing debate over materiel and morale among Red Army officers and shows that while differences existed between this debate and the German one, there were also remarkable similarities. After describing French views on modern warfare and how the next war should be fought, Braginskii discussed Taysen's criticism and agreed with him for the most part. He thought the German author was right to fault the way that the French planned on slow, deliberate advances rather than working out some way to maneuver freely on the battlefield, although he had doubts about some of Taysen's criticism of the tank.[66] It was with Taysen's outraged denial that technology could replace the infantry that the Soviet author most completely agreed:

> The German criticism concerns, for the most part, that type of weapon which was created for the direct combination of moral, physical, and material forces, that is, the infantry. Of course the infantry, based in its organization exclusively on the strength of the individual man, experiences a difficult crisis during a period of rapid technological progress. For the drive to arm the individual man as much as

63. Ibid., 825–26.
64. Ibid., 826.
65. Ibid., 827.
66. M. Braginskii, "Germanskaia kritika frantsuzskikh ustavov i vliianie etoi kritiki na Frantsuzov," *Voina i Revoliutsiia*, no. 10 (1926): 148–50, 154–56.

possible has a fixed limit – his physical capabilities. To step across this boundary means to convert the infantryman into the servant of his own weapon, that is, to liquidate him completely. From this came the drive to increase the technical types of forces at the expense of the infantry. For increasing it otherwise is impossible. In this connection we acknowledge as correct the opinion expressed by Taysen.[67]

Taysen's denigration of the French was echoed by many of those who opposed reliance on materiel. A retired Lieutenant Colonel Rath looked at France as an example of a country that needed to rely on technology both because it had fewer and fewer men of the right age for military service and because its economic and physical powers were lessening. The French had attempted to make up for these problems by using "colored" troops, but "[t]he inner worth of the white troops and in particular the troops drafted for the duration will be unfavorably influenced by this." To cover up their shortcomings, the French were thus forced to use materiel instead. Dependence on machines would, he argued, destroy offensive thought and in the end, materiel would triumph over man.[68] The French were especially taken with the tank, but of course the tank could never completely replace man. Like any other vehicle it could only pave the way for the victory of the infantry, as history had already shown that "the multitude of war machines of antiquity and modern times were never the army itself, but always only auxiliary vehicles of the individual fighting men, the infantry."[69] Finally, the use of modern technology demanded much more thorough training than did earlier weapons and was therefore another reason not to fear the French, since "a magazine-fed rifle in the hands of a well-trained German infantryman is something completely different than one in the hands of a Negro."[70]

A letter from an unnamed staff officer to Joachim von Stülpnagel in March 1925 agreed with Rath and Taysen that technology was overrated. Stülpnagel was a member of a large family, many of whose members were in the military. At this point in his career he was the head of the Army Department (Heeresabteilung) of the Truppenamt, a high-ranking position from which he would attempt to influence Seeckt and German doctrine. The anonymous staff officer naturally knew this when he wrote to Stülpnagel in an attempt to change the army's views of technology. He began by acknowledging that technology was as necessary a part of modern warfare as tactics. However, the pendulum had swung too far in the direction of technology and had to be checked. There were many ways in which the German army and others had overestimated the worth of some technology, such as the semiautomatic rifle. The other example was the tank: "has not our technology on this field also

67. Ibid., 162.
68. Oberstleutnant a.D. Rath, "Mensch und Material," *Das Wissen vom Kriege*, no. 19, suppl. to *Deutsches Offiziersblatt* 30 (1926), 73–74.
69. Ibid., 74.
70. Ibid., 75.

failed? And is the progress made in this field – and in other technical fields – in the six and a half years after the war so very great?" The technological breakthrough of the scientist was the easy part; application in real battles was something else, and relying solely on the work done in laboratories was thus open to objection. Some of the claims put forward on behalf of technology even reminded the writer of the kind of wild hopes "awakened by fantastic literary descriptions and the spirit of the time (occultism, mysticism, etc.)," as if a magical piece of technology could have saved Germany in the last war. This had not been the case in the past and "just as little will this be the case in the future. The Russians, English, or Americans will not get us out [of our difficulties], but we will do it by ourselves, or rather our own strong will, our proud national spirit, will do it. The other things are aids, in part important aids, but still only secondary."[71] As with so much else written by German and Soviet officers, the underlying supposition was that the machine was useful as long as it knew its proper place.

Men such as Volckheim, specialists who continued to seek support for their views about technology and the tank, came under special attack from morale advocates. In October 1925 Volckheim published an article in which he argued for the value of the tank by asserting the need to focus on both materiel and morale. Although his line of argument was close to that of the writers discussed above, Volckheim spent more time on the usefulness of technology, and especially on the worth of the tank, than did those who thought that morale would conquer all.[72] A few weeks later, an anonymous officer challenged Volckheim's praise for the tank by arguing that, of the three modern weapons, gas, airplanes, and tanks, tanks were by far the least valuable. Among other objections, he said that airplanes and gas attacked the rear, where helpless women and children were to be found, but "[t]he tank will only be a threat on the front, where the people best trained for battle, physically and morally, stand: men with strong wills and iron armament."[73] Others criticized the growing power of specialists like Volckheim. Rath, for instance, equated a rise in the influence of technicians with a decline in the power of the infantry, which would only lead to technology and materiel ruling the army and destroying the concept of the battle of annihilation.[74]

Another major element in German arguments against materiel was spirited disagreement with the arch-enemies of the morale supporters, Fuller and Soldan. Fuller's ideas were in the main labeled as sheer fantasies that did not merit serious refutation. A review of one of his books was typical, lightly mocking his concepts

71. "Aus einem Brief an Stülpnagel," 29 March 1925. BA-MA. N221/40; see also "Taktik und Technik, Moral und Material," *Heerestechnik*, no. 1 (1925): 20.

72. Ernst Volckheim, "Die Waffe des Zukunftskrieges," *Militär-Wochenblatt*, no. 14 (1925): 465–68.

73. "Zum Wesen der Waffen des Zukunftskrieges," ibid., no. 18 (1925): 622–23.

74. Rath, "Mensch und Material," 74–75.

about warfare in general and "the hypermodern Fuller-army" in particular.[75] Rath also thought the expectation of replacing the infantry with tanks was just a fantasy; it would indeed be the complete triumph of materiel, but how would one pack a million-man army into tanks? Where would they find the room?[76] Soldan attracted even more negative language, perhaps because he was French. Each of his ideas was analyzed and shown to be not only wrong but highly dangerous. One of the first reviews of his book *Man and the Battle of the Future* argued that no responsible, self-aware people would entrust their fate to a small minority of their number. More than that, the officer continued, "love of the fatherland, the struggle for existence, the will of the leader will also drive the physically and psychically weak into the trenches and precisely the machine [in the hands of the enemy] will also make these [men] into remarkable fighters."[77]

It is not surprising, given this hostility to the idea of machine warfare that German officers, like their Soviet colleagues, pointed to the various technological and tactical problems with the tank as a practical reason not to depend too much on materiel. Taysen, of course, emphasized the tank's poor technical capabilities, pointing out that, among other things, it was too vulnerable to machine-gun and artillery fire, too blind, too frail, and too cumbersome.[78] Other officers followed Taysen in trying to show that the tank was not the best weapon for modern warfare. They wrote that tanks had serious technical and tactical deficiencies; that they were far too dependent on huge logistical organizations; and that they were vulnerable to defensive countermeasures, a problem which no future technological developments could overcome.[79] Even a former officer who had fought with the German tank corps during the world war declared that "the idea of the battle wagon is outdated."[80] From a tactical standpoint, morale supporters also thought that the tank and other types of materiel were either created for, or would help to create, the wrong sort of war: one like the world war involving trenches and slow positional warfare. They equated a reliance on morale, on the other hand, with maneuver and

75. Frentsch, "Gegenwartsgedanken zu 'Die Zukunft des Landkrieges'" (review of Fuller's The Reformation of War), *Das Wissen vom Kriege*, no. 19, suppl. to *Deutsches Offiziersblatt* 30 (1926), 75.

76. Rath, "Mensch und Material," 74.

77. Oberstleutnant a.D. Müler-Loebnitz, "Der Mensch und die Schlacht der Zukunft" *Deutsches Offiziersblatt* 19, no. 34 (1925): 265. See also Generalmajor a.D. v. Vorries, "George Soldan: Der Mensch und die Schlacht der Zukunft," *Das Wissen vom Kriege*, no. 1, suppl. to *Deutsches Offizersblatt* 30 (1926), 2–3; Alexander Rühle von Lilienstern, "Schlacht der Zukunft," *Militär-Wochenblatt*, no. 40 (1926): 1443–44. For a more nuanced view of Soldan, see Oberst a.D. Blümner, "Mensch und Material," ibid., no. 1 (1926): 6–9.

78. Taysen. *Matériel oder Moral?*, 20–27, 53–54.

79. Frentsch, "Gegenwartsgedanken zu 'Die Zukunft des Landkrieges,'" 75–76; Oberleutnant Czimatis, "Die Waffen des Zukuntskrieges," *Militär-Wochenblatt*, no. 18 (1925): 620; "Zum Wesen der Waffen des Zukunftskrieges," 622.

80. Oberleutnant d.R. a.D. Larsen, "Als Tankkommandant," *Militär-Wochenblatt*, no. 42 (1926): 1533.

quick decisions. Since German officers, from Seeckt on down, were unanimous in their desire to return mobility to war and to avoid the dreaded stalemate of the Western Front, this gave the tank considerable appeal. Taysen, as noted above, was one of the first to contrast the systematic materiel assault of the French with the highly mobile warfare of the German. He also thought that it was materiel that had created positional warfare in the first place, and therefore should be avoided by the German army.[81] The anonymous officer who had criticized some of Taysen's ideas likewise equated materiel with unmoving fire and morale with mobility. He thought that both of these were necessary components of any battle, but one was obviously more important than the other. "Just as morale is always to be valued higher than materiel, so also must movement, the sign of moral power, be described . . . as the decisive factor, ahead of fire which is the materiel component. Movement, the assault forward into the opponent is always the goal of battle, while fire is only the means for this. For winning means attacking!"[82]

Yet another reason not to rely the tank and other materiel, the supporters of morale argued, was the ability of the German army to find successful countermeasures to new technological developments. The "lessons of history" showed that soldiers had found defenses against battle wagons in the past and therefore "proved" that modern militaries would discover the appropriate response to the tank.[83] More broadly, these officers believed that for every new weapon a means of defense would be found. Technology in particular progressed so slowly that there was always enough time to allow the proper antidote to be found, just as had been done in the case of the tank. After antitank weapons had been developed, the German army had quickly overcome the "tank horror" of the world war, and today troops that did not lose their nerve had no reason to fear armor forces.[84]

The prostrate economy that Germany, like the Soviet Union, faced during the twenties further bolstered these arguments against the new technology. Weimar Germany suffered several major shocks in the early twenties from which it recovered briefly only to sink once again after the American stock market crash. Between these two crises the Weimar governments had to be concerned with balancing budgets and could not increase spending on the army. There was also resistance from some administrations to giving more money to the military in general.[85] The Reichswehr officer corps realized that building a modern high-technology army would be difficult without a major revival of the economy and a change in state pol-

81. Taysen, *Material oder Moral?* 58.

82. "Material oder Moral?" 827; see also Vorries, "George Soldan: Der Mensch und die Schlacht der Zukunft," 3.

83. Larsen, "Als Tankkommandant," 1533.

84. "Von der Kriegstechnik," *Militär-Wochenblatt*, no. 29 (1925): 853–54.

85. Harold James, *The German Slump: Politics and Economics 1924–1936* (Oxford: Clarendon Press, 1986).

icy.[86] This was, in fact, one of the few areas where every officer, regardless of his views on mechanization, could agree, concluding that lack of money for the time being precluded the large-scale production of tanks and other expensive new weapons. Thus, an article describing the general mechanization of the British army commented that the displacement of muscle power by machines represented healthy progress, but that the greatest obstacle to mechanization was the "money question" since one could not count on an increase in the military budget.[87] Later discussions of armor forces recognized that expensive weapons like tanks were something that only rich nations could afford, especially given the poor track record of armor during the last war.[88] Even when the economy improved somewhat between 1924 and 1929, the German high command continued to consider extensive mechanization out of the question, for budgetary reasons alone, until after Hitler came to power.

While materiel supporters held up these economic and technological problems as objective reasons to refrain from even considering mechanization, believers in morale saw them as challenges to be overcome. German officers who argued that tanks, and materiel in general, would play an important role in future warfare also stressed the same improvements in technology and developments by other nations as did Soviet materiel advocates. But Germans could also emphasize the commonly accepted idea that the next war must be more mobile, as a decisive reason that the Reichswehr could not neglect the new and improved tank. As in the Soviet Union, however, German materiel advocates felt obliged to agree with the basic philosophical foundations of the morale idea. Man, and in particular the foot soldier, was still the basis for their thought about future warfare, while tanks and other materiel were but auxiliary weapons for the infantry.

Volckheim's work, which broke new ground in tank tactics, also attempted to answer, point by point, the objections of Taysen and other morale advocates. His second, more radical book of 1924 began with a chapter entitled "Are Tanks Necessary in Modern Armies Or Not?", a question that he answered by saying that the tireless perfecting and construction of tanks by Germany's former enemies as well as the prohibitions of Versailles were reason enough to believe that they would indeed be necessary.[89] He added that opinions about the tank within German military circles were, however, divided, and proceeded to repeat Taysen's arguments

86. See "Denkschrift über die Ziele und Wege der nächsten Jahre für unsere Kriegsvorbereitungen," 1925. BA-MA. RH 8/v. 1365. pp. 15–19.
87. "Gedanken über eine allmähliche Mechanisierung in der englischen Armee," *Militär-Wochenblatt*, no. 23 (1924): 649–51.
88. Czimatis, "Die Waffen des Zukunftskrieges," 619–21; "Vom Tank," *Militär-Wochenblatt*, no. 29 (1926): 1034; Larsen, "Als Tankkommandant," 1529–33.
89. Quite a few materiel advocates used this as an argument. See Friedrich Sonnenberg, "Neuzeitliche Heerestechnik," *Militär-Wochenblatt*, no. 43 (1925): 1327; and Volckheim, *Der Kampfwagen in der heutigen Kriegführung*, 1–3.

about the future uses of armor. After conceding that one had to be clear about the
disadvantages of tanks that had inspired these views, and agreeing that the types
of tanks currently available in France would not be useful in a future war, he continued by stating that the tank was being constantly improved. It was now smaller
(and therefore offered less of a target), faster, and more maneuverable – all qualities that future German armor experts would see as indispensable in tanks.[90]

Volckheim then looked at Taysen's claim that armor harmed the fighting spirit
of the infantry. He agreed that this had happened to the French during the war, but
continued: "this unfavorable effect of the tank on the French infantry can . . . by no
means be applied to a morally strong army. To be spoiled by the tank represents
without a doubt a danger for the infantry. This danger can however [be avoided]
through training, which must work on this, and accustom the infantry to fighting
without tanks." The use of tanks would then only strengthen the troops, not
weaken them.[91] He believed that one of the most important reasons that German
officers viewed the tank as unnecessary was simply sour grapes – the Reichswehr
had no tanks, and therefore they could not be decisive. This view had to change because armor was vital for future warfare. The strongest power of an army, he concluded, naturally remained morale, that is the offensive will of the German soldier.
This could however "by the correct use of mechanical weapons only be fundamentally strengthened. Thus the tank, in increased quantities, will remain in the future
a decisive *auxiliary arm of the infantry.*"[92]

Volckheim's final chapter dealt with an issue usually ignored by morale advocates, but continually emphasized by those who supported the tank: the future
technological and tactical development of the weapon. He discussed the need for
tanks that would be faster and smaller, but have stronger armor and greater
weaponry; tanks able to cross any kind of terrain, fight at night, shoot accurately,
and have better observation capabilities. He concluded that it would be impossible
to unite all these characteristics in one "universal tank," and thus the army would
need to build tanks for every imaginable mission. Volckheim, unlike the morale
supporters, saw the tank as a flexible and eminently improvable weapon, which
could be molded to meet any of the changing needs of the army.[93] In a later article
he was even more convinced of the promising future that the tank had before it,
pointing out the way that almost all the deficiencies of the first tanks had been corrected; for example, the tank could now move across almost any terrain, and was
no longer so vulnerable as it had been since it was much faster.[94]

And this was one of the chief differences between morale and materiel support-

90. Volckheim, *Der Kampfwagen in der heutigen Kriegführung,* 1–3.
91. Ibid., 4–5.
92. Ibid., 5–6; my emphasis.
93. Ibid., 81–89.
94. Volckheim, "Die Waffe des Zukunftskrieges," 467–68.

ers. The former believed in an ever brighter future for the technology created during the world war, while the latter thought that technology had already reached its limits and therefore would never be able to fulfill the fantastic claims of the engineers and specialists. Former General Schwarte thus asserted that the "Age of Technology," which had begun a quarter of a century before, had not yet reached its peak and that more successes were still to come. In particular he noted that the tank, although currently confined to positional warfare, was being transformed by the French and British into a weapon that would be useful also in mobile warfare.[95] Like others who believed in materiel, he offered comfort for German soldiers, repeating Taysen's belief that a spirited, morally unweakened warrior could lessen the effect of a mass tank attack, since this primarily worked on morale.[96]

German military thinkers who supported the tank and materiel agreed with Schwarte's emphasis on the growing perfection of the machine. They too stressed the fact that the tank had moved beyond most of its technological problems and believed that engineers would find solutions for current difficulties.[97] The next logical step was to conclude that the new tanks should be used in completely different ways from the slow-moving vehicles of the world war. The tank tactics of the new French and British tanks would be as far from those of the war tank usage as the management of a racehorse were different from that of a cart-horse, one officer wrote. He suggested following some of Fuller's ideas on tanks, although always keeping in mind that no country's industry could mass-produce tanks and also that tanks still could not travel on all terrains. He foresaw the creation of independent tank forces which, combined with other light mobile weapons and infantry on motorized transport, would completely replace the cavalry. At the end of his article he noted that these remarks were valid only for the present state of tank technology, and "the young tank weapon will quickly develop further technically. We must, then, free ourselves from the old tactical views and use every progress of technology to form new principles for using [tanks]."[98]

Tank supporters argued, too, that improvements in technology might revolutionize warfare in general.[99] With their speed, powerful armament, and ability to travel long distances, new French and British tanks had become purely offensive weapons meant for a war of movement. No longer would the tank be found only in trench warfare and slow systematic battles for positions; instead tank forces would

---

95. Generalleutnant a.D. M. Schwarte, *Die Technik im Zukunftskriege: Ein Handbuch* (Charlottenburg: Verlag "Offene Worte," 1924), 6–7, 191.

96. Ibid., 194–96.

97. See for example "Neuzeitliche Kampfwagen," *Das Wissen vom Kriege*, no. 8. suppl. to *Deutsches Offiziersblatt* 30 (1926): 31.

98. Mügge, "Betrachtung über die Kampfwagenverwendung," *Militär-Wochenblatt*, no. 22 (1925): 771–72.

99. See e.g. Oberst a.D. Frhr. v. Weitershausen, "Geschütz – Kampfwagen – Flugzeug," *Militär-Wochenblatt*, no. 13 (1926): 442.

move much faster than the infantry who would need to be motorized in order to keep up with them. Even the heavy tanks would find new uses, since they too would be much faster, able to travel far ahead of the light infantry-accompanying tanks and break the enemy's resistance.[100] One writer concluded that tanks could basically replace the other forces, since "the light tank forces will themselves be the infantry and the heavy will be the artillery."[101]

The army of the future implied by these views of technology was a comparatively small one, consisting of professional soldiers and equipped with relatively large numbers of machines. Not coincidentally this was precisely the vision on which Seeckt had predicated his leadership of the army. In fact, many of the materiel advocates supported, and were supported by, the head of the army. But they went even further than Seeckt, making a virtue out of an army that Seeckt saw as a necessity forced by Versailles. By lessening the number of men on the battlefield, the small army of the future would create the room to maneuver that the large army of the past had lost after 1914. On the battlefield itself the use of motor vehicles, airplanes, and trains would make the army a "wonder of mobility," able to move quickly and attack decisively, putting all its weight into any desired section of the battlefield. Yet the small, technologically advanced army would need to reach a quick decision, since behind the front each side would be rapidly mobilizing all the men and materiel that lack of money had prohibited it from stockpiling before the war. If the war was not decided before these could be inserted into the battle, a positional war would ensue, without decision or victory for either side.[102]

The idea of such a force was not popular with everyone in the German army. As one officer pointed out, those who supported the idea were doing so because they were forced to by circumstances beyond their control, namely Versailles. More than that, the new technologies of the future would require able-bodied citizens to remain at home as technicians, specialists, and workers creating tanks and airplanes, rather than joining the army as soldiers. This was unacceptable, since a smaller army, unless of higher quality, almost always lost to the larger mass army.[103] The following year Stülpnagel entered the debate, arguing that technology demanded not fewer men, but a larger number of well-trained men. He agreed that a small army was no match for a mass army, but also predicted that greater technical preparation

100. "Der Einfluß des neuzeitlichen Kampfwagens auf die Kriegführung," Militär-Wochenblatt, no. 26 (1926): 913–18; "Der Kampfwagen der Jetztzeit und der Zukunft," ibid., nos. 43–45 (1926): 1559–62, 1591–95, 1628–30.

101. "Der Kampfwagen der Jetztzeit und der Zukunft," 1630.

102. "Der Mensch und die Schlacht der Zukunft," Militär-Wochenblatt, no. 30 (1926): 1066–67; Major Dr. Lothar Rendulic, "Über die Formen eines künftigen Krieges," ibid., no. 7 (1926): 231–34. See also "Haruspex," "Massenheer oder Technik," ibid., no. 40 (1927): 1473–76.

103. Hauptmann Dittmar, "Vom kleinen Zukunftsheer," Militär-Wochenblatt, no. 18 (1926): 631–35.

would give any military an edge over its opponents. The question was therefore not mass army versus quality army, but rather how to create a large quality army.[104]

For many German officers the theoretical nature of the entire debate meant that it was a wasted exercise. Instead they looked for the evidence of actual combat or extensive maneuvers to prove conclusively which side was right. Tank supporters in Germany, like those in the Soviet Union, pointed to recent successes of tanks in British maneuvers as proof that armor would play an important role in future warfare. During the 1924 exercises German observers were impressed by the Vickers Mark I, a light fast tank that was able to speed ahead of the infantry and cavalry for the first time.[105] The results of special exercises held in July 1926 by the British army to test the new tanks against cavalry were more ambiguous; not even those who supported the tank were able to prove that the "modern units" had held their own against the "orthodox."[106] On the other hand, the obvious success of British target practices that same month gave renewed hope to those who believed in the tank. German armor supporters argued that, now that tanks could hit targets while moving, they were much more dangerous opponents than the old world war vehicles, which had had dismal records at accurate shooting.[107] The 1927 British exercises with an experimental motorized brigade were greeted with even more fanfare, as newspapers followed with growing excitement the developments on Salisbury Plain.[108] The British achievements gave powerful ammunition to the tank supporters, as they pointed to the successes of actual maneuvers as proof that they had been right to see the future of warfare in the tank.

Yet as the debate developed, some German officers became concerned by what they saw as extremism on both sides. As early as February 1924, Stülpnagel delivered a lecture to a group of officers entitled "Thoughts on the War of the Future" in which he sought to find a middle ground. He began by stating that a war of "liberation," that is, liberation from Versailles and the French, was inevitable.[109] But what would this war of liberation be like? First and foremost the entire nation would need to participate in the struggle. However, the people of the nation had to

104. Joachim von Stülpnagel, "Die zahlenmässig beschränkte Qualitätsarmee und das Massenheer in ihrer wechselseitigen Bewertung in künftigen Kriegen von Standpunkt moderner Waffentechnik. Wo liegen für beide die oberen und unteren Grenzen ihres Umfanges?" (lecture, 28 January 1927), BA-MA. RH 8/v. 1365, pp. 85–99.

105. "Die englischen Manöver 1924," *Militär-Wochenblatt*, no. 26 (1925): 761–63.

106. "Alfred," "Kampfwagen und Kavallerie," *Militär-Wochenblatt*, no. 16 (1926): 553–55.

107. "Das Schießen vom fahrenden Kampfwagen," *Militär-Wochenblatt*, no. 19 (1926): 681–83.

108. "Englische motorisierte Versuchsbrigade," *Militär-Wochenblatt*, nos. 14–17 (1927): 501–7, 540–43, 570–71, 607–8; and "Neues von den englischen Manövern," ibid., no. 16 (1927): 568–69.

109. As he put it, might made right, and it was against both nature and experience to try to "ring in" eternal peace. Joachim v. Stülpnagel, "Gedanken über den Krieg der Zukunft" (lecture, February 1924), BA-MA. N 5/10, p. 4.

be morally trained for war. The preparation of the nation would include national and military education for German youth; the fomenting of hatred against the enemy; the education of the people in the ideas of the state and in the duty to work; and a state-led struggle against international communism and pacifism, that is, against all that was "un-German." The idea of duty had to be cultivated as well as the categorical imperative to fight and die for the Fatherland. If this spiritual steadfastness of the masses was not attained, Stülpnagel warned, then the new troops, quickly assembled and badly trained, would not long withstand the stresses of modern war.[110]

A second characteristic of the war of liberation would be the overwhelming superiority of the French in materiel. This would force the German army to find new ways to conduct war which, strengthened by a spiritually powerful people and "carried out in the grandest form, must affect the French, who depend on their armaments and act very systematically, in a surprising and bewildering way. German spirit must be victorious over French materiel!" One of the weakest points of the French draft army was "the irresistible urge of the French to protect and hide their men, who were badly exhausted in the world war, behind armor, which has little mobility, in a future war." Yet he also argued that the Reichswehr should strive to have its own materiel, of at least the same quantity as the French, since morale without materiel was as useless as all materiel and low morale.[111] In a second lecture delivered a year later, Stülpnagel gave an even more balanced appraisal of the relative worth of morale and materiel, stating that both were equally necessary for victory, and in January 1927, although he still stressed the inner worth of the soldier, he argued that more highly developed states had always been victorious, through their technology, over less developed states.[112]

The German debate over mechanization was, in many ways, summed up in the discussion of the use of tanks and automobiles in place of horses which paralleled that over the replacement of man by machine. The majority of the German officer corps conceded that the world war had shown the futility of massed cavalry charges, but some officers went further, arguing that with the development of faster tanks and cars, the horse was no longer necessary at all. Some of the most severe critics of the tank, and machines in warfare generally, were older cavalry officers, who rightly saw that the motor was a direct threat to their existence. The attack was led by the head of the cavalry, General von Poseck, who had argued immediately after the end of the world war that no machine could replace the cavalry.[113] Poseck spent a great deal of time from 1924 to 1927 trying to show why the

110. Ibid., 9–11.
111. Ibid., 17–18.
112. Joachim von Stülpnagel, "Wechselbeziehungen zwischen Land-, See- und Luftkriegführung: Ein Beitrag zum Problem des Zukunftskrieges" (lecture, 5 March 1925), BA-MA. N 5/11, p. 40; Stülpnagel, "Die zahlenmässig beschränkte Qualitätsarmee," 85–89.
113. See above, chapter 1.

horse, and especially fighting from a horse, was still necessary even with the advent of the new weapons.

Poseck's crusade to save the cavalry from what he saw as intolerable criticism was inspired by an exchange in the *Militär-Wochenblatt* in 1924. An article by an anonymous officer had appeared, claiming that the missions of the cavalry could be done quicker, more easily, and with less loss of life by motorized and air forces.[114] Another officer answered a few weeks later that the cavalry was as modern as any of the other forces and still just as necessary. He admitted that airplanes were very useful for certain tasks, but the replacement of the horse by tanks would have a "very doubtful success" since tanks could not use bridges, travel through woods or cross large rivers.[115] Poseck joined in the debate, and much of his wrath was directed against those who championed the tank, as he tried to show that the horse was a better means of combat than any machine. First he belittled the notion that the tank could ever replace the horse, stating that tanks were useless in many kinds of terrain and therefore were incapable of performing reconnaissance missions. In addition, the tank was "deaf and half-blind and could not halt in order to observe," was so loud that any enemy would be able to find it, and at the same time was vulnerable to artillery fire.[116] As for mobility, he argued that the horse was able to maneuver better and faster than any machine. Vehicles had breakdowns and were dependent on manmade supplies like oil and gas while the horse could find "fuel" anywhere. He even supported the use of the lance, arguing that the world war had shown it was necessary for the cavalryman on the Eastern if not the Western Front, and that it would allow the cavalry to remain a true fighting force. Here as elsewhere, he also stated that only cavalry officers had the right to discuss the future uses of cavalry, since only they were qualified to do so. This arrogation of the privilege to express opinions laid the basis for his later attacks on tank supporters.[117]

Poseck's article, and the responses to it, consumed a large portion of the German officer corps's attention over the next three years. As in the dispute over Taysen's support of man in battle, the basic argument was whether living forces would be able to hold their own on an increasingly mechanized battlefield. At first officers tended to criticize the cavalry obliquely and only partially, using the works of foreigners to show their own thoughts. During 1925, for instance, two articles appeared in the *Militär-Wochenblatt* ostensibly describing the opinions of French and English military authorities on the cavalry question. Both foreigners quoted here were extremely critical of the chances of using the horse successfully in modern

---

114. "Beitrag zu den Gedanken über Kavallerie in den Aufsätzen 'Material und Moral,'" *Militär-Wochenblatt*, no. 24 (1924): 687–89.

115. "Zum 'Beitrag zu den Gedanken über Kavallerie in den Aufsätzen "Material und Moral,"'" *Militär-Wochenblatt*, no. 29 (1925): 849–53.

116. General der Kavallerie v. Poseck, "Heereskavallerie," *Militär-Wochenblatt*, nos. 37–38 (1925): 1121–25, 1158–61.

117. Poseck, "Heereskavallerie," *Militär-Wochenblatt*, no. 39 (1925): 1201–3.

battle, but while the first German officer, looking at the views of General Camon, described the French officer's ideas without much comment, the second, on Sir Ian Hamilton, was more critical.[118] Here the officer tried to show that Hamilton's conclusion, that there was simply no place for cavalry in future armies, was not completely wrong. The cavalry certainly could not fight as it had before the world war and would have to find new tactics and ways of employment in order to be useful. Even this modest critique was too much for the real cavalrymen, such as Poseck, who issued a blistering censure of Hamilton and the German author of the article several weeks later. Poseck once again used examples from the world war to show that the cavalry had performed wonderfully in battle and that it had already adjusted its tactics to meet the demands of modern warfare. On the other hand, vehicles and especially heavy tanks could not even use roads, while an automobile detachment had failed to enter battle at the right time during a recent French maneuver because of the rain![119] Use of vehicles would be all the more difficult during a war, when, for instance, bomber attacks would make bridges unusable. "This all proves," he concluded, "that the machine still will often fail, where only the horse moves forward."[120]

The editorial board of the *Militär-Wochenblatt* added a postscript to Poseck's article stating that they would adjourn for a time the exchange of ideas over the cavalry, but feelings about the future of the cavalry still ran high on both sides of the debate.[121] Only a few months later, a former officer attempted another mildly negative assessment of the cavalry, showing that airplanes, modern motor transport, and increased firepower had made possible the tactical envelopments that the cavalry was apparently no longer able to perform. The cavalry could not perform reconnaissance as well as these machines, nor should it use lances any longer in battle. The writer advocated, however, the use of mounted charges to support the infantry and thus a modification of cavalry organization and tactics rather than the abolishment of the horse.[122] Once again Poseck jumped at the chance to protect his cavalry from even minor criticism, citing a multitude of experiences from the world war that showed why cavalry was still able to perform reconnaissance and fight with lances.[123] The results of the British maneuvers of July 1926, featuring

118. "Zur Kavallerie-Frage," *Militär-Wochenblatt*, no. 41 (1925): 1260–63; Geyer, "Eine englische Ansicht über Kavallerie," ibid., no. 10 (1925):326–29.

119. Heavy vehicles and tanks in particular will tear up paved roads.

120. General der Kavallerie v. Poseck, "Ansichten über Kavallerie," *Militär-Wochenblatt*, no. 18 (1925): 609–13.

121. Ibid., 613.

122. Generalmajor a.D. Frhr. v. Rotberg, "Wichtigste Kriegserfahrungen der Kavallerie und ihre Auswerkung," *Militär-Wochenblatt*, no. 37 (1926): 1315–21.

123. General der Kavallerie v. Poseck, "Über Kriegserfahrungen und Ausbildung der Kavallerie," *Militär-Wochenblatt*, nos. 46–47 (1926): 1664–68, 1702–5.

cavalry on one side and tanks on the other, were interpreted by cavalrymen to support their position.[124]

Yet during late 1926 and 1927 the public debate over the cavalry began to swing in favor of those who criticized the horse in battle. In an article on the horse and the motor vehicle in the modern army, one officer went further than others had dared in print, writing that while for the moment one could not completely do without animals, at some future date this might happen. Motor vehicles could easily replace the horse already in most instances while the tank would take the place of the horse-drawn artillery. While this officer did not wonder that there were those who supported the use of the horse in war, the fact was that technology would indeed replace it.[125] Poseck, although retired from his position in 1927, refused to give up easily. In March 1927 he published an article that listed more instances from the world war in which the cavalry had used the lance effectively, but he no longer received the backing from other officers that he had enjoyed earlier.[126] Instead he was answered three months later by a fellow retired officer who gave counterexamples to illustrate the negative impact of the lance on warfare, concluding that the only solution was "away with the lance!"[127] A more serious attack on the horse in battle argued only a few weeks after Poseck's article that the tank was the cavalry of the future. The modern cavalry would still be useful in wars, but its tasks would be very different from those of the earlier cavalry, whose main mission, movement and fire in movement, would now be taken over by the tank. The new fast tank would, like the cavalry of old, fight far ahead of the infantry as the battle-deciding weapon. The old cavalry, which fought almost exclusively on horseback, had disappeared, argued this officer, but its spirit had risen again in the mobile tank forces.[128]

An answer to this author came several months later, in an article which in many ways summed up the attitude of the morale supporters. Most were willing to admit that they had lost the struggle against a further mechanization of warfare, but they still hoped that in the end man would be able to triumph over machine. In this article the officer conceded that the army of the future would be one of motor vehicles and armor, but this was not the whole story. Although the cavalry would surely be completely replaced in the future by even more perfected machines, and motorized and mechanized units would appear, still "in the end, dead machines are not decisive in the struggle between peoples, but rather the will and *the heart of the men*

---

124. "Alfred," "Kampfwagen und Kavallerie," 553–55.

125. L. D., "Pferd und Auto im heutigen Heere," *Das Wissen vom Kriege*, no. 12. suppl. to *Deutsches Offiziersblatt*, 30 (1926), 45–46.

126. General der Kavallerie a.D. v. Poseck, "Soll die Kavallerie die Lanze beibehalten oder abschaffen?" *Militär-Wochenblatt*, no. 36 (1927): 1315–19.

127. Generalmajor a.D. Frhr. v. Rotberg, "Soll die Kavallerie die Lanze beibehalten oder abschaffen?" *Militär-Wochenblatt*, no. 1 (1927): 1–6.

128. "Kampfwagen und Kavallerie," *Militär-Wochenblatt*, no. 38 (1927): 1405–6.

who stand in them and behind them. May we take care that this is strong and bold, as that of a horseman of Zieten or Seydlitz once was."[129] The cavalry and perhaps even the infantry might be swallowed up by machines, but their spirit would live on in the armor troops that replaced them.

The debate over the horse ended during 1927, with an article by Seeckt on the future of the cavalry. As we have seen above, Seeckt's view of the tank became much more favorable after 1924. During the materiel or morale debate he had, however, consistently taken a middle course, arguing, for instance, that "[m]ateriel, technology are superior to the living and dying masses, not to the living and undying spirit of man."[130] In this article he followed much the same line, commending Poseck for the fine work that he had done and agreeing rather ambiguously that he, too, thought that the cavalry would still serve a useful purpose in the next war.[131] Neither the advent of the automobile and its ability to carry a greater weight further and faster nor the superior visibility afforded by the plane had made the horse superfluous. Motor vehicles would supplement rather than replace the cavalry, modernize them rather than make them obsolete. After all, motor vehicles, including automobiles, armored cars, and tanks, did have severe limitations in terms of both terrain and refueling. Yet the cavalry could well use vehicles to carry heavy loads and ought to work in concert with tanks. Massed cavalry charges were a thing of the past, but the German cavalry would still fight as they had traditionally done, for "the days of cavalry, if trained, equipped and led on modern lines, are not numbered, and . . . its lances may still flaunt their pennants with confidence in the wind of the future."[132]

By the middle of 1927 the entire debate over materiel and morale within the Red Army and the Reichswehr was drawing to a close, but not without leaving its mark on both armies. In particular, the debate had set the parameters for future discussions about the usefulness of tanks, automobiles, airplanes, and other military technology. In the end, both armies decided that it was not a question of "Materiel or Morale," but rather of "Materiel *and* Morale," with the only real issue being which factor would be (somewhat) stronger than the other. In the Soviet Union the discussion ended with a new unanimity that represented a compromise between the two extreme positions. Books and articles on the future of mechanization adopted the philosophical reasoning of the morale supporters while at the same time acknowledging that tanks and other technology would be vital for future warfare. The Red Army had to have the very latest in new military technology, and in

129. "Noch einmal Kampfwagen und Kavallerie," *Militär-Wochenblatt*, no. 1 (1927): 10–11.

130. "Generaloberst v. Seeckt über Heer und Krieg der Zukunft," *Militär-Wochenblatt*, no. 38 (1928): 1458.

131. The discussion following is taken from Hans von Seeckt, *Thoughts of a Soldier* (London: E. Benn, 1930), 81–107.

132. Ibid., 107.

large amounts, but it was man and the mass army that would ultimately decide battles, not machines.[133]

One result was the Soviet decision to begin a limited three-year tank building program while retaining an old-fashioned tank doctrine. A special "Commission on Organizing the Domestic Production of Tanks," created to report to the RVS on the problem, recommended building three different types of vehicle: an escort, maneuver, and positional tank. A directive from the RVS allocated, however, only three to five million rubles for the production of these tanks. Given these financial limitations, even the man charged with overseeing the work suggested producing only 150 tanks by 1930.[134] Although convinced that tanks were a necessary part of future warfare, the Soviet high command still did not believe that they deserved the highest priority, and instead spent its limited funds on the infantry, the artillery, and even the air forces. Finally, two official declarations on armor doctrine showed just how cautious Soviet views of the tanks remained. The Provisional Field Service Regulations from 1925 hailed the tank as a strong mobile source of firepower, but only in positional warfare. Tanks had to cooperate closely with the infantry and their main mission was aiding the forward movement of the foot soldiers by clearing obstacles from their path.[135] The second examination of armor doctrine appeared in 1927, about the same time that the German army began to rethink seriously the role of the tank in future warfare. Although discussing in detail the improvements made in tank technology, the authors decided that the lessons of the world war and the Russian Civil War were decisive in determining tank doctrine. The tank remained, therefore an auxiliary weapon, designed to support and escort the infantry in positional warfare.[136]

In Germany, on the other hand, while many high-ranking members of the officer corps remained skeptical about the worth of the tank, a new cadre of tank sup-

133. See among many others Tukhachevskii's attack on Verkhovskii, Fuller, and Soldan in RGVA, f. 4, op. 1, d. 1147, ll. 53–54; the long refutation of Fuller et al. with a defense of tank warfare in V. Triandafillov, *Kharakter operatsii sovremennykh armii* (Moscow: Gosudarstvennoe izdatel'stvo Otdel voennoi literatury, 1929), 25–29; much the same thing in Modest Rubinshtein, *Imperialisticheskie voiny budushchego* (Moscow: Izdatel'stvo Kommunisticheskoi Akademii, 1929), 32–36, 58–59, 185, 190–191; and V. Sukhov, *Razvitie voennogo iskusstva v XX veke* (Leningrad: OGIZ – Molodaia Gvardiia, 1931), 106. Only in 1933 was Tukhachevskii able to support Fuller's ideas in "Tau" [Tukhachevskii], *Motorizatsiia i mekhanizatsiia armii i voina* (Moscow: Gosudarstvennoe voennoe izdatel'stvo, 1933), 35–39, 105–39.
134. Memo from Poliakov, Assistant Chief of 2nd Department of the AU for Mechanical Draught (Machines), "Tezisy k dokladu o trekhletnem plane tankostroeniia," 17 January 1927, RGVA, f. 4, op. 2, d. 262, ll. 91–89.
135. *Vremennyi Polevoi Ustav R.KKA. Chast' II-ia (Diviziia i Korpus) Shtab RKKA* (Moscow: Gosudarstvennoe Voennoe Izdatel'stvo, 1925), 15, 304–6.
136. S. Derevchov and A. Pushkin, *Spravochnik po bronevomu delu dlia komandnogo sostava RKKA vsekh rodov voisk* (Moscow: Gosudarstvennoe Izdatel'stvo Otdel Voennoi Literatury, 1927), 53–54, 90.

porters was able to contest their dominance, using the arguments first articulated in the "morale or materiel" debate. By the end of the twenties, even those officers most critical of mechanization were more willing than before to acknowledge that machines, and tanks in particular, would play important and necessary roles in the next war.[137] Like the Red Army, the Reichswehr continued, however, to declare that man and his morale were the deciding factors in battle, stressing that the regular infantry would always be the center and heart of the army.

137. Poseck admitted that armored cars could be useful for reconnaissance, although he made it clear that the machines served the horse and not the other way around. M. von Poseck, Gen. der Infanterie a.D, *Aufklärungsdienst der Kavallerie nach den Erfahrungen des Weltkrieges* (Berlin: Mittler, 1927), 82–87. Even Stülpnagel began to change his views of the specialists and their claims about the future of warfare. Stülpnagel to Rabenau, 14 May 1926. BA-MA. N5/21. p. 13. One of the final examinations of the question of morale and materiel, two short articles by Generalleutnant a.D. von Metzsch forming part of a larger study of "fallacious conclusions and misleading doctrines" also shows the new emphasis on materiel *and* morale. Generalleutnant s.D. v. Metzsch, "Trug-schlüsse und Irrlehren. I. Mensch oder Material?" *Militär-Wochenblatt,* no 13 (1928): 493–95; and "Trugschlüsse und Irrlehren. III. Die Entseelung des Krieges," ibid., no. 19 (1928): 735–37.

CHAPTER THREE

Technology Triumphant

Early German-Soviet Collaboration, 1927–1929

JUST AS the debate over the mechanization of warfare ended, theorists in Germany and the Soviet Union introduced the first truly innovative ideas on armor in battle and the armies of both countries became serious about producing tanks for future warfare. The breakthrough in armor affairs was influenced by a number of factors that coincided with the development of the new fast tank. Of special significance were the experiences of the British army, which from 1926 to 1929 had the world's most advanced ideas on tank use; the writings of Fritz Heigl, whose work was read by soldiers and assigned in the military academies of both the Soviet Union and Germany; and the ideas of certain influential military thinkers in the Reichswehr and the Red Army.

At the same time there were changes in both the international climate and the internal political circumstances of the two countries that encouraged the Soviet and German high commands to believe that they might be able to produce substantial numbers of tanks, and that they therefore needed to think more realistically about how to use armor forces in the next war. Versailles and the Bolshevik takeover had already led Soviet Russia and Weimar Germany to consider making common cause as the outcast nations of Europe. German political and military leaders argued that cooperation with the Soviets offered a way around the conditions of the hated peace treaty, while the new regime in Moscow believed that German technical aid would allow it to speed up the development of weapons for its technology-starved army. Representatives of the two countries met and discussed possible military collaboration in 1920, and solidified plans for cooperation on technology and tactics after 1924.[1] Both countries understood that it would be years before the collaboration bore fruit, but were also encouraged by the promise of modernization that it offered. Meanwhile the policies of Stalin, after 1927 the true ruler of Soviet Russia, held before the Red Army the real possibility that it would have the military hardware necessary for modern war. In early 1927 Soviet political leaders began warning their citizens that the encircling imperialist nations were about to start the long

---

1. For a complete description of the collaboration see Manfred Zeidler, *Reichswehr und Rote Armee, 1920–1933: Wege und Stationen einer ungewöhnlichen Zusammenarbeit* (Munich: Oldenbourg, 1993).

anticipated assault on the socialist homeland.[2] Whether deliberately started by Stalin to solidify his political position, or simply used by him once rumors of war began to circulate, the "war scare" allowed Stalin to keep the country in a continual state of emergency that justified the most extreme measures. As part of his plan to meet the "threat" from abroad, Stalin urged the rapid industrialization of the Soviet Union and the creation of a vast military-industrial base. Red Army commanders were ordered to develop plans to equip the army with massive quantities of the latest military technology. As we shall see, in some ways production helped to dictate Soviet armor doctrine rather than the other way around.

Almost simultaneously the German officer corps began to believe that it too would soon have enough tanks and other materiel to prepare the Reichswehr for the next large-scale war. Cooperation with the Soviets was one part of an overall plan including passive resistance, negotiations with the Western powers, and financial manipulation to undermine reparations payments, that right-leaning politicians hoped would gradually revise Versailles and re-create Germany as a great power. The impending removal of the Inter-Allied Control Committee prompted Kurt von Schleicher in December 1926 to argue that the Reichswehr could now begin serious preparations for rearmament.[3] The following January, the new head of the Truppenamt, Werner von Blomberg, asked his staff to integrate armaments planning into an overall program for rebuilding the army. The program that was finally approved by Seeckt's replacement as chief of the Army Command, Wilhelm Heye in September 1928 contained detailed plans for a sixteen-division army as a first step to full rearmament.[4] With the covert support of politicians like Foreign Minister Gustav Stresemann – even though they might feud with the high command over political issues – the army believed that its deepest desire, a strong army in a strong Germany, would be fulfilled.

Inspired by these factors, the number of German and Soviet officers who looked for more sophisticated ways to use tanks expanded rapidly. Like Seeckt, they began to emphasize a sharp dichotomy between the old, slow machines, fit only for positional warfare, and the new vehicles that would fight in a fresh and unconventional

2. For the latest thinking on the "war scare" see David Stone, *Hammer and Rifle: The Militarization of the Soviet Union, 1926–1933* (Lawrence: University Press of Kansas, 2000), 43–63. Lennart Samuelson, *Plans for Stalin's War Machine* (London: Macmillan, 2000), 34–36, 203; Sally Stoecker, *Forging Stalin's Army: Marshal Tukhachevsky and the Politics of Military Innovation* (Boulder, Colo.: Westview, 1998), 14, 35, 45–48. James J. Schneider, *The Structure of Strategic Revolution: Total War and the Roots of the Soviet Warfare State* (Novato, Calif.: Presidio, 1994), 201–6; and John Erickson, *The Soviet High Command: A Military-Political History, 1918–1941* (London: St. Martin's, 1962), 283–85, also have good discussions of the war scare.

3. Edward W. Bennett, *German Rearmament and the West, 1932–1933* (Princeton, N.J.: Princeton University Press, 1979), 24–25.

4. Wilhelm Deist, *The Wehrmacht and German Rearmament* (Toronto: University of Toronto Press, 1981), 10.

way. Within the Reichswehr, the paradigm shift affected not only lower-ranking officers, such as Heinz Guderian, but the very highest echelons as well. In late 1926
Heye agreed with his predecessor that the "continuous technical perfecting of the
tank, above all in speed and radius of action, will also result in an alteration in the
tactical employment of this force." Heye was especially impressed by the English
maneuvers of 1926, which he believed had shown that the previously accepted main
mission for the tank, direct support of the infantry's advance, was no longer valid.
In the maneuvers tanks had had distant objectives and had been used for huge
swings around the enemy's flanks accompanied by other mobile troops (cavalry,
motorized infantry, and artillery). Heye concluded that "other performances by the
tank in foreign armies in the past year have also demonstrated that modern tanks,
in cooperation with mobile forces or in independent units, are in a position to carry
out missions with far-flung objectives, against the flanks and rear of the enemy, and
also to fight quickly and successfully and at the battle's decisive point."[5]

In general, the rest of the high command agreed with Heye's understanding of
modern technological warfare. In a lengthy memorandum written in late 1926,
Friedrich von Rabenau, at that point a major attached to the Operations Section of
the Truppenamt (T-1), went even further, asserting that only the extensive use of
motor vehicles in combat would make it possible to achieve Schlieffen's dream:
surprise and a complete envelopment, culminating in a blow on the enemy's flanks
and rear.[6] Inspired by men like Rabenau, T-1 officially concluded, in a report published by the chief of the section and later chief of the Army Command, Werner von
Fritsch, that armor forces would have a huge impact on operations, not just tactics,
and that tanks could form independent units, like the British armor brigades.[7] Another Truppenamt officer, Ludwig von Radlmaier, also strongly supported the armor forces and was one of the first proponents of organizing tanks into distinct
mechanized and motorized units. He too argued that keeping tanks in close contact with the infantry or cavalry was an outmoded idea, even asserting that the tank
was the supreme battle weapon. Writing throughout the twenties and early thirties,
he pushed a view of the battlefield in which the timing of an attack with tanks and
infantry, the point at which the infantry would move forward and the artillery would
begin to provide covering fire, would be arranged to suit the tanks rather than the
other forces.[8]

Heinz Guderian was also among the officers who became interested in the high-
speed tank and its impact on warfare. Much has been written about Guderian and

5. Memo by Heye "Betr. Darstellung neuzeitlicher Kampfwagen," HL IV. Nr. 601.26 geh., In 6
(K), 10 November 1926, BA-MA. RH 39/155 Teil 1, p. 58.

6. See the discussion of this memorandum in Michael Geyer, *Aufrüstung oder Sicherheit: Die Reichswehr in der Krise der Machtpolitik, 1924–1936* (Wiesbaden: Steiner, 1980), 93–94.

7. Memo with signature of von Fritsch, "Betrifft: Ausbildung in der Führung motorisierter
Kampfverbände," T1 Nr. 762/27 g. Kdos. II., 5 December 1927, BA-MA. II H 539.

8. Discussed in Zeidler, *Reichswehr und Rote Armee*, 196–97.

the influence that he had on German armor doctrine and organization in the late thirties.[9] In fact, however, a great deal of the rethinking of armor doctrine had already been done by other officers during the mid- to late twenties. Guderian wrote little about tanks until 1936, long after other men had articulated the ideas that became known as "blitzkrieg." But he did absorb the new ideas on armor doctrine current within the staff and begin to formulate a few innovations of his own. Like others in T-1, he was already intrigued by the idea of large armor units that would fight independently from the slower foot soldiers.[10] His primary concern at this point, however, was to raise the mobility of the army as a whole and he therefore concentrated on the motorization, rather than the mechanization, of the Reichswehr.[11] This inclination, combined with the fact that he held only minor positions before Hitler came to power, meant that Guderian's impact on armor during its formative period was minimal.[12] Yet his zeal for the new ideas and the way that he inspired those who worked with him set him apart, and ensured that he attracted attention both to the armor forces and to himself.

By early 1927, then, officers within the German staff had developed a broad outline for how the new tanks would fight in future war: concentrated in independent units that would work closely with the other forces while assaulting the enemy on his flanks and rear. The details of the new tactics were extremely vague, however, and would need years of intensive work before they became clear. At this important juncture Heigl issued the second edition of his "tank pocketbook," in which he provided a precise delineation of tank tactics. The influence of this work is impossible to quantify, but it was read by both German and Soviet military thinkers, including Guderian and Tukhachevskii, and contained several ideas that were later made part of armor doctrine in both countries. Like so many others, Heigl now concluded that the latest high-speed tanks demanded completely different tactics from those de-

9. Dermot Bradley, *Generaloberst Heinz Guderian und die Entstehungsgeschichte des modernen Blitzkrieges* (Osnabrück: Biblio, 1978); Kenneth Macksey, *Guderian: Creator of the Blitzkrieg* (New York: Stein and Day, 1975).

10. For a good short discussion of the "Young Turks" on the staff, see Michael Geyer, "German Strategy in the Age of Machine Warfare, 1914–1945," in *Makers of Modern Strategy from Machiavelli to the Nuclear Age*, ed. Peter Paret (Princeton, N.J.: Princeton University Press, 1986), 558–60. Nehring would later contend that it was in fact Guderian who first came up with the idea of large independent armor units, an assertion not supported by the documentary record. Walther Nehring, *Die Geschichte der deutschen Panzerwaffe 1916 bis 1945* (Berlin: Propyläen Verlag, 1969), 56–59. Manstein, on the other hand, agreed that the staff was already thinking about such units long before Guderian. Erich von Manstein, *Aus einem Soldatenleben 1887–1939* (Bonn: Athenäum, 1958), 240–43.

11. See his articles "Straßenpanzerkraftwagen und ihre Abwehr," *Der Kampfwagen (Beilage zum Militär-Wochenblatt)*, no. 1 (October 1924); "Aufklärung und Sicherung bei Kraftwagenmärschen," ibid., no. 2 (November 1924): 13–16; "Die Lebensader Verduns," ibid., no. 4 (January 1925): 28–31; "Bewegliche Truppenkörper," *Militär-Wochenblatt* no. 18 (1927): 650–53; no. 19 (1927): 687–94; no. 20 (1927): 728–31; no. 21 (1927): 772–76; no. 22 (1927): 819–22.

12. Guderian worked in T-1 from 1927 to 1930 and then spent the next few years as head of a motorized detachment. Kurt J. Walde, *Guderian* (Frankfurt: Ullstein, 1976), 31, 32.

scribed in his earlier work.[13] The two decisive new features of the vehicles were of course their speed and operational mobility, which would enable them to do much more than simply fight in cooperation with the infantry in a frontal attack. Although this kind of old-fashioned action was within their scope, high-speed tanks would not slow for the sake of the infantry and therefore their connection with foot soldiers could easily be lost. A better solution would have the tanks attack the enemy's flanks and rear lines of communication. They could make far-reaching turning maneuvers and, at the end of the battle, cause the retreating enemy to disintegrate.[14]

Heigl then presented three options for an armor assault: the tanks alone but in great strength; in union with cavalry and mounted artillery; or with motorized artillery and infantry in trucks. He thought that the first method was the least dangerous way of fighting. The second could cause problems, since it was entirely uncertain that cavalry would be able to keep up with tanks, while horses and riders offered vulnerable targets on the battlefield. The third method was actually the most obvious, but armies had to work out certain difficulties such as dealing with air attacks and creating better tractors for the artillery, while trucks could not take infantry very far forward in combat. He therefore concluded that the future belonged to tanks accompanied by motorized artillery and infantry in lightly armored cross-country vehicles, although it would take time to build and distribute all these machines.[15] While the army waited for the construction of the vehicles, there would be a transitional period in which foot soldiers and tanks would still need to work together on the battlefield. Heigl recognized that the differential in speed of the two arms meant that infantry-tank cooperation posed a major dilemma for his armor tactics, and suggested two possible solutions. In the first the infantry would work their way forward, tanks would overtake them in a rush from the rear, and then the foot soldiers would take advantage of the confusion caused by the tank attack to secure the objective. The tanks could then push on further into the enemy's rear. The second possibility was to divide tanks into waves, one moving ahead to pin the enemy down while the other would come from behind, catch up with the infantry, and hit the defensive positions at the same time as the foot soldiers.[16] Heigl was so uncertain about the connection between the forces in both kinds of assaults that he personally supported having the main armor attack take place either alone or with just the cavalry against the flanks and rear of the enemy.[17]

The key points of Heigl's discussion – the need for an army that was completely mechanized and motorized (especially its infantry and artillery); the use of high-

13. Fritz Heigl, *Taschenbuch der Tanks, Ergänzungband 1927: Räder-Raupenfahrzeuge, Moderne Tanktaktik, Neue Tanks* (Munich: Lehmanns, 1927), 113–40.

14. Ibid., 140–42.

15. Ibid., 142–44.

16. Ibid., 146–48.

17. Ibid., 148.

speed tanks to attack the flanks and rear of the enemy; and even his description of tank echelons – would all appear in later German and Soviet armor doctrine. Just as significantly, his recognition of the problem of infantry-armor cooperation would prove prescient, as neither Reichswehr nor Red Army would find answers to the problem of coordinating the two forces during his "transitional" phase.

While certain officers were intrigued by Heigl's ideas and the new appreciation of the tank, not all agreed that the machine would transform warfare. There was stiff opposition to treating armor as a main branch of the army, on a par with the cavalry, infantry, and artillery. As we have already seen, cavalry commanders felt particularly threatened by the new weapon and, as the tank showed its new technical potential, became even more insecure and hostile. Major points of contention also involved the problem of infantry-armor cooperation described by Heigl and others, and around logistical support and the value of antiarmor weaponry. If the vehicles were used in the rapid assaults favored by Heigl and others, they could outdistance their vital infantry and supply support, find themselves surrounded by unsuppressed enemy resistance, and be neutralized. Officers argued, too, that antitank weapons had improved dramatically, keeping up with, and perhaps even surpassing, the advances in tank technology. The "eternal duel" between armor and projectile could only end with the victory of the latter. The innovative ideas expressed by Heigl must, therefore, be compared with an official outline of armored car and tank tactics for officers, which taught that tactics for the newer and lighter tanks were basically the same as those for the older machines. All tanks were to cooperate with the infantry, seldom fight by themselves, and would usually be subordinated to infantry units. During attacks they would not, however, "cling tightly" to the infantry, but could instead make full use of their mobility.[18] This much, at least, had changed forever in the German high command's appreciation of armor warfare.

Almost simultaneously the Soviet army was coming to similar conclusions, although for very different reasons. As discussed above, 1926 had seen the emergence of a Soviet three-year plan for tank production that was on a far larger scale than anything conceived by the German army. During the war scare, officials within the Soviet army and government argued that even more had to be done if the nation was to survive in the face of encirclement by its capitalist enemies. Stalin and his supporters used the threat of war and other social and political justifications to push for the adoption of the first Five Year Plan, a huge undertaking to industrialize the Soviet Union as quickly as possible.[19] At first the Soviet high command saw

---

18. "Ausbildungsunterlagen," 24 June 1927, signed Geyer, BA-MA. N 221/9.

19. There were of course other reasons for the adoption of the Five Year Plan, including a desire for economic independence and a perceived need to increase the size of the industrial proletariat. Raymond Hutchings, *Soviet Economic Development* (Oxford: Blackwell, 1982), 46–47. Eugène Zaleski

armor as marginal to the military version of the plan, which promoted self-sufficiency in armaments and the modernization of the army as a whole. When Tukhachevskii, now the chief of staff, submitted his thinking on the military plan (which he envisioned as a four-year plan), he listed rifle forces armed with strong artillery, strategic cavalry, and aviation as the decisive forces in future conflict. Armor forces or tanks were not even mentioned.[20]

When Soviet tank production began in 1927, therefore, it followed the old three-year program, while discussion over the shape of a military five-year plan continued throughout the next two years. Production was at first very slow, but one factory did manage to manufacture the first small tank in early April 1927.[21] Named the MS-1, the tank was supposed to act as a direct escort for the infantry. The handful of vehicles available officially joined the Red Army at the end of September.[22] These tanks and a few older ones, six machines in all, then took part in Moscow Military District maneuvers that fall.[23] Unfortunately, the first indication of trouble with industry appeared about the same time, and Kartel', the head of the AU, felt compelled to warn Aleksandr Tolokontsev, the chief of the Military-Industrial Directorate (VPU), that he should not curtail the tank construction program for any reason.[24] The latest mobilization plan, Variant no. 8, did not ignore the difficulties with production and foresaw industry manufacturing only 108 MS-1 tanks during time of war.[25]

The decision to proceed with the three-year plan was not an expression of overwhelming support for armor as the miracle weapon of the future, but instead a

emphasizes Stalin's desire to ensure the primacy of the socialist sector over the capitalist sector in the Soviet economy: *Planning for Economic Growth in the Soviet Union, 1918–1932* (Chapel Hill: University of North Carolina Press, 1971), 70. For a closer look at the political and philosophical debate over the shape that industrialization should take, see Moshe Lewin, *Political Undercurrents in Soviet Economic Debates: From Bukharin to the Modern Reformers* (Princeton, N.J.: Princeton University Press, 1974), 3–124. Finally, David Stone shows that military production had a much larger impact on the plan than previously thought. He also demonstrates that the push for militarization of industry and the country as a whole would have a lasting impact on Soviet economy and society. Stone, *Hammer and Rifle*, 110–11 and passim.

20. Theses by Tukhachevskii on the four-year plan, 10 May 1927, RGVA, f. 4, op. 1, d. 561, ll. 7–16. See also A. Ryzhakov, "K voprosu o stroitel'stve bronetankovykh voisk krasnoi armii v 30-e gody," *VIZh*, no. 8 (August 1968): 105.

21. Memo from Khalepskii and Poliakov, 25 November 1929, RGVA, f. 31811, op. 1, d. 1, ll. 11–12.

22. Sbornik sekretnykh prikazov RVS, no. 529/99 (29 September 1927), RGVA, f. 4, op. 3, d. 2950, l. 331. "MS" stood for "Malyi Soprovozhdennyi" or "small escort" tank.

23. Description of maneuvers of 17–26 September 1927, RGVA, f. 4, op. 2, d. 151, ll. 5–6.

24. Letter from Kartel', Chief of the Artillery Directorate, to the Chief of the Military-Industrial Directorate, 2 September 1927, RGVA, f. 20, op. 21, d. 4, l. 61.

25. Report by Pavel Dybenko, Chief of Supplies of the RKKA, "Obespechenie mobilizatsionnoi gotovnosti po variantu N⁰ 8 osnovnymi predmetami snabzheniia," arrived in archive 1 February 1928, RGVA, f. 33987, op. 3, d. 93, ll. 134–35.

more cautious acknowledgment of the tank's usefulness in a certain type of warfare. As earlier, Red Army officers still thought that a future war might be positional, like the world war, and that tanks would then play a decisive role. The high command thought, too, that they would be facing capitalist nations, such as Poland, which had many more tanks than their army currently possessed. Finally, they agreed with British theorists that tanks had to be used in large numbers if they were to be successful. Beyond this, the majority of the high command was unwilling to go. An exchange of views between Pavel Dybenko, the head of the Supply Directorate, and various officers of the Soviet high command illuminates the boundaries of the discourse taking place within the Soviet army. At the end of August 1927 Dybenko submitted a report to the RVS on increasing the firepower of infantry companies by more fully exploiting tanks. He dismissed the usual Soviet answer to the firepower problem, battalion artillery, arguing that the artillery's distinct logistical demands did not entirely suit it for close cooperation within smaller infantry units and that the experience of the world war had been inconclusive on the usefulness of the guns. He suggested instead that the tank was the obvious solution to the problem of infantry fire support. The Polish army, he stressed, already had huge numbers of tanks and was even giving them to each attacking infantry battalion. In the Red Army escort tanks could simply replace battalion artillery, although in the near term the army's limited financial resources would keep the actual quantity of tanks low. In his comparison of the relative value of artillery and tanks, he argued that tanks could provide five times as much firepower and that their logistical support would be easier. There were, he admitted, a few instances when tanks could not follow the infantry closely, since their supply vehicles would be unable to travel on all terrain, but company artillery would be on hand to cover those gaps.[26]

To elicit as many comments on the suggestion as possible, the RVS forwarded copies of Dybenko's report to the Red Army staff and the Main Directorate.[27] In November the staff submitted a formal memorandum on Dybenko's proposal that clarified their official position on tank doctrine. The core of the note was a seven-point rebuttal of Dybenko's reasons for replacing artillery with tanks. Deputy chief of staff S. Pugachev wrote that the staff had concluded that tanks could not replace battalion artillery because they were an offensive weapon primarily designed for positional warfare. Battalion artillery, on the other hand, had to fight directly with infantry in every sort of combat: defensive and offensive, positional and maneuver. None of the nations that had used tanks during the world war thought that tanks could completely replace battalion artillery; even the Poles did not have enough

26. Report by Dybenko, "O zamene batalionnoi artillerii tankami," 30 March 1927, RGVA, f. 4, op. 2, d. 262, ll. 103–2, 101.

27. Directive (draft) of the RVS, "Po dokladu NS RKKA tov. DYBENKO o zamene batalionnoi artillerii tankami," 28 September 1927, RGVA, f. 4, op. 2, d. 262, l. 105. Form cover letter with Dybenko's report as enclosure sent by Upravlenie Delami to the Main Directorate (GURKKA) and Chief of Staff, 22 September 1927, RGVA, f. 4, op. 2, d. 262, ll.104, 97.

tanks to do that. Foreign military authorities all agreed that tanks were a powerful means for attacking strongly fortified positions en masse. Dybenko's suggestion, which implied using tanks in small groups, would allow them to fall easy victim to the artillery fire of the opponent. Pugachev also noted that tanks had several significant weaknesses, such as an inability to carry large numbers of shells, slow speed during actual battle, need for cleaning and repair after ten hours of action, and heavy demand for fuel, which greatly limited their ability to follow the infantry closely and support them as needed during combat. The Red Army staff, Pugachev concluded, did not think that it was possible to replace battalion artillery with tanks, while financial and industrial circumstances prevented the army from arming with both artillery and tanks.[28]

Sergei Kamenev, the head of the army's Main Directorate and the deputy to Kliment Voroshilov, Frunze's replacement, was more supportive of the use of tanks, yet agreed with Pugachev's conclusions. He thought, for instance, that tanks were a better means for supporting an infantry attack than battalion artillery, although both needed the cooperation of other types of artillery to be truly effective. On the other hand, tanks had more complex logistical needs than artillery and therefore their use would complicate rather than ease supply problems. He agreed with the staff that tanks did not have as much firepower as Dybenko claimed, and that the organization which Dybenko suggested would not allow the necessary mass use of tanks. He added that since tanks could not travel in all terrain, needed help in reaching the battlefield, and even then were unable to fight for long periods of time, they would have great difficulty supporting the infantry. The straightforward substitution of tanks for battalion artillery he therefore thought was "unsuitable and unfeasible." He suggested instead using tanks to supplement artillery fire by organizing them as a general HQ reserve.[29]

Other official descriptions of armor tactics confirmed that the Soviet army did not see the tank as anything more than one of the necessary, if imperfect, elements of modern warfare. They also show that there continued to be a split between those who focused on the current limitations of the machines and other, more optimistic commanders, who saw only the inevitable progress of technology. A textbook on military technology thus emphasized the same technical shortcomings as earlier writing and even refused to acknowledge the recent gains in tank speed. Although there were two possible tasks for tanks listed, breakthroughs of strongly fortified positions and direct escort for infantry, both were still closely tied to the foot soldier and a walking pace.[30] A second guide was more optimistic, stressing im-

28. Report by Pugachev, 14 November 1927, RGVA, f. 4, op. 2, d. 262, ll. 107–6.

29. Report from the chief of the Main Directorate (GURKKA), "Zakliuchenie (sekretno) k dokladu NS RKKA za No. 2164/s. po voprosu o zamene batal'onnoi artillerii tankami soprovozhdeniia," RGVA, f. 4, op. 2, d. 262, ll. 100–199.

30. Vl. Lishchintskii, *Tekhnika v budushchei voine i oborona SSSR* (Moscow: Gosudarstvennoe Izdatel'stvo, 1927), 47–48.

provements made in speed and other technical areas.[31] The future of armor development was apparently bright; it might even be possible to build flying tanks, and technical difficulties, such as problems of observation or aiming, were viewed optimistically as challenges to be met rather than crippling failures.[32] The guide kept nevertheless to world war tactics, noting that tanks could not take or hold ground and were suited only for positional combat and attacks on fortified areas.[33]

Yet even though not convinced of the overwhelming importance of armor forces, the Red Army thought enough of tanks to agree to the German plan for designing and testing them on Soviet soil. After the initial contacts, the Reichswehr had cooled toward the idea of working with the Soviet Union to circumvent the stringent conditions of the Versailles Treaty. Only in the mid-twenties did the high command, including Seeckt, conclude that the easiest and least detectable way to foster tank development (as well as aircraft design) was by creating a small number of models with which industry and the army could experiment. When the models had been extensively studied and tested – and when it became politically feasible – the country would proceed to actual manufacturing.[34] The main difficulty with this idea was finding suitable testing grounds for the vehicles. In the mid-twenties there were two possibilities before the German army: either to exploit earlier established links with Swedish industry or to deepen the military collaboration with the Red Army.[35] Sometime in 1926 the German General Staff and Seeckt decided to concentrate on the Soviet option, although continuing their contacts with Swedish firms.[36] After several months of negotiations, Hermann von der Lieth-Thomsen, an air force officer and the German representative in the collaboration, signed a three-year agreement with Ian Berzin, the head of Soviet military intelligence, to set up a tank school at Kazan. Other agreements were signed to work on poison gas (code-named "Tomka") and aircraft development at Lipetsk. At Kazan the Germans agreed to pay all expenses while the Soviets would oversee repairs and reconstruction of living and working quarters at the former Kargopol barracks. Leadership of the school was in German hands, although they were to take into consideration Soviet wishes, and the school was to open in July 1927. The school's

31. S. Derevchov and A. Pushkin, *Spravochnik po bronevomu delu dlia komandnogo sostava RKKA vsekh rodov voisk* (Moscow: Gosudarstvennoe Izdatel'stvo, Otdel Voennoi Literatury, 1927), 16–17, 20.

32. Ibid., 25–28, 50–51, 56.

33. Ibid., 53–54.

34. "Generaloberst v. Seeckt über Heer und Krieg der Zukunft," *Militär-Wochenblatt.* no. 38 (1928): 1457–60.

35. Hammerstein would later call the two factories in Sweden Germany's greatest secret. These enterprises were put to other uses as well. Guderian, for instance went to Sweden during October 1928 on an official trip where he learned to drive a German First World War tank. Klaus Müller, "So lebten und arbeiteten wir 1929 bis 1933 in Kama" (unpublished manuscript, May 1972), 4. I am grateful to Willi Esser's widow for giving me a copy of this manuscript.

36. From Staatssekretär v. Schubert, e.o. R.M. 716, 21 May 1927, PA-AA, R31900.

table of organization and plan of study, included with the agreement, showed only three tanks for a full schedule of theoretical and practical, technical and tactical training.[37] The financial support for Kazan, as with the rest of the illegal rearmament, was hidden in the official German budget by setting the cost of permitted weapons too high and then transferring the extra funds to a "black" budget for use on the illicit ones.[38]

While the Germans hoped to produce a handful of finished machines for later production, their Soviet counterparts had very different plans for the Kazan installation.[39] Within the larger context of industrializing the Soviet Union, the Red Army hoped to use German engineering and manufacturing expertise to aid the Soviet tractor and tank industry.[40] Voroshilov and Stalin were extremely cautious about allowing the Germans too much influence over the collaboration and over the Red Army, but both believed that it was necessary to jump-start the Soviet economy. The decision to sign the agreement with the Reichswehr was thus one small part of Stalin's overall drive to fulfill the plan and prepare his country for war. Unfortunately for the Soviets, they would need German cooperation in any widening of the enterprise and the Germans had no intention of helping. They did not want to give away technical or military secrets to the Soviets, were ambivalent about helping to create a strong, modern army near their borders, and did not have enough money to help the Soviets even if they had wished. Because the Germans financed the entire installation, they could dictate how funds were spent at Kazan and the basic form that the school took was, therefore, very like what the Reichswehr had originally conceived. It was perhaps inevitable that these fundamentally different

37. Agreement between Berzin and Lieth on setting up tank school at Kazan, 2 October 1926, RGVA, f. 33987, op. 3, d. 295, ll. 58–60, 62–65. Lieutenant. Colonel Malbrandt was sent to the Soviet Union in 1926 to find land for the future tank school and chose the former artillery barracks with a nearby firing range. To disguise the purpose of the station, the Germans called it "Kama" after [Ka]zan and [Ma]lbrandt. By an unfortunate coincidence this was also the name of a stream which emptied into the Volga near Kazan, making "Kama" useless as a cover name. Müller, "So lebten und arbeiteten wir," 6–7.

38. F. L. Carsten, The Reichswehr and Politics 1918 to 1933 (Oxford: Clarendon, 1966), 274.

39. The German army had not always seen the collaboration just as a way to design and test equipment. In 1922 Seeckt sent a memorandum to Brockdorff-Rantzau in which he advocated using private German firms to build up the Soviet armaments industry. Memo from Seeckt to Brockdorff-Rantzau, "Germany's Attitude to the Russian Problem," 11 September 1922, in John W. Wheeler-Bennett, The Nemesis of Power: The German Army in Politics 1918–1945 (New York: St. Martin's Press, 1954), 137–38. Those who visited Soviet Russia at this time thought that damage from the Civil War and Revolution were too severe and too costly for any German participation in the reconstruction of industry. See Gustav Hilger and Alfred G. Meyer, The Incompatible Allies: A Memoir-History of German-Soviet Relations 1918–1941 (New York: Hafner, 1971), 195.

40. Iosif Unshlikht argued, in a meeting with German officials during spring 1926, that it would be mutually beneficial for the Germans to use the collaboration to help build up the Soviet Union's industrial base. Report from Unshlikht to the Politburo, 10 April 1926, RGVA, f. 33987, op. 3, d. 151, ll. 95–102.

conceptions of the collaboration would eventually lead to serious problems between the two countries.[41]

Indeed the enterprise almost fell apart not long after the Kazan agreement was signed, although for entirely different reasons. In December 1926 the *Manchester Guardian* printed an article about a delivery of (illegal) artillery shells to Germany from the Soviet Union. The exposé was taken up and used by the German Social Democrats against their political opponents then in power.[42] The Soviets were outraged and embarrassed at the exposure and suspected that Stresemann himself might have leaked the news for his own political gain. The deputy chair of the RVS, Iosif Unshlikht, who was in overall charge of the collaboration, argued that because the Germans had failed to fulfill the stipulations of an important project and because of these revelations, the Politburo should reexamine the whole question of cooperation with the Reichswehr.[43] Rather than go to such extremes, the Soviet government ordered the army on 24 February 1927 to confine the military collaboration to "legal forms." Unshlikht wrote to Stalin a few days later to say that he had prepared measures to transform the secret installations, including the school at Kazan, into "legal" enterprises and that he had ordered Berzin to tell Thomsen about the decision of the Politburo in an "extremely polite way." The Reichswehr representative had protested that the exposure was the fault of Otto Gessler — the civilian minister of defense who was despised by the majority of the German high command. Unshlikht thought that even if this were true, the Soviets had to be cautious since they could no longer count on the Reichswehr Ministry to keep the collaboration secret.[44] A little over two weeks later, he reported to Voroshilov that Thomsen had handed him a statement on converting the installations. Oskar Ritter von Niedermayer, who had been involved in the earliest stages of the collaboration and spoke fluent Russian, personally informed his Soviet colleagues that the statement had the complete agreement of the German government and ministries. The statement itself, provided in translation for Voroshilov, suggested describing the tank enterprise as an institution for studying automotive affairs.[45]

To make certain that the German government was fully involved in the coopera-

---

41. On the different aims of Germany and the Soviet Union in the military collaboration as a whole, see Jon Jacobson, *When the Soviet Union Entered World Politics* (Berkeley: University of California Press, 1994), 212–15.

42. On the *Guardian* leak and its repercussions, see E. H. Carr, *Foundations of a Planned Economy, 1926–1929*, vol. 3, pt. 1 of *A History of Soviet Russia* (London: Macmillan, 1976), 38–40.

43. Memo from Unshlikht to Stalin (copies to Voroshilov and Litvinov), 3 January 1927, RGVA, f. 33987, op. 3, d. 151, l. 26. and memo from Unshlikht to Stalin, 12 January 1927, RGVA, f. 33987, op. 3, d. 151, l. 27.

44. Memo from Unshlikht to Stalin, 4 March 1927, RGVA, f. 33987, op. 3, d. 151, l. 87. Unshlikht was skeptical about German motivations for collaborating from the very beginning. Report from Unshlikht to the Politburo, 10 April 1926, RGVA, f. 33987, op. 3, d. 151, ll. 101–2.

45. Cover memo from Unshlikht to Voroshilov, 11 March 1927 and copy of letter to Berzin, 8 March 1927, RGVA, f. 33987, op. 3, d. 151, ll. 91–92. For more on Niedermayer, see Carsten, *The Reichswehr and Politics*, 136–38.

tion, and thus to safeguard against any more revelations, Litvinov, the minister of foreign affairs, was asked to approach the German Foreign Office and obtain a communication to the effect that there would be no political reservations raised against the intended furnishing of Kazan. At a meeting held in May at the ministry, Stresemann, Heye, Gessler, and Blomberg discussed this request. Stresemann commented that he could agree to the statement despite certain reservations.[46] Ambassador Brockdorff-Rantzau, after reading the communication written by the Foreign Office, also declared himself in favor since the German side had the predominate interest in the school at Kazan. He thought, however, that the statement would need to be stronger than that proposed by the government as the initiative for Kazan had come from the German side and he was convinced that the Soviets placed no particular value on the tank school.[47]

Officers within the Reichswehr were meanwhile arguing strongly in favor of continuing the cooperation on the grounds that if it were broken off, the Soviets would go to the French.[48] Contacts between the Reichswehr and the Red Army would in fact expand rather than contract during 1927. Berzin reported to Voroshilov that three Soviet officers took part in field trips and eight, including Vladimir Triandafillov, participated in maneuvers and tactical studies. Ieronim Uborevich (commander of the North Caucasus military district), Robert Eideman (head of the Frunze Academy) and Ernest Appoga (an instructor at the same school) were also sent to study in Germany for over a year at an academy for German officers. The Germans, meanwhile, had six high-ranking officers study or attend maneuvers in the Soviet Union.[49]

Yet by the summer of 1927, three months after the request from the Soviet side, the German government had still not declared its support for Kazan, nor had it sent any tanks or other equipment. The Soviets, already suspicious about German intentions, viewed these delays as part of some plot by the capitalists to defraud them. The Germans did have a very good reason for dragging their feet over the collaboration, but it had nothing to do with what the Soviet government feared: German industry had simply been unable to produce even one tank for testing. The problems with production were not easily fixed. As described above, the Waffenamt had made its first request for tank prototypes in May 1925, and pushed especially for a medium sixteen-ton tank, known by the code name "Large Tractor."[50] The earliest description of the vehicle stated that it was slow, but had a large-caliber gun and

46. Memo from Streseman, Blomberg, and Schubert, signed Köpke, 18 May 1927, PA-AA, R31900, H111738–H111739.

47. From Staatsekretär v. Schubert, e.o. R.M. 716, 21 May 1927, PA-AA. R31900, H111736.

48. Military leaders told the government that even if there were a political decision to stop the collaboration, they would continue to work with the Soviet Union. Hilger and Meyer, *The Incompatible Allies*, 205.

49. Memo from Berzin to Voroshilov, [1927], RGVA, f. 33987, op. 3, d. 87, l. 125.

50. See above, pp. 51–52, and Walter J. Spielberger, *Die Motorisierung der deutschen Reichswehr, 1920–1935* (Stuttgart: Motorbuch Verlag, 1979), 281–83.

several machine guns.[51] Even at that time Henschel, one of the firms charged with developing the tank, reported that it could guarantee to meet the specifications only insofar as existing experience in the motor manufacturing industry in general, and in the motor vehicle manufacturing industry in particular, provided the basis for fulfilling any agreement.[52] The stiff wording of the memorandum suggested that Henschel knew it would have trouble with tank construction, and in fact only the other companies, Rheinmetall and Krupp would, in the end, deliver viable versions. This, though, was far in the future. During 1927 none of the companies was able to produce a single machine and the only action at the Kazan school was the arrival of a German engineer to set up the buildings and other physical equipment necessary to get the station working.[53]

While waiting for Kazan to produce results, the German and Soviet armies worked diligently on refining their understanding of how their soon-to-be-manufactured tanks would alter the conduct of war. The Reichswehr, like Heigl, now directly confronted the most intractable problem of machine warfare; how to keep fast-moving tanks and slow-moving infantry working together. One school of thought argued that close cooperation between the two was no longer possible, that tanks were now so much faster than soldiers on foot that the vehicles should not even attempt to stay with the infantry. Tanks had to exploit their speed to its fullest for their own safety – driving slowly only gave the enemy's artillery more time to find the range. Early on certain officers also argued that motorized units could not carry the infantry into the battle itself, but only bring soldiers up to the battlefield and then unload them and their equipment.[54] This would create a discontinuity between the two types of forces, but had the advantage of allowing the new tanks to fight on their own terms. Another group within the staff warned that any loss of contact between infantry and armor could only lead to disaster. These officers thought that at least a few of the high-speed tanks would need to stay with the infantry, maintaining a close connection that would allow the two arms to support each other on the battlefield.

The Reichswehr was aided in attempts to solve this seminal problem by faster, motorized dummy tanks. Although the army ordered the development of a small tank (the "Light Tractor") in July 1928 as a complement to the heavier "Large Tractor," the failure of industry to produce a tank and a desire to keep up at least an outward appearance of compliance with Versailles meant that the army continued to

51. "Beschreibung Gr. Tr." [no date or other title], BA-MA, RH 8/v. 2669.

52. "Stellungnahme zu den Baubedingungen für einen Grosstractor," [February 1927], BA-MA, RH 8/v. 2669.

53. Müller, "So lebten und arbeiteten wir," 7.

54. See, for example, Oberleutanant Wiesner, 1. (Pr.) I.R., "Selbstfahrer oder Räderraupenschlepper in motorisierten Divisionen," *Deutsche Wehr: Zeitschrift für Heer und Flotte* 32, no. 21 (1928): 449.

rely on mock-ups for testing armor doctrine.[55] Older dummies had either been pushed around the practice field by soldiers or consisted of bicycles with wooden mock-ups of tanks built around them.[56] Neither contraption had given the Reichswehr the best opportunity to form an accurate picture of what real armor combat would look like. The newer motorized dummies, made by Hanomag, were a significant improvement, since they had quite good cross-country performance.[57] Perhaps because the situation had been so bad before the arrival of the new mock-ups, they made, in the words of one officer, "a great impression on all participants [in one exercise] and were described as especially instructive."[58]

One of the first exercises with the new dummy tanks, led by the chief of motorized troops, Otto von Stülpnagel, was held in Grafenwöhr during May 1928.[59] Here for the first time the German army used its mock-ups in a new and innovative way, practicing the tactics and cooperation with the infantry that high-speed tanks would employ in future war. The plan of the exercise, designed by Alfred von Vollard-Bockelberg, the Inspector of the Motorized Forces, divided the armor units into three separate waves.[60] The first two groups of tanks would break through the enemy's front and head directly for his machine gun zone and artillery positions. The third wave would move more slowly in order to cooperate closely with the infantry, even turning back to help if the tank crews noticed that their accompanying soldiers were not with them.[61] Not surprisingly, given the regard in which German officers held British thought on armor affairs, the three-wave system was almost a direct copy of British tactics, although it built on earlier world war experience and perhaps the writings of Heigl as well.[62]

The divisional commander and the commander in chief of the exercise forces suggested to Stülpnagel and Bockelberg that there was a serious flaw in the tactics used in the maneuvers. In particular, they thought that it would be better to have the infantry follow the first wave of tanks, rather than wait for the third wave. In the latter case, the heavy infantry weapons that were to protect the tanks by combating

55. Spielberger, Die Motorisierung der deutschen Reichswehr, 317.

56. One table of organization for a dummy tank company showed that the former type of mock tank required two men to push it. "Etat einer Kampfwagennachbildungkompanie," BA-MA, RH 53–5/101, 90–91.

57. Müller, "So lebten und arbeiteten wir," 3.

58. Stülpnagel to Bockelberg, 27 June 1928, BA-MA, RH 53–5/101, 86.

59. See Heinz Guderian, Erinnerungen eines Soldaten (Heidelberg: Kurt Vowinckel, 1951), 18–19.

60. Bockelberg was well-known for his openness to innovation in armor affairs. See W. Heinemann, "The Development of German Armoured Forces 1918–40" in Armoured Warfare, ed. J. P. Harris and F. H. Toase (London: Batsford, 1990), 54.

61. "Infanterie-Führer V, Betrifft: Kampfwagenlehrübung am 18.5, 'Übungsverlauf,'," 14 May 1928, BA-MA, RH 53–5/101, 74–77.

62. The British three-echelon system is described in depth in a report by Uborevich and Khalepskii, "Opytnye ucheniia mechanizirovannoi brigady v 1932 godu v belorusskom voennom okruge," 13 October 1932, RGVA, f. 31811, op. 2, d. 101, ll. 58–59.

the enemy's defensive positions would not be close enough to do any good. In addition, the enemy's remaining forces could simply take cover until the approach of the infantry before showing themselves and firing on the foot soldiers. After the exercise ended, Stülpnagel wrote to Bockelberg to give his assessment of the tactics Bockelberg had suggested, and of the criticism leveled by these two officers. He concluded that the second objection was not valid since the third tank wave could protect the infantry against individual pockets of resistance. The first objection could not be so easily dismissed. However, placing heavy infantry weapons in hidden forward positions before the beginning of the assault would allow them to adequately cover the attack.[63]

Bockelberg replied about a week later with a look at the two different kinds of tanks, slow Renault-type tanks and fast Vickers types, and their uses in modern warfare. As so many others had, he describe the mission of the slow tanks as direct support for the infantry. Even the French knew, however, that slow tanks were "becoming extinct" and would soon be replaced by the faster new machines. The high-speed tanks would fight deep inside the enemy's positions and would not as a rule accompany the infantry. The full effect of the tank could then come to bear and the infantry would exploit this effect, somewhat as they did with the artillery. The beginning of the infantry assault and further advance thus depended on the effect of the tanks and not on an interval that could be rigidly predetermined.[64] He then laid out a modified view of the ideal tank attack that, as earlier, was predicated on a combined-arms approach to battle with armor. The assault would occur in three waves, as in his maneuver plan, but the first wave would have as its objective the enemy's deeply placed defensive weapons and artillery, while the second would accompany the infantry and the third would act as a reserve, ready to mop up any pockets of resistance. The first wave would use its speed to the utmost, seeking either to draw enemy fire away from the infantry or, if the artillery refused to engage them, attempting to reach and destroy the artillery. He thought that these tactics should answer the objections raised by the two skeptical officers.[65]

The observations of three Soviet commanders who attended these and similar maneuvers showed that the commitment of Bockelberg and others to reinventing tank tactics was shared by many within the German officer corps. Upon their return from studying at the military academy and attending maneuvers. Uborevich, Eideman, and Appoga submitted a report to Voroshilov on what they had observed and learned. Among many other things, they described "secret" games, where the Germans looked at questions such as motorization and the use of tanks. They wrote that the Reichswehr attached great importance to tanks and was studying thoroughly the experiences of the English and French. Like the English, the Ger-

---

63. Stülpnagel to Bockelberg, 27 June 1928, BA-MA, RH 53–5/101, 85–86.
64. Bockelberg to Stülpnagel, 5 July 1928, BA-MA, RH 53–5/101, 87–88.
65. Ibid. 88–89.

mans thought that tanks, even at the present stage of technical development, were capable of large-scale independent operations especially when combined with motorized units of infantry and artillery. The example that the three observers gave to prove this point was the war game carried out under the supervision of Bockelberg and Stülpnagel. The Germans, when using tanks against a fortified position, would have two waves attack, one heading directly for the rear and the artillery while the second, consisting of several echelons, would attack the infantry and the forward lines of the defense. The surprise attack had to be in massive numbers, and involved the close cooperation of infantry, artillery, and airplanes.[66]

The innovative ideas of Bockelberg, Stülpnagel, and others within the General Staff were counterbalanced by the opinions of officers who did not believe that the new tanks were important for future war. In their view, Germany might be able to avoid the expense of mechanizing and yet be secure against an armor offensive if the army procured large numbers of antitank weapons and passive defenses, leaving the wasteful creation of machine armies to more foolish nations. No one was certain, however, that the defenses were as strong as the tanks themselves, and the question of tank versus antitank weapon evolved throughout the late twenties and thirties into one of the pivots in the struggle between supporters and detractors of the tank. In one of the first articles on the problem, written in late 1928, an officer gave examples showing that the defense had been stronger than tanks during the world war. Although he cautioned that there was not yet enough evidence to decide how modern tanks would fare against the latest antitank weapons, he did think that these weapons had improved even faster than tanks, suggesting that tanks would once again fall victim to the defense in overwhelming numbers.[67] Another officer speculated that antitank defenses were so effective and the enemy could prepare so extensively beforehand for any attack that many tanks would be disabled on the field, creating obstacles that would slow or even completely halt offensives. In that case, a fully mechanized army could then just as easily lead to a war of positions as to greater strategic mobility.[68] As a third officer added, "antitank weapons are only at the beginning of a very promising development, whereas the possibility of strengthened armor protection is limited by the absolute need for swift mobility." Tanks would therefore continue to act as direct escorts and auxiliary weapons for the infantry, while the infantry and artillery remained the backbone of the army.[69]

66. Report from Uborevich, Eideman, and Appoga to Voroshilov, [early 1928], RGVA, f. 33987, op. 3, d. 329, ll. 1–101.

67. "Kampfwagen oder Kampfwagen-Abwehrwaffen," *Militär-Wochenblatt*, no. 20 (1928): 790–92.

68. "Das Gesicht des wirklichen Krieges," ibid., no. 21 (1928): 817–23. The writer also noted that the very speed of the new vehicles would place immense strains on supply lines and command mechanisms, as the tanks outran the ability of the rest of the army to keep up with them.

69. Major a.D. von Keiser, "Die Begleitwaffen der Infanterie," *Wissen und Wehr*, no. 10 (1928): 624–25.

In contrast to the dissension within the German army, Soviet commanders over the next few years would move together toward a new appreciation of the tank's usefulness and a new view of armor doctrine. The curious paradox in the Soviet army was that tactics in some ways followed production rather than determining it. The high command did not decide how it would use tanks in a future war and then procure vehicles to fit this doctrine. Instead, the decision to produce large numbers of tanks, made in 1928–29, sprang from the war scare, a perceived need to modernize the Red Army, and estimates of foreign tank arsenals. Once the army had the promise – and then the reality – of large numbers of tanks, a new way to use them was found.

The exception to this general rule was the writings and thought of Mikhail Tukhachevskii, who would now produce his first serious study of armor warfare. Before 1928 Tukhachevskii had written about other kinds of military technology, particularly aircraft and artillery, and how they might transform warfare. He had also begun to formulate his own ideas of what modern war as a whole would look like, primarily in opposition to what strategic thinkers such as Trotsky or Frunze had proposed. Perhaps his most important contribution was the concept of continuous operations, in which an army would link one operation directly to the next without pausing to resupply or allowing the enemy to reinforce himself. First articulated in an article entitled "Questions of the High Command," the idea had probably suggested itself to Tukhachevskii during his drive on Warsaw, when it became apparent that modern wars no longer depended upon a single decisive battle of annihilation. Instead, an army had to engineer successive operations that would culminate in the defeat of the enemy.[70]

Despite this emphasis on speed and continuous movement, for reasons that are not entirely clear Tukhachevskii ignored armor forces in his descriptions of future operations. Only in early 1928, with the publication of a lengthy, top secret study called "Future War," did he endorse the idea that the tank might make a real difference in modern combat. This study was not entirely his creation, and in fact it is difficult to say just how much of the final draft he authored. However, he did commission the study in 1926 when he first became chief of staff, and approved it when it was circulated two years later. In "Future War" Tukhachevskii and his co-authors recognized that the next conflict would demand huge numbers of motorized troops and tanks (as well as aircraft, artillery, and chemical weapons). Yet the Soviet Union did not have the necessary technology to fight such a war and would therefore be unable to meet the encircling capitalist nations as equals on the battlefield. Even worse, the army would be incapable of carrying out the continuous operations that

70. M. N. Tukhachevskii, "Voprosy vysschego komandovaniia," translated Richard Simpkin, *Deep Battle: The Brainchild of Marshal Tukhachevskii* (London: Brassey, 1987), 88–92; See also David M. Glantz, *Soviet Military Operational Art: In Pursuit of Deep Battle* (London: Frank Cass, 1991), 20–22, and Schneider, *Structure of Strategic Revolution*, 174–92.

Tukhachevskii believed were indispensable for the next war. The inescapable conclusion: the Red Army had somehow to obtain huge numbers of vehicles for motorized units and armor forces, enough to equal or better the strength of its potential enemies, and these could only be gotten through a quantum leap in military-industrial output.[71] Significantly, neither here nor elsewhere did Tukhachevskii outline exactly how these masses of tanks would fight in future wars. Apparently he, like other Red Army commanders, believed that it was enough to have a huge armor force and that a suitable doctrine could be found for it afterward.

Unfortunately, just as this point Tukhachevskii fell afoul of the intrigues that so characterized Stalin's Russia. He had been involved in a running debate with Voroshilov about the relative strength of the staff and the War Commissariat. Tukhachevskii had argued that the staff needed more authority to make the decisions necessary for preparing the army and nation for war, and Voroshilov had naturally resented this attempt to undermine his position. As with Trotsky, Tukhachevskii's obvious ambition also made him an object of concern to Stalin, as a possible "Bonaparte" who would use the army to challenge his claim to power. Faced with clear signals from both of his superiors that the staff would not be granted the authority he thought it deserved, Tukhachevskii resigned as chief of staff and was reassigned to the Leningrad military district. There he would produce some of his most innovative ideas on warfare, but at a distance from the political center of power. The result was to intensify his estrangement from the men that he needed most to retain his position: Stalin and Voroshilov.

Tukhachevskii's new attitude toward armor forces – and his focus on neighboring countries' armaments as the measure of what the Soviet Union needed – was shared by other Soviet commanders. In one report sent to Voroshilov, the tank was described as the weakest and technically most backward weapon in the Red Army. The army was far behind foreign militaries and in particular the Polish army, which was arming every battalion with escort tanks.[72] An inspection of Soviet tank forces showed just how bad things were with the deteriorating vehicles captured in the Civil War the only ones available for combat. The Inspector of Infantry and Armor Forces declared the 3d Tank Regiment, the army's premier tank force, "unfit for action." The commander of the district in which the unit was stationed, explained the reasons for this judgment in a report to Unshlikht. The men in the unit were demoralized because of bad living conditions, while the dilapidation and obsolescence of their tanks had caused the middle command staff to lose interest in their work. Only about half of the large and medium tanks were guaranteed for wartime use; thirteen of the nineteen mediums did not even have guns.[73] Dybenko,

71. This discussion of "Budushchaia voina," is from Samuelson, *Plans for Stalin's War Machine*, 22–28, and Stoecker, *Forging Stalin's Army*, 148–52.

72. Draft directive for Voroshilov's signature, March 1928, RGVA, f. 4, op. 1, d. 662, l. 28.

73. Report from Kuibyshev, Temp. Commander of Military District (MVO), and Bulin, Member of District RVS, to Deputy Chairman. RVS SSSR, 3 June 1928, RGVA, f. 4, op. 1, d. 344, ll. 143–56.

who had already shown himself anxious to add to the number of tanks in the Red Army arsenal, argued that the Soviet Union could not allow this to happen, and in particular had to at least equal or better the number of tanks in the Polish army.[74] In April the Executive Session of the Council of Labor and Defense (RZ STO), a defense cabinet created in early 1927 in the wake of the war scare, heard a report on the new tank production plans that argued along much the same lines. The unnamed speaker – perhaps Dybenko – began his statement by defending the need for more tanks. Tanks were the most powerful means for defeating weapon emplacements and, according to the best military authorities, any army without tanks would lack offensive power and suffer huge loses during an attack on fortified positions. Recognizing the importance of tanks, the RVS had followed developments in foreign armies very closely and seen that other countries were working diligently to improve tanks and "saturate" their armies with the vehicles – the examples he chose to dwell on were the French and Polish armies – and the speaker concluded that it was intolerable for the Red Army to fall behind foreign armies in this regard.[75]

With their own weaknesses and the worrisome strength of their capitalist neighbors in mind, defense officials called for a great leap forward in tank production. Dybenko and Gregorii Kulik, the new head of the AU, concluded that to keep up with other nations the Red Army needed 900 MS-1 tanks for thirty tank battalions and six heavy tank regiments (for the army reserve) with 30 maneuver tanks each, while every rifle regiment should have six Liliput tankettes for reconnaissance, or 1,800 of these light vehicles in all.[76] A few weeks later Dybenko and Lukin, the head of the Financial Planning Directorate (FPU), delivered a paper to the RVS in which they compared the number of tanks demanded by Variant no. 8 (108 MS-1 tanks) with these latest figures (2,880 in all). The huge difference in quantity was also reflected in tanks to be manufactured during the first year of war: 150 vehicles versus 1,050.[77] The deputy chief of staff agreed that the Soviet Union had to produce more tanks and attached a staff memorandum commenting on Dybenko and Lukion's report that asked for even larger increases in tank numbers.[78] In a closed meeting of the RVS held on 9 March, Nikolai Efimov, head of the staff's Organization and

74. His figures show that the Red Army had only seventy-four captured tanks at this time. Report from Dybenko, "Obespechenie mobilizatsionnoi gotovnosti po variantu N° 8 osnovnymi predmetami snabzheniia," arrived in archive 1 February 1928, RGVA, f. 33987, op. 3, d. 93, ll. 134–35.

75. Report for the signature of Voroshilov "V Rasporiaditel'noe Zasedanie Soveta Truda i Oborony," April 1928, RGVA, f. 4, op. 1, d. 662, ll. 22–26.

76. Dybenko, "Obespechenie mobilizatsionnoi gotovnosti po variantu No. 8 osnovnymi predmetami snabzheniia," February 1928, RGVA, f. 33987, op. 3, d. 93, ll. 134–135; Kulik, Chief of AU, to Chief of Supply, 23 December 1927, RGVA, f. 20, op. 21, d. 4, l. 71.

77. Report from Dybenko and Lukin, "DOKLAD RVS Soiuza SSR o meropriiatiiakh po obespecheniiu RKKA traktorami i tankami," February 1928, RGVA, f. 4, op. 1, d. 662, ll. 35–43.

78. Report from the Deputy Chief of Staff, 7 March 1928, RGVA, f. 4, op. 1, d. 662, l. 46.

Mobilization Directorate, followed suit. The council approved, calling for 1,600 MS-1, 210 maneuver, and 1,640 Liliput tanks by 1933.[79]

The fundamental problem with these demands was the severe backwardness of the Soviet military-industrial base. In line with similar optimism about the Five Year Plan as a whole, the army's ambitious schemes far exceeded the capabilities of industry.[80] During January 1928, even before commanders began submitting their expanded orders for tanks, the heads of the Supply, Production, Design, and Artillery directorates learned that the first tankettes would not be ready until October, while an experimental model of the maneuver tank would take more than a year to produce.[81] Dybenko's own estimates of maximum tank production showed that current factory capacity would be unable to produce the machines required by the plans.[82] Another report to Voroshilov was even more explicit. During 1927–28, factories could only manufacture 25 MS-1 tanks and would reach a mere 300 MS-1, 75 maneuver, and 150 Liliput tanks by 1931–32. Comparing the needs of the Red Army with these figures, the writer said, showed that the speed and scope of current production capacity would never permit the fulfillment of the army's needs.[83]

Regardless of the limitations of current factory capabilities, the army as a whole was becoming convinced, by the twin arguments of modernization and foreign developments, that the Soviet Union had to have tanks and quickly. Tukhachevskii, now identified as one of the chief supporters of armor forces, proposed the procurement of large numbers of the machines when he presented a final version of the military's five-year plan in April 1928. As earlier, he focused on the army's technological backwardness in comparison to other European militaries and wrote that the army had to equip itself with high-speed tanks and long-range aircraft. To accomplish this, the nation would have to build a military-industrial complex and construct many new factories. Unlike in his previous plan, Tukhachevskii now wanted tank production to increase, although changes in armor organization were limited to the creation of a few new tank companies and the rearming of older formations with the new MS-1 tanks.[84] Unshlikht too urged the creation of a domes-

79. "Protokol No. 16 zakrytogo zasedaniia RVS SSR," 9 March 1928, RGVA, f. 4, op. 1, d. 761, ll. 232–33.

80. Alec Nove, *An Economic History of the U.S.S.R* (London: Penguin, 1989), 135–36, has a discussion of the excessive optimism about the Five Year Plan as a whole.

81. Memo from Lukin to the Director of Affairs of the Military Commissariat and RVS SSSR, "Dlia doklada Zamnarkomvoenmor"a pred. RVS SSSR," 13 March 1928, RGVA, f. 4, op. 1, d. 662, l. 49.

82. Dybenko and Lukin, "DOKLAD RVS Soiuza SSR o meropriiatiiakh po obespecheniiu RKKA traktorami i tankami," February 1928, RGVA, f. 4, op. 1, d. 662, ll. 35–43.

83. Report for the signature of Voroshilov, "V Rasporiaditel'noe Zasedanie Soveta Truda i Oborony," April 1928, RGVA,. f. 4, op. 1, d. 662, ll. 22–26.

84. "Protokol No. 20 zakrytogo zasedaniia RVS SSSR," 27 April 1928, RGVA, f. 4, op. 1, d. 761, ll. 179–87; G. Isserson, "Zapiski sovremennika o M. N. Tukhachevskom," VIZh, no. 4 (April 1963): 66.

tic tank industry, emphasizing the widespread mechanization of Western European armies and the need to match these developments. The industrialization of the Soviet Union, he added, would allow the army to stop purchasing tanks abroad and concentrate on building them in Soviet factories.[85] A version of the military five-year plan, confirmed by the government on 30 July 1928, followed staff planning and Tukhachevskii's report closely, although authorizing fewer tanks.[86] Meanwhile, another look at the productive capabilities of the factories that would manufacture these thousands of tanks seemed to indicate that industry was capable of producing in amounts much closer to those desired.[87]

This is not to say that the army was able to obtain everything it wanted without a fight. In the summer and fall of 1928 the army's budget became involved in the ongoing struggle between Stalin and the "Right Opposition" led by Nikolai Bukharin, Aleksei Rykov, and Mikhail Tomskii. The Right believed that Stalin's push to industrialize the country was too extreme and would lead to economic disaster and the alienation of the peasantry. During 1928 Rykov, who was the chairman of the RZ STO, used his position to push for financial restraint and in particular a limitation of the military budget. Voroshilov and Unshlikht would spend much of the year pushing for more money to be spent on the weapons needed to create a military on a par with those of the encircling imperialist powers, in effect supporting Stalin in his struggle with the Right. The eventual result was the downfall of the Right and the triumph of both Stalin's vision for the Soviet Union and the staff's vision of future masses of airplanes, tanks, and artillery meeting and defeating capitalist technology on the field of battle.[88]

Soviet industry had to deal with realities, however, not hopeful predictions. Not long after the decision for increased production was made, the army high command became aware that there were serious obstacles to fulfilling their plans and that it might be necessary to seek help from outside the Soviet Union. Dybenko informed Voroshilov's deputy on 27 September that although the Bolshevik factory should have produced the first twenty-three MS-1 tanks by 1 October, they would not be finished until mid-December.[89] At about the same time the army ran into additional difficulties with the development of the tankette and a new light tank, reflecting a critical shortage of engineers to design new machines. Boris Shaposhnikov, who had replaced Tukhachevskii as chief of staff, and Efimov, now head of

85. Report by Unshlikht, "V Sovet Truda i Oborony (Rasporiaditel'noe zasedenie)," 2 October 1928, RGVA, f. 4, op. 1, d. 662, ll. 2–3.

86. A. Ryzhakov, "K voprosu o stroitel'stve bronetankovykh voisk krasnoi armii v 30-e gody," VIZh, no. 8 (August 1968): 105.

87. "Protokol (sov. sek.) soveshchaniia sostoiavshegosia 11 maia [1928] v Glavmetalle u Chlena Kollegii tov. Oborina po voprosu piatiletnei zaiavki NKVM na tanki i traktory," RGVA, f. 4, op. 1, d. 662, ll. 17–20.

88. Stone describes the struggle over the military budget in 1928 in Hammer and Rifle, 91–95.

89. Report from Dybenko to Deputy Military Commissioner, 27 September 1928, RGVA, f. 4, op. 1, d. 662, l. 5.

the staff's Second Directorate, had to write to Voroshilov in early 1929 to ask that the army develop the second tank from a modified MS-1, since the cost of creating an entirely new light tank was clearly prohibitive. They also suggested asking the Germans to design the tankette because the army would be unable to finish this task by the fourth quarter of the 1928–29 fiscal year. Soviet industry could then build the tankette using the foreign blueprints and specifications.[90] In late 1928 the management of the Soviet design bureau also approached the German designer Josef Vollmer about his dual-drive tank and, after protracted negotiations, signed an agreement with him to develop the machine for the Red Army.[91]

While help from abroad offered a solution to engineering weaknesses, the military collaboration with Germany, supposedly the main source of foreign aid and advice, produced more mixed results. In a report from the end of 1928, Berzin calculated that the Germans had spent one and a half to two million marks on the construction of the tank school and workshops, but noted that the school had only one dismantled experimental tank and that tactical studies had not begun. The latest estimates called for courses to commence no sooner than early spring 1929, and these would train only ten Germans and ten Soviets at a time.[92] Unlike the year before, the Germans now had a political reason for delaying their involvement in Kazan – the Shakhty show trials which, because of their openly antiforeign orientation, were perceived by the Germans as a blatant provocation.[93] The Shakhty affair had, of course, little to do with the Germans and much more to do with internal political calculations, specifically Stalin's struggle with the Right opposition and the remnants of the tsarist specialists. Only on 15 August, after the conclusion of the trials, did the German government issue a statement endorsing Kazan.[94] Educational exchanges and attendance at maneuvers continued throughout these political upsets, and did assist in some problem areas, as Soviet commanders learned German techniques for military training, education, and organization.[95] Officials who attended courses in Germany, including Eideman, used their experiences to

90. Report from Shaposhnikov and Efimov, Chief of the II Directorate of the Staff, to Voroshilov, 10 January 1929, RGVA, f. 4, op. 1, d. 799, l. 2.

91. Report from K. Neiman, Deputy Chief of Arms Formations, and A. Adams, Chief of N.T.U., to Uborevich, 8 August 1930, RGVA, f. 4, op. 1, d. 1276, l. 141.

92. Report by Berzin, "O sotrudnichestve RKKA i reikhsvera," and "Information" on Kama, 24 December 1928, RGVA, f. 33987, op. 3, d. 295, ll. 74, 80. The school at Lipetsk, by comparison, cost 8.6 million marks to construct. l. 81.

93. See e.g. Harvey Leonard Dyck, *Weimar Germany and Soviet Russia 1926–1933: A Study in Diplomatic Instability* (New York: Columbia University Press, 1966), 97, 129–44.

94. Kurt Rosenbaum, *Community of Fate: German-Soviet Diplomatic Relations, 1922–1928* (Syracuse, N.Y.: Syracuse University Press, 1965), 240. For a closer look at the Shakhty trial and its surprising lack of effect on German-Soviet relations, see Carr, *Foundations of a Planned Economy, 1926–1929*, 51–53, and Louis Fischer, *Russia's Road from Peace to War: Soviet Foreign Relations, 1917–1941* (New York: Harper & Row, 1969), 183–85.

95. See memo from Voroshilov to Stalin, 28 February 1928, and memo from Berzin to Voroshilov, February 1928, RGVA, f. 33987, op. 3, d. 87, ll. 123 and 125.

reshape study at the Frunze Academy on the German model and to make changes in training methods.[96]

During meetings of the military leadership, the effect of contact with the Germans was obvious, most particularly in the tendency of commanders to compare their own army unfavorably with the Reichswehr. Aleksandr Egorov, at this point chief of a military district but later the Red Army's chief of staff, remarked that the Soviet army did not even understand how the Reichswehr operated, let alone have the capacity to copy its skills.[97] Tukhachevskii quoted the German military attaché in Moscow on Soviet deficiencies.[98] Iona Iakir, head of the Kiev military district, compared the Red Army's lack of mobility, activity, decisiveness, and independence with the Reichswehr's constant envelopments and attacks on flanks.[99] Not everyone thought that the cooperation, and subsequent changes in Soviet opinion, were all to the good. Budënnyi, now the head of the cavalry and a true believer in Russian competence, had complained earlier in the year that the Reichswehr had undue sway over tactics and certain training practices and charged that the reports delivered at one meeting came straight from the Germans. He justified his opposition to German influence on the grounds that such a country was no example for the Soviet Union to follow.[100] Levichev also thought that "idealization" of the Germans was inappropriate for a socialist army. He said that all this talk of German talent for tactics and officer preparation was not even true; they had to have the same problems as did the Soviets.[101]

Yet there is no direct evidence that German influence extended to Soviet ideas on armor doctrine. Soviet tank tactics in 1928 resembled, in certain ways, those of the Reichswehr, but they were like British ideas, world war tactics, and earlier Soviet thought as well. Since the school at Kazan had not yet opened, while other close contacts with the Germans centered more on military training and education than concrete tactical practices, it seems reasonable to assume that the resemblances in doctrine came from common sources: the British exploitation of the new tank technology on Salisbury Plain, modifications of world war tactics, and widely read experts like Heigl.

The similarities between Soviet ideas and those of the Germans and British were

96. See for instance report from Hempel to von Dirksen on trip by Mittelberger to the Soviet Union, 10 May 1928, PA-AA. R 31681K, E671665–E671666. At the annual meeting of the high command, Eideman commented that the Red Army had learned much from the Reichswehr, and mentioned especially the use of referees in maneuvers. "Stenogramma zasedaniia RVS 27 Nov. 1928," RGVA,. f. 4, op. 1, d. 756, ll. 78–79.

97. Record of meeting of district commanders and RVS, January–February 1928, RGVA, f. 4, op. 1, d. 749, ll. 5–6.

98. Ibid. ll. 235–36.

99. "Stenogramma zasedaniia RVS 27 Nov. 1928," RGVA, f. 4, op. 1, d. 756, l. 47.

100. "Stenogramma zasedaniia RVS SSR i RVS Okrugov i Morei ot 30-go ianvaria 1928 g.," RGVA, f. 4, op. 18, d. 34, l. 194.

101. Ibid. ll. 104–5.

most apparent in two draft field manuals, the *Preliminary Instructions for the Battle Use of Tanks in the Red Army* and PU-28. This latter work would, after some significant changes, become PU-29, the main statement of Soviet military doctrine until the publication of PU-36 seven years later. Both drafts dealt extensively with the tank and presented the latest official thinking on armor tactics, although the *Preliminary Instructions* were more cautious when examining the new developments in tank design. They began, for instance, by listing the good and bad characteristics of tanks, a throwback to the days when technical failings were the primary factor determining tank tactics.[102]

The armor doctrine in the *Preliminary Instructions*, however, was more daring, reflecting the forward thinking of its author, Konstantin Kalinovskii – a close friend and collaborator of Tukhachevskii.[103] As in German studies on the subject, Kalinovskii stressed that there were now two different tactics of armor warfare: close cooperation with infantry and freely maneuvering tanks. In the first type of combat, tanks would stay in fire and eye contact with the infantry, working closely with foot soldiers to create a path through the opponent's defensive system. Yet even these tanks could at times fight far from the slower infantry. Kalinovskii in fact assumed that tanks would outrun the infantry and should only use a more methodical coordination when the opponent's defenses were well organized.[104] In the second kind of combat tanks, along with artillery and cavalry, would attack deeply into the opponent's rear without direct contact, exploiting fully the new speed of the vehicles. They would at first coordinate their actions with small groups of infantry, using their maneuverability to attack several objectives at the same time. As the attack developed, coordination with the infantry would be lost and then each tank unit would act on the initiative of its own commander, striving to strike where it would facilitate the advance of the infantry to the greatest degree.[105] Like German and British officers, Kalinovskii added that it was also possible to combine the two ways of fighting by dividing the tanks into echelons, one of which would head directly towards the rear while the other fought in close contact with the infantry to suppress the enemy's firepower.[106]

The armor doctrine described in PU-28 was similar to that outlined by Kalinovskii. Tanks could fight with either the infantry or cavalry and in offensive or defensive actions.[107] One echelon of tanks could head directly for the enemy's rear

102. *Vremennaia instruktsiia po boevomu primeneniiu tankov RKKA (Proekt)* (Moscow: Nauchno-ustavnyi Otdel Shtaba RKKA, 1928), 5–8, 14.

103. For Kalinovskii's role in writing the *Preliminary Instructions*, see report from A. Burov, Chief of the Scientific Regulatory Department of the Red Army Staff, 19 January 1927, RGVA, f. 7, op. 1, d. 229. l. 64; and report from Burov, 10 February 1927, RGVA, f. 7, op. 1, d. 229. l. 76.

104. *Vremennaia instruktsiia*, 26, 28–29.

105. Ibid., 30–31.

106. Ibid., 20, 23–24.

107. *Polevoi ustav 1928 goda (Proekt)* ([Moscow]: Nauchno-Ustavnyi Otdel Shtaba RKKA, 1928), 6, 75.

artillery positions or, if cavalry was present, the machines could fight them on the flanks and rear of the opponent.[108] The detailed description of an offensive with tanks had the first echelon fighting in the enemy's rear against the artillery and then turning to attack the flanks from the rear. Meanwhile, the other echelons would co-operate with the infantry to suppress the enemy's fire and centers of opposition. The attack was to be a combined-arms operation, closely tied to the artillery and air force.[109] Cooperation with the cavalry was given special emphasis, with descriptions of breakthroughs and pursuits combining horse and tank units.[110]

The revolution in Soviet doctrine reflected in these two manuals would remain purely theoretical during the next few years, for the major difference between the Reichswehr and the Red Army was the deplorable state of Soviet tactical capabilities. This failing meant that the Soviets were almost as handicapped as the Germans when it came to trying out their theories in practice. The 1928 Kiev maneuvers, for instance, one of the first in which the Red Army tried to use tanks, were not (to put it mildly) a success. The official report on the army's preparation for the year noted that commanders did not understand how to employ tanks. There was even a case of someone subordinating tank units to the commander of an artillery regiment, while joint action with cavalry, infantry, and artillery was very unsatisfactory.[111] Tukhachevskii, from his new post as commander of the Leningrad military district, reported that the infantry had not even known how to follow tanks, a report seconded by Mikhail Levandovskii, another district commander, who added that infantry had no conception of cooperation with tanks.[112] Exhortations in the annual report on battle preparation show that the military was determined to change all this. The army now had a new mission: the practical mastery of armor combat and of antitank defenses. Given the lack of large numbers of machines with which to practice, the RVS suggested using mock-ups, in the form of tractors or motorcycles, to give tank forces a more realistic organization.[113]

Fortunately the next year would finally provide an avenue for putting the new armor doctrine into practice: the school at Kazan became fully operational during the summer of 1929 with the arrival of the first German experimental tanks. The year did not start well, however, and setting up the school proceeded too slowly for the

108. Ibid., 78.

109. Ibid., 99–100, 110–11.

110. Ibid., 112, 122–23.

111. "Stenogramma zasedaniia RVS 27go noiabria 1928 goda," RGVA, f. 4, op. 1, d. 757, ll. 143–44.; f. 4, op. 1, d. 761, ll. 37, 39.

112. Ibid., RGVA, f. 4, op. 1, d. 756, ll. 16, 23. German observers also commented on the Soviet lack of skill in using tanks, and their poor tactics. Oberstleutnant Geyer, "Bericht über militärische Erfahrungen einer Russlandreise v. 23.8. bis 26.9.29," 14 October 1929, BA-MA, N 221/10.

113. "Prikaz (sekretno) RVS SSSR No. 393/79 3 Dek. 1928: Ob itogakh uchebno-takticheskoi podgotovki RKKA na osnove opyta manevrov 1927–28 uchebn. goda i uchebnye tseli na 1928–1929 goda," RGVA, f. 4, op. 1, d. 761, l. 42.

Soviets. Voroshilov, who was consistently suspicious of the Germans, reported to Stalin in March that ten German tanks were due to arrive at Kazan after sea navigation opened that spring, long months after the Soviets had requested them. He also wrote that in order to get around Versailles, the Germans wanted the Soviets to sign an agreement with Rheinmetall to buy the tanks and then both sides would destroy the contract. This would allow the German government to shift all blame onto the manufacturers if news about the tank shipment leaked to the outside world. Voroshilov advised Stalin that he supported this fiction only because no possible political damage could accrue to the Soviet Union if it was discovered.[114] Stalin decided, however, not to proceed with the fictitious contract. Avgust Kork, the military attaché in Berlin, informed Walter Behschnitt, a T-3 specialist, in early April that there were "insurmountable difficulties" and that the army had not received permission to proceed. Kork then asked Behschnitt when the tanks would arrive in the Soviet Union and was told again that the Germans would send them as soon as the Leningrad port was open.[115]

But in fact the first tanks, six "large tractors" from the three German firms, arrived in Kazan only during July, although the school as a whole began operations before then.[116] Because of the strict rules to preserve the secrecy surrounding the development of the vehicles, none of them had been tested in Germany, which inevitably created serious problems. Both Daimler tanks, for instance, had design flaws that kept them from moving at all the first year.[117] In general, though, the testing of the tanks' driving and shooting abilities, treads, and radio equipment was productive, at least for the Germans.[118] Meanwhile ten German officers and an equal number of Soviet commanders participated as students in the courses taught at Kazan.[119] As had been provided for in the original agreement, the command staff at the school was almost entirely German, as was the armor tactics instructor for the Soviet students.[120] This, along with the fact that Radlmaier was appointed the first director at Kazan, ensured that Soviet commanders were exposed to the very latest German thought on tank combat.[121] Yet the fact that the Kazan school was opened after the appearance of the *Preliminary Instructions* and PU-28 shows that the Soviet high command had already developed its new ideas on ar-

114. Memo from Voroshilov to Stalin, March 1929, RGVA, f. 33987, op. 3, d. 295, l. 50.

115. Report no. 11 from Kork, 8 April 1929, RGVA, f. 33987, op. 3, d. 295, l. 34.

116. Müller, "So lebten und arbeiteten wir," 10; minutes of a meeting between Voroshilov, and General Hammerstein, and Colonel Kühlentahl, 5 September 1929, RGVA, f. 33987, op. 3, d. 375, ll. 2–5.

117. Müller, "So lebten und arbeiteten wir," 14.

118. Ibid., 14–18.

119. Ibid., 12, 15.

120. Willi Esser, *Dokumentation über die Entwicklung und Erprobung der ersten Panzerkampfwagen der Reichswehr* (Munich: Krauss-Maffei, 1979), 59.

121. Discussed in Zeidler, *Reichswehr und Rote Armee*, 196–97.

mor doctrine before direct exposure to the similar concepts that had evolved within the German staff.

The Soviet high command was of course pleased that the school opened and from late 1929 through the end of the cooperation Kazan became increasingly important for producing the armor engineers and designers that the Red Army lacked. Kulik in fact called for the army to exploit more fully the opportunities that the installation offered for becoming acquainted with German technology, and recommended that seven of the engineers and commanders studying at the school be sent to work in the AU, and that five more engineers be sent to Kazan for further instruction.[122] A high-level meeting held that autumn between Voroshilov and Kurt Freiherr von Hammerstein-Equord, then head of the Truppenamt and soon to succeed Heye as chief of the German Army Command, shows that the Soviet high command also still hoped to realize its original, more ambitious, plan for Kazan. Hammerstein began by stating that both experimentation with tanks and training in tank warfare was going well, but Voroshilov only vaguely agreed with this and then pointed out the main problem with the collaboration: the Germans were primarily interested in a base for experimenting with new tanks, educating tank personnel, and studying tactics. All this interested the Soviet army, but he wanted in addition to receive technical help. He asked if the Reichswehr would be willing to exchange blueprints and data on tanks and suggested setting up a joint design bureau with German specialists. Even more importantly, he wanted German tanks to be constructed in Soviet factories under the German supervision. Hammerstein had two different reactions to these proposals. At first he flatly stated that the Reichswehr did not want to set up a design bureau at Kazan; the engineers there were only trying to find faults in tanks already constructed. Later, under pressure from the Soviets, he said that, in principle, he was of the same opinion as Voroshilov, but that there were only a few experimental tanks at Kazan. First the engineers had to work out which were the best tanks and then they could discuss production and a design bureau. Voroshilov stressed that the Red Army did not want to waste time since the important work being done at Kazan was connected to Soviet production.[123] The conversation ended, however, without any concrete agreements and with only a few vague promises from the German side. Voroshilov's tone during the conversation shows that he thought Hammerstein was being evasive and probably duplicitous about the collaboration, which only served to fuel his (and Stalin's) concerns about allowing these foreigners so much influence on Soviet soil.

The reason the Germans signed no contracts was that unlike the Soviets, they were satisfied with the progress made at Kazan. Until Versailles could be safely defied,

122. Report from Kulik, 25 October 1929, RGVA, f. 4, op. 2, d. 504, ll. 42–46.
123. Minutes of a meeting between Voroshilov, General Hammerstein, and Colonel Kühlentahl, 5 September 1929, RGVA, f. 33987, op. 3, d. 375, ll. 2–5, 6–7.

the Reichswehr was content to produce only a few tanks while conducting an intense theoretical discussion about the technical and tactical needs of an armor force. On the technical side, by 1929 officers agreed that the most important requirements for a tank were mobility, firepower, and low cost. One possible solution was the dual-drive tank, a vehicle first championed by Oswald Lutz, an officer in the motorized troops, during 1925–26.[124] This tank, which could switch from tires to treads at need, combined the advantages of an armored car (high speed on roads and therefore strategic mobility) with those of a light tank (fire power, armor protection against light infantry weapons, and tactical mobility).[125] The other strong interest was in an ultrasmall tank, similar to Fuller's one- or two-man vehicle, that would be cheap and easy to mass-produce and distribute widely throughout the army. Although one small-tank enthusiast admitted that larger tanks were probably more useful in battle, he argued that at times military needs had to bow to economic necessities. The low cost of the small tank outweighed its obvious shortcomings.[126] Majority opinion favored a larger vehicle, but over time the arguments of small tank supporters, as well as economic and production realities, would make the ultralight vehicle more appealing. In time the German high command would produce tactical justifications for smaller tanks, and come to believe that these were indeed the best choice for a modern army. This crucial decision, made under financial pressure and not informed by sound tactical thinking, would have far-reaching consequences for later German armor doctrine.

German thought on tactics was more unsettled than technical thinking. By 1929 there was a wide spectrum of views represented in the Reichswehr, ranging from officers who believed tanks would fight as they did during the world war, in close cooperation with the infantry, to those who saw the tank as the weapon of the future and dreamed of huge tank masses attacking the enemy's rear or enveloping and destroying whole armies. It was unclear which theory would succeed in impressing the high command as the most practical, because the German army still faced the problem of no experience with actual tanks in warfare or maneuvers. Theorists throughout the late twenties and early thirties proposed a multitude of mutually conflicting scenarios for how future war with tanks would play out, but for lack of practical data the army clung to the lessons of the world war (of doubtful worth now that the new tanks had appeared), the experiences of the British (always open to dispute), and the limited evidence of their own maneuvers with mock-ups. As in previous years, a major concern was the strength of antiarmor defenses. One

124. See James S. Corum, *The Roots of Blitzkrieg: Hans von Seeckt and German Military Reform* (Lawrence: University of Kansas Press, 1992), 116–18.

125. "Beschreibung des leichten Räderraupenkampfwagens M28." BA-MA, RH 8/v. 1672. p. 6. The idea of a workable car-tank hybrid would occupy German and Soviet thought on tank development until well into the next decade.

126. Dipl.-Ing. Wim Brandt, Leutnant a.D., "Kleintanks," *Militär-Wochenblatt*, no. 43 (1929): 1751–52.

author compared tanks to a herd of elephants. Nothing could stand in their way, but they could also be easily diverted and destroyed with defensive weaponry: "classical foot soldiers forced the monsters to turn back with firebrands. Modern infantry will slit through their stainless steel hides with armor-piercing shells. And speed will not be able to protect them from these lightning-fast projectiles." Infantry could also carry large-caliber machine guns, the best antitank weapon, rather than depending on artillery to perform this mission. Given this vulnerability of the tank, the only practical use for tanks was as transports for infantry and artillery like "the draft elephant of the Indian army."[127] In a reply to this article, an anonymous author argued that it underestimated the tank: it was entirely questionable whether defensive weapons would cancel out the tank's effect.[128]

Other officers ignored this controversy, perhaps because it was a question that only the experience of war could answer, and concentrated instead on the details of how to organize armor forces and how they would fight. From the masses of articles, reports, and manuals produced by German officers, it seems likely that the majority adopted a "moderate" position: they accepted that fast tanks would play important roles in future war, but rejected the Fulleresque vision of completely mechanized combat, deep thrusts into the enemy's flanks or rear, and an independent armor force. An explanation of the F.u.G. that served as an update of that seminal manual, reflected this desire to use the new tanks and the latest lessons from Britain, yet without going beyond certain boundaries. The author still thought that tanks should fight in the closest association with the infantry, but provided very different missions for light and heavy tanks. Light tanks would be subordinated to the attack infantry, while heavy tanks would fight against deep and strongly built-up defensive and flanking installations, thus clearing the way for the light tanks.[129] This idea of heavy tanks aiding light tanks, first proposed in the years immediately after the world war, would return in the thirties as a dominant strand in German armor doctrine.

In 1929 Friedrich von Cochenhausen, the head of the Army Training Section, produced the latest edition of the *Truppenführung* – the basic field manual for officers – which reflected the trend toward moderation. He envisioned dividing up the tanks among the infantry, apportioning a tank company to every infantry battalion. Although the two arms could fight in close harmony, the greater speed of modern tanks also allowed them to fight independently, in envelopments or far from the infantry.[130] In his closer examination of these two ways of using tanks, however, he

127. Friedrich Wilhelm Borgman (Alberga-Finnland), "Vertikale strategische Umfassung: Ein gedankliches Experiment," *Wissen und Wehr*, no. 10 (1929): 600–601.

128. "Vertikale strategische Umfassung?" *Militär-Wochenblatt*, no. 28 (1930): 1087–90.

129. Major Friedrich Siebert, *Atlas zu F.u.G. I*, "*Führung und Gefecht der verbundenen Waffen*": Ein Anschauungs-Lehrbuch (Berlin: Verlag Offene Worte, 1929), 52.

130. Oberst Friedrich von Cochenhausen, *Die Truppenführung: Ein Handbuch für den Truppenführer und seine Gehilfen*, 5th ed. (Berlin: Mittler, 1929), 274–75.

had a much clearer conception of how the tanks would cooperate with the infantry than of how they would fight independently. Close cooperation with the infantry was more suitable for the older tanks, which would use their speed to the fullest, attacking in waves with the infantry following to suppress the enemy's artillery and areas of resistance.[131] The newest tanks would be most effective in purely mobile warfare, exploiting their maneuverability to its fullest. Yet he was careful to say that they could not advance too far forward, and did not specify many tasks that they could perform.[132]

Supporters of a more ambitious exploitation of tanks did not allow these "moderate" ideas to go unanswered. An anonymous officer of the "moderate" school, describing French views on cooperation between the tank and the infantry, wrote that tanks would always be attached to the infantry, that tanks could not hold land, and that they could never replace the infantry.[133] Several weeks later, another officer took exception to each of these claims. Tanks should not always be attached to the infantry as they had been in the last war because the latest improvements in technology meant that armor could now complete independent missions, separate from the infantry. The deployment of tanks to hold land depended entirely on the terrain and the enemy. If one's opponent was badly armed or the terrain provided enough cover, then tanks could hold land for long periods of time. As for the final point, tanks could never completely take the place of the infantry, but they could and would, in as far as their technical development allowed, replace some of the infantry, artillery, and cavalry.[134]

This view of armor doctrine, seen as "radical" by many officers, actually came in several versions, most of which tried to be more practical than the "fantasies" of Fuller. An article examining the battle of Cambrai was typical of German attempts to describe the future of mechanized war in a more realistic way. The author concluded that tanks now had three different missions. First, their armor protection and cross-country mobility made them into infantry battering rams in a tactical breakthrough and the battle in the infantry zone. Next, they could carry their armor-protected weapons into the enemy's artillery zone in order to suppress it. Finally, their speed enabled them to penetrate deeply and complete a strategic breakthrough.[135] The lessons of Cambrai were thus twofold: the tank attack must be

131. Ibid., 275–78.

132. Ibid., 278.

133. "Zwischen Infanterie und Tanks: Französische Grundsätze in der Zusammenarbeit," *Militär-Wochenblatt*, no. 13 (1929): 490–92.

134. "Zwischen Infanterie und Tanks," ibid., no. 17 (1929): 650–652. Heigl wrote later to warn that while tanks could partially replace the infantry and hold ground, the army should tell this only to the tank troops and not to the infantry. It would be suicide to inform ordinary soldiers that they had been superseded by machines. Dr. Heigl, "Die französischen Tanks im neuen Infanterie-Reglement," ibid., no. 22 (1929): 843–44.

135. "Nutzanwendungen aus der Tankschlacht von Cambrai II," *Militär-Wochenblatt*, no. 24 (1929): 926.

concentrated and it must unfold in several strong waves, each of which would have a special, sharply defined mission. Somewhat like the exercises conducted by Stülpnagel and Bockelberg in 1928, this author foresaw using the first two waves to break through the zone of infantry resistance without getting involved in battle with the infantry, and to head towards the enemy's artillery. Another wave could co-operate with foot soldiers in the enemy's defensive systems, while the final two waves would remain as a tactical reserve.[136] The most important lesson of Cambrai, he concluded, was that the battlefield had to be saturated with armor.[137]

In the fall of 1929, Bockelberg ordered a modification of armor organization that reflected this new thinking on tanks rather than the "moderate" position. The changes that he required showed that he, like some others within the high command, supported large formations that would be entirely mechanized and motorized, an important first step on the way to the armor divisions of the next decade. Following his orders, the three companies of the 6th Motor Transport Battalion were transformed into a motorcycle company, a dummy armor reconnaissance company, and a dummy tank company.[138] A parallel reorganization plan, developed at the same time, foresaw the eventual formation of motorized infantry battalions consisting of rifle companies carried in cars built to travel cross-country. It also called for a transformation of the motorized forces that would result in units combining armored cars, tanks, antitank defenses, and motorcycles.[139] In late October the 3d Company of the 7th (Bavarian) Motor Transport Battalion was reorganized to reflect these ideas, which were predicated on tanks fighting in large independent units but in close cooperation with motorized infantry and other support forces.

In his report on training, the head of the 3rd Company concluded that the composition of company, reconnaissance, and liaison forces had proven successful. In the exercises, the company had tested the various ways that the high command had envisioned using armor: for envelopments on open flanks, in independent employment (without infantry), and as the advance guard for large units. On the basis of his experiences, the company commander argued strongly for using armor in combined-arms operations, rather than for independent missions. The high command, he wrote, should employ tanks after the infantry assault had forced enemy defensive forces to betray their positions by firing. The tanks would then come to the assistance of the infantry, cooperating with them to suppress enemy resistance. The number of waves in the actual tank assault depended on several factors, but it was important that commanders keep armor as concentrated as possible. His description of the armor assault showed that the most important element for success

---

136. Ibid., 927.

137. Or as he put it "Tanks, everywhere tanks." Ibid., 928.

138. Kurt J. Walde, *Guderian* (Frankfurt: Ullstein, 1976), 32.

139. List of planned organizational changes, 1 October 1929, BA-MA, RH 1/v. 14, pp. 166, 169.

was close cooperation between infantry, artillery, and armor, each working to support and aid the other's efforts. Unfortunately he, like the rest of the German officer corps, was unsure how exactly armor support for the infantry would take shape. If the advanced infantry companies were each allotted a tank platoon, the individual platoons would be unable to cooperate with each other in a desirable mass and the weight of the tank attack would be dissipated. At the same time platoons divided up among the infantry would be able to follow the orders of the (infantry) company commander more quickly. There was in any case a major problem for close cooperation between infantry and armor: a reliable means of communication. Signaling with flags provided a poor solution, but was the only one available at the time.[140]

The battalion commander forwarded this report to Military Area Headquarters VII with a memorandum saying that he concurred for the most part with the company commander's conclusions. He thought, for instance, that a platoon of Carden-Loyd tankettes (the ultrasmall British tanks favored by some in the army) would meet the requirements for reconnaissance pointed out by the company commander. He also generally agreed with the company commander's ideas on tank tactics. He too viewed the tank as a heavy infantry weapon, a sort of mobile artillery that would accompany the foot soldiers into the enemy's defensive positions where regular artillery could not provide observed fire support. Armor would therefore not attack with the foot soldiers, but only after the first infantry assault had clarified where tanks could make the most difference. His one point of agreement with more "radical" ways of viewing the tank was that armor unit commanders should have complete control over their units and that tanks should not be divided up among infantry platoons, a measure that only led to a dissipation of the armor attack.[141]

While the Germans slowly worked out the details of armor technology and tactics, the seemingly more united front maintained by the Soviets provided no solution to a growing dichotomy between words and deeds. Throughout 1929 plans for building an armor force and for its use in battle grew ever more ambitious, far outstripping the ability of Soviet industry to produce the actual machines. In late April Unshlikht presided over a meeting with industrial leaders in which they discussed the problems with completing the latest plans for tank production. The protocol of the meeting noted that there was a huge delay in fulfilling the orders for the

140. Report from 3rd Company, 7th (Bavarian) Motorized Battalion, "Erfahrungsbericht über die Verwendung der Kompanie als Kampfwagennachbildungskompanie mit Linke-Hofmann-Stumpf-Raupenschleppern," 24 October 1929, National Archives, T-79, Roll 33, Records of the German Army Areas, Frames 000403–417.

141. Memo from 7th (Bavarian) Motorized Battalion to Wehrkreiskommando VII, "Erfahrungsbericht der Kampfwagennachbildungskompanie," 29 November 1929, National Archives, T-79, Roll 33, Records of the German Army Areas. Frames 000394–402.

present year and that there was a real possibility that the entire tank construction program would fail.[142] Taking no notice of these difficulties, the latest army mobilization plan, Variant No. 10, required twelve light tank battalions and one detached heavy tank battalion in the short term. Some cavalry units would also have tank regiments or batteries attached to them, bringing the number of tanks to over fifteen hundred by January 1931. For actual deployment in time of war the army would need an additional twenty-six hundred tanks, putting the total wartime demand for tanks at a much higher level than the slightly more than sixteen hundred tanks that industry had promised to deliver by January 1932.[143]

The army reached its figures for Variant No. 10 using the same methodology as in the previous year. Rather than deciding how to use and organize the machines and then settling on a quantity of tanks that would best fit this doctrine, the military planners simply pointed to capitalist tank numbers and estimated the country's maximum tank production potential. To their pleased surprise, when the Politburo heard the figure for tanks and armored cars that the army hoped to have by the end of the Five Year Plan, it directed the high command to quadruple the numbers. Although the government then retreated somewhat from this demand, the final figure agreed upon was two or three times as high as the military had originally requested.[144] Along with raising production in every other category of weaponry, the Politburo called for forty-five to fifty-five hundred tanks to be built in the period of the Plan.[145] Like the Red Army high command, the government had not thought about how exactly the tanks would fight, merely informing Voroshilov that the increases were realistic because Soviet industrial capacity would expand.[146]

The government's change of heart was an acknowledgment that the Red Army was right: the Soviet Union could not allow the encircling capitalists to surpass them in military technology. In its resolution, the Politburo stressed that the technological base of the Soviet Union was much more feeble than that of bourgeois countries.[147] A recent incident in China had shown the extent of Soviet military

142. Protokol no. 8, "Soveshchaniia s promyshlennost'iu pod predsedatel'stvom tov. Unshlikhta ot 20-ogo aprilia 1929g.," RGVA, f. 4, op. 1, d. 1075, ll. 3–6.

143. "Tablitsa potrebnosti tankov, tanketok, bronemashin po var. No. 10 (utv. iu-1929g.) i orgmeropriiatiiam 1930g. i 1931g." (dated on verso December 1930), RGVA, f. 31811, op. 1, d. 11, l. 115.

144. Khalepskii would later report the new numbers as fifty-five hundred tanks by 1932–33. Report from Khalepskii to Voroshilov, 30 November 1929, RGVA, f. 4, op. 1, d. 1021, ll. 17–21.

145. Resolution of the Politburo, "O sostoianii oborony SSSR," 15 July 1929; with attachments, GARF, f. 5446, op. 55, d. 1966, ll. 43–31. The author wishes to thank David Stone for this source.

146. "Stenogramma zasedaniia RVS SSSR ot 29 Okt. 1929 g.: Ob itogakh boevoi podgotovki RKKA i Flota," RGVA, f. 4, op. 1, d. 1071, ll. 265, 277. This is from the original stenographic report. The corrected copy, published and distributed to the high command, said only that the Politburo had ordered a tripling of tank production above the RVS request.

147. Resolution of the Politburo, "O sostoianii oborony SSSR," 15 July 1929, GARF, f. 5446, op. 55, d. 1966, l. 41.

weakness. On 10 July 1929 Chiang Kai-Shek's troops had seized the Chinese Eastern Railway in Manchuria and expelled its Soviet employees. Despite efforts to dislodge the invaders and regain control of the railway, the Red Army had been
powerless to do so until several months later. This attack on the sovereignty of the
Soviet Union and the exposure of the frailties of its army provided a major impetus
for expanding military industry in general and tank production in particular.[148]

Only at this point, while the government and high command were in the process
of deciding to acquire large masses of the machines, did the army determine which
tanks were necessary for future warfare and how they would fight. During late
spring the RVS quickly put together a draft directive on tank construction which defined the tanks that the high command thought most useful for modern warfare.
The directive called for six models in all. A light and fast dual-drive tankette (one
with both treads and tires) was designed for reconnaissance and surprise attacks.
Another light tank, armed with a 37 mm main gun and able to travel at 25–30 kph,
would act as the shock element of large mechanized units, creating breakthroughs
in maneuver warfare. The directive noted that the MS-1 could fulfill this particular
need as long as the AU could find some way to increase its maximum speed. A
medium tank, weighing fifteen or sixteen tons and armed with a 45 mm main gun,
but still as fast as the small tank, would create breakthroughs in fortified areas in
maneuver or positional combat. Finally, a heavy tank would fight against well-for-
tified positions and would weigh sixty to eighty tons, carry a 76 mm main gun, and
yet be able to travel at 25–30 kph.[149]

To get as much input as possible on the problem of mechanization, the Red
Army's most senior commanders were asked to comment on the draft during June
and July. All those who responded pointed out that the directive called for too many
tank models and that this would lead to serious production problems. Thus Kork,
who had taken Dybenko's place as head of the Supply Directorate, recommended
that the army develop only a tankette with treads (already in the design process)
rather than the new dual-drive vehicle mentioned in the draft.[150] The chairman of
the Military-Scientific Research Committee of the RVS, Mikhail Dmitriev, argued in
the same vein that the army did not need a heavy tank because of its weight, high
cost, and lack of military usefulness. He also stressed using foreign help as fully as
possible to make up for technical problems with production and design.[151] Inno-
kentii Khalepskii, employed at this time in the Military Technical Directorate,
thought that existing factories charged with tank production were not being fully

148. See R. W. Davies, *The Soviet Economy in Turmoil, 1929–1930* (London: Macmillan, 1989),
444–46.

149. Draft directive of the RVS, 18 July 1929, RGVA, f. 4, op. 2, d. 504, ll. 3–4.

150. Memo from Kork and the Deputy Chief of AU, "Predlozheniia US RKKA o vnesenii izme-
neniia v proekt postanovleniia RVSR o sisteme tanko-traktoro-avto-brone vooruzheniia RKKA,
predstvlennyi shtabom RKKA," RGVA, f. 4, op. 2, d. 504, l. 26.

151. Memo from Dmitriev, Deputy Chair of the Military-Scientific Research Committee of the
RVS, to Litunovskii, Director of Affairs of the RVS, 22/23 July 1929, RGVA, f. 4, op. 2, d. 504, l. 30.

exploited, since they did not make this their top priority. He also noted that Soviet production methods – constructing special parts and factories for every tank type – hampered standardization and wasted time and money.[152]

The most extensive comments came from the chief of the Operations Directorate, Vladimir Triandafillov, who used the opportunity provided by the draft directive to discuss his (and the staff's) evolving thought on the issue of mechanization. Triandafillov was one of Tukhachevskii's closest friends and had collaborated with him in writing the 1926 field regulations.[153] He was also intensely interested in the future of tanks in modern war and would be instrumental in elaborating Soviet doctrine. His study of the directive, "On the Red Army's System of Tank-Tractor-Auto-Armor Weaponry," was a seminal work for the Soviet armor forces and would have far-reaching influence.

Triandafillov began his analysis by outlining the opportunities and challenges that the new system of weaponry presented. On the plus side it was now possible to consider both the formation of independent mechanized units as well as a more widespread mechanization and motorization of the army as a whole. At the same time the army had no experience with the entire question and did not have the technical specialists it would need to develop the weapons. Like Dmitriev, he thought that it would be necessary to turn to the outside world for the resolution of both problems. To work through the details of large mechanized formations, the army could follow the example of America and England and create an experimental unit, while guidance on designing the new machines would have to come from (unspecified) foreign countries.[154]

Triandafillov then examined in detail the twin issues of mechanization and motorization. On mechanization he foresaw two possibilities: partial mechanization, where the tank would play only an auxiliary role in combat; and complete mechanization, where the machines would be the main force within large motorized and mechanized units. He agreed with accepted Soviet and German thought that the evolution of the tank, and especially the latest improvements in speed, made it absurd for the vehicles to use the same tactics as the technically defective models of the world war.[155] It was imperative for the army to exploit the new speed of the tank to its utmost, although this did not lessen the need for coordination between tanks and the infantry. His answer to the problem of infantry and tank cooperation that troubled German officers was brief, suggesting that he also had no solution to this dilemma. He began with the assumption that the path to cooperation did not lie in reducing the speed of the tank, nor in combined operations of tanks and infantry, but rather in working out concrete methods of cooperation. It was more important,

---

152. Report from Khalepskii to Voroshilov, 8 July 1929, RGVA, f. 4, op. 2, d. 504, ll. 34–35.

153. Report from Triandafillov to Voroshilov, "O sisteme tanko-traktoro-avto-brone-vooruzheniia RKK Armiia," 5 June 1929, RGVA, f. 4, op. 2, d. 504, ll. 5–18 both sides. See also Philip A. Bayer, *The Evolution of the Soviet General Staff, 1917–1941* (New York: Garland, 1987), 107.

154. Report from Triandafillov to Voroshilov, 5 June 1929, l. 5.

155. Ibid., l. 5v.

in other words, for the two arms to coordinate their actions using the same kinds of tactics than to be in close physical contact.[156]

Having set the parameters for discussing mechanization, Triandafillov then divided tanks into two basic categories, determined by technical and tactical characteristics. Arguing that the categories should follow the example of artillery, which was separated into field and headquarters pieces, Triandafillov proposed that one category would consist of vehicles that could travel anywhere, directly following behind the other forces, while the other would include those tanks that had to be carried to battle by rail. He based his classification system on weight, which in turn was grounded on the load capacity of a country's highway bridges and railroads. Since Soviet bridges on strategic roads could only bear up to eight tons, he set this as the absolute upper limit for the tanks in the first category. The weight limitation meant that these "field" (or light) tanks would have to be small in size and have limited armor, but they needed sufficient striking force to push through fortified positions and over trenches.[157] The light tanks required the aid of even lighter tankettes with greater operational mobility to perform reconnaissance and carry out raids on the enemy's rear and flanks. The second category of armor vehicles would include the medium tanks, designed to break through fortified zones. Since they did not have to follow directly behind the other forces, the heavy machines could have very thick armor and be fairly slow.[158] This advocacy of the medium tank was based purely on transport considerations; the payload capacity of Soviet flat cars was insufficient to allow the army to transport the heavies on all railroads.[159]

Triandafillov next turned to the proper organizational structure for the vehicles. Overall, he thought that the question needed more study and that it would take time and experience with the machines to decide how best to organize them. The technological development of armor forces had been so phenomenal, however, that he was convinced that they had become a separate branch of the military.[160] The speed and operating radius of the lighter tanks separated them decisively from all other types of land forces; it would be utterly wrong for the army to simply assign these machines to the cavalry or infantry and thus renounce the full use of their advanced capabilities. Instead, the army had to create special independent mechanized units. The fundamental principle for organizing these units had to be uniformity of operational mobility and cross-country ability for all the vehicles that made them up.[161] Within each mechanized formation would be several subunits, all mechanized and motorized to allow the formation to work as one whole. The main strik-

---

156. Ibid., l. 6.
157. Ibid.
158. Ibid., l. 6v.
159. Ibid., ll. 6v–7. For his closer analysis of the four types of tanks see ibid., ll. 7–10v.
160. His proposed organization into independent units was good only for the lighter machines; the heavies and mediums would form what he called an "Armor Reserve of the High Command" and would be at the disposal of the army headquarters. Ibid., ll. 15v–16.
161. Ibid., l. 15.

ing core would consist of light tanks supported by self-propelled artillery and assisted by infantry detachments in transporters that would follow the tanks everywhere. These infantry units were necessary because the tank could not hold land, but they had to be kept to a minimum because too many would create an excessively large organizational structure for the mechanized formations and far outweigh any tactical advantage that they offered.[162]

Triandafillov argued that such mechanized and motorized units would wage a new kind of warfare that would have nothing in common with ordinary infantry combat. The army commander would deploy them on a wide front, choosing the area for the main blow during the process of battle itself. Without exception, the tactical mission of the units was not a "shattering blow" (sokrushenie) but rather "attrition" (iznurenie) and paralyzing the opponent.[163] Triandafillov, in other words, envisioned his mechanized formations using their speed to outflank or wear down the enemy rather than annihilate him, an interesting contrast to German thought, which favored an idealized "battle of annihilation."[164]

In the middle of July, just after the Politburo had ordered the immense increase in tank production, Triandafillov delivered his report at a two-day meeting of the RVS. After hearing the first part of the report, on technical/tactical developments, the council approved a revised version of its draft directive, leaving out the development of a heavy tank.[165] The second half of his report, on the establishment of large mechanized units, led the RVS to order the creation of an experimental unit to test his idea in action – again following the British example.[166] A mechanized regiment was set up not long afterwards and took part in the fall exercises held in the Belorussian military district. Because of the successes experienced at these maneuvers, the regiment formed the basis for a later mechanized brigade.[167]

Triandafillov's ambitious plans for the tank should be compared to the ideas in his major publication, The Nature of Operations of Modern Armies, which appeared in 1929. This book, in which Triandafillov refined the concept of "operational art," a complement to the more established tactical and strategic arts, would have immense influence on Soviet military thought during the interwar period. If tactics were the art of leading men in a particular battle, then operations were the art of linking separate battles to fulfill the ultimate strategy of the high command. One attack or breakthrough would follow directly on the next, occurring so quickly that the enemy would not have time to regroup or counterattack.[168] As noted above,

162. Ibid., ll. 12v–13, 14.

163. Ibid., ll. 12–12v.

164. Ibid., l. 12v.

165. "Vypiska iz protokola No. 29 zasedaniia RVS SSSR ot 17–18 iiulia 1929 goda," RGVA, f. 4, op. 2, d. 504, ll. 31–33.

166. Ibid., l. 36.

167. G. K. Zhukov, Vospominaniia i razmyshleniia, 10th ed., vol 1 (Moscow: Avtor [nasledniki], 1990), 190.

168. See for example V. Triandafillov, Kharakter operatsii sovremennykh armii (Moscow: Gosudarstvennoe Izdatel'stvo, Otdel Voennoi Literatury, 1929), 136–37.

Tukhachevskii had first conceived of linking separate engagements into continuous operations, but in this work Triandafillov proposed a major innovation, arguing that the operation even in its initial phase would seek to "overcome all depths of the opponent's tactical position."[169] At this point he thought that tanks and automobiles could aid armies in accomplishing this goal, but that they would not radically alter the way in which battles were fought. Tanks, as in the last war, would create the initial breakthrough necessary for the operation to begin, and aid the artillery in suppressing the enemy's resistance. Motorized and mechanized units could also help to encircle and envelop the enemy's army, attacking on the enemy's flanks at the same time as the breakthrough.[170] He noted that because of their higher speed, greater maneuverability, and wider radius of action, tanks could take an active part in pursuit.[171]

This gave additional significance to armor, because in the concept of linking battles into continuous operations, pursuit was the essential connection between each attack. Motorized units could aid pursuit, helping to encircle and attack the flanks and rear of the opponent.[172] Tanks and automobiles would also permit deeper penetrations and advances than in the last war, with the original battle 25–35 km in depth and the pursuit operation reaching up to 250 km.[173] Triandafillov's vision of future operations in this publication stopped short of endorsing the ideas of Fuller and other supporters of complete mechanization. He emphasized in his opening remarks that man was still the basis of warfare, that a million-man army was absolutely necessary even if motorized and mechanized, and that Fuller and the others only supported a small army because they feared the "inevitable" revolution.[174] The tank would help man forward, but would not decide the battle. Within months of the publication of *The Nature of Operations*, however, Triandafillov had changed his mind about the decisive nature of mechanization and was supporting, and even adding to, the rather grandiose schemes of the Red Army high command.[175]

Triandafillov was not alone in his new support for a broad mechanization of the

169. Ibid., 116.

170. Ibid., 120–24.

171. Ibid., 19–20.

172. Ibid., 21, 137–59.

173. Ibid., 116, 159, 166–69.

174. Ibid., 25–29, 69, 85.

175. The reaction of the Soviet officer corps to Triandafillov's ideas is just as interesting as the ideas that he articulated. It is clear that the book and his report based on it made a deep impression at the annual meeting of the RVS and force commanders. RGVA, f. 4, op. 1, d. 1071, ll. 192–93, 230. The introduction to the second edition of the book said that it was a "most original and serious" work, "in the fullest sense progressive," and that it made an "exceptionally immense contribution to Soviet military literature." V. Triandafillov, *Kharakter operatsii sovremennykh armii*, 2d ed. (Moscow: Gosudarstvennoe Voennoe Izdatel'stvo, 1932), 3–4. By 1936 improved industrial conditions and changes in doctrine resulted in an introduction that was critical of his views of tank usage. V. Triandafillov, *Kharakter operatsii sovremennykh armii*, 3d ed. (Moscow: Gosudarstvennoe Voennoe Izdatel'stvo, 1936), 5–6.

Red Army and a more pervasive use of the tank. The latest army textbook on armor stated that tanks could fight as a "freely maneuvering group," fulfilling missions in the depths of the opponent's defenses without any direct connection to the infantry.[176] N. Varfolomeev, in a book on the weapons of modern armies, described three different types of tanks, each with wide-ranging mission. Light tanks could cut through enemy positions and fight in their rear, attacking transport, staffs, and so on. Together with motorized detachments and cavalry, they could seize lines, areas, and points (at least for a while), gather intelligence, attack enemy columns on the move, take part in pursuit, or protect withdrawals. Like artillery, medium tanks would escort infantry into battle, clearing the way for them. Their most important mission was overcoming the opponent's firepower for which they had to have a large radius of action. Finally, heavy tanks were designed to break through fortified areas.[177]

The new commitment to mechanization and the tank did not mean that Soviet commanders endorsed Fuller, or other theorists whose ideas were seen as too extreme. Like Triandafillov, the military as a whole made very clear its support for a large mass army that would use tanks to aid the infantry rather than replace it. In late 1929 Tukhachevskii praised tanks as powerful weapons, but also said that their main mission was to advance with the infantry and supplement artillery. He rejected utterly Fuller's call for a small mechanized military, defending the mustering of a mass army as a basic tenet of Marxist philosophy.[178] Verkhovskii, on the other hand, had become known as a supporter of Fuller's small technologically advanced army and as such was attacked by both Tukhachevskii and Triandafillov.[179]

Like the infantry, the cavalry was also supported by the Soviet high command, but there was now pressure from certain quarters to modernize the arm. Budënnyi interpreted this pressure as an attack on his precious horses. At the annual fall 1929 analysis of army preparation, he openly charged that certain officers wanted to destroy the cavalry, replacing it with motorized and mechanized units and aircraft. "The Germans," he added ominously, "have turned the heads of our young men."[180] In his view of events, a struggle between two different philosophies, one European and one Eastern, was taking place within the Red Army. The European

176. S. Ammosov and A. Sluchkii, *Vzaimodeistvie tankov s pekhotoi v rote, batal'one i polku* (Moscow: Gosudarstvennoe Izdatel'stvo, Otdel Voennoi Literatury, 1929), 10–11.

177. N. Varfolomeev, *Vooruzhenie sovremennykh armii: Lektsiia shestaia* (Moskva: Gosmedizdat, 1929), 23–24.

178. "Stenogramma doklada tov. Tukhachevskogo sdelannogo 16-go Dekabria 1929 goda v Kommunisticheskoi Akademii po voprosu 'O kharaktere sovremennykh voin v svete reshenii VI-go kongressa Kominterna,'" RGVA, f. 4, op. 1, d. 1147, ll. 42, 53–54.

179. Ibid. ll. 53–56; Triandafillov, *Kharakter operatsii sovremennykh armii* (1929), 26n.

180. "Stenogramma rasshirennogo zasedaniia Rev Voen Soveta Soiuza SSR ob itogakh boevoi podgotovki RKKA i F za 1928–1929 god i ob uchebnykh tseliakh na 1929–30 god," 28–29 October 1929, RGVA, f. 4, op. 16, d. 3, l. 29.

tendency wanted to destroy the cavalry completely, and Budënnyi accused several commanders, such as Tukhachevskii, Iakir, and others, of agreeing to this pernicious idea. Iakir in particular had lived among the Germans and they had "twisted his brains," so that now he thought that he could do better on foot than on horseback.[181] In fact no one at this meeting or any other suggested ridding the army of its prestigious Red Cavalry, not least because of its strong connection to Stalin and Stalin's closest supporters. A few commanders did, however, mention supplementing cavalry with the striking power of the tank and the automobile.[182] Only Triandafillov was a little more critical, pointing out that cavalry commanders, even when given tanks and armored cars during exercises, chose not to use them and instead depended only on the shock of a horse assault. He thought that this tendency was a result of insufficient preparation of the cavalry command staff and a "peculiar conservative viewpoint."[183]

Notwithstanding the commitment by the high command to the infantry and cavalry, PU-29, the first official statement of Red Army doctrine, reflected the new thinking in the army. Written by Triandafillov, Tukhachevskii, and other innovators, PU-29 went even further than the 1928 draft in its recognition of the major changes that had taken place in tank technology and their effect on tactics. No longer would armor forces participate only in short breakthroughs closely tied to the infantry. PU-29 listed four types of possible tank combat: cooperation with infantry units; independent missions deep in the opponent's positions in cooperation with infantry and artillery; cooperation with the cavalry on the opponent's flanks; and, in motorized units, attacking flanks or creating breakthroughs.[184] The two emerging strands of thought on the future use of the tank were reflected in the types of armor combat described as most important: acting as infantry weapons in infantry strike forces and fighting against the opponent's artillery or other remote objectives.[185] PU-29 affirmed that the basic task of the tank remained paving the way for the attacking infantry, but added that commanders should divide the main mass of tanks into two echelons: a "PP" ("infantry support") force to accompany infantry; and another, intended to combat artillery and disorganize the opponent's rear, designated "DD" ("long-range").[186] DD tanks would also protect infantry

181. "Stenogramma zasedaniia RVS SSSR ot 29 Okt. 1929 g. 'Ob itogakh boevoi podgotovki RKKA i Flota,'" RGVA, f. 4, op. 1, d. 1071, l. 126.

182. See Levandovskii's and Kalinovskii's speeches in "Stenogramma rasshirennogo zasedaniia Rev Voen Soveta Soiuza SSR ob itogakh boevoi podgotovki RKKA i F za 1928–1929 god i ob uchebnykh tseliakh na 1929–30 god," 28–29 October 1929, RGVA, f. 4, op. 16, d. 3, ll. 30, 35–36.

183. "Stenogramma zasedaniia RVS SSSR ot 29 Okt. 1929 g. 'Ob itogakh boevoi podgotovki RKKA i Flota,'" RGVA, f. 4, op. 1, d. 1071, ll. 11–12.

184. *Polevoi Ustav RKKA* (1929) (Moscow: Gosudarstvennoe Voennoe Izdatel'stvo, 1933), 96–97.

185. Ibid., 64.

186. Ibid., 97. The Soviets also used "PP" and "DD" to describe types of artillery and their different missions.

support tanks by engaging and eventually destroying the opponent's artillery.[187] The manual concluded, however, that regardless of the great advances made in tank design and tactics, tanks could still not take or hold ground, but could only aid the infantry in this all-important task. The foot soldier thus remained the decisive force on the battlefield.[188] The greatest problem that tank commandeers would face, given the distances between the areas of DD tank combat and the infantry battle, was coordinating the actions of the two types of forces.[189] As with German doctrine, then, the Soviet army had not determined how the slower forces would keep up with the fast tanks, nor precisely how tanks and infantry would cooperate on the battlefield.

The very real obstacle to fulfilling any of these ambitious plans for armor tactics and organization continued to be failures in production. Kulik presented a report on 25 October that described the Artillery Directorate's views of the new tank construction ordered by the RVS, and the problems that he foresaw with its completion. The AU considered the light tank to be the main type for maneuver warfare and thought that the new T-19 would fulfill this mission admirably. After describing the various difficulties that industry had experienced in developing the vehicle, he concluded that it would not be ready for serial production until spring 1932. Despite staff opposition, the Soviet Union had decided to go ahead with development of a light dual-drive tank, but Kulik noted that the army was dependent on the German designer Vollmer to fulfill this requirement. As for the MS-1, the AU recognized that its armaments and speed did not meet staff requirements and was working to update these by early 1930. Since the modernized MS-1 would not go into full-scale production for several years, he suggested producing an intermediate type of tank, the T-20. The staff had issued specifications for this small tank in July 1928 and the first experimental machine would be ready in December 1930. The final tank type, the medium T-12, was similar to the German experimental "large tractor," which had some interesting design aspects, but still had far to go in development. Soviet industry could begin production of their own medium no earlier than the 1930–31 fiscal year.[190]

About this time the high command concluded that one of the biggest obstacles to mechanizing the Red Army was the AU itself. As early as February 1927 some within the Red Army had expressed interest in the creation once again of a separate armor force directorate. In an anonymous letter to Dybenko a member of the Politburo suggested some sort of "Mechanical Section" that would combine the functions of the Auto Section of the Military Technical Directorate and the AU's Mechanical Traction Section. He argued that the army needed to have coordination

187. Ibid., 99.
188. Ibid., 98–99.
189. Ibid., 98.
190. Report from Kulik, 25 October 1929, RGVA, f. 4, op. 2, d. 504, ll. 42–46.

between the mechanization of the army and the question of armament design and production.[191] No action was taken on the question until the summer and fall of 1929 when the army began to consider the formation of an independent Directorate of Mechanization and Motorization (UMM). Kulik then agreed with the Politburo member; the new agency should be created from various sections of the AU plus part of the Auto Section.[192] In mid-October, Kalinovskii described the founding of the UMM as "dragging on" and thought that the army should simply unite all the departments and personnel which dealt with the questions of motorization and mechanization.[193] This was in fact what happened, although it would not be until November, and after much more discussion, that the directorate began to function.[194] The regulations for the UMM envisioned a department that combined technical, production, supply, training, and, to a more limited extent, tactical functions.[195]

Khalepskii, experienced already in technical matters from his five years as head of the Military-Technical Directorate, was appointed head of the new UMM and within a few days was hard at work on the problem of production failures. His first report was even more brutal than Kulik's, noting that the army had ordered 300 MS-1's for 1928–29 but there was no chance that the factories could fulfill the order, let alone meet demands to modernize the machines. He also reported that attempts to produce the new medium tank on schedule had failed completely.[196] Overall the tank-building plans for the fiscal year 1928–29 had been fulfilled only 20 percent.[197] One week later Khalepskii and another commander produced an analysis of the state of the tank-building program for the high command. They concluded that there was no way that the current plan for converting factories to tank production would succeed. The Supreme Council of the National Economy (VSNKh), responsible for controlling industry and coordinating overall production, had done nothing to guarantee the fulfillment of the program. They noted that there was no support for design, tank manufacturing was not connected with tractor production, and there were no medium tank or tankette models. Meanwhile, Voroshilov

191. Letter from "Member VKP(b)" to Pavel Efimovich [Dybenko], February 1927, RGVA, f. 31811, op. 1, d. 24, ll. 146–47.

192. Report from Kulik, 25 October 1929, RGVA. f. 4, op. 2, d. 504, l. 46.

193. Report from Kalinovskii to Voroshilov, 16 October 1929, RGVA, f. 4, op. 1, d. 1021, l. 4.

194. See "Skhema upravleniia mekhanizatsii i motorizatsii Armii," 22 October 1929, RGVA, f. 31811, op. 1, d. 14, l. 3.

195. Voroshilov, "Polozhenie ob upravlenie po mekhanizatsii i motorizatsii RKKA," 22 November 1929, RGVA, f. 31811, op. 1, d. 14, ll. 10–11. and "Sekretnyi prikaz RVS No. 367/82," 22 November 1929, RGVA, f. 4, op. 3, d. 3154, l. 152.

196. Report from Khalepskii and Poliakov, Chief of the Tank and Tractor Department, 25 November 1929, RGVA, f. 31811, op. 1, d. 1, ll. 11–12.

197. "Postanovlenie Rev Voen Sovet SSSR 'O polozhenii s tankostroeniem,'" 21 March 1930, RGVA, f. 31811, op. 1, d. 4, l. 70.

had not yet issued the final technical requirements for all the types of tanks.[198] Two days later Khalepskii wrote a draft resolution for the Politburo that would formally recognize these problems and call for decisive action to correct them. The resolution noted that industry would not be able to produce any of the four types of tanks that the army wanted. The light MS-1, the only tank that Soviet factories had produced in any quantity, did not have suitable armament, and industry would not be able to produce the minimal 1929–30 plan. Khalepskii called for speeding up production and for Kuibyshev, Voroshilov, and Ordzhonikidze to take personal charge of the fulfillment of the plan.[199] The actual resolution passed by the Politburo was less severe but still required more to be done to safeguard tank production.[200]

Khalepskii also argued that it was useless to maintain the outmoded captured tanks, and that the UMM should instead receive extra funding for a complete motorization and mechanization of the army. In his reports he emphasized the numerous problems with the old machines, describing their breakdowns during the last maneuvers and the impossibility of ever obtaining spare parts, which left several tanks permanently out of service. Replacing them with the new MS-1s made much more sense.[201] He put the total financial needs for the army's tanks, including repairs and new machines, at over twenty million rubles for the ten-year period 1929–39; along with armored cars, trains, and tractors, the UMM would need more than fifty million rubles during that time.[202] At a meeting of the RVS on 17 December, he formally asked for 47,655,000 rubles to motorize and mechanize the Red Army. The council approved.[203]

Khalepskii's other strategy for accelerating tank production was to rely even more heavily on foreign designs. Throughout the autumn several commanders had suggested that, given the poor state of Soviet technology and design and the failures in tank production, the Soviet army should look abroad while continuing to

198. Memo from Khalepskii to Litunovskiii, 1 December 1929, RGVA, f. 4, op. 2, d. 504, ll. 38–40.

199. Draft resolution from Khalepskii "po voprosu o tankostroenii," 3 December 1929, RGVA, f. 31811, op. 1, d. 1, ll. 46–48.

200. "Postanovlenie Politbiuro 'Po voprosu o vypolnenii Tanko-Traktornoi programmy,'" adopted without changes, according to a handwritten note by Khalepskii, on 5 December 1929, RGVA, f. 31811, op. 1, d. 1, l. 52.

201. "Tezisy k dokladu nachal'nika UMM RKKA tov. Khalepskogo po voprosu o material'nom i finansovom obespechenii mekhanizatsii i motorizatsii RKKA k zasedaniiu RVS SSSR 13/XII-29 goda," RGVA, f. 31811, op. 1, d. 41, ll. 1–2; "Analiz Ispolnitel'no-zagotovitel'nogo material'nogo plana 1929–1930 goda po Tankovomu, Traktornomu, Avtomobil'nomu, Bronevomu i Brone-poezdomu Imushchestvu," c. 10 December 1929, f. 31811, op. 1, d. 41, ll. 11–15.

202. "Tezisy k dokladu nachal'nika UMM RKKA tov. Khalepskogo po voprosu o material'nom i finansovom obespechenii mekhanizatsii i motorizatsii RKKA, k zasedaniiu RVS SSSR 13/XII-29 goda," RGVA. f. 4, op. 1, d. 1029, ll. 3–8.

203. "Protokol No. 40 zasedeniia RVS SSSR 17-go dek. 1929 goda," RGVA, f. 31811, op. 1, d. 4. l. 8; "Vypiska iz protokola No. 40 zasedeniia RVS SSSR ot 17 dekabria 1929 goda," f. 4, op. 1, d. 1029. l. 46.

develop a domestic tank industry. Kalinovskii thought that the Germans could be particularly useful since they were working in the Soviet Union itself on the very areas where the Soviets were experiencing problems, tank design and technology. The army could order tanks now from German industry and, with the completion of testing at Kazan, also request the best tanks which that experience produced. Another possibility would be to put money aside for the purchase of the newest tanks from France, Britain, and the United States.[204] By late November the army had taken his advice and was in the process of making several deals with foreign manufacturers, including agreements for buying Carden-Loyd and Vickers tanks in Britain, the nine-ton Christie and T1E1 in the United States, and the German Vollmer tank.[205] Khalepskii also hoped to conclude contracts with Krupp and Daimler for technical help in reorganizing Soviet tank factories, for designing tanks, and for the right to send Soviet engineers to study in German factories. With this in mind, he requested permission to travel to Germany by the first of the new year to set up these agreements.[206] During December the staff convened a special meeting to discuss Khalepskii's trip abroad and the tanks that he should buy. Shaposhnikov, though not generally known as a supporter of foreign aid in technical innovation, agreed that the Soviet Union had to seek help abroad if the army was going mechanize quickly. He suggested the purchase of several machines, and the final schedule for the trip called too for a first stop in Berlin to hold talks with private German firms about assistance with Soviet military-industrial production.[207]

For the Soviet military, 1929 thus ended where 1927 had begun: with the Red Army determined to use its connections with Germany (and other countries) to further its industrialization and mechanization plans. The production of tanks remained on shaky ground and there were no guarantees that industry would ever be able to manufacture anything like the number of the vehicles that the army's grandiose plans required. The push had begun, however, and there was a great deal of excitement over even the possibility of creating huge mechanized armies. The question

204. Report from Kalinovskii to Voroshilov, 16 October 1929, RGVA, f. 4, op. 1, d. 1021, ll. 1–4.

205. Report from Khalepskii to Voroshilov, 30 November 1929,. RGVA, f. 4, op. 1, d. 1021, ll. 17–21. Shaposhnikov had held a meeting at the end of September with Kork and others in which they decided to buy three of Vollmer's tanks and four motors. "Protokol Zasedaniia u Nach. shtaba RKKA po voprosu proekta koliesno-gusenichnogo tanka – inzh. FOL'MAR ot 30 sentiabria 1929 goda," RGVA, f. 4, op. 2, d. 504, ll. 40–41. A commission under the leadership of Shaposhnikov approved a draft agreement to purchase Vollmer tanks but the RVS had not yet done so in mid-December. "Tezisy k dokladu nachal'nika UMM RKKA tov. Khalepskogo po voprosu o material'nom i finansovom obespechenii mekhanizatsii i motorizatsii RKKA, k zasedaniiu RVS SSSR 13/XII-29 goda," RGVA, f. 4, op. 1, d. 1029, l. 3.

206. Report from Khalepskii to Voroshilov, 30 November 1929, RGVA, f. 4, op. 1, d. 1021, ll. 17–21.

207. Report by Shaposhnikov, 13 December 1929, and Khalepskii, "Plan Poezdki Komissii Zagranitsu," RGVA, f. 4, op. 1, d. 1029, ll. 19, 20–21, 24–27.

of how to employ the masses of tanks that industry would deliver was still unsettled, but with the ideas worked out by Tukhachevskii, Triandafillov, and Kalinovskii, the high command could feel satisfied that a good foundation had been laid for forward-looking thinking about how to use armor in the next war.

The Reichswehr could also feel pleased with the progress made as the decade ended. The command staff as a whole had decided that tanks would fight in completely different ways from the old, slow tanks of the world war, and had begun to think about organizing the vehicles, along with other motorized forces, into independent mechanized formations. The collaboration with the Soviet army had not yet borne fruit, but the Germans had every reason to be confident that, in the new decade, the station at Kazan would produce the perfected, fast machines that would transform warfare.

1. Official photograph of I. A. Khalepskii. (RGVA)

2. Tukhachevskii speaking at the Seventeenth
Party Congress in 1934. (RGVA)

3. The five Marshals of the Soviet Union, 1935:
Tukhachevskii, Budennyi, Voroshilov, Egorov,
and Bliukher. (RGVA)

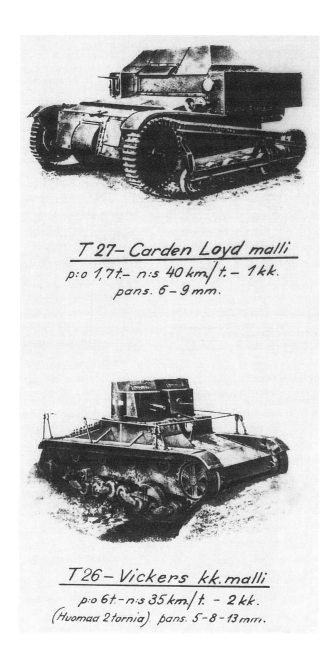

T 27 – Carden Loyd malli
p:o 1,7t. – n:s 40 km/t. – 1 kk.
pans. 6 – 9 mm.

T 26 – Vickers kk. malli
p:o 6t. – n:s 35 km/t. – 2 kk.
(Huomaa 2 tornia). pans. 5 – 8 – 13 mm.

4. Top: The Soviet Carden-Loyd;
Bottom: The famous T-26. (NARA)

5. Christie tank chassis, August 1931. (RGVA)

6. The Soviet B-T or "Fast Tank." (NARA)

7. The BT-5 in testing. (RGVA)

8. The medium T-28. (NARA)

9. The heavy T-35. (NARA)

10. The first German tank, the light Pz. I. (NARA)

11. The larger Pz. II with gun. (NARA)

12. The Pz. III, the main Wehrmacht
battle tank in 1941. (NARA)

13. The Pz. IV, a version of the Pz. III with larger main gun. (NARA)

CHAPTER FOUR

Consensus and Conflict, 1930–1931

ESPITE the high hopes with which the Reichswehr and the Red Army began the new decade, the first two years of the thirties were stormy for both Germany and the Soviet Union. In Germany the Communists on the left and extremist parties on the right increased their share of votes in national elections, and the Nazis began to wield a power in high places far outweighing their actual membership. The economic circumstances of the early thirties almost seemed to have been deliberately created to encourage extremism, as the worldwide slump that began in 1929 deepened into depression. Soviet internal affairs also reached a crisis point, one of many, brought about by the decision to push the collectivization and industrialization drives to a fever pitch. The nation would complete the Five Year Plan in four years, Stalin said, while simultaneously peasants would join collective farms, voluntarily or involuntarily, and the kulaks would be "destroyed as a class."[1]

Military affairs in the two countries were affected by their differing crises, though less so in Germany than in the Soviet Union. Funding for the Reichswehr, for instance, increased even during the Depression, and most German officers did not yet pay heed to Hitler's antics.[2] At the same time, the Reichswehr still could not afford either financially or politically to produce large numbers of tanks and thus was compelled to continue developing an armor doctrine on a mostly theoretical plane. In the Soviet Union, however, the new urgency to fulfill the Plan forced industry to overcome the most serious of its difficulties with tank production. This is not to say that problems did not remain, nor that army planning for tank manufacture became more realistic. As earlier, commanders ignored difficulties with production and called for ever greater numbers of the machines. But the ambitious schemes, and the fact that industry was able to produce at least some of the vehicles required by the Plan, worked together with the new trends in doctrinal development to produce the radical concept of armor doctrine known as "deep battle."

---

1. For a good description of Stalin's "revolution from above" see Robert Tucker, *Stalin in Power: The Revolution from Above, 1928–1941* (New York: Norton, 1990).

2. For the Reichswehr budget, see in Walther Nehring, *Die Geschichte der deutschen Panzerwaffe 1916 bis 1945* (Berlin: Propyläen Verlag, 1969), 54.

Soviet commanders would enthusiastically adopt this new concept of combat, proposed and developed by Kalinovskii, Triandafillov, and Tukhachevskii, and dedicate the first years of the decade to working out its details.

Tukhachevskii had already realized the implications of industrialization, but now he went even further. In January 1930 he wrote to Voroshilov, Shaposhnikov, and other commanders to explain how he thought the changes in the Soviet Union would transform war forever. His provocative memorandum would create an uproar within both the high command and the political leadership. It also fueled Stalin's suspicions about Tukhachevskii, and led to an investigation that almost destroyed the commander's career. Tukhachevskii's thesis was that

> the successes of our socialist construction, the accelerating tempo of our country's industrialization, and the socialist reconstruction of agriculture set before us in all its magnitude the task of reconstructing the armor forces, taking into account the newest factors of technology, the possibility of mass military-technical production, and also the improvements occurring in the countryside.[3]

Stalin's ambitious programs transforming the Soviet Union were all connected – and could only work for the good of the army. The destruction of the kulaks as a class and the collectivization of the instruments of production would, Tukhachevskii wrote, allow the army to use peasant masses as never before – in territorial forces that included not only infantry and cavalry, but also massive amounts of technology. The successful conclusion of the Five Year Plan would help to create a huge military while increasing the army's mobility and raising its offensive capabilities. Finally, the quantitative and qualitative growth of the various forces would produce new structural changes and the reconstruction of the army would in turn give rise to new forms of operational art.[4]

Based on his country's increased manufacturing capacity, Tukhachevskii envisaged a quantum leap in the army's technical forces and in their combat usage. Rather than two to four thousand tanks as he had requested in 1928–29, he thought that the Red Army could have fifty thousand tanks available by 1932–33.[5] This quantity of tanks, and the thousands of airplanes and other technical forces for which he called, would make the army capable of huge maneuver battles and operations. He cautioned that it would be a mistake to think that the army's reconstruction would only make possible earlier views of operations or strategy. The massive numbers of tanks and airplanes in fact allowed a completely new type of combined-arms battle, with 150 divisions attacking on a front of 450 kilometers or more at the same time. Even more significantly, he thought that the new battles

---

3. Memo from Tukhachevskii to Voroshilov, 11 January 1930, RGVA, f. 7, op. 10, d. 170, l. 11.
4. Ibid., ll. 13–14.
5. Ibid., ll. 15–17.

would take place in great depth, of 100–200 kilometers. To reach this depth, he suggested using both airplanes and special tanks, to deposit infantry in the enemy's rear and disrupt lines of communication. Airplanes and chemical weapons would cooperate with these troops, while the main forces (tanks, regular infantry, and artillery) destroyed the enemy's army.[6]

Tukhachevskii's proposal was a radical departure from previous Soviet thinking about future war and met with a stormy reception from both Stalin and the staff. In a lengthy memorandum Shaposhnikov suggested that neither the nation nor the economy would be able to provide the material and manpower resources that Tukhachevskii believed possible, although he took care not to criticize the proposal directly. Voroshilov passed on both the original proposal and Shaposhnikov's analysis to Stalin, writing in his cover letter that Tukhachevskii's proposition showed that the commander wanted to be "original" and "radical." In his reply Stalin agreed that the plan was "fantastic," in fact "science fiction," and lacked any realistic appraisal of the country's current economic, financial, and cultural situation. Ominously, he wondered how a Marxist commander could possibly divorce military matters from the country's underlying economic realities, and commended Shaposhnikov for his prudence in dissociating himself from the flawed plan. Voroshilov would later use the criticism of both Stalin and Shaposhnikov in the fall meeting of the high command to chide Tukhachevskii for his bad habit of sketching unrealistically huge vistas for the army that only served to discourage people.[7]

None of this kept Tukhachevskii from continuing to dream of even more ambitious plans for the Soviet army and economy. In December 1930 he sent another memorandum to Stalin, in which he argued that by converting the existing motor industry to tank production in wartime, it would be possible to manufacture a tank for every tractor and every automobile and not one for every two tractors as he had earlier thought. Keeping in mind current industry capabilities, he believed that the Soviet Union could turn out a hundred thousand tanks every year. No capitalist country or even coalition of anti-Soviet forces could produce tanks on such a huge scale. Significantly, to support his ideas about the automobile and tractor industry as the perfect basis for tank production, Tukhachevskii quoted Liddell Hart's book on *The Remaking of Modern Armies*, showing that he had read and at least partially agreed with the conclusions of that seminal work.[8]

Of course Tukhachevskii's proposals went far beyond the capacities of Soviet industry. The less ambitious tank-building plans for fiscal year 1928–29, had been fulfilled only 65 percent by the middle of March 1930. The program for 1929–30

---

6. Ibid., l. 17.

7. Samuelson discusses the interchange between Stalin, Voroshilov, Shaposhnikov, and Tukhachevskii in *Plans for Stalin's War Machine* (London: Macmillan, 2000), 90–120.

8. Tukhachevskii to Stalin, December 1930. RGVA, f. 33987, op. 3, d. 400, ll. 74–79.

was in worse condition: at the very moment when Tukhachevskii was predicting an army of fifty thousand tanks that would overwhelm any aggressor, factories within the Soviet Union had not managed to manufacture even one tank for that year's quota. Naturally the RVS, after looking at the capacity of industry, said that their original plan could and should be fulfilled. Voroshilov ordered several measures to ensure that the responsible military agencies paid more attention to their work and that the factories had the necessary material to build the tanks. In addition, Tukhachevskii was made personally responsible for seeing that factories in Leningrad fulfilled their part of the national plan.[9]

In spite of these actions, problems continued to plague the tank industry – clear proof, if anyone needed it, that Tukhachevskii's ideas were unrealistic. A report on the status of tank manufacturing issued at the end of May made it clear that orders were unfulfilled across the board. Factories ought, for instance, to have produced ten tankettes and thirty T-12 medium tanks for 1929–30, but it was now apparent that in the best case they would only finish four experimental tankettes by the end of the fiscal year. The report noted too that the plans for 300 T-12s and 290 tankettes would have to be revised – the Soviet Union was simply not capability of manufacturing that many machines.[10] The bad news continued through the autumn. Khalepskii reported in September that one of the most important tank plants was still unable to produce T-24 tanks according to plan. The responsible factory personnel thought that they would be able to fulfill the 1929–30 orders, although seriously delayed. The RVS noted, however, that judging from the first ten days of September, even the extended period for meeting the quota would be insufficient.[11] By October the tank program had only been fulfilled 18–20 percent. Although in other sectors of the Soviet economy "wreckers" were being put on trial for deliberately sabotaging the socialist industrialization drive, Voroshilov did not blame industry's failings on individuals, but on "our feebleness."[12]

The truth was that the Soviet industrialization drive as a whole had run into trouble by late 1929. As with military planners, government and industrial managers had set unrealistic goals for the Plan as a whole and, once some positive results were achieved, pushed their quotas even higher. By early 1930 not only did shortages of labor, capital, and raw materials afflict the overheated economy, but also a lack of training for new workers, the purge of the Right Opposition, and the problems resulting from collectivization added to the chaos.[13] Matters only worsened

9. "Postanovlenie RVS SSSR 'O polozhenii s tankostroeniem,'" 21 March 1930, RGVA, f. 31811, op. 1, d. 4, l. 70.

10. Report from Nemitts to Voroshilov, 26 May 1930, RGVA, f. 33987, op. 3, d. 306, l. 63.

11. "Protokol No. 20 zasedaniia RVS SSSR," 13 September 1930, RGVA, f. 7, op. 1, d. 172, ll. 51–52.

12. "Stenogramma rasshirennogo zasedeniia RVS SSSR s 22–26 oktiabria 1930," RGVA, f. 4, op. 1, d. 1403, ll. 716, 721.

13. R. W. Davies has an excellent discussion of the dilemmas facing the economy in *The Soviet*

throughout the year. The result was an overall slowdown in production gains, affecting the manufacturing of tanks as much as the rest of industry. Officials in charge of the economy had to face the real possibility that the Plan might not be fulfilled.

During 1930 the Soviet army looked at two possible solutions to its difficulties with armor production: concentrating on just one tank model and exploiting foreign expertise. In June, Khalepskii reported that the army had a program on the table to produce a bewildering variety of tanks, including four different sorts of small tanks, five mediums, and two tankettes. This did not include three German tanks, which the high command also hoped to copy and mass-produce.[14] Limiting the army to just one tank type would simplify production considerably, and there was a movement afoot within the Soviet army to concentrate on a machine that united all "imaginable qualities." In his December memorandum to Stalin, however, Tukhachevskii argued that there were good tactical and technical grounds for rejecting this idea. In the first place, the newest armor tactics required several echelons of tanks, each with its own technical specifications. The first echelon demanded a tank capable of suppressing antiarmor guns while the second echelon required tanks able to neutralize enemy infantry, machine guns, and artillery. Furthermore, Soviet industry was incapable of developing a general-purpose tank from existing automobile and tractor factories, yet mass production of tanks had to be based on the automobile industry.[15]

If the army could not concentrate on one tank type to resolve production problems, there was an alternative solution already in place: using the expertise of foreign armor manufacturers. The most ambitious attempt to exploit this source of assistance, besides Kazan, was Khalepskii's "shopping tour." While this had apparently been successful, it was unclear whether his purchases and consultations would help or hinder the Red Army's attempts to produce large numbers of tanks. By 8 January, Khalepskii had visited Rheinmetall, Krupp, Mafei, Daimler-Benz, and Linke Hoffman, and discussed building tanks with all of them. He informed the Germans that the Soviet army did not want help in the construction of tanks that already existed, but rather assistance in creating new tanks built to Soviet specifications.[16] Following a lengthy stay in Germany, Khalepskii traveled to England,

---

Economy in Turmoil, 1929–1930 (London: Macmillan, 1989), 370–77. For the frustration of the military at the slowdown in production, see David Stone, *Hammer and Rifle: The Militarization of the Soviet Union, 1926–1933* (Lawrence: University Press of Kansas, 2000), 162.

14. Report from Khalepskii to the RVS, 16 June 1930, RGVA, f. 31811, op. 1, d. 1, ll. 83–84, 92; "Protokol No. 17 zasedeniia RVS SSSR," 13 August 1930, RGVA, f. 7, op. 1, d. 172, ll. 72–77.

15. Tukhachevskii to Stalin, December 1930, RGVA, f. 33987, op. 3, d. 400, ll. 74–79.

16. Report from Khalepskii to Voroshilov, 8 January 1930, RGVA, f. 33987, op. 3, d. 350, ll. 17–18. While Khalepskii was abroad these several months, Kalinovskii became the acting head of the UMM. Report from Kalinovskii to Voroshilov, 6 April 1930, RGVA, f. 4, op. 1, d. 1276, ll. 59–60. This accounts for the confusion over who exactly was the first head of the UMM; see G. Isserson,

France, and America, returning in June with twenty Carden-Loyd tankettes, fifteen six-ton and fifteen twelve-ton Vickers, and two Christie tankettes.[17] Yet after his return at least one commander argued that testing, blueprint creation, and the lengthy decision-making process, let alone actual production, would make it a long and arduous procedure to include these in the Red Army's arsenal.[18]

Voroshilov agreed that Khalepskii's trip had ambiguous results, although he still supported the use of foreign expertise to jump-start the Soviet armor industry – a rather surprising stance for such a staunch opponent of copying other nations' ideas. But Voroshilov had never been known for his innovative thinking, and may simply have been following (as he always did) Stalin's lead. He had also shown himself not averse to exploiting the advanced technology of the capitalists when it was possible to do so without allowing them too much influence. Thus in late April he wrote to the commissar of trade, Anastas Mikoian, partially blaming the failure of the tank construction plan on the reluctance of Narkomtorg (the trade commissariat) to fulfill import orders for tank-manufacturing equipment. To have enough funds to pay for Khalepskii's purchase of tank models abroad, Narkomtorg had reduced these imports by one million rubles. Voroshilov said that this was unacceptable; the foreign orders should not influence the development of internal Soviet tank production. It was useless, in any event, to have the tanks if the Soviet Union did not have the means to produce experimental models based on them.[19] Mikoian replied that Narkomtorg had not limited the allocation of any single industrial trust, but rather there had been a general reduction in imports of production equipment.[20]

The reduction in funding for foreign technology was prompted by three considerations. There were, first, the funding troubles experienced by the industrialization drive as a whole. With so many demands for capital from every sector of the economy, it was simply impossible to meet them all. Secondly, regardless of their desire to exploit capitalist expertise, the Soviet government and army did want to create a fully independent military-industrial complex capable of meeting all the Red Army's needs. Thus one of the aims of the latest mobilization plan, Variant No. 10, was to free tank construction from dependence on imports.[21] There was also the unarguable fact that many agreements that the Soviets tried to conclude with Western firms ended in frustration for both parties. Negotiations with Vickers-Armstrong to buy a heavy tank, which took place from May through December

"Razvitie teorii sovetskogo operativnogo iskusstva v 30-e gody," VIZh, no. 1 (January 1965): 38, where Kalinovskii is called the first head of motorization and mechanization.

17. Report from Khalepskii, with cover letter, 9 June 1930, RGVA, f. 4, op. 1, d. 1486, l. 44.
18. Report from Nemitts to Voroshilov, 26 May 1930, RGVA, f. 33987, op. 3, d. 306, ll. 63–64.
19. Voroshilov to Mikoian, 21 April 1930, RGVA, f. 4, op. 1, d. 1276, l. 65.
20. Mikoian to Voroshilov, 6 May 1930, RGVA, f. 4, op. 1, d. 1276, l. 67.
21. Although this apparently did not include foreign intellectual property. "Protokol zasedenii Komissii po tankostroeniiu 12 ianv. 1931g.," RGVA, f. 31811, op. 1, d. 101, l. 17.

1930, were typical. Soviet specifications for the vehicle were very precise, but technically impractical. They requested a tank that was extremely heavy and yet could move at 30 kph. As Vickers's engineers also pointed out, the two huge guns that the Soviets wanted on the tank would take up too much space. Khalepskii refused to accept these "excuses" and asked that the British firm live up to the agreed-upon specifications. Some changes were possible, but in the end the British were unable to create a machine that would meet the Soviets' demands.[22] The Vollmer tank project, one of the first joint enterprises that relied on a foreign design, also fell apart in 1930. By August plans and designs for the tank were advanced enough to allow production.[23] A few weeks later the RVS realized that, with two other tanks that fulfilled the same needs as the Vollmer, it did not make sense to produce the vehicle: over two years of intense negotiations with the German inventor came to naught.[24]

If every such effort had ended badly, Voroshilov and other Soviet planners might not have placed any hope at all on help from abroad. Decision making over the issue was complicated by the fact that not every agreement failed to deliver. Vickers was able to ship the Carden-Loyd tankettes that the UMM had ordered, while contacts that Khalepskii made in America eventually lead to full-scale production of a tank based on the Christie vehicle.[25] Several of the new "Soviet" tanks produced from 1930 onward were in fact little more than modified versions of American, British, or German vehicles. Thus, in some cases, foreign design did allow the Soviet army to leapfrog preproduction and design difficulties and push straight into manufacture.[26] As a result, when production of a new tankette and light tank ran into trouble in August, the RVS ignored the snags in earlier cooperation and again called for foreign help.[27]

While the army struggled to find an answer to its difficulties with production, the Politburo decided to rein in the military budget in order to focus attention on problem areas in the civilian sector.[28] Just one year previously the specter of a Japanese threat on the eastern borders had led the government to push the Red Army high command to agree to a tripling of its demands for tanks and armored cars.

22. Specifications for tank from Kalinovskii to Vickers, 8 May 1930; letter to Mr. "Zvavitch" at Arcos Ltd. from Vickers, 9 July 1930; Khalepskii to Begunov at ARKOS, 6 December 1930, RGVA, f. 31811, op. 2, d. 11, ll. 12–39.

23. Report from K. Neiman, Deputy Chief of Weapons Formations, and A. Adams, Chief of the N.T.U., to Uborevich, 8 August 1930, RGVA, f. 4, op. 1, d. 1276, l. 141.

24. "Protokol No. 17 zasedeniia RVS SSSR," 13 August 1930, RGVA, f. 7, op. 1, d. 172, ll. 72, 74; "Kontrol' protokola No. 17 RVSS," RGVA, f. 4, op. 1, d. 1276, l. 181.

25. Letter from Vickers on shipping of "Carden-Loyd Light Armoured Vehicles," RGVA, f. 31811, op. 2, d. 11, l. 59; for the Christie tank see, e.g., "Proekt konspekta doklada nach-ka UMM RKKA tov. Khalepskogo," dated June/July (?) 1930, RGVA, f. 31811, op. 1, d. 1, l. 108.

26. Report from Khalepskii to the RVS, 16 June 1930, RGVA, f. 31811, op. 1, d. 1, ll. 83–84, 92; "Protokol No. 17 zasedeniia RVS SSSR," 13 August 1930, f. 7, op. 1, d. 172, ll. 72–77.

27. "Protokol No. 17 zasedeniia RVS SSSR," 13 August 1930, RGVA, f. 4, op. 1, d. 172, l. 75.

28. See Davies, *Soviet Economy in Turmoil*, 453–54.

Now it was the RVS that demanded more money for mechanization while the Polit-buro tried to apply the brakes. By late summer there were three competing military budgets for the army to choose from: that of the RVS, which asked for almost one billion rubles; Voroshilov's, which requested 750 million; and the Rykov commission (or RZ STO) plan, which asked for fifty million less. Rykov was as usual concerned about fiscal responsibility and preventing an overheating of an already stretched economy. The Politburo approved Voroshilov's purchase plan, giving the military only about half what the RVS had already agreed upon with industry for all armaments. In a letter to Voroshilov, Rykov, and Lazar Kaganovich, Ieronim Ubore-vich – now the head of a newly created Armaments Directorate – complained that this was unacceptable, especially attacking Rykov who had dared to call for a re-duction in spending over the previous year. The armor forces were hard hit by the new budget and yet, he argued, these (and the air forces) were the most important branches for the army's future. The RVS, he wrote, asked the Politburo to recon-sider its decision and grant the funds that would meet the minimum defensive needs of the USSR.[29] At a meeting in August, however, it was the RVS that backed down, agreeing to lessen its expenditures for motorization and mechanization, al-though still asking for sixteen million more rubles than the Politburo had decided to give it.[30]

True to form, army proposals throughout 1930 recognized neither budgetary nor manufacturing restraints, calling for ever greater numbers of tanks and even re-quiring a higher proportion of the more expensive, and more difficult to produce, light tanks rather than the small tankettes. The latest mobilization plans, Variants Nos. 10 and 12, now called for thirteen hundred tanks to be manufactured during 1930–31, rising to over twenty-eight hundred by 1932–33. If war were to break out, Unshlikht forecast production increasing even more abruptly, from around sev-enty-six hundred in 1930–31 to almost twenty-two thousand by 1932–33. Light and medium tanks would make up the bulk of the vehicles, with tankettes constituting a much smaller percentage of total production.[31] A draft list of organizational changes from 1930 also foresaw the creation of two more tank regiments, the ex-pansion of existing regiments, and the formation of numerous smaller units dur-ing 1931 and 1932.[32]

The Red Army high command may not have allowed production and funding dif-ficulties to distract them because factories were able to deliver some tanks. Even if

29. Memo from Uborevich to Kaganovich, Voroshilov, and Rykov, 31 July 1930, RGVA, f. 33987, op. 3, d. 112, ll. 88–93.

30. "Protokol No. 17 zasedeniia RVS SSSR," 13 August 1930, RGVA, f. 7, op. 1, d. 172, ll. 82–83.

31. Report from Unshlikht, Deputy Chair VSNKh, and Smigla, Chief of the Mobilization Plan-ning Directorate, "Tankovaia Programma (Zapiska)," 12 September 1930, RGVA, f. 4, op. 1, d. 1276, l. 164–67.

32. "Perechen' organizatsionnykh peropriiatii na 2-iu polovinu piatiletki," RGVA, f. 31811, op. 1, d. 11, l. 112.

much fewer than the number ordered, the new vehicles were more than enough to keep the army busy testing the concepts articulated in Triandafillov's work, in PU-29, and in the temporary armor field manual. By April, several armor and tank companies had been created, including a few for the cavalry.[33] The most important step came in February, with the formation of an experimental mechanized brigade, consisting of artillery, infantry, armored car, tank, and engineering units, with almost three thousand men, sixty-six tanks, and over 340 other vehicles. The brigade was to be formed provisionally that summer and become a permanent entity during the fall.[34] Malevskii was named commander of the unit, and by the autumn it had assumed a slightly different configuration.[35] Designed for self-sufficiency and based on the British model, the unit now had an armor regiment, an infantry battalion, an artillery battery, and chemical and anti-air units. The armor regiment itself consisted of two tank battalions (sixty tanks in all), twelve armored cars, and more than 350 other vehicles to transport troops and supplies.[36]

Exercises with the unit and other mechanized forces showed that more tanks and a new organizational structure did not mean that the Soviets had overcome their difficulties with implementing doctrine. The unit conducted its first war games, working against motorized infantry, during early July. An analysis by Khalepskii of the maneuvers stressed the unit's failures, including the inability of the command staff to organize battle and the poor training of the drivers.[37] Later that autumn Triandafillov developed plans for more extensive testing. In one exercise the brigade was to take part in the pursuit of a cavalry division, cut off its withdrawal, and attack it on the flank. This did not occur because the brigade consumed all its fuel and could not even keep up with the cavalry.[38] The results of other exercises held that fall were almost uniformly disappointing. In some cases the failures were caused by simple mechanical problems, as when a unit of MS-1 tanks from the Moscow military district took part in the Volga military district maneuvers and broke down continually.[39] In other cases the problem was a lack of understanding

33. Orders from April 1930 to be fulfilled by 1 October 1930, RGVA, f. 31811, op. 1, d. 11, ll. 80–90.

34. "Sekretnyi Prikazy NarKomVoenMorDela SSSR and RVS SSSR No. 017127," 22 February 1930, RGVA, f. 31811, op. 1, d. 11, ll. 41, 45. See also A. Ryzhakov, "K voprosu o stroitel'stve bronetankovykh voisk krasnoi armii v 30-e gody," *VIZh*, no. 8 (August 1968): 106.

35. Table of organization for experimental brigade, April 1930, RGVA, f. 31811, op. 1, d. 11, l. 78.

36. Brigade organization table by Pushkin, Chief of 2nd Department USU UMM, 18 October 1930, RGVA, f. 33987, op. 3, d. 297, ll. 102–5.

37. "Prikaz Nachal'nik Mekhanizirovannykh Voisk No/ 2/1," 11 July 1930, RGVA, f. 31811, op. 1, d. 84, l. 1.

38. K. A. Meretskov, *Na sluzhbe narodu*, 4th ed. (Moscow: Vysshaia shkola, 1984), 98.

39. As a rule, after going into action, one or two of the tanks remained on the field, unable to move. Report from Force Commander PRIVO, "Otchet ob okruzhnykh manevrakh PRIVO 1930 goda," RGVA, f. 33987, op. 3, d. 334, l. 47.

of the new doctrine and tactics on the part of the commanders involved. One no-torious example was the maneuvers held in Leningrad military district, which included both motorized and mechanized units. The report on the exercises ex-plained that the motorized units were supposed to carry troops to the battle area where they were to dismount and fight like regular infantry. The crews of mecha-nized units, on the other hand, were to stay in their machines. The commander pre-senting the report said that the problem was that the two concepts, motorization and mechanization, were not well understood in the district and therefore the lo-cal officers had used the motorized units as if they were mechanized, that is, the men had fought from their vehicles. In addition, the commanders on the field had used the tanks only to directly support the infantry. The author commented that this outdated method of using tanks was left over from the world war, when the com-batants had possessed only low-speed tanks. The high-speed vehicles needed to be used in DD (long-range) groups to attack the enemy's artillery. The best way to at-tack artillery positions was with the DD group far ahead of the infantry, attacking the flanks and rear of the artillery batteries. "It is strange," the commander com-mented. "We demand grand maneuvers and tanks with their great mobility are not used for any such maneuvers and like turtles move directly in front of the infantry." The Soviet army, he concluded, had wonderful new high-speed tanks, but old-fash-ioned tactics.[40]

Other commanders agreed that the troops had serious trouble implementing the new ideas on tank usage. Khalepskii, in a report to Uborevich, confirmed that the troops did not know how to use tanks in DD groups. He thought that the MS-1 was partially to blame since it did not have enough penetrating power, but the majority of the problems were due to a lack of "technical culture."[41] The mechanized brigade had done slightly better, especially when used as an independent unit, al-though it had still experienced trouble with command and control and coor-dination with the infantry.[42] Shaposhnikov was more critical. The army did not understand at all how to coordinate armor units with the other forces, he said at the

40. Report from Tummel'tau, Deputy Chief of the 30th Department of the IV Directorate of the Staff to the Chief of the IV Directorate of the Staff and the Chief of the V Directorate of the Staff, "Otchet o manevrakh LVO 1930g.," 30 September 1930, RGVA, f. 33987, op. 3, d. 334, ll. 75–79. Stülpnagel agreed that the Soviets used their tanks badly. Report by Stülpnagel, "Bericht über meine Reise nach Russland von 16.IX. bis 13.X.1930," 12 November 1930, BA-MA, RH 1/v, 14, pp. 15–16.

41. Report from Khalepskii to Uborevich, "O boevoi podgotovke tankovykh, avto-bronevykh mekhanizirovannykh i motorizovannykh chastei RKKA," 15 October 1930, RGVA, f. 33987, op. 3, d. 297, ll. 94–101, and "Stenogramma rasshirennogo zasedaniia RVS SSSR, 'Ob itogakh boevoi podgotovki RKKA i F za 1929–30 god i ob uchebnykh tseliakh na 1931 god.,'" RGVA, f. 4, op. 18, d. 36, l. 83.

42. Report from Khalepskii to Uborevich, "O boevoi podgotovke tankovykh, avto-bronevykh mekhanizirovannykh i motorizovannykh chastei RKKA," 15 October 1930, RGVA, f. 33987, op. 3, d. 297, ll. 94–101.

yearly meeting of the high command, while commanders had used tanks incorrectly, ignoring the regulations in the new manuals.[43] He thought that the brigade had done just as badly as the other mechanized units. Although this kind of unit demanded quick decisions from commanders, they had moved very slowly, cautiously ordering it first to one area and then to another and not using it for its primary task – attack. The mechanized brigade, he said, ought to be used actively, decisively, and to strike strong blows on the enemy's rear and flanks.[44]

Malevskii was somewhat more positive in his examination of the brigade's experiences, stressing that the unit had managed to participate in twelve maneuvers. He agreed, however, that serious problems remained. As Triandafillov and PU-29 had warned, actual experience had now shown that there was a decided lack of coordination between the brigade's two echelons. The first echelon, designed for reconnaissance, was composed of Fords and other light wheeled vehicles and traveled at 20–25 kph. The second or offensive core of the brigade was made up of MS-1 tanks that could move at only 7–8 kph. The gap in speed meant that reconnaissance vehicles moved far ahead of the striking force without the firepower to protect themselves. This, he said in an understatement, "extraordinarily hampers and complicates the operational-tactical work of the army."[45] For the rest of the thirties, the Soviet military, like the Reichswehr, would wrestle with this seminal problem of coordinating slow and fast vehicles into a coherent attack force.

If the army needed guidance in implementing its new ideas, there was one source of expert advice already on hand: the group of German officers working in the Kazan school. Military cooperation between the Reichswehr and Red Army in fact went very well during 1930, and the Soviets would assure their German partners that they were greatly helped by the tactical and technical training provided by the Reichswehr.[46] In recognition of the usefulness of the school, the Red Army increased the number of students participating in the courses at Kazan from ten to thirty.[47] In contrast to previous years, there were also no difficulties with a lack of tanks; six "Small Tractors" arrived at Kazan during May and June.[48] As the Red Army would shortly realize, however, the aid provided by their German partners

---

43. "Stenogramma rasshirennogo zasedeniia RVS SSSR s 22–26 oktiabria 1930," RGVA, f. 4, op. 1, d. 1403, ll. 41, 43, 47–48. Khalepskii agreed that coordination between tanks and the infantry was terrible and suggested joint training to correct this problem. Ibid., l. 689.

44. Ibid., ll. 50–51. Others present at the meeting agreed. See Levandovskii's description of how high-speed tanks ought to fight. Ibid., ll. 346–48.

45. "Stenogramma rasshirennogo zasedaniia RVS SSSR, 'Ob itogakh boevoi podgotovki RKKA i F za 1929–30 god i ob uchebnykh tseliakh na 1931 god.,'" RGVA, f. 4, op. 18, d. 36, ll. 62–64.

46. Stülpnagel, "Bericht über meine Reise nach Russland von 16.IX. bis 13.X.1930," 12 November 1930. BA-MA, RH 1/v, 14, p. 52.

47. Klaus Müller, "So lebten und arbeiteten wir 1929 bis 1933 in Kama" (unpublished manuscript, May 1972), 20.

48. Ibid, 21, 22.

could not fully correct the complex series of problems with tactics, technology, and industry that plagued their armor forces.

If the Soviets now began to benefit from the installation at Kazan, an extensive report by Otto von Stülpnagel showed that the Germans had gained even more. During the fall he and Heinz Guderian visited Russia to inspect the school, speak with Kalinovskii, and watch various maneuvers.[49] Kazan, Stülpnagel concluded,

> is at the present time the only place where really positive work on the area of tanks can be achieved. Clear insight into the true worth of the tank, the effect of its weapons, the possibilities for its employment, the tactics to follow, etc., can only be acquired there, with the actual materiel. The most detailed study of foreign literature, the best theoretical reflections and well-prepared experimental exercises with tank mock-up units, can only yield an approximate value.[50]

The army should exploit the school further, he argued. It could use Kazan not only to explore technical capabilities, but also to develop tactical skills, train tank crews, and use the knowledge so acquired to determine the best organization for tank defenses.[51]

Turning to that year's technical and tactical developments at Kazan, Stülpnagel thought that the "large tractors" had performed certain tasks well, although any outside observer might not have agreed. He wrote in glowing detail about the performance of the Rheinmetall vehicle, but in fact it had traveled only two hours nonstop and was still experiencing technical difficulties. But Stülpnagel had hopes that the future development of the vehicles would correct the problems because, unlike most Reichswehr officers, he felt that the larger tank had definite advantages vis-à-vis the smaller one. Interestingly enough, his report confirms the existence of internal discussions then taking place within the Soviet army, noting that the Russians agreed with him on this point and had even suggested jointly building a heavy tank.[52] There were, however, good reasons to put the development of a larger tank on the back burner. The fine performance of the "light tractor" surprised both him and the others involved in the testing. Although this was partially due to chance circumstances such as the weather and the condition of the ground, they all thought that based on these tests, it would be possible to have a tank ready for emergency construction in case of war within about two years. The technical developments that Stülpnagel described were also significant. First, he thought that it was possible to recognize and fight objectives effectively from a moving tank and secondly, radios put capable command and control of tank units within reach. As would be

49. For the presence of Guderian see ibid., 25.

50. Stülpnagel, "Bericht über meine Reise nach Russland von 16.IX. bis 13.X.1930," 12 November 1930, BA-MA, RH 1/v, 14, 5.

51. Ibid., 5–9.

52. Ibid., 10.

recognized later, both of these advances were vital for the further development of armor doctrine.[53] Stülpnagel knew how important Kazan had become for the Reichswehr and called for a continuation of the technical experiments that had taken place during 1930, even suggesting an expansion of the workshops and experimental equipment while adding personnel and material.

But not surprisingly, given the two very different militaries involved, all was not well with the cooperation. For instance, the Germans disagreed with the Soviets about how best to use Kazan to form a trained corps of tank specialists. Because they were limited to a small army by the terms of Versailles, the Germans thought it best to move slowly and systematically, creating a well-trained core of men who would act as teachers for the larger group of specialists to follow. The Soviets wanted to train massive numbers of men and then choose the best of these for further education. Stülpnagel tried to convince them that the German idea of cadre formation was better, but reported in the end that he doubted he had succeeded since the situations in the two countries were so different.[54] There were other signs of tension between the partners. Stülpnagel's first meeting with Kalinovskii did not go well. The German spoke frankly with the Soviet commander about the Reichswehr's concerns and its plans for the next two years of cooperation, but Kalinovskii was cool and suspicious toward him. Their second conversation went better, with Kalinovskii agreeing to all the points that the Germans wanted and suggesting a new contract with them. A draft of the points that Stülpnagel discussed with Kalinovskii was indeed frank, pointing out a multitude of problems with the program at Kazan and asking the Soviets to improve matters.[55]

While Stülpnagel complained about the help that the Reichswehr was receiving from the Soviets, he was correct in acknowledging that Kazan was the only place where the German army could test ideas on armor. Whereas the Soviet drive for industrialization gave the Red Army enough capital and factory space to begin (if not complete) large-scale tank production, the German army had but the few tanks at Kazan to establish which vehicles would be suitable for future warfare and how exactly to use them. Tank tactics were in an even more precarious position than the technology itself. It was possible to find and correct technical defects in the machines at the school, but without large numbers of tanks for maneuvers the army was still forced to depend on theory and the observation of other armies to determine its armor tactics.

The Reichswehr's new dummy tank units provided some assistance in choosing an organizational structure, though the unrealistic size and speed of the machines

53. Ibid., 11–12. Soviet participants in the Kazan course agreed that they had learned much on a tactical level from the Germans. Report no. 2 by Braverman and Pavlovskii, 29 March 1930, RGVA, f. 31811, op. 1, d. 331, ll. 87–88.

54. Stülpnagel, "Bericht über meine Reise nach Russland von 16.IX. bis 13.X.1930," 12 November 1930, BA-MA, RH 1/v. 14, 12–13.

55. Ibid., 17–22.

made them less helpful for tactical purposes. In 1930 a company of the vehicles from the 6th Motorized Battalion, reorganized into the new structure tested the previous year in the 7th Motorized Battalion, participated for the first time in a large-scale exercise. The 6th Battalion was one of the first to have the better Hanomag tank mock-ups and so was a natural subject for the organizational experimentation.[56] On the basis of this exercise, and others like it, the Reichswehr Ministry decided to use the 6th Battalion as the model for other battalions.[57] The new units would combine an armored car and a motorcycle company, together constituting the elements for an armor reconnaissance regiment, plus one tank and one antiarmor company.[58] This structure, it is worth reemphasizing, was predicated on the idea of larger mechanized formations that would be able to fight in a combined-arms battle with the infantry. For 1931–32, the Motor Inspectorate set only a few other organizational goals: the creation of motorized reconnaissance and of motorized antiarmor detachments for inclusion in infantry divisions.[59]

The modest organizational planning for the armor forces was paralleled by the Reichswehr's mobilization and war plans, both of which anticipated serious weaknesses in overall force structure. The standard plans for 1929–30 foresaw the army growing from seven to sixteen infantry divisions in time of war, although the high command had formulated another mobilization plan that called for a trebling of the army, from seven to twenty-one infantry divisions.[60] Even with the extra divisions, war games predicted that Germany would have to take the strategic defensive in the event of an unprovoked attack from the east, that is, Poland.[61] An operational problem set for 1931 had a more active role for the army, with Germany in a war with France with the possibility of an attack by Czechoslovakia. The Reichswehr would, however, remain at a considerable disadvantage in armor forces, with only a few armored car units and two light and one medium tank battalions to face far greater numbers of enemy tanks.[62] Even this exaggerated the German army's armor strength, which in the spring of 1931 consisted of six medium and three light tanks.[63]

Recognition of the army's real weaknesses prevented the German officer corps

56. Edgar Graf von Matuschka, "Organisation des Reichsheeres," in *Handbuch zur deutschen Militärgeschichte 1648–1939*, ed. Hans Meier-Welcker and Wolfgang von Groote, vol. 4: *Reichswehr und Republik (1918–1933)* (Frankfurt am Main: Bernard & Graefe, 1970), 305–43.

57. Adolf Reinicke, *Das Reichsheer, 1921–1934* (Osnabrück: Biblio Verlag, 1986), 162.

58. Heinz Guderian, *Erinnerungen eines Soldaten* (Heidelberg: Kurt Vowinckel, 1951), 19.

59. Nehring, *Geschichte der deutschen Panzerwaffe*, 61–62.

60. Erich von Manstein, *Aus einem Soldatenleben 1887–1939* (Bonn: Athenäum, 1958), 111–14. In 1921 Seeckt had envisioned raising the number of infantry divisions from seven to twenty-one and a study by the Truppenamt in 1925 agreed that twenty-one divisions was "the maximum figure for an orderly and efficient increase." S. J. Lewis, *Forgotten Legions: German Army Infantry Policy 1918–1941* (New York: Praeger, 1985), 28.

61. Manstein, *Aus einem Soldatenleben*, 126, 131.

62. Operational Exercise 1931, signed Adam, BA-MA, RH 2/103, 3–7.

63. F. L. Carsten, *The Reichswehr and Politics 1918 to 1933* (Oxford: Clarendon, 1966), 357.

from reaching a consensus over armor doctrine. The optimistic visions of men like Bockelberg, Stülpnagel and others in the high command were predicated on large mechanized armies, for which industry might not be able to produce the vehicles. The result was an intensification of attacks on the new ideas of tank use and an attempted resurgence of the "moderate" line. The most important areas of discussion among the groups interested in the tank continued to be cooperation between tanks and other forces, logistics and supply, antitank defenses, and whether the tank was able to take and hold ground. This last point was in many ways the most contentious. With the exception of a few officers, almost everyone in the Reichswehr agreed that the tank could not hold ground and therefore large numbers of infantry were still necessary. The train of logic went something like this: only the infantry could hold ground; holding ground was essential in order to win a war; therefore, the tank had to work with the infantry to attain victory. This syllogism, believed implicitly by the majority of officers in Germany as well as in the Soviet Union, and strengthened by a firm belief in combined-force operations that the materiel-morale debate had cemented, ensured a central role for infantry in each nation's armor doctrine. A few armor supporters tried to contest this, arguing for instance that perhaps the enemy's army and not his territory should be the proper objective of warfare, but they were shouted down.[64] Throughout the early thirties majority German opinion on armor warfare, even from many tank supporters, would continue to stress the need to take and hold ground and thus the corollary that tanks had to have other forces – especially the infantry – to aid them in battle.[65]

With this realization, German officers came back to the intractable problem of coordinating a combined-arms battle involving armor. As we have seen, staff officers in both Germany and the Soviet Union had already recognized that differences in speed and objectives would create difficulties for tank-infantry cooperation. During the summer of 1930 Reichswehr officers began to explore the depth of the problem as well as the related issue of coordinating armor and artillery. They concluded that there were four possible solutions, but that it would be impossible to decide which was most effective without another war. The first method was to have tank forces mass and attack without accompanying foot soldiers, much as the cavalry had done in the past. This solution appealed to only the most ardent armor supporters since it violated at least two accepted principles of German doctrine: that the tank could not take and hold ground and that all forces had to fight together to win a battle. The second solution, tight coordination with the artillery and infantry, found greater support, but was open to the criticism that it would force the tanks

64. "Hat Fuller recht?" Militär-Wochenblatt, no. 21 (1929): 808–9; "Nochmals: Hat Fuller recht?" ibid., no. 26 (1930) 1010–12. See also Rittmeister Crisolli, "Kampfwagenverwendung auf Grund der englischen und französischen Kampfwagenvorschrift," ibid., no. 40 (1931): 1563.

65. See e.g. "Kann die Krise des Angriffes überwunden werden?" ibid., no. 36 (1930): 1401–5, and lecture on "Aufgaben und Organisation eines Heeres, die verschiedenen Waffengattungen und ihre Aufgaben," 9 December 1931, BA-MA, RH 17/v, 19.

to move at a walking pace. As we have seen, this was no longer acceptable to the high command. By January 1931 the Reichswehr Ministry would issue a statement that in battle *"Every vehicle is to be driven as fast as possible. Only in this way is the full benefit of vehicle transportation derived. Troops and vehicles are in this way most protected. The relinquishment of a large close-marching column caused by this is the normal case. The exploitation of speed is more important than military uniformity!"*[66] The third answer was the one already suggested by men like Heigl: to raise the mobility of the infantry and artillery by motorizing them so that they could accompany tanks onto the field of battle without slowing the machines down. The main objections to this sensible solution were that it would take a great deal of time and money to build the vehicles and that having so many machines on the battlefield would make an already difficult logistics and supply situation impossible. Finally there was the "moderate" answer – to have armor attack in waves with infantry supporting the tanks but not closely tied to them. The machines would speed against a nearby target, use their weapons briefly but intensely, return quickly, and then charge anew. At no time would the tempo of tank units and infantry match, but all the forces would attack the same enemy on the same battlefield at the same time and thus (hopefully) coordinate their actions.[67] These last two views, with their advocacy of loose-order advance on the opponent, conducted at high speed regardless of whether direct contact between forces was maintained, were again an outgrowth of the stormtroop tactics developed by the German army at the end of the world war.

The question of cooperation between tanks, infantry, and artillery was vital, argued many German officers, for more than solving the problem of seizing ground and reinforcing successes won by any one arm. Tanks had to have the support of other arms to maintain their vital fuel supplies, while antiarmor defenses were a serious threat to tank assaults, demanding infantry and artillery to neutralize them. German officers realized early on that machine warfare had completely different requirements from earlier forms of combat. Armies that consisted chiefly of tanks and other vehicles needed a continuous supply of oil and gas or their advance could literally stall and then be rolled back by the enemy.[68] As one officer pointed out, the

66. A study by the Reichswehrministerium, "Kraftwagen-Transportverbände," 23 January 1931, BA-MA, RH 1/v. 11, p. 74. Emphasis in original.

67. "Zusammenarbeiten der Waffen mit Kampfwagen," *Militär-Wochenblatt*, no. 2 (1930): 35–37; "Zusammenarbeiten der Waffen mit Kampfwagen," ibid., no. 6 (1930) 202–4; "Zusammenarbeiten der Waffen mit Kampfwagen," ibid., no. 9 (1930) 328–29; "Zusammenarbeiten der Waffen mit Kampfwagen," ibid., no. 11 (1930) 406–8. For the very similar arguments over armor-artillery cooperation, see "Zusammenarbeit von Kampfwagen und Artillerie beim Angriff," ibid., no. 48 (1931): 1885–86; "Zusammenarbeit von Kampfwagen und Artillerie beim Angriff: Zu 'Militär-Wochenblatt' No. 48 vom 25.6.31, Sp. 1885/86," ibid., no. 5 (1931) 175–76; "Zusammenarbeit von Kampfwagen und Artillerie in der Angriffsschlacht," ibid., no. 18 (1931): 647–649.

68. See e.g. "1946: Gedanken eines Unmodernen," ibid., no. 32 (1930) 1246–47.

question of whether Fuller was right or not depended not so much on the technical abilities of the tank as on problems of fuel, logistics, and industrial preparation in advance of war.[69]

Critics of Fuller's "tank-only" army also stressed that enemy antitank defenses would play a significant role in slowing any armor offensive.[70] One commander tried to show that just as coastal defensive artillery had successfully turned back Britain's fleet in the Dardanelles, mobile artillery (tanks) would be useless when confronted by defensive guns. Now that the British had invented more effective antiarmor weapons, they too were experiencing a crisis of confidence in the tank.[71] German officers who denigrated the usefulness of the tank in the face of new antiarmor defenses had strong support within the high command, as Wilhelm Adam, the newest head of the Truppenamt, agreed that tanks would be basically useless in direct confrontation with antiarmor weaponry. In November 1931 Adam traveled to Moscow to discuss the ongoing cooperation with the Soviets. About halfway through their conversation, the German general digressed to explain his views of the tank and the mechanization of warfare. Adam said that he categorically supported the opinion "that tanks in future war will play an auxiliary role and that we need to pay special attention to antitank weapons; with good antitank weaponry tanks will not have great significance." When Voroshilov asked why antitank weapons were needed if tanks would not be significant in the next war, Adam replied that

> Tanks are very expensive weapons and only rich states will be able to have them. I am of the opinion that you have to keep up development in this field. You have to spend money on development, on experimentation, and acquire tanks only when the testing fully persuades you that they are suitable. That is my personal view. . . . I agree that for antitank protection, tanks are also necessary. But some people say that tanks decided the war. I can't agree with that. Tanks attained such great significance at the end of the war only because we – the Germans – were already weakened. The tank did not decide the war. One has to see that tanks were destroyed when defenses were good. During the world war on my divisional sector out of thirty-six tanks, in twenty minutes, twenty-four were shot up. And I emphasize that it is not true that tanks decided the war . . .

Adam thought that tanks would be useful for reconnaissance but again stressed antitank weapons and the fact that large battles would never be decided by tanks. Voroshilov challenged this assumption, agreeing that it was easy to organize defenses on a positionally stable front, but that with high maneuverability it would be much more difficult. Adam replied that good artillery plus a tank to fight other

---

69. "Nochmals: Hat Fuller recht?" ibid., no. 26 (1930): 1010–12.
70. See e.g. "1946: Gedanken eines Unmodernen," ibid., no. 32 (1930): 1246–47.
71. "Hat Fuller recht?" ibid., no. 25 (1930): 975–76.

tanks would be all that was necessary to neutralize the enemy's armor forces. One had to have tanks to fight tanks, "but if you ask the question where to spend the money, then I place tanks in last place – that is my personal opinion, it contradicts many viewpoints."[72]

Adam's opinion chiefly clashed with that of the supporters of the new tank tactics. No exercise was realistic enough to prove which theory was correct, but men such as Bockelberg had to believe that the tank could overcome antiarmor defenses – their ideas about future war (speeding through the enemy's positions to disrupt his rear) demanded it. They therefore argued that tanks could hide from artillery by using terrain, employing a variety of avenues to approach their objectives, and even destroying the guns that threatened them.[73] Antiarmor defenses might be powerful and dangerous, but the tank still had an even chance of escaping their reach and completing its mission. Some officers went even further, arguing that there was little hope for static tank defenses at all: only tanks themselves had any chance of stopping a full armor offensive.[74]

By the end of 1931, the "moderate" position on armor doctrine, which avoided the extremes of Adam on the one hand and Fuller on the other, had strengthened somewhat. The officers who held this position were especially suspicious of the British notion of large independent armor units, which they saw as vulnerable and of doubtful overall worth. In a typical article from February 1931, one officer argued that motorized units were a luxury that developed nations might find too expensive for the benefit they gave.[75] The British attempt to establish large independent mechanized units had shown that tanks needed the close support of other troops.[76] He doubted whether there was any future for the sort of "armor brigades" that contained every branch of the service in mechanized or motorized form. Much more likely was a unit with tanks as the backbone, armored artillery to support the fight against enemy antitank weapons, and armored cars for reconnaissance. These units would act exactly like modernized army cavalry, cooperating with cavalry units, but without a tight connection, and attacking where the command sought great decisions. Whether armor would in the future come to dominate the battlefield remained to be seen, since "even in the Middle Ages there were still unarmored troops next to the armored horsemen."[77]

72. "Zapis' Besedy Narkomvoenmora t. Voroshilova s Nachal'nikom Genshtaba (truppenamt) Reikhsvera gen. Adamom. (19.XI.31 – 19–22.10)," RGVA, f. 33987, op. 3, d. 375, ll. 26–32. Voroshilov thought this conversation important enough to send a copy of the minutes to Stalin and set up a meeting to discuss them with him. Memo from Voroshilov to Stalin, 11 November 1931, RGVA, f. 33987, op. 3, d. 375, l. 21.
    73. "Vertikale strategische Umfassung?" Militär-Wochenblatt, no. 28 (1930): 1087–90.
    74. "Motorisierung und Kampfwagenverwendung," ibid., no. 47 (1930): 1854–56.
    75. "Motorisierung: Begriffe, Tatsachen und Betrachtungen," ibid., no. 30 (1931) 1155–57.
    76. Ibid., 1156–57.
    77. Ibid., 1157–58.

Other officers who supported a "moderate" position agreed that fairly limited goals for tanks were best. A typical description of tank tactics had armor forces attacking the enemy's front or rear in waves. After achieving their objectives most of the vehicles would reassemble for further advance, while the remainder would be kept back in case of an enemy counterattack with tanks. But this modest view of the tank's usefulness depended on the terrain. If some of the ground was unsuitable for armor vehicles, the tanks had to wait to attack until after the infantry had taken it. While it was of course best to employ tanks en masse, this officer, like many others, thought that the machines could achieve good results in fewer numbers, if inserted at the decisive moment.[78]

Though the German high command had not yet settled on the exact shape of armor doctrine, like the Soviet army, it had to make decisions about tank design. The foremost question in many military thinkers' minds was whether to build a strongly armored and armed tank or one which was fast and mobile, for German authorities agreed with Tukhachevskii that one tank could not have both sets of characteristics. As we have seen, the German military leadership decided to build two types of tanks, one large and one small yet fast, but published sources and official reports and memoranda show that sentiment within the army generally favored speed, if a choice had to be made. The basic argument was that every tank had the same mission, and therefore it made no sense to build different models; that it was a mistake to construct a large, slow tank that would be vulnerable to artillery fire; and that therefore the army had to concentrate on one small fast tank that presented a limited target, cost less, and could speed through the enemy's positions.[79]

Of course not every German officer agreed that a very small tank could fight modern wars on its own, as the example of Stülpnagel shows. An anonymous officer noted that even the British, who had built and extensively tested the Carden-Loyd, thought that it was suitable only for certain types of mobile combat. If the enemy had the chance to create any sort of defensive positions, then the small tank was practically useless.[80] In the latest edition of his guide to tanks, Heigl recognized the problems with the small tank, but again suggested that armies should build large numbers of the fast machines, for financial as well as tactical reasons, but also produce a smaller number of mediums to accompany and protect the lighter vehicles.[81]

78. "Motorisierung und Kampfwagenverwendung," ibid., no. 47 (1930): 1854–56; see also Oberleutnant v. Wedel, "Verwendung eines selbständigen Panzerverbandes," ibid., no. 31 (1931): 1200–1204; Oberleutnant v. Wedel, "Verwendung eines selbständigen Panzerverbandes," ibid., no. 32 (1931): 1237–43, in which the author does not give an independent armor unit any major role in the battle.
79. "Schwergepanzerte Riesen oder bewegliche Zwerge?" ibid., no. 10 (1931): 377–79.
80. "Schwergepanzerte Riesen oder bewegliche Zwerge?" ibid., no. 22 (1931): 792–95.
81. Fritz Heigl, Taschenbuch der Tanks. Ausgabe 1930: Strassenpanzer. Neue Tanks. Panzerzüge (Munich: Lehmanns, 1930), 11, 106–7.

After actual comparative testing of the army's "light" and "large" tanks in 1930 and 1931, two different opinions emerged. On the one side were those, like the Chief of T-1 who wanted to concentrate on the smaller vehicle.[82] The other side pointed out that the small-caliber gun on the light tank could penetrate armor and destroy antiarmor guns, but had no blast effect. The indecision over which tank would best serve the army led Guderian and other officials to decide to keep both vehicles until they could make personal judgments in Kazan.[83] Meanwhile the high command ordered the construction of an even lighter "small tractor" during early 1931 to act as a reconnaissance vehicle for mechanized units. This tank, which would soon be renamed the "agricultural tractor" (LaS), weighed only 3.5 tons and was armed with a machine gun, but it was very fast and maneuverable.[84] The LaS was in fact a direct descendant, if not a direct copy, of the British Carden-Loyd tankette.[85]

As Reichswehr officers continually stressed, one of the most important reasons for favoring a light tank over the larger machine, beside tactical considerations of speed, was the lower cost of smaller tanks and the greater ease with which they could be built. Unfortunately for any hopes on this point, the army began to experience the same two difficulties that the Soviet army was already dealing with: organizational confusion and industrial ineptitude. In a memorandum from May of 1930, the chief of T-1 spoke against the current system of tank construction, which had one army department assigning the task, another making the funds available, and a third constructing and testing the vehicle without keeping the other two departments informed. This had already led to problems, because the order could prove to need changes at any stage of development, on tactical, financial, or technical grounds. He urged each of the departments to speak to each other more often and to share plans or experiences even during the developmental stage.[86]

If organizational difficulties created delays and wasted effort, the covert military-industrial complex was also showing itself less than completely efficient. The clearest example of this was the problems that Krupp, the most respected German armaments manufacturer, experienced in producing the LaS in the time allotted by

82. Memo from Chief of T 1 to Section Head of T 1, 10 May 1930. BA-MA, N 221/10.

83. Müller, "So lebten und arbeiteten wir," 25.

84. Reichswehrministerium, Heereswaffenamt, "Btr: Kl. Tr.," 2 June 1931, BA-MA, RH 8/v. 2674 (Krupp), p. 125; "Kl. Tr. Beschreibung," BA-MA, RH 8/v. 2674 (Krupp), zu 125.

85. German firms were just as keen as the Soviets to obtain interesting and possibly usable tank parts from foreign companies. Letter from Werkzeugfabrik "Franken" Bernstiel & Wenzel to Firma Zahnradfabrik A.G., 15 August 1931. BA-MA, RH8/v. 2674 (Krupp); cover letter for above from Wa Prw 6 to Krupp, 27 August 1931, BA-MA, RH8/v. 2674 (Krupp); Müller, "So lebten und arbeiteten wir," 36; Wa Prw 6 V, "Niederschrift über die Besprechung am 18.9.31 betr. Kl. Tr. Kp.," 18 September 1931, BA-MA, RH 8/v. 2674 (Krupp).

86. Memo from Chief of T 1 to Section Head of T 1, 10 May 1930, BA-MA, N 221/10.

the Waffenamt.[87] Although pledged to manufacture a chassis for the machine by 1 June 1931, Krupp acknowledged that it would be unable to do so.[88] Officials at the firm blamed their inability to meet the deadline on many different discussions about the tank and the resulting repeated, fundamental alterations in the order made by the army.[89] On 17 June, Krupp told the Waffenamt that it would be able to construct the essential components for the small tank by the end of August.[90] By mid-August, the company had produced only a wooden model of the vehicle and was asked by the army to submit the main designs by the October 1.[91] After these repeated delays it is no surprise that Krupp could not manufacture the first LaS until a year later, in July 1932.[92] Of course it must be kept in mind that at this point the Reichswehr did not view the LaS as its main combat tank. The high command still considered the light machine a reconnaissance platform or at best a stop-gap while industry perfected a heavier main battle tank.

Throughout the Reichswehr's attempts to create a modern tank and tactics to suit it, the cooperation with the Soviet army ran like a red thread. As Stülpnagel had pointed out, the most important experiments on tank design and tactics could only take place at Kazan and it was here that vital decisions about the future of the tank forces were made. During 1931 the collaboration deepened and expanded. In the summer, along with the usual tactical training at Kazan, two small tanks and a larger Rheinmetall vehicle took part in Soviet exercises. One of the most important discoveries from experiments done that year was that Stülpnagel was right: it would be possible to install radios in the light tanks that would allow them to keep in constant contact with each other and with the higher command.[93] Here was an answer to problems with command and control that both the Soviets and the Germans faced, since commanders would have full control over armor forces even when fighting at great distances from each other. Not every officer in the Reichswehr was

87. For the story of Krupp's involvement in the secret rearmament of the German army, see William Manchester, *The Arms of Krupp, 1587–1968* (Boston: Little, Brown, 1964), 344–58.

88. Reichswehrminister, to Firma Fried. Krupp A.G., Nr. 188/6.31 WaPrW6V, "Betr: Konstruktion eines Fahrgestells für einen Kl. Tr.," 9 June 1931, BA-MA, RH 8/v. 2674 (Krupp).

89. Reichswehrministerium, Heereswaffenamt, "Betr: Kl. Tr. Fahrgestell-Konstruktion, A. Nr. 6065," 10 June 1931, BA-MA, RH 8/v. 2674 (Krupp).

90. "Niederschrift über die Besprechung in Berlin am 17. Juni 1931, Betr: Kl. Tr.," 17 June 1931, BA-MA, RH 8/v. 2674 (Krupp).

91. "Niederschrift über die Besichtigung des Kl. Tr.-Holzmodell am 14.8.31 in Essen und anschließende Besprechung," 14 August 1931. BA-MA, RH 8/v. 2674 (Krupp).

92. Müller, "So lebten und arbeiteten wir," 36. For the continuation of the story of the LaS see below, pp. 000–00. Perhaps because they knew of the German desire to create their own ultrasmall tank, the Soviet firm Avtodor presented the Reichswehr with two Carden-Loyd small tanks during 1931. "Bericht Nr. 10/3T Land: Sowjetunion," 1931, BA-MA, RH 2/2746, p. 27.

93. Müller, "So lebten und arbeiteten wir," 24.

convinced that the new communication technology was such a great advance. The head of T-1, for instance, argued that radio equipment, which was technically not yet very advanced and tactically "*completely unnecessary*," was not essential for the light tank.[94] This was a minority view, however, and it was testing at Kazan that convinced the army of the radio's usefulness.

Other areas of cooperation were likewise successful, but there were again clear signs that all was not well with the relationship between the two countries. As in the previous year, the number of Soviet trainees at Kazan rose, this time to forty.[95] The Germans as before sent only ten men, but the high quality of the officers involved in exchanges made up for the small number of students. Among those who traveled to the Soviet Union in the summer and fall of 1931, for instance, were Adam, Wilhelm Keitel (then head of T-2, the Organization Section of the Truppenamt), and Walter von Brauchitsch (chief of T-4, the Training Section of the Truppenamt) with his assistant Walter Model, and Erich von Manstein, who was working in T-1.[96] All would go on to hold high-ranking positions in the Reichswehr and Wehrmacht. On the Soviet side, Egorov spent several months studying in Germany and praised German teaching methods and the Reichswehr.[97] Uborevich also lived a year in Germany and his letters show that he became an admirer of the German military in general and its war academy in particular.[98] The tensions between the two countries were, however, apparent in a conversation between Adam and Egorov. He made clear German concerns over the recent Soviet overtures to France and Poland, which could be taken either as a signal that Soviet interest in the cooperation was lessening or, even more ominously, as an anti-German step. The question of Poland in particular, a most sensitive issue for both countries, dominated the talks.[99]

Adam's discussion with Voroshilov about the tank school showed the strains in the relationship as well. Because the Reichswehr controlled the installation, a right conferred by the original treaty and cemented by the large sums of money that Germany had invested in Kazan, work at the school had thus far conformed to German plans rather than those of the Soviets. The Reichswehr had a safe proving ground

94. Memo from Chief of T 1 to Section Head of T 1, 10 May 1930, BA-MA, N 221/10. Emphasis in original.

95. Müller, "So lebten und arbeiteten wir," 23.

96. Wilhelm Keitel, *The Memoirs of Field-Marshal Keitel* (New York: Stein and Day, 1966), 16; Walter Görlitz, "Keitel, Jodl and Warlimont," *Hitler's Generals*, ed. Correlli Barnett (London: Weidenfeld and Nicolson, 1989), 143; Walter Görlitz, *Model: Strategie der Defensive* (Wiesbaden: Limes, 1975), 42–43; Manstein, *Aus einem Soldatenleben*, 138.

97. Egorov to Voroshilov, 6 March 1931, RGVA, f. 33987, op. 3, d. 280, ll. 109–21.

98. See, e.g., Uborevich to Voroshilov, 5 April 1931, RGVA, f. 33987, op. 3, d. 280, ll. 123–47.

99. Copy of a report from von Dirksen on a conversation between General Adam and Egorov in November 1931, 20 November 1931, Leplevskii documents, RGVA, f. 33987, op. 3, d. 70, ll. 270–72.

for the small number of vehicles that its industry could produce and had been able to work on tactical and technical problems. The Soviet government and certain commanders within the Red Army, including Voroshilov, thought that their country had gained far less from Kazan. Although now aware that it would be impossible to depend on Germany for the further development of their military-industrial complex, Soviet leaders did still hope for aid with their weakest spot: the design and engineering of new tanks. This they thought the German army was suspiciously reluctant to provide. In his talks with Adam, Voroshilov openly expressed his, and the Soviet government's, distrust of German intentions.

> Our comrades never complained to me that the German army ever hid anything from them. But I personally sometimes think that we perhaps don't know everything about you. I'll be frank. Let us take tanks for example. I think that here there is something unclear. I already spoke somewhat about this with Herr Niedermayer. Take the Kazan school. It seems to me that something is not right with it. If I didn't know the German army then I would have said straight away that there was wrecking (*vreditel'stvo*) here. You know the significance of this term. I, frankly speaking, cannot believe that you don't have more than [what is] at Kazan. Three years fooling around at Kazan and no new materiel. All the same tanks as you brought at the beginning. I said "Send designers and we will both have tanks." If you actually do not have any more – I'll say directly that I don't envy you, but it may be that this is not everything, or they are deceiving you. We are ready to assist with everything but you must actually help also.

Adam explained that tanks were very expensive and quickly became obsolete, and that therefore it was difficult to provide more of them. Voroshilov answered:

> Already when Her. Hammerstein was here, I laid before him the necessity to send more types and designs of tanks. We already have an industrial base, but we still have very few people – i.e. designers. You have people, we thus thought that your side would furnish models, blueprints, drafts, ideas, designs, in a word, that we would have laboratories both for you and for us. None of this has happened.

Adam commiserated with Voroshilov, but noted that it was difficult to figure out what was happening in Kazan without traveling there personally. Voroshilov took a very tough line:

> I'm afraid that I will be misunderstood. I do not have the least doubt that your people are working conscientiously and well. But I say again completely frankly – I do not understand why every opportunity is not being exploited. Perhaps, all the same, they are hiding something from us, or for some reason or other they do not consider it necessary to do everything. This is not just my opinion. I myself am not seeing to this personally, I am a member of the Government and report to them.

They say to me – there is a risk, and where are the results, show the tanks and there is nothing to show, three years of joint work and zero usefulness.[100]

Voroshilov was not alone in expressing official dissatisfaction with the course of the cooperation. Tukhachevskii, in a meeting with General Adam, Ernst Köstring, Edmund Hoffmeister (a staff officer in T-3, the Foreign Army Section of the Trup-penamt) and Manstein, also stressed the need for more materiel at Kazan and the other schools.[101] He went even further in a meeting with Herbert von Dirksen, the German ambassador, accusing the Germans of holding back supplies and new technology from the Soviet army.[102] Tukhachevskii may have been prompted to express this anger by Adam's refusal to grant most of the Soviet's concrete requests for the Kazan school.[103] Many of the Germans were obviously not enamored with the Soviets any more than Voroshilov was with them. In a meeting with high-rank-ing officers held in April 1931 Hammerstein called the collaboration with the Soviets "a pact with Beelzebub," countenanced only because the Reichswehr had no other choice.[104] Dirksen was pessimistic about the collaboration as well, com-plaining at a meeting with top officials that he was against giving the Soviets too many "military presents."[105] What he did not know was that the Soviets were fully informed of his remarks, as they had an agent who was either present at this (and other) confidential meetings, or who stole the documents relating to the meetings and passed them on to the OGPU.

While Dirksen's reaction was not far from earlier views expressed within the German government on the collaboration, the bold expression of dissatisfaction by the Soviets was new and made possible because the formerly outcast nation was no longer completely dependent on Germany for contact with the outside world.[106]

100. "Zapis' Besedy Narkomvoenmora t. Voroshilova s Nachal'nikom Genshtaba (truppenamt) Reikhsvera gen. Adamom. (19.XI.31 – 19–22.10)," RGVA, f. 33987, op. 3, d. 375, ll. 26–32.

101. "Spravka o prieme t. Tukhachevskim generala Adama, Kestringa, Gofmeistera i Man-shteina 10.XI.1931 g. (Prisutstvovali: Petrenko, Sukhorukov)," RGVA, f. 33987, op. 3, d. 375, ll. 162–63.

102. Report from von Dirksen to von Twardowski, 13 November 1931, "Zapis' o besede s zames-titelem narodnogo komissara – TUKHACHEVSKIM," Leplevskii documents, RGVA, f. 33987, op. 3, d. 70, ll. 259–62.

103. "SPRAVKA O peregovorakh sovetskoi i nemetskoi storon v otnoshenii raboty sovmestnykh predpriiatii (na osnovanii peregovorov Narkoma, t. Tukhachevskogo, t. Alksnisa i t. Derevtsova s Adamom i Gofmeisterom v noiabre m-tse 1931 g.)," RGVA, f. 33987, op. 3, d. 375, ll. 16, 18–19.

104. Thilo Vogelsang, "Neue Dokumente zur Geschichte der Reichswehr, 1930–1933," Viertel-jahreshefte für Zeitgeschichte 2 (1954): 409.

105. "Zametka o besede posla, Gofmeister, fon-Nidermaiera, fon-Tvardovskogo,"- 25 Novem-ber 1931," Leplevskii documents, RGVA, f. 33987, op. 3, d. 70, ll. 273–75.

106. Riekhoff argues that by the late twenties the Germans recognized close ties with the Soviet Union as a liability rather than an aid to revising Versailles and that they became even more am-bivalent towards the collaboration. Harald von Riekhoff, German-Polish Relations, 1918–1933 (Balti-more: Johns Hopkins University Press, 1971), 226–94.

During 1931 the Soviets held meetings with French and Polish officials that would culminate in nonaggression pacts with both countries the following year.[107] Knowing that they no longer had to look only to Germany gave the Soviets the freedom to inform their partners about their frustrations with the military cooperation for the first time. Yet, in spite of their new friends and the quarrels with the Germans, the collaboration continued to be useful, and in November Voroshilov would inform Dirksen that nothing would change so far as cooperation was concerned. To reassure the Germans he told the envoy that the talks held with France were only on economic matters, while as for Poland, the nonaggression pact certainly had nothing to do with German-Soviet relations.[108]

For the Soviets there was an additional reason to rely less on contacts with the Germans: their industry had begun to catch up with the army's production plans. According to a report from the UMM, by May 1931 industry had manufactured almost all the tanks required by Variant No. 10.[109] A special commission, set up to oversee the fulfillment of the tank programs for the first half of 1931, reported in July that factories were producing light tanks on schedule. The army would have 300 by January 1932 and 1,350 by the end of 1932.[110] Unlike earlier production predictions, which always ran into unforeseen snags, this one came true: by the end of 1931 industry had indeed made 300 light tanks.[111] Voroshilov agreed in a report to Molotov that production of the small vehicles was progressing well, although noting that the manufacture of other tanks remained unsatisfactory.[112]

The dilemma for industry was that once the army began receiving larger numbers of tanks, the high command doubled and even tripled its orders. As noted above, this was a feature common to the first Five Year Plan as a whole: once factories began to meet orders, targets were consistently revised upwards, putting still more strain on the economy.[113] The latest army plans for 1931 were as optimistic now as Tukhachevskii had been the year before, calling for 12,000 T-26 light tanks based on a Vickers model, 16,000 tankettes, and a reserve of 2,000 T-26s for wartime (that is by the fall of 1932). By 1933 the USSR had to be able to produce

107. See Adam B. Ulam, *Expansion and Coexistence: Soviet Foreign Policy, 1917–73*, 2d ed. (New York: Praeger, 1974), 209–11.

108. Report by von Dirksen, 12 November 1931, "Zametka o besede s voennym komissarom VOROSHILOVYM [perevod s nemetskogo]," Leplevskii documents, RGVA, f. 33987, op. 3, d. 70, ll. 253–58.

109. "O mobgotovnosti, sostoianii i razvitii tekhniki RKKA po linii UMM RKKA," RGVA, f. 31811, op. 2, d. 57, ll. 1–3.

110. Protocol from Tukhachevskii's Commission, 5 July 1931. RGVA, f. 31811, op. 2, d. 52, ll. 46–48.

111. "O tankovoi programme (proekt)," RGVA, f. 31811, op. 1, d. 101, ll. 26–28.

112. Report from Voroshilov to Molotov, 16 June 1931, RGVA, f. 31811, op. 2, d. 52, ll. 38–39.

113. Peter Rutland, *The Myth of the Plan: Lessons of Soviet Planning Experience* (London: Hutchinson, 1985), 87.

28,000–35,000 tankettes a year.[114] During early January 1931, the Politburo agreed to dramatically increase tank production, but tried to move away from the emphasis on tankettes to the larger light tanks. The Soviet government thought that industry should be able to manufacture 11,800 light tanks, 2,000 mediums, and 4,000 tankettes during the first year of war.[115] A special Commission on Tank Construction, consisting mainly of military men, reported to Stalin a month later and set the needs for the army during wartime at approximately the same levels as had the Politburo. The commission also decided that the army should create, by armoring and arming tractors and automobiles, a second echelon of tanks that would accompany the infantry.[116] A draft directive from Khalepskii's office, prepared for Molotov's signature as head of the Defense Commission (the replacement for the RZ STO), disagreed with this turn away from tankettes and proposed making these ultralight vehicles more central to the armor forces. It requested the same quantity of light and medium tanks, but wanted four times the number of tankettes in the first echelon.[117] The final plans fell somewhere between these two proposals, with large numbers of tankettes, but with the light tank as the central focus for operations with armor.

The decision to produce large numbers of light tanks was, as in Germany, shaped by both technical and tactical considerations. Technically, the Soviet Union continued to experience difficulties with the design and engineering of the complex vehicles. A light tank made sense both because it employed the same basic technology as that used in the growing Soviet tractor and automobile industry, and because just at this moment of decision two Western sources, the British company Vickers-Armstrong and the American inventor J. Walter Christie, provided the Soviet Union with excellent small tanks.[118]

At first negotiations over the Vickers had run into the same trouble as other attempts to conclude deals with Western companies. Throughout 1930 Vickers would send over the latest blueprints for the tank and receive return letters asking why Soviet specifications were not being met. In February 1931, Khalepskii had a meeting with a representative of the company in which he questioned him harshly about various apparent failings in the tank. He especially did not like the way that the motor ran and was also suspicious because the company had not informed him

---

114. Protocol from Tukhachevskii's Commission, 5 July 1931. RGVA, f. 31811, op. 2, d. 52, ll. 46–47.

115. Report from Ordzhonikidze to the Central Committee, 6 January 1931, RGVA, f. 4, op. 1, d. 1433, ll. 25–29.

116. Report from Uborevich to Stalin, 19 February 1931, RGVA, f. 31811, op. 1, d. 101, ll. 50–51.

117. "Postanovlenie Komissii Oborony SSSR" (undated draft), RGVA, f. 31811, op. 2, d. 52, ll. 63–64.

118. B. Fel'dman, K kharakteristike novykh tendentsii v voennom dele, 2d ed. (Moscow: Gosudarstvennoe Voennoe Izdatel'stvo, 1931), 71–72.

about a new sixteen-ton tank that Vickers planned to produce.[119] Once the tank arrived later that winter his tone changed. In a report to the RVS on the testing of the light Vickers, now called the V-26, he wrote that the tank, which was extremely fast and maneuverable, was well suited for use in large mechanized units.[120] Soon afterwards the V-26 was renamed the T-26 and production began. The three hundred light tanks produced during 1931 were all T-26s and the VSNKh was so pleased with it that directorate heads proposed acquiring more technical help from Vickers, including blueprints and machine tools.[121]

Discussions with Christie over his dual-drive tank were more straightforward. As discussed earlier, the late twenties had seen an increased interest in tanks of this type in both Germany and the Soviet Union. The hybrids combined the cross-country capability of the tank with the speed on roads of the automobile, thus creating a vehicle which, it was hoped, would significantly increase an army's operational mobility.[122] Christie had developed his version of this sort of vehicle for the U.S, army, but found himself rebuffed and searching for other buyers.[123] He sold one prototype to Khalepskii during that officer's trip abroad and the vehicle impressed those Soviets who saw it in action. Tukhachevskii – soon to be made head of the Armaments Directorate – and the commissioner of the RVS charged with ordering equipment for "special purposes" (the cover name for military materiel) both agreed that the tank was worthwhile and should be included in the Red Army's arsenal.[124] The Soviet high command, however, placed great significance on the outside world's impression of the tank for their own decision making, and intently followed discussions in other armies on the Christie before making any decision. Berzin, for instance, sent Voroshilov a transcript of a debate over the vehicle that took place in a U.S. Congressional commission during December 1930. He said that all the American officers were very pleased with the tank.[125] Even Stalin used a foreign source, Heigl's handbook of tanks, to keep informed about the various versions of the Christie tank.[126] The concern that Stalin showed over the se-

---

119. Report from Khalepskii to Voroshilov, 6 February 1931, RGVA, f. 33987, op. 3, d. 297, ll. 134–38.

120. Report from Khalepskii to RVS, 7 April 1931, RGVA, f. 31811, op. 2, d. 22, ll. 2–8.

121. "O tankovoy programme (proekt)," RGVA, f. 31811, op. 1, d. 101, ll. 26–28.

122. See above, chapter 3, and Ernst Volckheim, 1st Lieutenant in the Staff of the 5th Division, "Sind Panzerkraftwagen durch schnelllaufende Kampfwagen ersetzbar?" *Militär-Wochenblatt*, no. 10 (1930): 361–65.

123. For how and why the U.S. army decided not to adopt the Christie see R. P. Hunnicutt, *A History of the American Light Tank* (Novato, Calif,: Presidio, 1992), 55–60.

124. Tukhachevskii to Khalepskii, 14 April 1931, RGVA, f. 31811, op. 1, d. 101, l. 24; report from Dyrenkov to Voroshilov, April 1931, RGVA, f. 33987, op. 3, d. 306, ll. 173–74.

125. Report from Berzin to Voroshilov, 28/31 March 1931, RGVA, f. 33987, op. 3, d. 306, l. 102; 103–35.

126. Khalepskii to Berzin, 20 November 1931, RGVA, f. 31811, op. 2, d. 55, l. 1.

lection of this tank was in fact extraordinary, and shows that the general secretary was well informed about, and closely involved in deciding, even the most minute details of his army's weaponry. In November 1931 Khalepskii fell ill and was sent to the Kremlin hospital to recuperate. Late in the month, Stalin called to grill him about the Christie tank, demanding to know whether it was true that Khalepskii had bought a tank that would now be capable of amphibious operations. Khalepskii explained in detail the construction of the Christie amphibious tank and told Stalin that only an iron mock-up of the tank existed and that Christie, for technical reasons, had decided not to produce it.[127] Influenced by Stalin's personal interest – and the support of foreign experts – a directive from the Defense Commission on tank construction declared that the army had to have the new Christie, or B-T ("High-Speed Tank"), as it was now called. By late 1931 it would be considered one of the Red Army's main battle tanks.[128]

These technical considerations were just part of the reason that the army concentrated on a lighter tank. Like Reichswehr officers, Soviet commanders were now convinced that speed was the tank's most crucial technical characteristic and this implied a fairly light tank. Unlike the Germans, however, they were also convinced that it was possible to produce a tank that would be fast and yet have significant armor protection and at least one gun.[129] It is no surprise, then, that although the German and Soviet armies decided to concentrate on what both called "light" tanks, all borrowed from foreign sources, the Soviet tanks were in fact much larger and, more importantly for later events, had thicker armor and heavier guns. The Soviet "light" tanks were in fact closer to what the Germans called "medium" tanks, while later Soviet "mediums" were as large as German "heavy" tanks. This difference in conceptions of what constituted the fast, mobile tank of the future would have devastating consequences when the two armor forces met on the battlefields of Spain and Russia.

As production of the light tanks seemed to overtake planning, Soviet commanders became ever more intent on understanding the military implications of their country's industrialization. Their basic conclusion was that Tukhachevskii had gotten it right: possessing large numbers of tanks forced the army to completely revise the technical, organizational, and tactical principles of its armor forces. As a manual of armor doctrine would later put it, "[t]he development of military technology – quality and quantity – compels [us] to seek more effective uses for its combat application, especially in the complex forms of offensive battle."[130] There

127. Ibid.; Khalepskii to Stalin, 20 November 1931, RGVA, f. 31811, op. 2, d. 55, ll. 2–3.

128. "Postanovlenie Komissii Oborony 'O tankostroenii,'" RGVA, f. 31811, op. 2, d. 52, ll. 22–23.

129. Khalepskii's only caveat about the T-26 was that its speed came at the expense of armor protection. Report from Khalepskii to RVS, 7 April 1931, on tests of the Vickers V-26 between 27 November 1930 and 5 January 1931, RGVA, f. 31811, op. 2, d. 22, ll. 2–8.

130. "Ukazanie po organizatsii glubokogo boia (proekt)," RGVA, f. 31983, op. 2, d. 20, l. 149.

were two possibilities for revising the technical principles of armor warfare. Khalepskii thought that five specific types of action demanded tanks. It would be possible to create tanks that could fulfill more than one of these missions, but not all of them, and therefore the army had to have as a minimum three types: a reconnaissance tank, an escort tank and a long-range tank.[131] Tukhachevskii, in contrast, thought that the army should manufacture a specific tank for every possible eventuality on the battlefield. The army would need six different machines: one for combating artillery; another for transporting infantry; a third for use against heavy machine guns; a fourth to accompany infantry; a special type for engineering and supply purposes; and finally a radio tank for communications.[132]

While commanders debated how best to further the technical side of armor affairs, they also reconsidered the question of how to organize the new masses of tanks. Although Khalepskii commented in the fall of 1931 that the best form for the Soviet armor forces was still not settled, in reality the Soviet army was more united on this question than other European militaries.[133] Rather than facing a choice between gathering tanks into large mechanized formations (the British example) or spreading tanks throughout the infantry to aid their advance (the French model), Soviet commanders, with the expectation of tens of thousands of tanks soon to arrive, decided that they could do both. In August the RZ STO continued the trend toward concentration that had begun the year before, ordering the creation of large mechanized units that would be capable of independently deciding missions both on the field of battle and in all operational depths of a modern battle front.[134] Tukhachevskii added the other side to the equation, calling for different organizational structures to fit the different technical capabilities of his tank types. Tanks that would accompany infantry would obviously need to be part of assault infantry divisions, while the DD tanks would form a reserve force at the disposal of the army command.[135] In November he described in greater depth a comprehensive reorganization of the entire army demanded by the Soviet Union's new production capabilities. He estimated that the Soviet Union would manufacture eighty-five hundred tanks by the end of 1933, and argued that not only should they be formed into "experimental units," but they should also be introduced into rifle and cavalry divisions. As he wrote, "the essence of the matter now is not that there are supporters or opponents of motorization (tankization) of divisions, but rather that

131. Memo from Khalepskii to Tukhachevskii, "Takticheskie trebovaniia, opredeliashchie sistemu tankovogo vooruzheniia RKKA," (spring 1931?), RGVA, f. 31811, op. 2, d. 77, ll. 14–15.

132. Memo from Tukhachevskii to Khalepskii, 3 March 1931, RGVA, f. 31811, op. 1, d. 101, ll. 18–22.

133. "Stenogramma rasshirennogo zasedaniia RVS SSSR ob itogakh boevoi podgotovki RKKA i F za 1930/31 god i ob uchebnykh tseliakh na 1932 god," 22–26 October 1931, RGVA, f. 4, op. 16, d. 11, l. 27.

134. Ryzhakov, "K voprosu o stroitel'stve bronetankovykh voisk," 107.

135. Memo from Tukhachevskii to Khalepskii, 14 April 1931, RGVA, f. 31811, op. 1, d. 101, l. 25.

growing technology compels reconstruction, and not elsewhere than in the basic organism of the army, but rather precisely inside it, in the main mass."[136] He suggested that the large number of tanks would be enough to mechanize about seventy-five rifle divisions and thirteen cavalry divisions, form twelve to fifteen tank battalions for the reserves, known as TRGK, and still create ten independent "moto-tank" divisions. These last divisions could be formed from existing rifle divisions and would consist of three tank regiments and one battalion of thirty lightly armored personnel transporters. The "moto-tank" divisions would also have mechanized artillery and a squadron of airborne troops.[137]

Actual new unit formation closely followed Tukhachevskii's suggestions, with the army creating both mechanized units as well as mechanizing infantry and cavalry units. The detached TRGK battalions, designed as tank reserves for use by the infantry, became tank regiments with three tank battalions each while three territorial tank battalions were created. The strength of the experimental brigade increased dramatically and now amounted to 119 tanks, 100 tankettes, a large number of self-propelled or towed artillery pieces, and 385 other vehicles. The brigade was structured into a reconnaissance regiment, a strike regiment (two tank battalions and two self-propelled artillery divisions), a battalion of mounted infantry, and an artillery group with antiair capability.[138]

The one major controversy over organization involved the cavalry. During the previous year Budënnyi had agreed, at least in internal communications, that the cavalry had to change in order to survive. In early February 1930, he submitted a memorandum to Voroshilov on reorganizing the cavalry so that it would be able to march further and faster, conduct war independently, and defend against motorized and mechanized units. To achieve this, he proposed reorganizing cavalry divisions around light mechanized and motorized units. The new divisions would have four cavalry regiments, an artillery regiment, and a mechanized regiment. This latter unit would include an armored car and tankette squadron and a full light tank "battery" of thirty tanks. He thought that the cavalry could use its tanks in encirclements and for attacks on the enemy's flanks and rear.[139] In public meetings, however, Budënnyi spent most of his time defending his beloved horses, and attacking Tukhachevskii, Iakir, and Triandafillov, whom he saw as the enemies of the cavalry.[140] At the 1931 fall meeting of force commanders he was especially con-

136. Memo from Tukhachevskii to Voroshilov, November 1931, RGVA, f. 33987, op. 3, d. 291, l. 44.

137. Ibid., ll. 44–47.

138. A. Ryzhakov, "K voprosu o stroitel'stve bronetankovykh voisk," 106–7; see also Khalepskii's speech in "Stenogramma rasshirennogo zasedaniia RVS SSSR ob itogakh boevoi podgotovki RKKA i F za 1930/31 god i ob uchebnykh tseliakh na 1932 god," October 1931, 22–26, RGVA, f. 4, op. 16, d. 11, l. 26.

139. Memo from Budënnyi to Voroshilov, 9 February 1930, RGVA, f. 33987, op. 3, d. 320, ll. 2–28.

140. Ibid., ll. 383–86, 691.

tentious, arguing that when the airplane first appeared some had said that this would replace the horse, but it could not and had not. Now, he continued, some were saying the same about armor forces. The truth was that the army needed, at the very least, to maintain cavalry in operational reserves.[141] In actual fact Tukhachevskii and other mechanization supporters, at least in public, continued to talk only of motorizing the cavalry, not of dispensing with it entirely.[142] In private they may have deplored a continued reliance on the horse, but they knew better than to attack openly the force that Stalin's closest friends had ridden to glory in the Civil War.

There was far less controversy over the tactics for the new tank units. In 1930 and 1931 the idea of a battle deep in the enemy's rear, first expressed by Tukhachevskii and Triandafillov, became widely accepted. In a seminal memorandum to Khalepskii in March 1930, Tukhachevskii took a sweeping view of the implications of the new doctrine which, for the first time, he publicly labeled "deep battle." His memo began with the presumption that the doctrine expressed in PU-29, grounded on the meager quantity of tanks available to the Red Army at that time, was already outdated. Soviet success in creating a motor industry, he wrote, required a complete reconsideration of the problem. The vital difference in the new armor combat, compared to tank use during the previous year, was that huge numbers of the machines would take part in battles, allowing the army to carry the fight directly into the depths of the enemy's defensive positions. Accompanying the infantry and helping them to push ahead was thus only one component of the new deep battle, since the employment of special tank-borne infantry in the enemy's deep rear would add a new operational element to the whole assault. He described how the first echelon, the DD tanks, would attack directly into the opponent's rear with strong artillery support. This echelon would destroy the enemy's artillery, headquarters and lines of communication and, by unloading the special tank-borne units in the enemy's rear, cut him off from both escape and reinforcement. After this echelon had passed the artillery would resume their assault on the opponent's infantry, and then the second echelon of tanks, followed by the infantry, would attack. In front of the foot soldiers would come the fast "tank-fighters," designated as "DPP," or "remote infantry escort," tanks, which would seek to destroy the enemy's heavy machine guns and tanks. Behind the DPP group would follow tanks of the "NPP" ("direct infantry support") echelon.[143] Working together, the three waves of tanks would allow the Soviet army to fulfill the vision of Tukhachevskii

141. "Stenogramma rasshirennogo zasedaniia RVS SSSR ob itogakh boevoi podgotovki RKKA i F za 1930/31 god i ob uchebnykh tseliakh na 1932 god," 22–26 October 1931, RGVA, f. 4, op. 16, d. 11, l. 124.

142. See "Stenograficheskii otchet komvoiskami okruga Tukh. o razbore okruzhnykh voiskovykh manevrov," 10 September 1930, RGVA, f. 25888, op. 15, d. 193, l. 62.

143. Memo from Tukhachevskii to Khalepskii, 3 March 1931, RGVA, f. 31811, op. 1, d. 101, ll. 18–22.

and Triandafillov of simultaneously suppressing the enemy's entire defensive structure.

Later that year Tukhachevskii used the occasion of the annual autumn meeting of the high command to detail his view of the contrast between the old doctrine and deep battle. He began his presentation by arguing that earlier armies had attacked the opponent from the front and sought to find an open flank to envelop him from the rear. One's adversary, however, rarely offered a flank and therefore in most cases the battle took shape as a frontal clash. Even when experiencing a serious defeat, the enemy often succeeded in retreating in good order by using the flexibility of machine gun defenses. Now, with the availability of the new weapons, he believed that it was possible to land forces by air and motor in the opponent's rear, while armored transporters could carry troops armed with machine guns across the defensive zone. Meanwhile, the "old" combined-arms attack with infantry, artillery, and NPP tanks would push through the enemy's front. Working together, the two assaults made it possible to drive a wedge between the opponent's defensive battle formations, and stop him from bringing up reserves from the deep rear. Tukhachevskii concluded, however, that the army would find it very difficult to implement the new deep battle idea in actual combat since "these new forms of battle are very complex. They raise anew the questions of command and control, the nature of battle training, and to a significant degree 'twist the brain.'"[144]

Tukhachevskii's final warning was not a mere afterthought. Although the RZ STO as well as the RVS adopted as official army doctrine the need "to pin down simultaneously the entire depth of the defense," the very essence of deep battle, the question of how to carry out the new idea and put into action its revolutionary tactical conceptions, proved far more problematic.[145] To work through these difficulties the army command set up several exercises in which the various aspects of the new form of combat, especially attacks into the depths of the enemy's positions with the DD echelon, could be mastered.[146] The RVS proposed, too, an ambitious plan to work on cooperation between armor units and the other branches of the army as well as among the various types of forces that made up the mechanized brigade.[147]

The speeches at that same meeting showed that there had been more failures

144. "Stenogramma rasshirennogo zasedaniia RVS SSSR ob itogakh boevoi podgotovki RKKA i F za 1930/31 god i ob uchebnykh tseliakh na 1932 god," 22–26 October 1931, RGVA, f. 4, op. 16, d. 11, l. 195.

145. Ryzhakov, "K voprosu o stroitel'stve bronetankovykh voisk," 107; "Stenogramma rasshirennogo zasedaniia RVS SSSR ob itogakh boevoi podgotovki RKKA i F za 1930/31 god i ob uchebnykh tseliakh na 1932 god," 22–26 October 1931, RGVA, f. 4, op. 16, d. 11, l. 26.

146. "Sekretnye prikazy RVS SSSR 1931, No. 031," 4 May 1931, RGVA, f. 4, op. 3, d. 3256, ll. 41–42, 49.

147. RVS resolution "O rezul'tatakh obsledovaniia mekh. brigady," to Khalepskii, 20 June 1931, RGVA, f. 31811, op. 2, d. 23, ll. 1–3.

than successes in these exercises. Egorov discussed the complexities inherent in the spatial character of deep battle: command, control, and communications over the kind of distances envisaged were especially difficult to work out.[148] Khalepskii reported that the use of DPP and DD echelons still needed refining, and that the deep battle idea as a whole was far from perfected. He said that no other country, including England, had yet solved the basic problem of simultaneously pinning down the entire depth of the defense.[149] Like officers of the Reichswehr, he noted that cooperation with the infantry remained a problem area, while his summing up suggested that little of the exercises had gone as the doctrine said it should. In particular he complained that

> we do not yet have unanimity in our understanding of the work of the DPP tank echelon. Often this latter is assigned as a basic mission the suppression of machine guns in defensive depths, along with suppression of antitank weapons that interfere with the NPP attack. In practice Group DD is assigned a main mission with near objectives, is very weakly studied, and gets mixed up with Groups NPP and DPP. As a result Group DD does not fulfill its basic mission – reaching artillery positions and the enemy's deep defensive positions to destroy and disorganize the system of artillery fire.[150]

The RVS order on battle training for 1930–31 concluded that the army had raised the mobility of its forces, but that the use of mechanized units and tankettes during a combined-arms battle was not at all settled.[151]

It is one of the many tragedies of the Soviet army during this period that the two men who might have been able to work through these problems with deep battle, Triandafillov and Kalinovskii, were killed that summer of 1931 in an airplane accident. As Grigorii Isserson would later write, this in effect "orphaned" the concept, leaving it without two of its chief supporters and innovators.[152] The tragedy was all the more pronounced because the army had now decided to expand the deep battle idea beyond its original tactical bounds into an operational doctrine. The differences between "deep battle" and "deep operations" were immense. In the first place, the army had to rework the idea of simultaneity which was no longer literally true when dealing with the large scale of an operation. Operations also demanded mechanized forces capable of carrying out independent deep missions, as well as a method for pushing these forces into the enemy's rear. Finally, there was the basic problem that the army began work on in the fall of 1931: turning a suc-

148. "Stenogramma rasshirennogo zasedaniia RVS SSSR ob itogakh boevoi podgotovki RKKA i F za 1930/31 god i ob uchebnykh tseliakh na 1932 god," 22–26 October 1931, RGVA, f. 4, op. 16, d. 11, ll. 43–44.

149. Ibid., l. 26.

150. Ibid., l. 28.

151. "Prikaz RVS No. 090," 26 October 1931, RGVA, f. 4, op. 3, d. 3256, ll. 120–23.

152. Isserson, "Razvitie teorii sovetskogo operativnogo iskusstva," 39.

cessful tactical break-in into an operational breakthrough.[153] Without the advice and thought of Triandafillov and Kalinovskii, it would be more difficult for the army to imagine how to transform and implement the deep operations concept.

As 1931 ended, armor doctrine in Germany and the Soviet Union, at least on the surface, seemed to be in very different positions. The German high command still believed that tanks would play a decisive role in the next war and had even re-created a (theoretical) organization for armor forces that reflected a desire for at least a few large, independent, mechanized units. Articles, reports, and even private conversations showed, however, that there was no unanimity in the officer corps about this organizational structure nor about doctrine. The high command as a whole was not convinced that tanks could overcome antiarmor defenses and dominate the modern battlefield. In contrast the Soviet army, encouraged by successes in production and stimulated by the exciting ideas of Triandafillov, Tukhachevskii, and the others, had unanimously adopted the deep battle idea. All that remained, apparently, was working out the details of the doctrine.

On closer inspection, however, Soviet armor doctrine was not as settled as it appeared. The Red Army had not been able to implement its new concept in any of its exercises, yet the expansion of deep battle into deep operations would require even greater facility at organizing, commanding, and controlling armor forces. As time passed, these failures to prove that the doctrine could work on the real battlefield would cause some commanders to doubt its practicality. Meanwhile, the one obvious source of outside aid for training in the practical side of deep battle, the collaboration with Germany, was imperiled by growing tensions between the two countries. The Soviet army would soon find itself alone in its attempts to prove that its new views of modern combat were sound.

153. Ibid., 40–41. The development of deep operations was also not helped by the fact that most of the young professors in the Frunze Operational Department died in Stalin's purges. See ibid., 41. Richard Simpkin discusses the "broadening" of the deep battle concept into the idea of deep operations in *Deep Battle: The Brainchild of Marshal Tukhachevskii* (London: Brassey, 1987), 35–37.

CHAPTER FIVE

A New Confidence?

The End of Collaboration, 1932–1933

Despite the growing ambivalence of the Soviet government, the military collaboration between the Reichswehr and the Red Army seemed to go well in 1932. Work at the three installations proceeded smoothly, multiple educational exchanges took place, and there was large-scale participation in joint exercises. At Kazan more Soviets than ever took part in the summer course; one hundred soldiers in addition to the usual number of students came to the installation to train in armor tactics and to work on tank technology.[1]

Yet, although the collaboration was apparently at its height, the powerful forces that had already begun to undermine friendship between the two countries reasserted themselves and led to the collapse of military cooperation within a year. The Soviet Union was about to "complete" (or at least declare successful) the Five Year Plan, a feat that would have ambiguous results for the country as a whole, but was an unalloyed success for the armor industry. As the Soviets grew more self-sufficient in tank production, there was further development of the deep battle/deep operations idea. Soviet officers gradually became convinced that their army had the most advanced technology and tactics in the world, while an expansion of contacts with France and other Western nations only added to their new confidence. Within two years both the Soviet army and government would no longer see any need for joint work with the Reichswehr.

The German army, in turn, had reason for confidence in its future, and less cause to continue the collaboration. Hitler came to power promising to reinvigorate and rearm the German nation, a defiance of Versailles that the officer corps applauded. After 1933 the high command could expect more money for the military in general and for the forbidden technological weapons of modern warfare in particular. The army was also more united on its evaluation of the tank and the shape of future war, although important differences still remained. Taken together these new factors meant that Germany would soon be equipped with the armor forces that both military and political leaders desired, and with the beginnings of a unified military

---

1. Willi Esser, *Dokumentation über die Entwicklung und Erprobung der ersten Panzerkampfwagen der Reichswehr* (Munich: Krauss-Maffei, 1979), 52.

doctrine. The Reichswehr therefore also had good reason to see the collaboration as irrelevant prior to its collapse in the fall of 1933, and to accept its passing with few protests.

As we have seen, even before Hitler came to power German officers (and some politicians) plotted the army's future course as if they had already overturned Versailles. By 1930 the economic crisis and resultant surge in popular support for the Nazi Party compelled even moderate political leaders to perceive a more forceful policy, and especially a push for rearmament, as necessary to retain the good-will of the people.[2] During 1932 these efforts intensified, spurred on – ironically enough – by the international disarmament conference then underway in Geneva. The Reichswehr and succeeding German cabinets viewed that gathering as their best hope of shifting the European balance of power in their favor without risking war. The German position for negotiations was the need for equality with the other great powers, either through a general disarmament (which seemed unlikely) or by allowing Germany to build weapons to match the other nations of Europe. In a confidential report entitled "The Hidden German Goal at the Disarmament Conference," the high command argued that negotiators had to seek more concrete concessions. As a first step they wanted the right to an armor unit, military aircraft, and manpower almost twice that allowed by Versailles. Both positions assumed that whatever the reaction of the Western nations, the disarmament conference would provide a path for rearmament without the risk of French or British intervention. A series of detailed plans for the future of the Reichswehr created by military officials during the autumn of 1932 reflected this belief. The "Six-week Program" only prepared Germany for a short war, but the "Billion Program" was a long-term rearmament plan predicated on an end to Versailles. The high command did not believe that either of these were adequate and argued forcefully for an even greater expansion of the army. Included in a rebuilt military would be the twenty-one divisions decided upon earlier in the decade as well as significant armor, heavy artillery, and air units – in short, all the weapons forbidden by the treaty. To conceal the nature of their radical plans, military planners described it as a "reconstruction" of the army, rather than rearmament.[3]

Thus, although still not able to build large numbers of tanks, the German army felt free to choose prototypes, organization structures, and tactics for armor units

---

2. Gaines Post, Jr., *The Civil-Military Fabric of Weimar Foreign Policy* (Princeton, N.J.: Princeton University Press, 1973), 7, 281–90.

3. Edward W. Bennett, *German Rearmament and the West, 1932–1933* (Princeton, N.J.: Princeton University Press, 1979), 53, 60–61, 174–75, 184–85, 236; Wilhelm Deist, "The Rearmament of the Wehrmacht," in Militärgeschichtliches Forschungsamt, *Germany and the Second World War.* vol. 1: *The Build-up of German Aggression* (Oxford: Clarendon Press, 1990), 406.

that anticipated an early liberation from the treaty. One of the more important changes in Reichswehr thinking about its future armor forces was greater support for a very light tank. Proponents of a larger tank remained vocal, but there were sound reasons for favoring a machine like the LaS that would be cheap and, presumably, easy to build. The depression that the country had entered in 1929; the slow, painful process of tank manufacture; and the satisfactory performance of the LaS, seemed to suggest that that the army could have a light vehicle immediately or wait several years until industry produced a better-armed and armored tank. In the short term, it was impossible to have both types of vehicles in large numbers. Over the next two years skeptical German officers thus reluctantly accepted the super light LaS as a viable main battle tank.

At the beginning of summer 1932, however, the high command still thought of the small tank only as a reconnaissance vehicle, a carrier for a small gun, or a draft machine.[4] Production of this supposedly easily built vehicle lagged far behind schedule. Oswald Lutz, the new Inspector of Motorized Troops (Kraftfahrtruppen), and a man who would soon play an influential role in the development of German armor doctrine, felt compelled to threaten Krupp with buying the Carden-Loyd directly from Britain if an LaS was not ready for testing immediately.[5] The first model was only available at the end of July and even then a Krupp engineer reported that though very maneuverable, it still suffered from (unspecified) "technical problems."[6] The Waffenamt was more precise, criticizing especially the motor which, one captain reported, was not strong enough and "in no way meets the expected performance of the Small Tractor."[7]

After a comparison test of the Carden-Loyd and the new tank in late September, the tone of comments by German officers changed. A Krupp representative wrote that Bockelberg and others from the Waffenamt had seen for themselves that the German tank had driven quickly and smoothly on rough terrain while the British machine had shaken a great deal and bumped along. The test, he reported, had ended in complete satisfaction.[8] Lutz also commented after the demonstration that he liked the looks of the small vehicle.[9] Weaknesses in industry meant that production would be slow, however. When Lutz asked a Krupp representative how

---

4. "Niederschrift über die Besprechung mit Prw in Essen am 25.6.32," 25 June 1932, signed Hagelloch. BA-MA, RH 8/v, 2675 (Krupp). p. 339. See also Walter J. Spielberger, *Die Motorisierung der deutschen Reichswehr, 1920–1935* (Stuttgart: Motorbuch-Verlag, 1979), 350.

5. Aktennotiz, Krupp, 5 July 1932, BA-MA, RH 8/v, 2675 (Krupp), 345.

6. "Vorführung des Kl. Tr. Fahrgestells in Meppen am 15./16.8.1932," BA-MA, RH 8/v, 2675 (Krupp).

7. Memo from Wa Prw 6/VI on the Small Tractor, BA-MA, RH 8/v, 2675 (Krupp).

8. "Niederschrift über Vorführung des Kl. Tr. in Wünsdorf am 28.9.1932," BA-MA, RH 8/v, 2675 (Krupp).

9. Spielberger, *Motorisierung der deutschen Reichswehr*, 357. Lutz's approval was noted with satisfaction by the Krupp representative. Aktennotiz, 13 October 1932, BA-MA, RH8/v, 2676 (Krupp).

much time the company needed to build just five of the light vehicles armed with machine guns, he was told five months.[10]

While the army began to focus attention on the very light tank, it did not abandon larger vehicles. Guderian especially favored a heavier machine, and after driving both the large and small "tractors" at Kazan in July, ordered further development of the larger tank with all possible speed.[11] Lutz tried out the vehicle for himself and the Krupp engineer present wrote that the tank had performed very well.[12] Later that summer German officers met with a Soviet delegation about improving the machine.[13] The army had other suggestions for larger tanks, including a multiturret medium tank, the euphemistically named "new vehicle," for which Lutz soon set out a design competition.[14] Yet if experiences with the small tank had been any indication it would be several years before heavier tanks would be ready for mass production. Lutz and Guderian reluctantly agreed that the very light LaS, soon to be called the Panzer (Pz.) I, might have to serve as a stopgap main tank until heavier vehicles began to come off the production lines. To make up for what they saw as obvious weaknesses, they suggested a larger gun for the tank, but the chiefs of the Waffenamt and Artillery Inspectorate disagreed. In the end, the two armor specialists settled on a smaller gun, although the majority of the machines that came off the assembly lines had only a machine gun.[15] The army recognized that the small tank was not adequate for all the missions before it and would decide later to follow the strategy first suggested by Heigl: build large numbers of the LaS and as many of the heavier machines as possible.[16] The larger tanks would support the small vehicles on the battlefield and take care of objectives for which the armaments of the lighter tank were insufficient.[17]

While decisions about tank design were still in process, the army held important maneuvers at the Grafenwöhr and Jüterbog proving grounds to clarify the tactics that the tanks would use. The exercises, six in all, were designed to work especially on the problems that had occupied German military thought for the last several years, including the strength of antiarmor defenses and cooperation between ar-

10. "Niederschrift über die Besprechung mit General Lutz in K. am 12.10.32, Betr: Gr. Tr.," 12 October 1932, BA-MA, RH 8/v, 2676 (Krupp).

11. Klaus Müller, "So lebten und arbeiteten wir 1929 bis 1933 in Kama" (unpublished manuscript, May 1972), 27.

12. "Niederschrift über die Besprechung mit General Lutz in K. am 12.10.32, Betr: Gr. Tr.," 12 October 1932. BA-MA, RH 8/v, 2676 (Krupp).

13. Spielberger, Motorisierung der deutschen Reichswehr, 313.

14. Ibid., 334.

15. The other two heads of inspectorates argued that the infantry had already adopted the same smaller gun and the army had to simplify armaments. Heinz Guderian, Erinnerungen eines Soldaten (Heidelberg: Kurt Vowinckel, 1951), 21–22.

16. See chapters 3 and 4 above.

17. Fritz Heigl, Taschenbuch der Tanks, Ausgabe 1930: Strassenpanzer. Neue Tanks. Panzerzüge (Munich: Lehmanns, 1930), 106–7; Guderian, Erinnerungen eines Soldaten, 21.

mor and other forces.[18] During the exercises involving antiarmor operations, Blue (Germany) was, of course, on the defensive against an assault by the Red side, which was armed with tank dummies.[19] The detailed instructions for the Red attack sounded very similar to German ideas on armor tactics. The tanks would advance in three waves with the first wave so timed that the machines would push through the line of their own forward infantry at "X" hour. Each of the waves had very specific goals, with the first wave to destroy enemy artillery and combat enemy reserves and reinforcements while the second would cooperate with the stormtroops. The third wave would act as a reserve at the disposal of the battalion commander. Artillery would meanwhile pound the forward enemy infantry area as the tanks were coming forward and an infantry assault would follow closely behind the tank advance.[20]

Afterward Lutz used these maneuvers to support his belief, and that of other armor supporters, that tanks were now capable of dominating the battlefield. First and foremost he argued that the tank was exclusively an offensive weapon which would fight at the critical point to achieve decision. In contrast to those officers who wrote about the dependence of armor on other forces, he argued that the maneuvers proved that tank units had to have independent combat missions and could even constitute the main force, whose demands all other arms had to take into account. Armor, he stressed, was not an auxiliary branch of the infantry and should not be subordinated to infantry regiments except when attacking limited objectives. Commanders were therefore to avoid creating a close link between the vehicles and slower forces since they would only waste the tank's principle combat advantages; speed, mobility, and range. Yet Lutz's other major lesson from the maneuvers was that only a combined-arms approach, which united infantry, artillery, aircraft, and tanks in battle, could ensure success. He had no real answer to the contradiction inherent in these two points, simply suggesting that the infantry who worked with the tanks should strive to follow them closely, falling upon the enemy's infantry while these were still "morally paralyzed" by the sudden appearance of the vehicles. Tanks, however, were not compelled to remain within the infantry combat zone: only the common objective would bind man and machine.[21] In No-

18. Heinz Guderian, *Achtung – Panzer!* tr. Christopher Duffy (London: Arms and Armour Press, 1992), 162; In 6 Nr. 536/32 geh. (I b). to T 4, 12 September 1932, signed Lutz, "Anregungen und Lehren aus den unter Leitung der Inspektion der Kraftfahrtruppen abgehaltenen Übungen der Kampfwagen-Nachbildungs-Bataillone zusammen mit Infanterie und Artillerie auf den Truppenübungsplätzen Grafenwöhr und Jüterbog," BA-MA, RH 12–6/v, 2.

19. Inspektion der Kraftfahrtruppen, "Übung in Grafenwöhr am 18.8.32," signed Lutz, BA-MA, RH 12–6/v, 6.

20. Instructions and "Rot Lage" for exercises held in Grafenwöhr on 20.8.32, BA-MA, RH 12–6/v, 6.

21. In 6 Nr. 536/32 geh. (I b). to T 4, 12 September 1932, signed Lutz, "Anregungen und Lehren aus den unter Leitung der Inspektion der Kraftfahrtruppen abgehaltenen Übungen der Kampfwagen-Nachbildungs-Bataillone zusammen mit Infanterie und Artillerie auf den Truppenübungsplätzen Grafenwöhr und Jüterbog," BA-MA, RH 12–6/v, 2, 10–13, 16r–v.

vember Lutz circulated his thoughts on the maneuvers more widely, emphasizing the need for surprise and the advantage that the tank's armor gave it vis-à-vis other types of weapons.[22]

In his official comments for the year Lutz was more blunt, asserting that the armor forces were now a "main branch" of the army, on a par with the infantry, artillery, and cavalry. Subordination to the infantry would therefore only occur as an exceptional case.[23] Guderian too thought that the exercises provided clear proof of the capabilities of motorized and armor units. In his memoirs he wrote that many younger cavalry officers, on the basis of the maneuvers, agreed with the armor specialists and became firm defenders of the new weapon.[24]

The official high command analysis of the maneuvers was more vague, showing that not every officer viewed the lessons of Grafenwöhr and Jüterbog as decisive. As in Lutz's report, the description of an armor offensive here contrasted sharply with Soviet descriptions of similar engagements, with suggestions and a broad outline of principles rather than ironclad rules. The overall vision of warfare thus presented left more leeway for decisions by officers on the spot, and was a natural outcome of the underlying German military principal of mission-oriented tactics. In this analysis, for example, the author recognized that an armor attack could occur in waves or in lines, depending on the judgment of the commanding officer.[25] Significantly, the official report did not endorse the idea of an independent armor force fighting as a separate branch of the military, the main innovation in Lutz's vision of tank warfare.

The older generation of cavalry officers was also unimpressed by the maneuvers and remained unenthusiastic about the tank, tenaciously resisting the replacement of their beloved horses by "soulless" machines. Their views are obvious in a series of *Militär-Wochenblatt* articles that dealt with the possible motorization of the cavalry. Lieutenant Colonel (later General) von Faber du Faur fired the opening salvo with an essay that directly attacked Lutz's organizational structure for the armor forces. He argued that the military had to assign mechanized units either to the army or to the cavalry corps; they could not constitute an independent command. He of course thought that the most suitable place for such formations would be within the cavalry where horseman and armor vehicle would fight shoulder to shoulder, but with the tank firmly subordinated to the cavalry.[26] Not long afterward

22. Memo from the Inspector of Motorized Troops critiquing 1932 exercises, November 1932, BA-MA, RH 12–6/v. 2, pp. 19, 29.

23. "Grundsätzliche Bemerkungen des Inspekteurs der Kraftfahrtruppen," 19 October 1932. BA-MA, RH 17/v, 19.

24. Guderian, *Erinnerungen eines Soldaten*, 23.

25. "Hinweise für die Ausbildung im Jahre 1932/33 auf Grund von Beobachtungen der Heeresleitung bei Truppen- und Herbstübungen im vergangenen Ausbildungsjahre," Zu Nr. 900/32g. T4 Ia.; Anlage 5, BA-MA, RH 17/v, 19.

26. Oberstleutnant v. Faber du Faur, 4. Reit. Rgt., "Neuzeitliche schnell bewegliche Verbände,"

Captain Crisolli, one of the younger cavalry officers who supported a more wide-spread use of the tank, wrote that the cavalry needed much more extensive motor-ization and mechanization than Faber du Faur suggested. He proposed that every cavalry division have at least one motorized unit consisting of a mechanized armor brigade including cross-country vehicles, mechanized artillery, and tanks.[27] Older cavalry officers were quick to see that Crisolli's organizational reform would effec-tively replace the horse with motor vehicles. A few weeks after the captain's article appeared, Colonel von Wiktorin argued vehemently that the presence of any motor vehicles could only change the basic character of the cavalry for the worse. In order to retain the cavalry's mobility and cross-country capability, the army had to pre-serve a force organized around the horse alone.[28] Faber du Faur was more moder-ate, but just as opposed to doing away with the horse altogether. He suggested that mechanized battalions would only take over some kinds of long-range reconnais-sance, leaving the horse to handle local or close reconnaissance. The two types of forces would thus complement rather than replace each other.[29] The German high command, like the Soviets dedicated to preserving the horse as an essential part of modern warfare, decided that Faber du Faur was right: cavalry and armor could work together in a mobile, combined-arms battle. The main army maneuvers for 1932, which pitted cavalry in mobile combat against an infantry division, had a dummy tank company cooperate with the horse troops.[30] A report on the results of the maneuvers suggested that strategic cavalry could follow the same principles as the infantry when cooperating with tanks, coming forward at the appropriate time to exploit any successes won by the vehicles.[31]

To outside observers such as Tukhachevskii, the attitudes of the senior cavalry officers and men like Adam toward mechanization were more striking than the strong interest in new tactics and organization expressed by certain sectors of the German officer corps. Tukhachevskii attended the Reichswehr's large-scale fall maneuvers in 1932, and reported back to the annual meeting of Soviet force com-manders that "the Germans regard the question of a mechanized army extremely skeptically. . . . All the generals declare that they are against mechanization and the maximum that they will allow is only partial motorization." He added that "[i]n this question they undoubtedly lag behind the English and even the French and are con-

Militär-Wochenblatt, no. 22 (1932): 721–24; Oberstleutnant v. Faber du Faur, 4. Reit. Rgt., "Neuzeitliche schnell bewegliche Verbände," ibid., no. 23 (1932): 756–61.

27. Rittmeister Crisolli, "Für und wider die Motorisierung der Kavallerie-Division," ibid., no. 29 (1932): 1028–32.

28. Oberst v. Wiktorin, "Die Motorisierung der Kavalleriedivision," ibid., no. 38 (1932): 1349.

29. Oberstleutnant v. Faber du Faur, "Mechanisierte Aufklärungsabteilungen in der opera-tionaln und taktischen Aufklärung," ibid., no. 46 (1932): 1609–11.

30. Adolf Reinicke, Das Reichsheer, 1921–1934 (Osnabrück: Biblio Verlag, 1986), 163.

31. Bericht über die Herbstübungen der Heeresleitung 1932 (Berlin: Reichsdruckerei, 1932), BA-MA, RHD 17/9, 26.

servative generals."[32] The changes occurring within the German staff would in fact not be apparent to the outside world until after 1934, when the Wehrmacht began to arm openly with the forbidden tanks, and older officers were forced by events to accept a thorough mechanization of the German army.

Given his close contact with the Germans in the military collaboration, Tukhachevskii should have been able to provide a more nuanced analysis of Reichswehr doctrine, but a growing estrangement between the German and Soviet governments may have encouraged him to be critical in his public remarks. As we have seen, both "pariah" nations had already increased their diplomatic contacts with the international community. The pace of these activities, especially on the part of the Soviet Union, accelerated after the Manchurian crisis of 1931 once again reminded Stalin of the vulnerability of his eastern borders, pushing him to increase the tempo of the industrialization drive and to seek allies to counterbalance the Japanese threat.[33] Over the next few years the Soviets not only signed formal agreements with France and Poland, they were also recognized by the United States and petitioned to become a member of the League of Nations. Germany, in response to these actions and for internal political reasons, also chose to depend less on the Soviet Union as its main source of international support. Although the final break between the two armies would not come until Hitler's rise to power, military cooperation was thus already under scrutiny in both countries, and outright suspicion in the Soviet Union. Voroshilov's comments in late 1931 showed that the Kazan school in particular was seen as a waste of effort or even as a liability.[34]

Not all Red commanders had such a poor opinion of the help that the army received from the Germans. In March 1932, Ivan Griaznov, the deputy chief of the UMM, sent a report to Voroshilov in which he listed the achievements of Kazan. He noted first that the school had allowed the army to train sixty-five men of the command staff for tank and motorized/mechanized units. The Germans had also shown the army how to teach tactics and techniques for driving the vehicles, and in the future the UMM hoped to use Kazan for acquainting commanders with German combat vehicles, and for studying methods of supply and the tactical use of tank units.[35] On the technical side Griaznov thought that Kazan had contributed

32. "Stenograficheskii otchet rasshirennoe zasedanie RVS SSSR, 20–25 October 1932," RGVA, f. 4, op. 18, d. 39, l. 109. The Soviet commander's poor opinion of the German army was more than reciprocated by German officers who believed in the decisive nature of the armor forces. See Erich von Manstein, Aus einem Soldatenleben 1887–1939 (Bonn: Athenäum, 1958), 146–50.

33. David Stone discusses the galvanizing influence of events in Manchuria in Hammer and Rifle: The Militarization of the Soviet Union, 1926–1933 (Lawrence: University Press of Kansas, 2000), 184–209.

34. See above, chapter 4.

35. Report from Griaznov to Voroshilov, 14 March 1932, RGVA, f. 33987, op. 3, d. 375, ll. 113–15.

profoundly to the Red Army's armor program. The Soviets had "borrowed" the Krupp suspension system (used in the T-28); the welded body of German tanks (used in the T-26, B-T, and T-28); the internal arrangement of the crew positions in the bow of the German medium tank (incorporated in the T-28 and T-35); German instruments for seeing out of the tank (adapted to form the viewing cupola of the T-26 and T-35, while German periscope tank sights formed the basis for experimental sights on the T-26, B-T, T-28, and T-35). Griaznov obviously believed that the work at Kazan still had a great deal to offer the Red Army, and even listed numerous ways that the Soviets could benefit from German technology and command techniques. At the end of the report, Griaznov asked for an increase in the number of Soviet officers and engineers studying at Kazan, an indication of his continued confidence in the value of German aid.[36]

But as Soviet industry became more proficient at producing tanks, an appeal to the technical help received from Germany no longer served as a justification for continuing the collaboration. In 1930–31 the country could produce "only" 740 tanks each year, a number which increased to nearly 4,000 by 1932–33.[37] From January to May 1932 tank production went up almost by half, and that of tankettes more than two and a half times. The army added 424 tanks and tankettes during this five-month period and mechanized units grew by one-fifth.[38] The latest mobilization plan, Variant No. 12, recognized the new reality in tank production while, like so many earlier plans, continuing to dream of even greater numbers of machines for the future. The plan, approved in May 1932, required 13,800 light tanks, 2,000 mediums, and 4,000 tankettes for the next war.[39] While there would be many reasons for the impending break in the secret military collaboration, the growing proficiency in production, and a corresponding independence from foreign help, were vital ingredients in the Soviet decision.

The increases in production also affected plans for organizing the new masses of tanks. In January 1932 two commanders submitted their proposals for armor units, one arguing that the corps should be uniformly armed with fast-moving B-Ts rather than mixing in slower tanks, while the other pushed for a complete

36. Ibid., l. 113.

37. M. Zakharov, "O teorii glubokoi operatsii," VIZh, no. 10 (October 1970): 11.

38. Report by Chief of the UMM on preparation of mechanized forces during winter period 1932, RGVA, f. 31811, op. 2, d. 194, l. 689. By January 1932 the number of tank regiments had increased to nine and to fifteen in June, while seven more mechanized brigades were brought into existence. List of chiefs of staff for new units entitled "O spisochnom sostave nachal'nikov shtabov stroevykh chastei za 1931 i 1932 gg.," October 1932, RGVA, f. 31983, op. 2, d. 18, l. 168. At the end of the year, the army had five detached mechanized brigades, two tank regiments, twelve mechanized regiments, four mechanized batteries (in the cavalry), and fifteen tank and sixty-five tankette battalions for rifle divisions. A. Ryzhakov, "K voprosu o stroitel'stve bronetankovykh voisk krasnoi armii v 30-e gody," VIZh, no. 8 (August 1968): 107.

39. Directive from Voroshilov's office and RKKA staff to Chief of the UMM, 6 December 1930, RGVA, f. 31811, op. 2, d. 6, l. 1.

rethinking of the army's ideas on armor.[40] This latter commander, the head of armor forces in the Leningrad military district, argued in particular that the terms "NPP," "DPP," and "DD" ("direct infantry support," "remote infantry support," and "long-range echelon") did not answer the actual conditions of battle, and wanted them replaced by a more specific partitioning of armor forces. He listed the five tasks that tanks should perform and then divided tank types along corresponding lines.[41] All these groups would coordinate their action with aviation and artillery, with the artillery concentrating on enemy artillery, not tanks. The air forces were also vital and he concluded that the best form of battle would employ at first only tanks, artillery, and aviation; the infantry could come later.[42]

To settle the question of armor force structure, the army high command set up a special commission in late 1931 to weigh the various possibilities. In March 1932 the commission recommended that the Red Army follow Tukhachevskii's concept of spreading tanks as widely as possible throughout the entire army. The army would create not only mechanized corps (consisting of mechanized brigades and other motorized elements bound organically together), but also TRGK brigades (reserve units for the combined-arms commander's use), mechanized regiments in the cavalry, and tank battalions in rifle divisions. The RVS reviewed the question two days later and decided to create two mechanized corps that would have rifle divisions as their core. Thus the 11th Rifle Division became the core for the 11th Mechanized Corps and the 45th Rifle Division was the basis for the 45th Mechanized Corps. The mechanized corps comprised a mechanized brigade of T-26 tanks (three tank battalions, a rifle–machine gun battalion, an artillery battery, engineering and antiair units); a second brigade of the same composition but with B-T tanks; a rifle brigade; and corps elements (reconnaissance, engineering, etc.) including an aircraft detachment.[43] Overall there were more than five hundred tanks and two hundred armored cars in each of the huge formations.[44] The mechanized corps would be a semiautonomous unit, acting as the central strike force for the army, and would have the burden of carrying out the majority of the missions associated with the deep operations concept.

While armor organization seemed settled by mid-1932, the exact shape of deep operations was much less certain. In July Aleksandr Egorov, now promoted to chief of staff, decided to take on this knotty problem and find a definitive solution. The result was a lengthy essay on "The Tactics and Operational Art of the Red Army at

40. Memo to Tukhachevskii and Khalepskii from Liapin, former chief of staff of the 45th Rifle Division, 14 January 1932, RGVA, f. 31811, op. 2, d. 232, ll. 166–69.

41. Booklet by V. S. Kokhanovskii, Chief of Armor Forces, "Novye tendentsii v boevom primenenii tankov," 13 May 1932, RGVA, f. 31811, op. 2, d. 110, ll. 1–3.

42. Ibid., ll. 5–6.

43. Ryzhakov, "K voprosu o stroitel'stve bronetankovykh voisk," 107.

44. G. K. Zhukov, *Vospominaniia i razmyshleniia*, 10th rev. ed., vol. 1 (Moscow: Avtor [nasledniki], 1990), 190.

a New Stage." Egorov began by agreeing that modern technology allowed one to "strike the opponent simultaneously at all depths of his position."[45] But what exactly did this mean? In his description, the attack had to be extremely mobile, based on a tight combination of all arms, and work to turn an initial break-in into an operational breakthrough. The assault would start with a short artillery barrage followed by the first forward motion of the infantry and the DD tanks. This armor group would consist of medium or Christie (B-T) tanks, which would destroy the enemy's artillery batteries, headquarters, communications, and so on, assisted by artillery and air forces. As the infantry came forward for their assault, tank group DPP (the second echelon) would move forward with them, overtake the slower foot soldiers, and attack heavy machine gun placements, antitank weapons, and forward artillery. NPP, the third echelon, would then attack with the infantry, using the disarray in the opponent's fire system to head quickly for the depths of his positions. The NPP tanks would work closely with the infantry, but once they had penetrated three to four kilometers into the enemy's positions, a crisis period would begin in which the exhausted infantry would be without their artillery support and might suffer a counterattack by the opponent. To make certain that the opponent's resistance was completely crushed, assault aircraft, which had been attacking the reserves and landing parachutists in the enemy's rear, would turn to concentrate on approaching reserves, while the DD tanks switched from their first objectives to take care of withdrawing or approaching enemy columns, the DPP tanks would support the infantry, while the NPP tanks destroyed the opponent's second echelons.[46] The depth of the attack during the first twenty-four hours could reach eighty to one hundred kilometers while aircraft went as deep as four hundred kilometers.[47] Egorov saw the problem central to this doctrine as the coordination of the thrust from the front with the assault on the operational depths of the opponent. If done properly – and the army did not yet know how to carry that off – the two attacks together would lead to a rapid break-in along the entire front and the encirclement and destruction of the enemy.[48]

A few months later, in their report on the results of testing with the new brigade, Egorov and Khalepskii suggested that the Red Army could look to the British military to find an answer to their questions about organizing deep operations. Not only were the British assumed to have the most advanced views on mechanized warfare, but it was now apparent that the echelon schemes proposed by Egorov, Triandafillov, Tukhachevskii, and others were very like British ideas. As they pointed out, the British system also had three waves: a "fire echelon" that forced the opponent to turn their antitank weapons on it; a "maneuver echelon" that attracted any

45. Egorov, "Taktika i operativnoe iskusstvo RKKA na novom etape," 10 July 1932, RGVA, f. 31983, op. 2, d. 18, ll. 161, 158–57.

46. Ibid., ll. 157–55.

47. Ibid., l. 136.

48. Ibid., l. 137.

remaining antitank fire; and the "echelon of the main blow" which attacked the enemy's flanks and rear, deciding the battle.[49] Throughout the early thirties Soviet descriptions of armor tactics would fluctuate between British and Red Army designations for the three echelons, showing that British thought was clearly influencing how Soviet commanders thought about armor warfare.

As these images of deep battle/deep operations show, the Soviet army had reached a consensus over the basic form of future warfare. The next conflict, presumably beginning as a positional war, would be decided quickly by the combined might of huge armor, artillery, and air forces organized in waves, which would strike the entire operational depths of the enemy. Yet the exact tactics that the army would use, the specifics of this overall doctrine, remained uncertain. The two questions that would consume the attention of the Red Army were exactly those that the German army also found most vexing: How would the echelons coordinate their assault over such vast distances? And how would the slow-moving infantry work with the tanks, which were supposed to drive as quickly as possible toward the enemy's rear? Over the next four years discussions on armor use within the Soviet military would focus on working out these details. The Soviets, like the Germans, believed implicitly that success in war was possible only when all forces cooperated closely, working together for the same goal.[50] In deep operations this aspect became even more important as armor, aircraft, infantry, parachutists, and even cavalry had to work as a unit on far-flung sectors of the battlefield (the front and rear) to achieve the simultaneous suppression of the enemy's forces.

During 1932 the army dedicated most of its attention to working out the coordination of all four main arms with the new armor forces. The role of aviation seemed simple. Air forces and mechanized armies were "two sides of one coin," as Tukhachevskii put it, and had to cooperate fully to bring about victory.[51] He so believed in the necessity of air power for deep battle that he would later invent the term "air-mechanization" to describe the new system of armaments (aircraft, tanks, radio, and chemical weapons), that had arisen from the world war.[52] Aleksandr Sediakin, who was in charge of combat training, agreed that the army had to accord aircraft almost equal status with tanks in deep battle, although he was concerned

---

49. Report by Uborevich and Khalepskii, "Opytnye ucheniia mekhanizirovannoi brigady v 1932 godu v Belorusskom Voennom Okruge," 13 October 1932, RGVA, f. 31811, op. 2, d. 101, ll. 58–59. Egorov again recommended the "English" concept of three echelons later that month. "Stenograficheskii otchet rasshirennoe zasedanie RVS SSSR," 20–25 October 1932, RGVA, f. 4, op. 18, d. 39, l. 4.

50. See e.g. "Tau" [Tukhachevskii], *Motorizatsiia i mekhanizatsiia armii i voina* (Moscow: Gosudarstvennoe voennoe izdatel'stvo, 1933), 102.

51. Ibid., 105.

52. M. N. Tukhachevskii, "Novye voprosy voiny," written 1931–32, translated and reprinted in Richard Simpkin, *Deep Battle: The Brainchild of Marshal Tukhachevskii* (London: Brassey, 1987), 136–37.

that airplanes were not yet able to bomb accurately enough to fulfill the tactics planned for them.[53] He saw the other component of air combat, parachutists who would disrupt communications and command centers, as equally vital. These landing forces could work with tank-borne troops in the deep rear to complete the encirclement begun by armor.[54]

The role of the cavalry in deep battle was more controversial. It was not unusual for Soviet commanders, like some German officers, to argue that mechanized units themselves were the cavalry of future war, able to fulfill the missions that the horse units once had, but more quickly and efficiently.[55] Other commanders asserted that the horse was still an integral part of modern warfare, and that horse and machine had to work together in order to achieve success. This was seen as especially true now that modern cavalry, with its tanks, artillery, and aircraft, was nothing like the earlier force of the same name.[56] Tukhachevskii, at least in public, condemned any "erroneous contrasting" of cavalry forces with mechanized forces, arguing that both were equally necessary. In a speech delivered in late October, he commented that some commanders had tried to say that the cavalry had had its day, but in fact precisely the opposite was true. Mechanization, rather than making the cavalry obsolete, had instead caused its role, when properly modernized, to increase dramatically. Yet in a telling sentence that showed his true thinking on the subject, he then warned that neither the cavalry nor the infantry could stay in their old forms, without mechanization.[57] Cavalry forces could survive, in other words, only if they became part of the machine army of the future.

Maneuvers held in Belorussia with the mechanized brigade confirmed that old-style horse-only cavalry would have great difficulty in combat against tanks. Commenting on one attack by tanks against cavalry, Uborevich and Khalepskii reported that although the machines had at first suffered severe losses, they were soon able to do exactly as they wished against the horse units. Their general conclusion was that "comparing these two types of forces in the given tactical episode speaks in favor of a small group of tanks against a large cavalry regiment. And this in spite of the fact that the cavalry began quickly and efficiently and the artillery opened fire in good time."[58] Their conclusion was supported by another study, which showed that in three different kinds of combat situations that matched cavalry against an

53. Stenogram of report by Sediakin at the Frunze Academy, 9 December 1932, RGVA, f. 4, op. 14, d. 1040, l. 13.

54. Ibid., l. 42.

55. See e.g. P. D. Korkodinov, *Motorizatsiia i mekhanizatsiia sovremennykh armii: Sredstva, moto-mekhanizirovannye voiska i ikh boevoe primenenie* (Leningrad: LOIZ, 1932), 66–67.

56. "Stenograficheskii otchet rasshirennoe zasedanie RVS SSSR," 20–25 October 1932, RGVA, f. 4, op. 18, d. 39, l. 61.

57. Ibid., l. 110.

58. Report by Uborevich and Khalepskii, "Opytnye ucheniia mekhanizirovannoi brigady v 1932 godu v belorusskom voennom okruge," 13 October 1932, RGVA, f. 31811, op. 2, d. 101, l. 22.

armor brigade, the tanks would have either destroyed or driven away the horse units.[59] In cooperation rather than competition with each other, both forces had done well, leading commanders to conclude that coordinating the action of a mechanized brigade with cavalry and aviation could achieve the complete destruction of a rifle division.[60] In the end, the Soviet high command chose to believe this latter lesson rather than experiences that seemed to show that the days of the horse were numbered: the Red Cavalry could not, and therefore would not, be disbanded.

If the issue of the cavalry's future was a sensitive one, the effect that mechanization and the adoption of deep operations could have on the infantry was downright explosive. The materiel versus morale debate may have ended with a compromise between the two positions, but the overwhelming successes of the industrialization drive, and the promise of deep operations, once again gave credence to the claims of those who saw the machine triumphant in modern war. Despite his earlier support for the "morale" side of the argument, Tukhachevskii would now write that during the world war the infantry became incapable of independently attacking a machine gun defense and that therefore the significance of the infantry as an offensive force was reduced.[61] Another commander went even further, writing that the infantry would play a subsidiary role compared to the armor units of motorized/mechanized formations. Infantry were not necessary for the strike but were present merely to strengthen the tanks' blow.[62]

Once Soviet theorists had gone this far they began to have trouble differentiating a socialist mechanized army from the imperialist tank army envisaged by Fuller. After all, the Soviets had been most critical of Fuller precisely when he had described the kind of military that the Soviet Union was now intent on building. Some writers, such as Ammosov, an instructor at the Frunze Academy who wrote the standard textbook on armor tactics, tried to argue that Fuller had corrected his earlier extreme "tankist" views, making it possible to agree fully with the British theorist. Fuller had realized, for instance, that tanks were unable to act without the aid of other forces and that mechanized units needed defensive capabilities as well as a strong striking force.[63] In a lecture delivered at the end of March 1933, an unidentified speaker went even further in his praise of Fuller. He called the British officer's ideas of 1919 "the first plan for a simultaneous blow on a significant depth of the opponent's positions."[64] Like deep battle, Fuller foresaw high-speed tanks breaking through to attack the enemy's rear, while other tanks with artillery and infantry

59. Ibid., ll. 31–37.
60. Ibid., ll. 44–46.
61. Ibid.
62. S. Ammosov, *Taktika motomekhsoedinenii*, 2d ed. (Moscow: Gosudarstvennoe Voennoe Izdatel'stvo, 1932), 15–16.
63. Ibid., 7–10, 12–13.
64. "Tezisy k dokladu: 'Mekhvoiska i glubokaia taktika,'" addressed to Stoinov, 31 March 1933, RGVA, f. 31811, op. 2, d. 183, l. 130–31.

attacked the front.[65] The speaker then spent a good deal of time discussing the development of Fuller's thought, disagreeing with his small army while honoring him as the "ideologist of mechanization . . . who first advanced a sound theory about a mechanized army and posed the question concerning the destruction of an opponent in a significant depth of his position." He even thought that Fuller's ideas about using partisans and dividing the army into an offensive "tank army" and a defensive "antitank army" were "interesting."[66] In his summing up, the speaker said that although Fuller's mechanized army was

> the expeditionary strike army of English imperialism . . . the idea itself, the proposition that is the foundation of its operation, is suitable for refinement and testing in practice (maneuvers). It may produce guiding principles that will be valuable for final working out [and] that by their nature demand the infliction of deep blows on the opponent's entire position, from the front line to the deep rear. Yet the activity of independent mechanized forces ought to be coordinated with the activities of the whole army ("occupying army" in Fuller's terminology), on the one hand, and with the ever deeper activity of the air forces, on the other.[67]

As these articles and others make clear, the manufacturing prowess of the Soviet Union had in fact created a troubling dilemma for the Red Army. On the one hand, the high command had an ideological commitment to a mass army consisting of the entire proletariat – every worker and peasant had to participate in the fight against capitalist encirclement. Yet technological progress, which socialism also believed was inevitable and good, seemed to dictate an increasing reliance on machines and a far more constrained role for ordinary human beings. Recognizing this problem, Tukhachevskii's armor specialist in Leningrad suggested that political workers in the army had to emphasize that there could be no division between men and materiel in armor forces, adding that "[t]he slogan 'Tankist and machine – one indivisible fighting whole' will be the truest [principle] for the organization of all political work in tank units."[68] In a speech before a meeting of force commanders, Voroshilov, too, sought to restore the balance between man and machine, which he thought had been lost over the last few years. "There is an extreme opinion," he began, "And it has its supporters in the Red Army, that motorized-mechanized forces are the prototype of future armies, that they ought to replace almost all other arms." But, he warned,

> That if you please is pure Fullerism. Such a theory we cannot hold here in the Red Army and, in my personal opinion, we ought not even to popularize such a theory.

---

65. Ibid., ll. 130–34.
66. Ibid., ll. 134–36.
67. Ibid., ll. 136–37.
68. V. S. Kokhanovskii, Chief of Armor Forces, lecture, "Novye tendentsii v boevom primenenii tankov," 13 May 1932, RGVA, f. 31811, op. 2, d. 110, l. 7.

This theory is not for the Red Army, not for the Soviet Union, not for a state that takes up one-sixth of the land on the globe. Our borders are very extensive and extremely diverse in terms of geography, climate, ethnography, and other characteristics. Such simplified Fullerism might in practice lead either to a belittling of the significance of the old types of forces or to a series of questionable expenditures – most importantly unnecessary experiments. And in both cases this could lead to a weakening of our defense. That is why this theory does not suit us, it can cause harm.

At the same time he cautioned against the other extreme, an attitude which said that "motorized-mechanized forces are nonsense; one ought not to take them seriously because good infantry, good cavalry with good artillery, with well-organized machine gun units and perhaps, yes, even with a small number of tanks, can destroy any motorized/mechanized unit. This other extreme is also incorrect and also harmful." The RVS and the state, he concluded, had decided that the newly created motorized/mechanized formations *and* detached tank units best met the interests and objectives of their country's defense. The Red Army unquestionably had to have independent mechanized formations, but a modern army also had to have infantry and cavalry strengthened by the motor and armor.[69]

With this definitive statement from the head of the military, commanders understood that they now had to criticize Fuller's "imperialist" ideas and clearly differentiate them from accepted Soviet doctrine. In one of his major works on motorization and mechanization, Tukhachevskii spent a great deal of space showing where Fuller was wrong and how his own ideas differed from those of the British writer.[70] The problem that the Soviets had with Fuller was, of course, his concept of a war of tanks, with infantry doing nothing more than serving and guarding the machines. This was "building a house on sand," Tukhachevskii now argued, since the mechanized army demanded human qualities like initiative, inventiveness, and heroism.[71] The Soviet commander could not, however, hide his admiration for Fuller as the man who had first described attacking at all depths and striking at the "brain" of the enemy army.[72] Some specific concepts, such as dividing the army between reconnaissance, holding, and pursuit armies were, he had to admit, interesting and practicable.[73] His contrasting examination of British and French ideas, the first representing complete mechanization and the latter simple motorization, showed that despite his superficial condemnation of Fuller, he actually agreed with the key components of Fuller's thought on the future of warfare.[74]

69. "Stenograficheskii otchet rasshirennoe zasedanie RVS SSSR," 20–25 October 1932, RGVA, f. 4, op. 18, d. 39, l. 139.
70. "Tau," *Motorizatsiia i mekhanizatsiia*, 105–33.
71. Ibid., 125.
72. Ibid., 37.
73. Ibid., 111–14.
74. Ibid., 176–79.

Other commanders also sought to counter what they viewed as a belittling of the human element in warfare or an "excessive" confidence in machines that admiration for Fuller might bring. A typical monograph argued that armor units were incapable of holding terrain or of deciding independent operational missions without the aid of infantry, strategic cavalry, and motorized formations.[75] One of the chiefs of military training even attacked commanders, men he called "mechanizers," who wanted to use tanks to help other tanks forward, rather than using them to aid the infantry in its advance.[76] The most comprehensive attack on Fuller appeared in a book on the four problems with Fuller's "pure" mechanized army. As the writer pointed out, it was "impossible to manage" without infantry; armor units were incapable of waging defensive warfare; tanks were practically helpless at night; and finally they were helpless on certain kinds of terrain.[77] "Fulleresque" units without infantry could exist only in union with infantry and cavalry in large combined formations, such as motorized and mechanized divisions. In any case, the author noted, Fuller's mechanized units were ill-suited to the character of the Soviet theater "since this [type of] unit will meet with difficulties on every step of its path, called by Fuller 'the infantry areas,' in which a machine without infantry cannot do anything (forests, defiles in swampy areas, river banks, etc.)."[78] The Soviet army acknowledged that tanks formed the basis, the "shock core," of mechanized units, he continued, but did not deny the importance of man. The infantry would have to be motorized and perhaps even protected by armor, but was absolutely vital for warfare.[79]

If the army had (once again) definitively answered the question of the infantry's worth in machine warfare, the experiences of the fall exercises failed to settle other problems with deep operations. The one bright spot was a series of studies of the experimental brigade, which seemed to show its worth as an independent unit, able to achieve operational objectives when cooperating with other forces.[80] Otherwise the exercises only raised new difficulties. One of these was a realization of the quickness with which situations would change on the new armor battlefield. Since time was extremely important in a battle of machines, the Red Army had to push its mechanized forces to use every minute wisely.[81] Soviet tankists had, however, lit-

75. Ammosov, *Taktika motomekhsoedinenii*, 25. Compare Korkodinov, *Motorizatsiia i mekhanizatsiia sovremennykh armii*, 25.

76. Questions on Egorov's essay "Taktika i operativnoe iskusstvo RKKA na novom etape" from Tkachev to Egorov, 2 September 1932, RGVA, f. 31983, op. 2, d. 18, l. 165.

77. S. N. Krasil'nikov, *Organizatsiia krupnykh obshchevoiskovykh soedinenii (Proshedshee, nastoiashchee i budushchee)* (Moscow: OGIZ – Gosudarstvennoe voennoe izdatel'stvo, 1933), 275.

78. Ibid., 265.

79. Ibid., 276–82.

80. Report by Uborevich and Khalepskii, "Opytnye ucheniia mekhanizirovannoi brigady v 1932 godu v belorusskom voennom okruge," 13 October 1932, RGVA, f. 31811, op. 2, d. 101, ll. 58–59.

81. See stenograph of report sent to Tukhachevskii by Sediakin, "Stenogramma doklada Nachal'nika Boevoi podgotovki RKKA tov. Sediakina v Voennoi Akademii imeni Frunze 9/XII-32 g.," RGVA, f. 31983, op. 2, d. 20, l. 565.

tle tactical experience and they did not take full advantage of the armor forces' speed during the exercises. The reassembling of armor forces after an attack was a procedure that obviously wasted precious time, and Khalepskii and Uborevich suggested quickly giving mechanized units new missions after their first objectives were attained.[82] This was but a minor point when compared to the other problems experienced by the new tank units. Egorov bluntly stated that the exercises showed the army did not know how to use motorized/mechanized forces at all. Commanders simply threw them around from one flank to the other without any plan and did not coordinate them well with the general mission of the army.[83]

Sediakin, the chief of military training, agreed with Egorov that the army needed more practice in the implementation of the new doctrine, but he had a more sophisticated explanation for the problem than simple incompetence. He noted that deep operations demanded a deep echeloning of forces and of mobile reserves, with motorized forces in both the rear and the front. The rear would have to be large, and demanded a quick establishment of lines of communication and supply.[84] Advance planning for deep operations would therefore have to be more detailed and comprehensive than anything attempted by the young Red Army. It was this planning that Sediakin now proposed to undertake. While Triandafillov, Kalinovskii, Tukhachevskii, and Egorov were the theoretical innovators of deep operations, it was Sediakin who developed the programs for maneuvers, exercises, and studies that would allow the army to put the deep battle part of the doctrine into practice.

Sediakin's concerns first surfaced during the autumn of 1932, when he became frustrated by what he saw as "abstraction" and philosophizing about deep tactics, rather than using common sense to work out what actual combat would look like. After a year and a half of talking about deep battle, he said, no one within the Red Army had worked concretely on the comprehensive exposition of the tactical-technical means for it.[85] The army had to decide, for instance, whether infantry or tanks should begin the action and whether the DD or DPP echelons should attack first.[86] The entire question of the DD echelon in fact was not thought through theoretically, let alone practically.[87] "[O]n maps, plans, on paper, and in exercises where

82. Report by Uborevich and Khalepskii, "Opytnye ucheniia mekhanizirovannoi brigady v 1932 godu v belorusskom voennom okruge," 13 October 1932, RGVA, f. 31811, op. 2, d. 101, l. 28, 60–61.

83. "Stenograficheskii otchet rasshirennoe zasedanie RVS SSSR," 20–25 October 1932, RGVA, f. 4, op. 18, d. 39, l. 2.

84. Stenograph of report sent to Tukhachevskii by Sediakin, "Stenogramma doklada Nachal'nika Boevoi podgotovki RKKA tov. Sediakina v Voennoi Akademii imeni Frunze 9/XII-32 g.," RGVA, f. 31983, op. 2, d. 20, l. 543.

85. Stenograph of report by Sediakin at the Frunze Academy, 9 December 1932. RGVA, f. 4, op. 14, d. 1040, l. 36.

86. Ibid., ll. 26–27.

87. Stenograph of report sent to Tukhachevskii by Sediakin, "Stenogramma doklada

there is no opponent, everything turns out well for us: tank regiments and battalions move as if they were immortal, move where they want and as they want. In so doing they move in formations which are unsuitable if one takes into account the reality of fire from antitank artillery . . . [88]

Sediakin's response to the air of unreality surrounding deep battle was to set up teams of planners, each of which was given a specific tactical problem to solve. There were a multitude of practical questions that had to be worked out, including what the army's operational structure ought to be and the use of the different types of forces (mechanized, combined-arms, air forces, and parachutists); how deep one could and ought to carry the effort; how to organize the operational development of the first break-in so that it would lead directly into an operational breakthrough, completely shattering the enemy; and how to isolate the first break-in from the enemy to prevent a concentration of his reserves against it.[89] Once the teams had gotten down to work, Sediakin gave them more specific issues to study.[90] Throughout 1932 and into early 1933 the teams reported back with their solutions to the many tactical and logistical problems associated with deep battle. By the beginning of 1933 Sediakin hoped to unite the experimental results into a scientific instruction manual that would provide commanders in the field with a detailed plan for fighting a deep battle. From 5 to 9 January there would then be a series of studies looking at the separate questions of deep tactics.[91] The entire enterprise was strikingly different from the attitude of the German army, which believed in training men in the basics of combat and then allowing officers on the spot to apply the principles in actual combat as conditions demanded. In contrast Sediakin followed typical Soviet military practice by trying, through his studies on deep battle, to give commanders a precise recipe for success. The officer in command had only to follow directions and victory would ensue.

The conclusions reached by Sediakin's groups were remarkable for their specificity. An analysis of the timing of tank attacks during deep battle showed all three echelons achieving their goals within twenty hours through a three-phase attack.[92] Another deep battle schedule was even more detailed, with a four-phase attack covering the first two hours of the offensive. By two hours after the start of the offen-

Nachal'nika Boevoi podgotovki RKKA tov. Sediakina v Voennoi Akademii imeni Frunze 9/XII-32 g.," RGVA, f. 31983, op. 2, d. 20, l. 547.

88. Stenograph of report by Sediakin at the Frunze Academy, 9 December 1932. RGVA, f. 4, op. 14, d. 1040, l. 18.

89. G. Isserson, "Razvitie teorii sovetskogo operativnogo iskusstva v 30-e gody," VIZh, no. 1 (January 1965): 42–44.

90. "Plan Izucheniia voprosov Glubokoi Taktike v U.B.P.," RGVA, f. 31983, op. 2, d. 20, l. 483.

91. Report by Tkachev, "Plan prorabotki voprosov glubokoi taktike v U.B.P.," RGVA, f. 31983, op. 2, d. 20, ll. 480–79.

92. Report by Stepnoi and Kolchigin, "Normy nasyshcheniia tankami s divizii i korpusa pri proryve oboronitel'no polosy v usloviiakh manevrennoi voiny na glavnom naprovlenii," RGVA, f. 31983, op. 2, d. 20, l. 340.

sive, all three echelons would have attacked, suppressed their first targets, and begun to neutralize their main objectives.[93] Investigations into another question, likely losses from antitank weapons, estimated that the enemy would be able to destroy 30 to 60 percent of the tanks employed in a deep battle offensive.[94] There were several reasons for the high losses, most importantly the expected strength of antiarmor defenses. An analysis done by Sediakin's teams in fact argued that deep battle could occur only when a favorable correlation of forces between offense and defense existed. If offensive firepower was insufficient and the defense strong, then deep battle might be unfeasible. From this fact the report concluded that the instructions which would come out of these studies were not meant to supersede PU-29, but rather to detail exactly under what conditions it would be possible to conduct deep battle. If it was impossible to organize deep battle, then the attack would be organized on the basis of PU-29, with some help from the new manual.[95]

Another report produced by Sediakin's teams tried to rationalize the command and control of the various forces and groups involved in the battle. The authors suggested that the central corps command would have control of the DD artillery and tanks as well as the assault aircraft, landing troops and parachutists. PP (infantry support) artillery and DPP tanks would be subordinated to divisional commanders; regimental commanders would command detachments of PP artillery and "sometimes" the DPP tank echelon; while commanders of battalions would control NPP artillery and tanks. Battalions would take charge of suppressing the enemy's defenses to a depth of two to three kilometers, divisions and regiments from three to four kilometers, and corps from six to fifteen kilometers.[96]

The most intractable problem with command and control was, however, the DD echelon. These tanks would penetrate the furthest into the enemy's rear and commanders would therefore have difficulty communicating with them, let alone keeping their activity in line with overall plans – especially without radios. This was not the only problem with the DD tanks. An investigation of the fuel expenditure by the echelon showed that the amount of gasoline the tanks carried in their own reserves would allow only thirty kilometers of movement during battle or forty-eight without battle.[97] Another report concluded that the shortcomings of the T-26 made

93. Report by Ernest, Assistant Chief of I Dept. I Directorate of the UMM, and Kolchigin, "Skhema Planovoi tablitsy boia . . . s divizii," RGVA, f. 31983, op. 2, d. 20, l. 332.

94. "K voprosu ob ispol'zovanii sredstv podavleniia v glubokom boiu," RGVA, f. 31983, op. 2, d. 20, l. 478.

95. "Vremennye, predvaritel'nye, iskhodnye, raschetnye materialy po 'Ukazaniia,'" RGVA, f. 31983, op. 2, d. 20, ll. 470–69. Tukhachevskii also did not see deep battle as a negation of PU-29. "Stenograficheskii otchet rasshirennoe zasedanie RVS SSSR," 20–25 October 1932, RGVA, f. 4, op. 18, d. 39, l. 110.

96. Report by Rubchov, "Plan Razrabotki ukazanii voiskam po voprosam 'Glubokoi taktiki,'" undated, RGVA, f. 31983, op. 2, d. 20, l. 491.

97. Report by Kolchigin, Chief of I Department of I Directorate of the UMM, and Kryzhanovskii, Assistant Chief of the I Department of the I Directorate of the UMM, "Spravka po raskhodu goriuchego i boepripasov tankovoi gruppy DD," 4 February 1933, RGVA, f. 31983, op. 2, d. 20, l. 349.

the DD echelon too weak.[98] One possible solution was to replace the light, and lightly armed, T-26 with a medium tank equipped with a heavy 76 mm main gun and machine guns.[99] Group DD could also be reinforced with "chemical tanks," which would destroy the crews of the enemy's tanks with fast-acting chemical weapons.[100] If further fortified by sapper tanks, self-propelled artillery, and infantry landing forces, the DD echelon would become a truly formidable force, able to carry out independent missions deep in the enemy's rear.[101]

The military training directorate's work culminated in the *Provisional Instructions for Organizing Deep Battle*, which was published on schedule in early 1933. The objectives of the *Provisional Instructions* were "to establish a unified view by the Red Army command staff on the organization and control of 'deep tactic' basics"; "to establish preliminary theoretical, and tactical, and technical standards, partially proven by experience, for calculating the combat use of the basic types of forces in deep battle"; and "to outline a system and method for educating the command staff and forces in deep tactics."[102] By following the prescriptions outlined in the *Provisional Instructions*, a commander would be able to achieve the ultimate goal of deep battle, the "almost simultaneous neutralization of the defensive zone in all its depth."[103] The neutralization would include not only the tactical rear of the opponent, but also his operational positions, leading to a complete rout.[104] The "simultaneous" part of the deep battle definition did not mean exact "astronomical" simultaneity, the *Provisional Instructions* noted; one could consider the principle observed "if the wedging-in of the means to neutralize [the enemy's defenses] and the attacks on the important deep objectives of the opponent's defense . . . disrupt the [enemy's] fire system and draw attention away from the main forces of the attacking infantry."[105] Deep battle was thus the ultimate answer to the offense's weakness in the last war, facilitating and speeding the infantry's attack during a break-in while preventing the opponent's reserves from repairing the breach.[106]

Reflecting the lessons learned from Sediakin's intensive work, the *Provisional Instructions* proposed that deep battle was possible only with a certain correlation of

98. "K voprosu ob ispol'zovanii sredstv podavleniia v glubokom boiu," RGVA, f. 31983, op. 2, d. 20, ll. 475–74.

99. "Ideia glubokoi operatsii i glubokogo boia," RGVA, f. 31983, op. 2, d. 20, ll. 188–87.

100. Report by Semenov, Chief I Sector I Directorate of Chemical Warfare of the RKKA, "Material po boevomu primeneniiu khimicheskogo orudiia v razrabatyvaemye UBP ukazaniia voiskam po voprosam 'Glubokoi taktiki,'" RGVA, f. 31983, op. 2, d. 20, ll. 390–80.

101. "K voprosu ob ispol'zovanii sredstv podavleniia v glubokom boiu," RGVA, f. 31983, op. 2, d. 20, ll. 475–74.

102. *Vremennye ukazaniia Po organizatsii glubokogo boia. (Nastupatel'nyi boi)*, Izdanie Upravlenie Boevoi Podgotovki Sukhoputnykh Sil RKKA 1933 god., February 1933, RGVA, f. 31983, op. 2, d. 33, l. 204. (unpublished draft)

103. "Ukazanie po organizatsii glubokogo boia (proekt)," RGVA, f. 31983, op. 2, d. 20, l. 149.

104. Ibid., l. 146.

105. Ibid., l. 145.

106. Ibid., ll. 148–47.

forces between offense and defense. If a favorable relationship did not exist, the
army would organize battle according to PU-29, although it was also possible to
seek to change the correlation.[107] In a bow to the pressure for more emphasis on
the aerial component of deep battle, the *Provisional Instructions* listed air power and
parachutists as the first element of the doctrine, with motorized/mechanized formations and mechanized cavalry as the second component.[108] The manual then
proceeded to provide detailed instructions for organizing, deploying for, and implementing deep battle. Every specific element of the new doctrine, from the types
and numbers of tanks, their organizational structures and cooperation with other
forces, to the precise timing of each phase of the attack was provided for.[109] The
lengthy appendices to the manual included much of the raw data used by Sediakin's
teams to form their conclusions. These showed that Sediakin had been right in his
judgment that one of the greatest problems with deep battle would be supply and
refueling — a problem to which the Soviets still had no answer.[110]

Soon after the manual appeared, the RVS issued Order No. 0100, naming deep
battle as the official doctrine of the Red Army, and defining the parameters of the
concept along the same lines as the new manual.[111] With the issuance of these two
coherent and consistent formulations of its armor doctrine, the Red Army's attitudes toward its German partners became much more critical. Soviet commanders
had always respected the Reichswehr for its professionalism, its superior educational and training methods, and its superb implementation of tactics. Now,
however, commanders felt themselves more advanced than the German army in
technology and doctrine. When Sediakin attended the September 1933 Reichswehr
maneuvers, he was not at all impressed with German use of armor, reporting that
a tank attack and antitank defense had not been shown in action or worked at in
the exercises, while the final tank attack could not be taken seriously.[112] He commented on the lack of "up-to-dateness" of the Reichswehr and concluded that

> diligence there is undoubtedly in both study and work. But if commanders and
> forces diligently strove to give a sample of their military art, then that military art,
> it ought to be admitted, already lags behind modern demands and is not a model
> for the Red Army. The Red Army, in spite of huge shortcomings in the culture of

107. Ibid., ll. 145, 103.

108. Ibid., l. 146.

109. *Vremennye ukazaniia Po organizatsii glubokogo boia. (Nastupatel'nyi boi)*, Izdanie Upravlenie
Boevoi Podgotovki Sukhoputnykh Sil RKKA 1933 god., February 1933, RGVA, f. 31983, op. 2, d.
33, ll. 208–55.

110. The T-26 could only travel 100 to 120 kilometers on the fuel allotted at the start of battle,
while the T-27 could advance 60 to 80 kilometers. Ibid., l. 288.

111. See e.g. "Stenograficheskii otchet rasshirennoe zasedanie RVS SSSR 16–18 noia. 1933 ob
itogakh 1933 g. i tseli 1934 g.," RGVA, f. 4, op. 18, d. 39, ll. 13, 50–51, 218.

112. Report by Sediakin to Berzin, 19 January 1933, RGVA, f. 31983, op. 2, d. 103, l. 201.
Tukhachevskii also attended the exercises. Ibid., ll. 149–48.

its technical command staff, in spite of huge shortcomings in its training, already has appreciably better organized and educated forces, undoubtedly tactically more modern training, and its leaders and staff have a higher military art.[113]

The Soviet army and government had other reasons to become critical of the Germans in 1933. Hitler had come to power in January of that year, promising to rearm his country and fight Bolshevism. His overt anticommunism was in some ways not that far from the more disguised attitudes of other leaders of Germany, including his immediate predecessor Franz von Papen.[114] Hitler's open hostility toward the Soviet Union was, however, an organic part of his worldview and as such was seen by the Soviets as irreconcilable with a continuation of normal friendly relations between the two nations. Although Soviet officials outwardly expressed their desire for continued good relations, by the summer of 1933, and especially after the Reichstag fire, they realized that a parting with Hitler's Germany was inevitable.[115]

One result of the new Soviet view of Germany was that it became impossible for Red Army commanders to express admiration for the Germans without first protesting their loyalty to Stalin and enumerating the failings of the Reichswehr. Sediakin's report is one obvious example of this attitude. Even more conspicuous is the swift change in tone by Mikhail Levandovskii, now the head of the Siberian military district, whose reports and letters clearly show the contrast between the old and new moods. Levandovskii spent several months in Germany studying at a military academy and his first letters held nothing but the highest praise for the quality of the soldiers, training, and exercises that he observed there.[116] His first comprehensive report, submitted to Voroshilov on 19 July 1933, was without ideological judgment or propaganda, consisting simply of a recital of events and his impressions of the German army, most of which were positive.[117] That same day he sent Voroshilov a revised version of the report, which was completely different in tone and content. He began with praise for Stalin, industrialization, the Red Army, and its new technology, and then moved on to criticize the Reichswehr and especially its armor doctrine.[118] Whereas the Red Army saw tanks as the decisive strike force element of warfare, affecting all tactics, the Germans did not know how tanks

113. Ibid., l. 200.

114. See Harvey Leonard Dyck, *Weimar Germany and Soviet Russia, 1926–1933: A Study in Diplomatic Instability* (New York: Columbia University Press, 1966), 250–55.

115. For outward Soviet wishes for a continuation of good relations see E. H. Carr, *German-Soviet Relations between the Two World Wars, 1919–1939* (Baltimore: Johns Hopkins University Press, 1951), 109–11.

116. See for example copy of a letter from Com. Levandovskii sent to Tkachev by Sukhrukov, 28 May 1933, RGVA, f. 31983, op. 2, d. 103, l. 322.

117. Report 1 from Levandovskii, commander of SibVO forces, to Voroshilov, 19 July 1933, RGVA, f. 33987, op. 3, d. 505, ll. 29–43.

118. Report 2 from Levandovskii to Voroshilov, 19 July 1933, RGVA, f. 33987, op. 3, d. 505, ll. 46–78.

should cooperate, did not use tanks in mass, and did not take them into consideration even when thinking about how to fight France or Poland, both of which had many tanks.[119]

Stalin's assessment of Hitler, and the new confidence inspired in the Soviets by successes in military production and doctrine, combined to produce a political decision to end the collaboration with Germany. By the spring of 1933 there were already signs that the Soviet government was considering a termination of the joint enterprises and by May the Germans became concerned enough to consult Tukhachevskii. Otto Hartmann, the new German military attaché in Moscow, spoke with the Soviet commander at length about the collaboration. He concluded that there was a serious and genuine desire on the part of the highest Soviet military figures to continue the collaboration, but that this line could only be pursued if political difficulties were settled in a form acceptable to the Soviets.[120] Tukhachevskii, however, one of the Soviet commanders most favorable toward the Reichswehr and the collaboration, was not representative of the general attitude of the Soviets toward the Germans.[121] Voroshilov and others in the government were a different matter. As we have seen, the Soviet political leadership had been dissatisfied with the results of the collaboration for the past several years and now almost welcomed the excuse to end it. Regardless of how he may have felt privately about this decision, Tukhachevskii too was bound to support his nation's policies.[122] The results of the decision were soon apparent. The Soviets did not permit any students to attend Kazan nor were there any exercises with Soviet forces in 1933.[123] The Red Army also decided not to send officers to inspect Reichswehr units as they had been accustomed to do.[124] Not all contacts were immediately cut off, but there was a more strained atmosphere when they did occur. On 11 July, Hartmann asked if Lutz could visit several men from the Red Army high command, including Khalepskii, to convey his gratitude for the cooperation at Kazan. On Berzin's memo relaying the request, Voroshilov wrote that "[w]hoever wants to make the visit may do so,

119. Ibid., ll. 62–63.

120. Report from T-3 Oberst Hartmann, military attaché in Moscow on chemical installation and collaboration, 18 May 1933, PA-AA, R31682K, E696254–E696255.

121. Even after the relationship was officially ended, the new German ambassador von Twardowski reported Tukhachevskii's remarks on the great sympathy that the Red Army had for the Reichswehr. Cover memo from von Twardowski to the Auswärtiges Amt, Tgd. Nr. A/2410, "Betr: Unterredung mit dem Stellvertreter des Kriegskommissars Tuchatschewski," 6 November 1933, BA-MA, RW 5/v, 461.

122. See e.g. report by Bockelberg on trip to the Soviet Union, 13 June 1933, BA-AA, R. 31690, p. 201a.

123. Müller, "So lebten und arbeiteten wir," 32.

124. Report from Berzin to Voroshilov, 9 August 1933, RGVA, f. 33987, op. 3, d. 504, l. 103.

but our people just shouldn't talk too much, that's all."[125] At the end of the summer, Voroshilov agreed to show certain German officers some Red Army studies and exercises, but the Reichswehr Ministry declined, with the excuse that officers were busy at summer training. In his report to Voroshilov on this development, Berzin said that the refusal was undoubtedly connected with the earlier refusal of the Red Army to send its own officers to Kazan. Voroshilov underlined the section of the report on the Reichswehr Ministry's refusal and Berzin's explanation and wrote in large letters across it, "Very good!"[126]

The change in Soviet policy soon affected the three schools as well, although there had been signs earlier in the year from the Germans that they too wanted to end this part of the cooperation. On 11 January Ernst Köstring had already told Egorov that the chief of the army command planned to close the installation at Lipetsk (the airplane school) in the fall of that year. The reason given by the Reichswehr was an urgent need to save money given the current financial situation in Germany.[127] Most of the impetus for the end of close collaboration at the three installations came, nonetheless, from the Soviet side. At Kazan, the liquidation of the school began on 20 June and by early September no Germans remained.[128] Berzin reported to Voroshilov in August that the Soviets had sent the first shipment of military material from Kazan on the eleventh of that month. He also submitted a list of every piece of equipment sent to Germany, including six large tanks and four small ones, with a note that the UMM had agreed to the shipments and that Khalepskii had no objections to sending back the materiel.[129]

If Tukhachevskii expressed regret over the ending of the collaboration, certain German officers also hoped that it might be possible to continue some sort of relationship. During May 1933 Bockelberg submitted a report on a long visit to the Soviet Union in which he spelled out why the collaboration should continue: for reasons of military policy and on grounds of armament technology.[130] He put his visit in the best light, describing his reception by the Red Army as "decidedly friendly" and noting that all its leading personalities (that is, Tukhachevskii) assured their visitors that they placed great value on close cooperation with the German army and German technology. Voroshilov and Egorov had made it plain, however, that close collaboration was possible only when the two countries pur-

125. Report from Berzin to Voroshilov, 11 August 1933, RGVA, f. 33987, op. 3, d. 504, l. 105.
126. Report from Berzin to Voroshilov, 9 August 1933, RGVA, f. 33987, op. 3, d. 504, l. 103.
127. Hartmann to Voroshilov, 22 July 1933, RGVA, f. 33987, op. 3, d. 504, ll. 54–55.
128. Report from Berzin to Voroshilov, 14 October 1933, RGVA, f. 33987, op. 3, d. 504, ll. 163–64.
129. Report from Berzin to Voroshilov, 14 August 1933, RGVA, f. 33987, op. 3, d. 504, ll. 106, 107–51.
130. Report by Bockelberg on trip to the Soviet Union, 13 June 1933, PA-AA, R. 31690, pp. 203–203a.

sued similar foreign policy goals.[131] The Germans' positive attitude continued even while the collaboration was ending. In his final report on the installations Berzin informed Voroshilov that

> in the initial period of the talks with the "friends" [i.e., the Germans], they tried to delay the liquidation of the enterprises, apparently assuming that in the process of the talks changes would occur and that their stay in the USSR would be extended for an indefinite time. At the same time, becoming convinced of the futility of this attempt, the "friends," to "save face," themselves have cut back comparatively quickly on the enterprises, declaring that this completely coincides with their wishes and that the present situation demands new forms of cooperation, which ought to persist even in the future after the liquidation of the enterprises.[132]

Blomberg also wrote Voroshilov in October, expressing his warm feelings for the Soviet army and his hopes that they would keep the same friendly relations that they had always had.[133] These feelings were reciprocated by Tukhachevskii when he parted from Twardowski after a meeting in the autumn of 1933. He insisted that it was only German policies that kept the two armies apart, but that "Soviet sentiment" remained very friendly toward the Reichswehr.[134] The implication was that if German policy changed, the cooperation could resume as it had before.

The Soviet high command may have had other reasons to regret the ending of their relationship with the Reichswehr, beside personal friendships with Germans or the desire to benefit technically or tactically. The collaboration had provided an important avenue for military and industrial espionage. For instance, unknown to the German high command, Voroshilov, too, read Bockelberg's report. On 26 September Berzin sent Voroshilov selections from the document that he thought important for Soviet policy, and summarized most of the rest.[135] He began, for instance, with Voroshilov's statement about the need for the foreign policies of the two nations to pursue the same goal if they wanted to work together. He also stressed Tukhachevskii's repeated remarks at a breakfast, wishing the Reichswehr had an air force of two thousand bombers as soon as possible so that Germany would be able to extract herself from her "difficult political situation." Voroshilov, ominously in view of later events, underlined this passage and scored it three times

131. Ibid., p. 194a.

132. Report from Berzin to Voroshilov, 14 October 1933, RGVA, f. 33987, op. 3, d. 504, l. 161.

133. Blomberg to Voroshilov, October 1933, RGVA, f. 33987, op. 3, d. 504, ll. 158–59.

134. Minute from von Twardowski to Auswärtiges Amt, 1 November 1933; attached to Tgd. Nr. A/2410, "Betr: Unterredung mit dem Stellvertreter des Kriegskommissars Tuchatschewski," BA-MA, RW 5/v, 461.

135. Memo from Berzin to Voroshilov, 26 September 1933, and excerpt from a report by Bockelberg on his trip through the USSR during May 1933, RGVA, f. 33987, op. 3, d. 504, l. 134, 135–38.

in the margin.[136] Berzin included Tukhachevskii's thoughts on tanks as well as the admiration expressed by Bockelberg for Soviet industry. He ended the report with Bockelberg's desire to continue the cooperation.[137]

Bockelberg's report was not the only prize recovered by Soviet intelligence from their "friends." The Fourth Directorate (the GRU) had been responsible for obtaining copies of several secret reports from Dirksen, including the ambassador's private thoughts on German-Soviet relations.[138] In September Berzin also sent Voroshilov a document, translated from German, that described a meeting Hartmann had had at the Reichswehr Ministry to discuss German-Russian relations. Hartmann painted a picture of relations between the two countries that was "not so dark," believing that the Russians "had not completely closed the door" and that deft diplomatic handling was necessary to better relations between the countries.[139] Ironically, that very year Hartmann had noticed how well-informed the Soviets were on even the latest innovations in German technology and had complimented Tukhachevskii on their industrial espionage.[140]

The Germans, in their turn, were not as honest with their partners as the close military relationship would suggest, hiding (or attempting to hide) technical knowledge that they thought too sensitive to share with the Soviets. Long before Bockelberg described Soviet disinterest in the "small tractor," Krupp had been informed that it was to develop the vehicle only for the Reichswehr Ministry and not for Kazan. Although there was the possibility of replicating the motors in the Soviet Union, the ministry wanted to keep what it thought might have to be the Reichswehr's main battle tank out of Soviet hands.[141] And later that year the new Soviet military attaché in Berlin reported to Voroshilov that during one trip to Germany his group was purposely shown only technology that they had already seen before.[142]

Apart from these problems of distrust, the military collaboration between Germany and the Soviet Union, by any objective standard, was extremely successful. Regardless of the complaints of Voroshilov and others in the Soviet government, the Red Army acquired a wealth of technical and tactical information from their partners, as Griaznov's list suggests. When the relationship ended, they were able to retain and use the capital improvements that the Germans had made at Kazan,

136. Ibid., l. 137.

137. Ibid., ll. 137–38.

138. See Leplevskii documents, 21 December 1931, RGVA, f. 33987, op. 3, d. 70, ll. 253–75.

139. Report from Berzin to Voroshilov, 20 September 1933, RGVA, f. 33987, op. 3, d. 504, l. 160.

140. Report from T-3 Oberst Hartmann, military attaché in Moscow, on chemical installation and collaboration, 18 May 1933, PA-AA, R31682K, E696254–E696255.

141. Memo "Diktiert Hagelloch": "Niederschrift über die Besprechung hier im Werk am 9.2.33; 9.2.33; Btr: Kl. Tr. Ka.," BA-MA, RH 8/v, 2677 (Krupp).

142. Report from Levichev to Voroshilov, 18 May [1933], RGVA, f. 33987, op. 3, d. 505, l. 21.

and in fact the school there remained one of the main testing and training grounds for Soviet and Russian armor troops.[143] The total value of equipment left to the UMM from Kazan was one million rubles, and the UMM also acquired another 220,000 rubles worth of technical equipment.[144] The German army in turn benefited, obtaining secure testing areas for the tanks that would serve them throughout the next war. The fact that German industry was able to begin large-scale production of tanks almost as soon as Hitler decided to rearm was directly due to the testing and decision making by industry and the army at Kazan.

Hitler planned to make good use of this aid with rearmament. In early February 1933, just days after his appointment as chancellor, he met with Hammerstein and other members of the high command to assure them that he had but one goal – to return Germany to political power by building up the Wehrmacht.[145] The details of this buildup were another matter. In *Mein Kampf* Hitler seemed to place himself on the "morale" side of the materiel/morale debate, writing that "The best arms are dead and useless material as long as the spirit is missing which is ready, willing, and determined to use them."[146] But later in the same work he argued that motorization, one of Germany's weakest areas, would be decisive in the next war.[147] His actions once taking power showed that his true sympathies lay with a mechanization of both war and society. One of his first projects was the creation of a "people's car" and highways to drive it on, and later he would show great interest in tanks in particular, like Stalin becoming involved in the minutiae of weapons procurement.[148] As we shall see, at a crucial juncture he would also support Guderian and other armor enthusiasts in their dispute with the high command.

Even with Hitler's support, and the assistance that Kama gave the Reichswehr in developing and choosing tanks, the army still had to depend on German industry to produce the machines. In late February 1933 the Procurement Branch in the Waffenamt requested an accelerated completion of its order for the light tanks. These were not to be used for experimentation but were intended for the troops and would be hidden in the budget as "automobile equipment."[149] About a week later a Krupp

---

143. For use of Kazan after the Germans left, see memo from Khrulev to Voroshilov, 17 November 1934, RGVA, f. 4, op. 14, d. 1147, l. 87.

144. Report from Berzin to Voroshilov, 14 October 1933, RGVA, f. 33987, op. 3, d. 504, ll. 163–64.

145. Thilo Vogelsang, "Neue Dokumente zur Geschichte der Reichswehr, 1930–1933," *Vierteljahreshefte für Zeitgeschichte* 2 (1954): 434–35. For Hitler's determination to make Germany "again able to defend herself" (*wiederwehrhaft*) see Michael Geyer, *Deutsche Rüstungspolitik 1860–1980* (Frankfurt am Main: Suhrkamp, 1984), 140.

146. Adolf Hitler, *Mein Kampf* (Boston: Houghton Mifflin, 1939), 459.

147. Ibid., 958; and Edward W. Bennett, *German Rearmament and the West, 1932–1933* (Princeton, N.J.: Princeton University Press, 1979), 319.

148. R. J. Overy, *War and Economy in the Third Reich* (Oxford: Clarendon Press, 1994), 68–89.

149. Report from Krupp representative Wilhelm Prillwitz, "Btr: Angebot auf 4 Kl. Tr. für Heereswaffenamt-Beschaffungsabtlg," 24 February 1933, BA-MA, RH 8/v, 2677 (Krupp).

representative informed the main company office that the Branch might ask them to deliver two more "small tractors."[150] These Krupp was able to produce, but when the Waffenamt requested a large number of the small tanks in late June, it was soon apparent that Krupp had overestimated its production capabilities. The army thought that it would have to use tanks from foreign firms to fulfill the order, although promising to use companies from Germany when it was possible to do so.[151] When the Waffenamt asked for delivery of the order to start December 1933, Krupp reported that it could do so only by February 1934, and foresaw a monthly production of a mere twenty-five vehicles. The last of the 150 tanks would not arrive until the end of May 1934.[152]

The controversy over the combat value of the very light tank did not end with the decision to proceed with more intensive production. In November 1933 an article appeared in the Militär-Wochenblatt arguing that the machine was thoroughly worthless for modern warfare. It had serious technical failings which created unbearable heat for the driver and jeopardized the operation of the engine when the hatch was closed for battle; a ground clearance of only twenty centimeters which made it unable to cross large obstacles or very uneven ground; and a machine gun with an arc of fire of only thirty degrees. The small tank, the anonymous officer concluded, was fine for parades where it could drive with the hatch open, but completely unsuited to actual combat.[153] An answer to this criticism appeared in an article that argued, among other things, that the British example had convinced many other states to arm with a small tank – and they would not have done so unless it was worthwhile; that the British high command would not favor the vehicles unless they were ready for production; and that the first officer must have considered only an older version of the machine since the latest models did not have the failings he mentioned. Whatever one might think about the worth of the small tank, he added, the fact was that in every country allowed to rearm the small tank was a major part of reconnaissance and tank units. Even in its current state the small tank was a weapon that one should not underestimate.[154]

Regardless of its tactical or technical failings, the small tank was the only machine available for immediate production when Hitler seized power.[155] With his

150. Prillwitz to Krupp/Krawa, 1 March 1933. BA-MA, RH 8/v, 2677 (Krupp).

151. "Niederschrift über Besprechung am 23./24.6.1933 in Essen," 23 June 1933, BA-MA, RH 8/v, 2679 (Krupp); Müller, "So lebten und arbeiteten wir," 36.

152. Spielberger, Motorisierung der deutschen Reichswehr, 363–64. Other firms also participated in the production of parts for the small tank, including Rheinmetall, Henschel, and MAN. Memo, 1 July 1933. BA-MA, RH 8/v, 2679 (Krupp). p. 7. After December 1934 an improved LaS was produced by MAN. Werner Oswald, Kraftfahrzeuge und Panzer der Reichswehr, Wehrmacht und Bundeswehr (Stuttgart: Motorbuch Verlag, 1973), 239, 252.

153. "Wertlose Kleintanks: Nach neuesten Kriegserlebnissen," Militär-Wochenblatt, no. 17 (1933):550–51.

154. "Mrs.," "Wertlose Kleintanks: Eine Entgegnung," Militär-Wochenblatt, no. 23 (1933): 745–47.

155. The "large tractor" was by this time clearly a dead end and the final specifications for a

encouragement, the army began serious planning to ensure that rearmament with both the small tank and the other forbidden weapons occurred as quickly, efficiently – and quietly – as possible. On 16 March T-1 issued a preliminary development and rearmament program for the entire Reichswehr. The main objectives of the plan were to create the greatest possible operational and tactical mobility for the field army and to strengthen its offensive power. To achieve these aims, the planners suggested an increase in the army's offensive firepower under armor protection, that is, tanks.[156] Because he was still uncertain of his hold on power Hitler refused to endorse this development publicly, but as the year progressed he became bolder. In October he ordered negotiators in Geneva to demand that all the other powers disarm to the level of the Reichswehr, or else Germany would no longer consider itself bound by the limits of Versailles. He was then able to blame the resulting collapse of the conference on the other powers, which had refused to live up to the principle of disarmament they themselves held. In December the Truppenamt as a whole could begin concrete planning for the three-hundred-thousand-man, twenty-one-division army that had always formed the basis for its strategic plans. Strangely enough, armor forces no longer played a central role. Neither the peacetime nor the wartime army described in the new plans reflected the March program's desire to exploit the tank and other vehicles to increase mobility and firepower. In time of war the army would expand threefold, to sixty-three infantry divisions, but would include only one light motorized division and one armor unit.[157]

One reason for the sharp difference between the two plans was the continued lack of unanimity within the highest ranks of the Reichswehr over the tank. Once again the contrast with Soviet armor doctrine is instructive. Among Red Army officers by this time there was disagreement only over the specific details of deep battle and over some minor points of implementation. There was certainly no longer any serious debate over the worth of the tank and motor vehicles in general in modern war. Despite Budënnyi's quibbling over the horse and Voroshilov's warnings to the contrary, the Soviet high command agreed that future war would take its character primarily from the tank, aircraft, and other machines. The German army as a whole had no such assurance about modern warfare, and large segments of the staff believed that foot soldiers and the horse would play the same roles in the next war as they had in the last. Guderian would later say that the fiercest struggle was between those who supported the tank as a decisive force in battle and the Cavalry

larger "medium tractor" were sent to Krupp in March 1933. Memo from Ritter, "Besprechung mit Hauptmann Striech in Berlin am 28.2.33; betr: Kl. Tr. und M. Tr.," 2 March 1933, BA-MA, RH 8/v, 2677 (Krupp).

156. Described in a draft memo from the Inspector of the Motorized Troops to the Wehramt, "Betr.: Ausbau der Kraftfahrkampftruppe," 3 August 1933, BA-MA, RH 12–6/v. 2, 71.

157. Memo from the Truppenamt (T-2), "Aufbau des künftigen Friedensheeres," 14 December 1933, BA-MA, RH 15/34, reprinted in Beck-Studien, no. 9, p. 340; Deist, "Rearmament of the Wehrmacht," 413–14.

Inspectorate. Lutz asked these "cavalryists" if they saw the future development of the cavalry as reconnaissance or battle forces. Contrary to all the lessons learned from the Western Front in the world war, General von Hirschberg, the Cavalry Inspector, declared himself in favor of using horsemen as battle forces but relinquished operational reconnaissance to the motorized forces. Hirschberg's successor, General Knochenhauer, was not willing to leave even this ground in the armor supporter's hands. He created a cavalry corps from the Reichswehr's three cavalry divisions while trying to make operational reconnaissance once again a mission of the horse troops.[158]

These disagreements can be seen in the writings of the cavalry proponents. As late as June 1933, some rejected the entire concept of linking motorized units with the cavalry in the order of battle. The grounds given by one were military-geographical and tactical. Motorized units would only be able to fight on certain types of terrain, while the cavalry could fight anywhere and at any time; the cavalry had to be kept light and independent from vehicles if it was to perform well.[159] Earlier that spring, Faber du Faur emphasized the many problems with the mass production of tanks and other machines – high cost, early obsolescence, and manifold technical and manufacturing difficulties – as well as his fears that the selfish interests of the motor vehicle industry were having an insidious influence on what should be objective military decision making.[160]

If cavalry officers provided the vocal opposition to new thought on the tank, officers within the larger and even more influential infantry arm were also lukewarm. Fritz Kühlwein's standard training manual for the infantry began by stating that it was the infantry that brought the decision in battle.[161] The main task of the tank was simply to make easier the infantry's push into the enemy's position.[162] As with many others who downplayed the role of the tank, Kühlwein emphasized the mass, fire, weight, and moral influence of the tank rather than its speed and maneuverability.[163] The largest tank unit in his tactical scheme was the regiment, not the battalion, and certainly not the massive mechanized corps that formed the basis for Soviet thought on armor organization.[164] In battle tanks had to cooperate closely with the infantry and other offensive forces, allowing the infantry to open the attack and then overtaking them and pushing into the enemy's positions.[165]

158. Guderian, *Erinnerungen eines Soldaten*, 20–21.

159. "Kavallerie im Rahmen der anderen Waffen. I," *Militär-Wochenblatt*, no. 1 (1933): 5–8; "Kavallerie im Rahmen der anderen Waffen. II," ibid., no. 5 (1933) 148–50.

160. Oberstleutnant von Faber du Faur, Reiter-Regt. 4, "Das Kraftfahrzeug für Aufklärung und Gefecht," *Militär-Wochenblatt*, no. 38 (1933): 1245–47.

161. Fritz Kühlwein, *Die Gruppe im Gefecht (Einheitsgruppe): Ein Handbuch für Lehrer und Schüler*, 3d ed. (Berlin: Mittler, 1933), 44.

162. Ibid., 47.

163. Ibid., 117.

164. Ibid., 118–19.

165. Ibid., 119–20.

These views of the tank were not the only ones current within the German army and government. Both Blomberg and Reichenau, the new leaders of the army, as well as Hitler himself, agreed with men such as Bockelberg, Stülpnagel, Lutz, and Guderian that the tank would play a decisive role in the next war. Guderian was able to demonstrate the motorized and mechanized elements of the army, including the Pz. I, to the new chancellor in 1933, and Hitler showed great enthusiasm. That this was not translated into immediate support for a modernized army was due, Guderian later said, to the inflexibility of the army's "official channels" and the negative stance of "competent authorities" in the General Staff.[166] Another officer suggested more likely reasons: Versailles and lack of money.[167] Hitler was not yet ready to defy the allies, and the country, although soon to begin a turnaround, was still in the depths of the Depression and could not afford huge tank armies.[168]

Analyses by German officers of the now famous 1932 British armor maneuvers showed the differences in views of the tank's role in future warfare. Adam's report on the maneuvers clearly reflected his own prejudices, as he cast doubt on the validity of exactly those parts of the exercises that went against his own view that tanks could not fight without the support of the infantry. He argued that although one exercise had seemed to show the success of an attack with tanks acting alone, in actual fact the vehicles had needed a simultaneous infantry assault to destroy or roll up a whole division.[169] A second exercise had apparently ended with Blue forces in full retreat from a superior Red tank force, but because the British had only used flags to represent Blue, it was difficult to know what exactly this part of the maneuvers meant.[170] Meanwhile an exercise on direct cooperation between infantry and tanks had "corresponded to German tactical conceptions" while another day's exercise, also studying cooperation between tanks and other forces, had made "the impression of a well-prepared battle picture."[171] He examined this last exercise in great detail, noting that the British timing of the engagement, with the tanks attacking the artillery well before the infantry assault, was unlike the "German concept." And the side using tanks had lacked good coordination between the infantry and armor, so that it was only the fact that it had had a large number of tanks – an entire brigade with about two hundred of them – and the fact that the other side had not been able to defend itself fully because of the speed of the entire battle, that allowed the armor force to successfully engage and destroy the artillery.[172] In ret-

166. Guderian, *Erinnerungen eines Soldaten*, 24.

167. Hptm. M. Braun, "Das Heer der Zukunft," *Militär-Wochenblatt*, no. 40 (1933): 1316–17.

168. See "Eine selbständige Panzerbrigade im Kampf," ibid., no. 41 (1933): 1340–43, for a discussion of the expense involved in arming with the tank.

169. Report from Adam, "England: Die Manöver der Kampfwagentruppen Sommer 1932," 16 May 1933, BA-MA, RH 2/2968, 6–10.

170. Ibid., 10–14.

171. Ibid., 20–23.

172. Ibid., 23–25.

rospect it was exactly those elements which Adam saw as incidental or accidental – the tremendous speed of the brigade, the use of large masses of tanks, and the surprise which had left the enemy force without time to use its antitank defenses – which would prove decisive in the next war.

Adam's negative assessment of the tank during these exercises can be contrasted with another analysis, which emphasized the power, speed, and destructive force of the armor unit. Here the author, a retired general, noted that the brigade had managed to destroy an entire infantry division without the aid of other forces and that despite the presence of numerous antitank weapons, it had attacked and pushed through the left wing of the infantry. Although suffering losses, most of the brigade had managed to win through to the infantry division's rear.[173]

These differences over the tank were not, however, reflected in the latest descriptions of doctrine, which still sought a middle ground between armor enthusiasts and critics. The Reichswehr issued its first official statement on doctrine since F.u.G., the *Truppenführung (T.F.)*, in October 1933. T.F. was primarily written by Ludwig Beck (in 1933 the chief of the Truppenamt) during 1931–32 and put together with the aid of experts from the army's various branches.[174] Although the basic principles of war described in T.F. were the same as those in F.u.G., the new manual was supposed to incorporate the lessons and technologies of the world war with their later refinements and improvements. T.F. would remain in print, with minor changes, until 1936. In most respects the manual expected the German army to fight the same sort of war as the last conflict. Although recognizing that the envelopment was more effective than frontal attacks, T.F. saw the latter as the most likely type of battle – perhaps even taking the same form as assaults during the world war. Flanking attacks, although desirable, demanded superior mobility and surprise and were not discussed in detail.[175] The emphasis was overwhelmingly on the infantry and its main support, the artillery. Thus the goal of any attack was described as bringing the infantry to the final decision against the enemy – making it possible for the foot soldiers to push through deeply and break the enemy's resistance definitively. The only way to achieve this goal was to have "lasting, close connections" among all forces cooperating in the assault and especially between the artillery and infantry whose cooperation "gives the course of the attack its character."[176] One small change concerned the cavalry, which the manual described as partially motorized. As in the last war, however, the horse troops were expected to

173. Generalmajor a.D. Zöltz, "Mechanisierte Brigade gegen Infanteriedivision: Aus Englischen manövern," *Militär-Wochenblatt*, no. 48 (1933): 1566–67.

174. Walther Nehring, *Die Geschichte der deutschen Panzerwaffe 1916 bis 1945* (Berlin: Propyläen Verlag, 1969), 67. One of the experts was Karl Heinrich von Stülpnagel, a younger relation of Otto von Stülpnagel, who would lead forces in the attack on the Soviet Union. Walter Goerlitz, *History of the German General Staff 1657–1945* (New York: Praeger, 1957), 293.

175. *Truppenführung. (T.F.): I. Teil (Abschnitt I–XIII): H.Dv. 300/1* (Berlin: Mittler, 1936), 119–21.

176. Ibid., 127.

take an active part in combat, a victory for the cavalry officers who had agitated for the continuation of this vital role for their branch.[177]

In view of this traditional image of warfare, it is not surprising that the armor doctrine discussed in T.F. was but another version of the "moderate" line. The manual encouraged, for instance, a loose connection between the infantry and the tank, reflecting the earlier triumph of those who had wanted to use the machine's speed to the fullest. Although tanks were expected to coordinate their attacks with the infantry, this did not mean a close physical tie which "robs the tank of the advantage of its speed and possibly leaves it to become a victim of enemy defenses." Tanks could, however, be directly subordinated to the infantry commander if they broke through with the foot soldiers, and would then take care of enemy forces hindering the infantry. This proviso was a bow to those who wanted it clear that the vehicles were to work as part of the overall combined-arms battle. During combat, the infantry would aid the tanks by suppressing antiarmor defenses, artillery would battle enemy artillery and general defensive emplacements, while aircraft supported the attack throughout, attacking artillery, reserves and even lines of communication. Artillery and motorized forces might also accompany the tank assault.[178] In sum, T.F. envisaged a combined-arms offensive predicated on substantial numbers of tanks closely supported by the other forces, but no independent role for large armor units.

The second statement of doctrine, drafted by Lutz in the form of a memorandum to the Wehramt in August 1933, took on this issue, which was becoming the pivot of the struggle over armor doctrine. Lutz forcefully argued that the army needed an independent armor force that would be the core of an offensive strike force. He began by asserting that only the motorization and mechanization of the German army would grant it the mobility and striking power necessary for modern warfare. The use of motor vehicles could compensate for the Reichswehr's inferiority, in numbers and modern weaponry, vis-à-vis its neighbors. The demand for operational mobility had been at the top of the Truppenamt's March development plan, he wrote, and only this could give the Reichswehr a chance of victory. "Aside from making full use of railways and road vehicles, this operational mobility can only be attained through fast mobile combat units, which are independent from other units in a new sense, and are employed far afield against the enemy's flanks and rear."

Lutz argued that a combination of both armor and "light" divisions containing motorized battalion-strength units with especially large numbers of automatic weapons, was necessary. The armor unit would provide the decisive fire and offensive power upon whose success the following light division could build. He stressed, however, that "[t]he armor unit is decisive and has priority. The light division – more or less a question of transportation – cannot carry out independent

177. Ibid., 288, 291.
178. Ibid., 133–34.

wide-ranging missions without the armor unit." The use of vehicles would increase tactical mobility by relieving both man and horse and by removing any constraints on the movement of individuals or of a unit.

> the previous framework, where foot soldiers provided the backbone for the bat-
> tlefields in land warfare, will – in contrast to the views of a FULLER – in the end
> still be crucial. But now also seems the time to use modern means of transport to
> their fullest – independently from the old framework – for the mobile conduct of
> war. And after they have proved that it is possible to employ them as an indepen-
> dent weapon, we should also use them as a weapon that will decide both battles
> and wars.[179]

Lutz then addressed directly the contentious issue of the organization of the new armor units. Should they be tied organically to existing structures, or should the army create an entirely new force consisting of independent units? Lutz agreed that the first option, giving tanks or other vehicles to existing infantry and cavalry divisions, would undoubtedly raise the fighting efficiency of these units. But in so doing, the army would renounce the fundamental advantage of motorized units: their operational mobility. It would also have to give up employing tanks as the main focus of an operation as well as their mass use which, he argued, was the sole factor that guaranteed success. Finally, a close connection with slower forces, which used a mostly frontal approach, would take from armor its surprise use against the flanks and rear of the opponent.[180] In contrast, the second option would give commanders a strong force suitable for special tasks and would permit as well the full exploitation of the tank's operational mobility for surprise use on the most effective spot. Lutz thought, too, that independent armor units would allow the modest tank forces that Germany possessed, at least at this point, to accomplish the maximum. Meanwhile the second solution still gave commanders the capability to use armor units in conjunction with the other arms to decide the battle. With all these points in mind, he concluded that "[t]he Inspectorate is therefore convinced that only the second way is advantageous."[181]

Lutz then made suggestions about how to implement each of the options. With regard to creating armor units in light divisions, he noted that they did not have their own experience on which to draw, only that of foreigners (the British), which was not yet fully verifiable. He thought therefore that this should be implemented only gradually, using what "foreigners" knew, and in the future exploiting the German army's own lessons learned through experimental units. Independently of this problem, the army should proceed with the formation of tank battalions on a long-

179. Draft memo from the Inspector of the Motorized Troops to the Wehramt, "Betr.: Ausbau der Kraftfahrkampftruppe," 3 August 1933, BA-MA, RH 12–6/v. 2, 74.

180. Ibid., 75.

181. Ibid., 75–76. It is significant the Lutz crossed out this sentence and wrote in his own hand "I *am* convinced that only the second way leads to the goal" (emphasis mine).

term basis. He suggested setting up seven tank battalions in regiments and motorizing an infantry battalion or cavalry regiment as a first step. By 1935 he wanted
an experimental unit, in effect an armor division, consisting of a reconnaissance
detachment, a tank regiment with two battalions, a motorized infantry battalion or
cavalry regiment, and a motorized artillery unit.[182] Finally he explained again why
he preferred the second option, the organizational separation of tanks and motorized units from the other branches of the service, over adding tanks to infantry divisions. "The training and use of the motorized battle force now falls outside of the
bounds of the [infantry] divisions. It has become an army branch with its own manner of fighting, its own principles of usage, which go considerably beyond the other
land forces." All the motorized and mechanized troops needed to be unified under
one command, just like the infantry or cavalry. He recommended therefore that he,
as the Inspector of the Motorized Troops, have all motorized units (including light
divisions and the section of the Waffenamt concerned with motor troops) put under his command, and that he answer directly to the chief of the army command.[183]

Taken together, these two statements on doctrine show that the high command
was more united than in the past over the use of armor in future war, with one important proviso. In particular the publication of T.F with its far-reaching vision of
the tank confirms that the negative views of Adam, and others like him, were mar-
ginalized and no longer influential by 1933. Armor would form the nucleus of a
combined-arms battle that would use tanks in new and daring ways to break
through and defeat the enemy. The major difference that remained was the question of organization. Lutz, Guderian and others supported the concentration of
most (if not all) tanks in large, independent formations, while Beck and the majority of the high command wanted some way for the vehicles to cooperate more
closely with the infantry.

In the short term, however, neither the ambitious plans outlined by Lutz, nor the
less grandiose ones of Beck, could be implemented. Although promised new support by Hitler, the Reichswehr as it stood in late 1933 was a weak and badly armed
force, barely able to fight a conventional war, much less an ultramodern war of machines. During December, in response to a threat of sanctions from the Allies,
Beck, now the head of the Truppenamt, produced a series of memoranda on military options available to the politicians. One of his most important conclusions
was that Germany could only conduct a war on more than one front defensively,
able to halt the enemy's offensives, but nothing more.[184] Until Germany recovered
from its economic woes, had a leader who was willing to defy Versailles, and the
Reichswehr agreed with the ambitious ideas of Lutz and others like him on the
tank, the dream of a mechanized army would remain just that.

182. Ibid., 76–77.
183. Ibid., 79.
184. Memo from Chef des Truppenamts on "Grenzschutz," 11 December 1933, BA-MA, RH 2/
25, pp. 52–53.

If German political and economic weaknesses acted as a brake on larger plans for the armor forces, the Soviet Union, at least on the surface, had no such problems. During 1933 the new Soviet military-industrial complex would produce thousands of tanks, while the Red Army created dozens of mechanized units and sought to implement deep battle in a variety of exercises and maneuvers. Griaznov reported that the number of tanks should almost double during the year, from 5,550 to 10,200.[185] By July these numbers had to be tempered somewhat, but his directorate still predicted an impressive production of 4,120 tanks during 1933 and another 9,725 to 11,575 tanks during the next Five Year Plan.[186] A list of mechanized formations showed that the Red Army had used its tanks and tankettes to create nearly forty units of various sizes in the four organizational structures (independent mechanized force, TRGK, infantry, and cavalry).[187]

A report from Egorov and Griaznov to Voroshilov on the different types of tanks in the army confirmed, however, that there had not yet been any rationalization of the bewildering variety of vehicles in the Red Army arsenal. The main tanks were still the light T-26, the dual-drive B-T, and the T-18, although the army was in the process of replacing this last tank. The T-37 light amphibious tank was to be everywhere by the end of 1933, as was the T-27 tankette. Other tanks included the T-24, the V-12 (used as a command vehicle), the medium T-28 (in certain brigades) and the heavy T-35; nine different tanks in all. Even more bewildering were the different units in which these tanks served: the T-35, T-28, and T-24 were only in TRGK brigades; the V-12 only in mechanized corps; the T-27 in rifle divisions; the B-T in mechanized corps and cavalry mechanized units; and different models of the T-26 in TRGK units, mechanized units, and tank battalions. Only the T-37 was in all the different varieties of mechanized and tank units in the Red Army.[188] In a move that could only confuse matters further, the RVS decreed in March that all mechanized cavalry units (with some few exceptions) would change their armament from B-T tanks to T-26 and T-37 tanks.[189]

In spite of the bewildering variety of tanks, which might have been a hindrance to smooth production, the army was confident that industry would be able to manufacture anything that their plans required. In a long report on how the military expected the next Five Year Plan to affect the motorization and mechanization of the army, Egorov could predict that the success of the industrialization drive would

---

185. Report from Griaznov to Voroshilov, 30 March 1933. RGVA, f. 4, op. 14, d. 889, l. 70.

186. Report by Ivanov, "Orientirovochnye dannye po planu zakazov UMM na 2-iu piatiletku (tanki)," 28 July 1933, RGVA, f. 31811, op. 2, d. 276.

187. Listing (in a pamphlet) of all mechanized units and mechanized BUZ's from August 1933, RGVA, f. 4, op. 14, d. 884, ll. 79–88.

188. Report from Egorov and Griaznov to Voroshilov, 14 February 1933, RGVA, f. 4, op. 14, d. 914, ll. 1–2.

189. Memo to the Chiefs of armor/tank forces of all districts from Griaznov, 12 March 1933. RGVA, f. 31811, op. 2, d. 168, l. 1.

transform forever the conduct of war. In his preface he credited the "use of the motor in military affairs with introducing a fundamental change in how war is conducted, in military art and tactics."[190] Aircraft and tanks had been introduced into the general military system, won the right to be independent branches of the army, and even taken the leading place in it. They were generally recognized by the imperialists as the decisive factors in future war, and the Party and state had decided to be stronger than their enemies in these two new weapons. His conclusion: "Mechanization and motorization was introduced into the Red Army as the *obligatory and decisive* factor for the military work of land forces."[191]

Turning to the results of the first Five Year Plan, he noted that the USSR had no special tank production and only ninety tanks, exclusively foreign made, at the beginning of the industrialization drive. In stark contrast, as of 1 May 1933 the Soviet Union had produced 5,644 tanks, including 2,430 T-27's and 1,550 T-26's. He emphasized, however, that tankettes and old T-18s still constituted close to 60 percent of the tank forces actually in the field.[192] The mobilization capabilities of Soviet industry were equally impressive. Egorov claimed that Soviet factories could produce forty thousand tanks a year in wartime and that currently they were capable of manufacturing twelve thousand tanks a year.[193] In comparison with foreign militaries, the Red Army was far ahead, with more tanks and the best organizational structure. Only England, with its experimental mechanized brigade, came close; most armies used the regiment as their basic unit.[194]

Egorov believed that the first Five Year Plan had created new operational and tactical capabilities for the Red Army upon which future technical developments would build. Mechanization had already proven an important corrective for tactics and raised anew the question of cooperation between the different types of forces — especially with artillery, which tanks both reinforced and partially replaced. Mechanized units had also changed operations, making it possible to deliver a simultaneous blow in all operational depths. He foresaw mechanization heading in three basic directions: the development of independent, ever larger mechanized formations; the introduction of tanks into regular forces; and the widest possible motorization of the rear. All this would logically lead to the complete mechanization of the army.[195] Unfortunately, the next Five Year Plan would not yet achieve this goal, but it should create an army capable of fulfilling operational missions. To do this, Egorov argued that the army had to have at least fifteen thousand tanks and that these vehicles had to be faster and more powerful, grouped into operational

190. Report by Egorov, "O razvitii mekhanizatsii i motorizatsii RKKA na vtoruiu piatiletku," 14 June 1933, RGVA, f. 4, op. 14, d. 978, ll. 9–10.
191. Ibid., l. 10. Emphasis in original.
192. Ibid., ll. 11–12. For how this armor force "permeated" the Red Army see ibid., ll. 13–15.
193. Ibid., ll. 15–16.
194. Ibid., ll. 20–22.
195. Ibid., ll. 26–31.

and strategic mechanized units with a strong tank reserve in the hands of the high command. The other forces, such as the cavalry and combined-force units, also needed their own organic mechanized units for reconnaissance and combat.[196]

This new army would be able to carry out deep battle and destroy the enemy's entire defensive position, reaching 100 to 150 kilometers by the end of the first twenty-four-hours of an attack. Mechanized units would destroy the operational reserves and airfields of the opponent, shut down or disorganize his rear, and even assault the untouched portions of the front from the rear to widen the breakthrough and destroy the opponent's retreating units. To achieve these results, the mechanized units had to work closely with motorized units, cavalry, parachutists, and the air force. Meanwhile, the mechanized units working with the combined forces would suppress artillery, tactical reserves, machine guns, and antitank weaponry, while directly supporting the infantry. Like German officers looking at armor warfare, Egorov pointed out that the speed of the new tanks made cooperation with the infantry very difficult, but had no suggestions as to how the army would overcome this problem.[197]

Voroshilov used Egorov's study in a report to Stalin and Molotov, as chairman of the Defense Commission, on the most appropriate system of tank weaponry for the second Five Year Plan. It is typical of Voroshilov's unimaginative imitation of his more thoughtful subordinates that he copied almost verbatim Egorov's suggestions in his own memorandum.[198] A month later the Defense Commission approved a temporary system of tank armaments for the Red Army that reflected Voroshilov's (Egorov's) proposals, and in some ways was yet more ambitious. They decided, for instance, that even these tanks would be replaced from 1935 on with more "perfected" designs.[199]

While the successes in production were indeed impressive, as Egorov's report implied, the Red Army was still experiencing a sizable gap between tanks manufactured and tanks actually present in field units. At a meeting to assess military training, held in February, the head of the First Directorate of the UMM noted that eleven "mechanized corps [sic]" had supposedly been set up, but that the units still lacked 70 percent of their materiel.[200] The Deputy Inspector of the Cavalry was

196. Ibid., ll. 31–33.
197. Ibid., ll. 34–36.
198. Report from Voroshilov to Molotov, 16 July 1933. RGVA, f. 4, op. 14, d. 994, ll. 50–53. This report was also sent to Stalin, Kuibyshev, Ordzhonikidze, Iagoda, Tukhachevskii, Egorov, and Khalepskii. RGVA, f. 4, op. 14, d. 994, l. 72.
199. Memo from Pavlunovskii, chief of the GVMU, Neiman, Director for Special Heavy Machine Trusts, and directors of tank factories to Ordzhonikidze (copies to members of the Defense Commission), 27 May 1935. RGVA, f. 4, op. 14, d. 1272, ll. 21–26.
200. Stenogram "Ob itogakh boevoi podgotovki chastei i BUZov po dannym na 15 fevraia 1933 goda," 27 February 1933, RGVA, f. 31983, op. 2, d. 32, l. 1. By "mechanized corps," the writer probably meant "mechanized units."

more scathing in his analysis of the cavalry's mechanized regiments, writing that "what are called "mechanized regiments" cannot at the present time be so named. Most of them . . . completely lack technology. Producing specialists for absolutely no reason. The mechanized regiment started studies in November [1932], but as far as technology goes, only its title changed, and in actual fact there is nothing, since they removed the equipment and did not give anything [to replace it]."[201] One month later, in a report to Sediakin on the results of cavalry training for the first half of the winter period 1932–33, the inspector would again complain that some mechanized regiments did not have their materiel.[202] Budënnyi added that the horse troops of at least one district did not have any sort of mechanized forces.[203] A huge survey of military preparedness, conducted by the army in February 1933, agreed that the new armor units were not ready for war. Seven different mechanized units were inspected during the survey, with the conclusion that most had been set up a only short time earlier and a significant portion were still in the process of formation.[204]

Even without the technology in place, the army worked diligently to improve the implementation of deep battle. In their introduction to the *Provisional Instructions*, Egorov and Sediakin had recognized the seriousness of the problem, writing that the army had to hold studies with the command staff to master the tactical-technical standards of deep battle and also the general principles for organizing and conducting the new tactics.[205] A few weeks later they backed up this suggestion with a directive that relayed Voroshilov's orders for the theoretical study of deep battle tactics. For the period March through May, officers were to master the theoretical basis for organizing and conducting deep battle for a rifle corps and the standards and methods for calculating the forces, means, and time necessary to carry out deep attacks.[206] In June Tkachev, Sediakin's temporary replacement as head of military training, issued a fifty-four-page document on how to organize deep battle when attacking a strongly fortified opponent. It detailed in particular the organization of cooperation between DD and DPP groups and artillery and between infantry and NPP groups.[207]

Attempts to achieve these varied goals consumed the training exercises held by

201. Ibid., l. 6.

202. Report from Kosolov to Sediakin, 25 March 1933, RGVA, f. 31983, op. 2, d. 26, ll. 51–52.

203. Budënnyi, "Zakliuchenie ob itogakh boevoi podgotovki konnitsy RKKA za 1933 god.," 15 October 1933, RGVA, f. 31983, op. 2, d. 32, ll. 332, 340, 344.

204. Report, "OBZOR sostoianiia boevoi podgotovki chastei i VUZ'ov RKKA po dannym obsledovaniia na 15-e fevralia 1933 goda," RGVA, f. 31983, op. 2, d. 32, ll 96.

205. Circular for the "Ukazanie po organizatsii glubokogo boia" from Egorov and Sediakin, 9 February 1933, RGVA, f. 31983, op. 2, d. 33, l. 385.

206. Directive from Egorov and Sediakin to all top military leaders, 26 February 1933, RGVA, f. 31983, op. 2, d. 33, l. 359.

207. Detailed instructions from Tkachev to all top military leaders on how to organize deep battle, 13 June 1933, RGVA, f. 31811, op. 2, d. 183, ll. 196–99.

the Red Army during 1933. The first war game of the year dealt with the most pressing problem: the DD echelon and how to support it.[208] Most of the other exercises for the year worked on the weaknesses recognized in the past year: coordinating the diverse forces involved in deep battle, assuring command and control, and providing the logistical support for the hundreds of machines involved in the simultaneous destruction of the enemy's defenses. Sediakin, true to form, tried to prevent the exercises from becoming unrealistic. In particular he warned that the army could not underestimate the enemy's ability to organize defenses using regular infantry forces. He also asked that special attention be paid to the forthcoming experimental studies which ought, by the end of summer 1933, to give sufficient material for formulating a realistic theory of deep battle "with a sober projection of the likely conditions of a future large-scale war."[209]

These early exercises experienced the same problems as in previous years. The Inspector of the UMM noted that men in the 3rd Detached Tank Regiment "do not have even the most elementary knowledge of the action of the vehicle [tank] as part of a platoon or about tank groups NPP, DPP and DD. For instance in the 7th Company they did not even know about the existence of published tank manuals, instructions, and so on." The commander of a platoon, working on the concept "The Battle Use of Tank Groups NPP, DPP, and DD," could not explain the difference between NPP and DPP groups and gave a description of their use that did not match that given in the armor manual.[210] The cavalry too, once they received their new tanks, had trouble understanding how to cooperate with the vehicles.[211]

In contrast, studies held that autumn showed better results. One of these, personally led by Tukhachevskii in the Leningrad district, worked on cooperation between tanks and artillery in a breakthrough, coordination of NPP groups with infantry and air forces, DD tank cooperation with parachutists, and more.[212] A report presenting the lessons drawn from the exercise was very optimistic, concluding that the district had worked out the question of cooperation between the different types of forces during all stages of battle. The commanders knew where tanks should be in battle and knew how to work with them, although there were still problems with communications with the other forces.[213] Several exercises

208. Description of war games held 20 January 1933, RGVA, f. 31983, op. 2, d. 20, l. 154.

209. Report from the Chief of Military Training of Land Forces, "O khode boevoi podgotovki," presented during May 1933 to the RVS, RGVA, f. 31983, op. 2, d. 26, l. 77. See also "Postanovlenie RVS SSSR (PROEKT) po dokladu nachal'nika boevoy podgotovki RKKA o khode boevoi podgotovki 5–5-33," RGVA, f. 31983, op. 2, d. 26, ll. 99–97.

210. Letter from Pakaln, Inspector UMM, r.e. inspection of 3rd Detached Tank Regiment on 15–21 April 1933, RGVA, f. 31811, op. 2, d. 167, l. 222.

211. Budënnyi, "Zakliuchenie ob itogakh boevoi podgotovki konnitsy RKKA za 1933 god.," 15 October 1933, RGVA, f. 31983, op. 2, d. 32, ll. 332, 340, 344.

212. "Otchet ob opytnykh ucheniiakh mekhchastei LVO za letnii period 1933 g.," RGVA, f. 31811, op. 2, d. 187, ll. 4, 2.

213. Ibid., l. 3.

with the original mechanized brigade, held in late September were also seen as positive experiences in working out deep battle.[214] The official analysis of the exercises said that the brigade had shown itself able to cooperate well with both cavalry and air forces.[215] It commented on the "unbelievable speed of battle" of the brigade, which had covered an average of 100 to 120 kilometers a day, with an average speed of 12–15 kph.[216] The analysis showed that the exercises had confirmed earlier reports on the cavalry in modern battle. Even though able to inflict losses of up to 20 percent on attacking tanks, the horse troops would suffer tremendous casualties in a surprise tank attack.[217] The report then proceeded to argue strenuously against direct tank assaults, since these would meet the full strength of the enemy's anti-tank defenses and cause huge losses. Instead, it offered the British army's version of armor combat, a three-echelon assault consisting of fire, maneuver, and "main strike" echelons, as the best way to organize deep battle. Finally, the report agreed with Khalepskii and Egorov's lengthy paper of the year before, noting that concentrating the tanks at an assembly point after the attack meant the loss of a precious thirty minutes. Tanks should instead work on destroying the opponent completely and then head toward his rear.[218]

Khalepskii had a mostly optimistic view of the maneuvers, pointing out that they had proven the army's views on armor-air cooperation. To the heads of the air force he suggested that the studies had shown the need for close cooperation between mechanized formations and the air force, which could be either an independent actor (cooperating operationally) or attached to a rifle corps. The exercises had in addition proven the worth of using parachutists. He then argued that mechanized formations and TRGK units were so intertwined with aircraft in combat that it was necessary to consider the question of "an organic drawing together of both types of forces" and "the organic inclusion of air detachments in mechanized and tank formations." He especially wanted the bureaucracies of the air forces and the UMM to work together on tactical and operational questions.[219] If implemented, Khalepskii's suggestion would have resulted in a greater centralization of all armor forces and perhaps even the subordination of the air forces to the mechanized command.

When the maneuvers had ended for the year, Egorov summarized the lessons learned from them in a massive one-hundred-page report. The first and most vital of his conclusions was that the basic theoretical principle of deep offensives had received full confirmation: it was indeed possible to achieve the almost simultane-

214. *Vyvody po operativnym opytnym ucheniiam provedennym v 1932 godu* (Moscow: Izdanie 1 Upravleniia shtaba RKKA, 1933), RGVA, f. 31983, op. 2, d. 113, l. 5.

215. Ibid., l. 32.

216. Ibid., ll. 22, 38.

217. Ibid., ll. 29–30.

218. Ibid., ll. 39–40.

219. Communication from Khalepskii to all the chiefs of VVS RKKA, 14 November 1933, RGVA, f. 31811, op. 2, d. 176, l. 556.

ous destruction of all depths of the defender's battle order.[220] The most important part of the exercises, an experiment with the echeloning of tank groups, had tested two different viewpoints. The first had suggested that the attack ought to start with DPP tanks, then the DD echelon, and finally the NPP group. The DPP force would not only suppress machine guns, but also antitank defenses, so that DD tanks would sustain fewer losses on their way to the enemy's rear. The Belorussian district and separate studies at Tochk had tried out this idea as it was described in the *Provisional Instructions*. The second viewpoint directly contradicted the first, stating that with artillery support, DD tanks would not suffer great losses and therefore would be able to fulfill their mission while in turn helping the DPP echelon to achieve its objective. The exercises at Tochk and Leningrad had explored this idea. In the end Egorov argued that the question could not be set in stone; there had to be room to take into consideration the particular circumstances of each battle and the state of the enemy's defenses.[221] Later that fall Egorov would argue more strongly in favor of the DD tanks leading the attack, perhaps because he saw the logic in allowing the echelon that had the farthest objectives to lead the assault.[222] This was an important point, because the real controversy was over whether it was possible for the DD group, and mechanized forces in general, to conduct independent operations in the enemy's depths separately from combined-arms formations.[223] The whole concept of deep battle, and deep operations even more so, hinged on whether the DD tanks could perform this crucial mission. By the end of the year Egorov certainly thought that they could, and pushed for greater independence for the DD echelon.[224]

While these analyses suggested that the army had made great strides toward implementing deep battle in 1933, there were other signs that implied something quite different. Soviet commanders, when discussing deep battle or deep operations, almost always mentioned the serious difficulties they were having with the logistics of mechanized formations.[225] One set of exercises with a mechanized brigade that took place in October showed that there were also many problems with command, control, and communication.[226] Although Khalepskii and others urged

220. Report by Egorov, "Vyvody iz opytnykh uchenii 1933 goda," 9 November 1933, RGVA, f. 4, op. 14, d. 1018, ll. 21–23.

221. Ibid., ll. 25–26.

222. "Stenograficheskii otchet rasshirennoe zasedanie RVS SSSR," 16–18 November 1933, RGVA, f. 4, op. 18, d. 39, ll. 17–18.

223. See Isserson, "Razvitie teorii sovetskogo operativnogo iskusstva," 44, 46.

224. See e.g. report by Egorov, "Vyvody iz opytnykh uchenii 1933 goda," 9 November 1933, RGVA, f. 4, op. 14, d. 1018, ll. 25–26.

225. See e.g. "Stenograficheskii otchet rasshirennoe zasedanie RVS SSSR," 16–18 November 1933, RGVA, f. 4, op. 18, d. 39, l. 12.

226. "Otchet po ucheniiu Shtaba Korpusa i Shtaba Mekhbrigady so sredstvami Sviazi, Razvedki i Komandirokimi boevymi mashinami na temu: 'Mekhbrigada v razvitii proryva,'" (the exercises took place 19 October 1933), RGVA, f. 31983, op. 2, d. 64, ll. 15–20.

close coordination between armor and air forces, Egorov, in a report delivered to the force commanders, pointed out that the army had not yet worked out this co-operation.[227] There was also the continuing problem of the speed differential between infantry and tanks. A commander in the UMM suggested that the answer to this particular dilemma was to mount the infantry on armored troop transporters, built on the T-26 chassis with caterpillar treads. The infantry would then be able to follow the tanks closely, developing their successes and holding terrain, while still allowing tanks to use their fullest speed.[228] There was just one problem with this sensible solution: the rest of the Red Army high command was not yet convinced that infantry transporters were the answer.

The question of whether the army had succeeded in implementing deep battle dominated discussion at the annual meeting of the high command. In addition to the problems noted above, several officers, including Sediakin and Egorov, pointed out that the speed of attacks during the exercises was a "mere" 10–12 kph, only half that demanded by Order No. 0100.[229] Despite the successes of the fall exercises, Tukhachevskii could bluntly conclude that the army had not yet learned how to organize deep battle.[230] After reviewing what the army had done that year he ended by saying: "I would say that the study of deep battle, to a certain degree, is progressing haphazardly. Neither the district commanders nor our central directorates achieved anything concretely until the RVS intervened in this question, and deep battle was not worked out this year."[231]

Uborevich, on the other hand, thought that his district had made substantial advances. He told the gathering of commanders that he and his staff had succeeded in working out a new organization of attack based on deep battle, including the successful maneuvering of large numbers of tanks and the cooperation of tanks and artillery. Given the achievements of the tank units, he was confident that the army could break through an opponent's front and get up to thirty to forty kilometers into the depths of his positions in twenty-four hours.[232] Where Tukhachevskii had been pessimistic about the army's chances for implementing deep battle, Uborevich concluded on an upbeat note; Order No. 0100, he said, had basically been fulfilled.[233]

Then on 14 November, Isserson submitted a lengthy report to Voroshilov called "The Fundamentals of Deep Operations." Compiled over the course of two years

227. "Stenograficheskii otchet rasshirennoe zasedanie RVS SSSR," 16–18 November 1933, RGVA, f. 4, op. 18, d. 39, l. 12.

228. Report from Kryzhanovskii, 29 August 1933, RGVA, f. 31811, op. 2, d. 405, ll. 20–22.

229. "Stenograficheskii otchet rasshirennoe zasedanie RVS SSSR," 16–18 November 1933, RGVA, f. 4, op. 18, d. 39, ll. 13, 50–51.

230. Ibid., ll. 217–18.

231. Ibid., l. 219.

232. Ibid., ll. 332, 336.

233. Ibid., l. 345.

by the Frunze Academy's Operational Department, of which Isserson was the head, the report had two purposes: first, to find a solution to some of the problems with the doctrine that were consuming the energy of the entire Red Army; and secondly, to provide the army with the projections necessary for its next war. In his cover letter to Voroshilov, Isserson cited the difficulties experienced during the fall exercises as the main reason that the army had to pay more attention to the Frunze Academy and its ideas, a clear signal that up to this point the high command had in fact ignored the institution. The army, he noted, had decided how deep battle would look – the three-echelon system was understood and supposedly being put into practice – and now the high command had to settle what exactly its operational equivalent would be like.

Isserson began by observing the basic dilemma with deep operations – that the socialist reconstruction of the Soviet Union and the Red Army demanded this completely new way of organizing warfare, and therefore Soviet commanders could no longer look to the past, could not study the last conflict – as was the wont of every military – when trying to understand what deep operations would look like. Given the enormity of the task before him, Isserson added that the academy's report could only attempt a partial solution, focusing on two of the most intractable problems: cooperation between the forces in the enemy's depth, and the initial period of deep operations. Finally, Isserson warned that no one should take the report's recommendations as hard and fast rules on how to organize battle in every circumstance, a reference to Sediakin's earlier work which was already being criticized as too "schematic." The academy's research, in contrast, showed "not how to do (not a ready-made category, a standardized norm) – only what to do (an idea, a directive)."[234]

The report came to four important conclusions about deep operations. First and foremost, Isserson argued that deep operations was a doctrine of the breakthrough. Whether organized against a stationary front, or during an encounter battle, its primary goal was to push through the front of the enemy's forces into his operational rear. However, unlike the linear tactics used during the world war, deep operations would not push through the entire line, but rather create a narrower and far deeper penetration. Only then would this break-in be widened from within, as ground and air forces destroyed not just the far rear, but also the entire tactical, operational, and strategic depth of the enemy's position. Just what Isserson meant by "narrow" was only apparent much later in the study, when he mentioned that the width of the main area of the initial assault would be thirty to forty kilometers.[235]

Secondly, Isserson argued that at the operational level, there would be just two echelons: the "attack echelon" and the "breakthrough development echelon." The

234. Report by G. Isserson, "Osnovy glubokoi operatsii," 14 November 1933, RGVA, f. 33987, op. 3. d. 553, ll. 8–11.
235. Ibid., 130.

attack echelon would create the initial break-in which the development echelon would then deepen and widen into a complete breakthrough. The difference in the two echelons was basically the speed at which they would move and the depths at which they would be expected to act. The attack echelon would contain slower-moving forces and would only operate in the tactical zone, between fifteen and twenty kilometers into the enemy's positions; the breakthrough development echelon would be expected to attack at the same time and yet travel all the way to the enemy's operational rear (one to two hundred kilometers) while destroying all of his defenses. In a more detailed look at the development echelon, Isserson optimistically predicted that it could achieve a full penetration and rolling-up of the entire enemy position in three days. This was a rather convenient estimate since, as Isserson himself commented, the development echelon tanks would be able to fight for only three days without resupply.

Isserson also noted, as had so many others, that deep operations would only be effective if all the forces worked together as one to achieve this grandiose scheme. Like his friend Tukhachevskii, Isserson put the air forces in first place, then the mechanized corps, cavalry (to which he gave special prominence), and the motorized infantry. How would they coordinate their action when operating independently deep within the enemy's positions or high overhead? Isserson argued firstly that the Soviet army needed to combine the different forces in much smaller units, for instance at the battalion level, rather than just in the corps or army. But this did not settle the question of how to coordinate the huge forces that would need to work together in deep operations. Isserson wrote that the key was for command and control to be organized, centralized, and uninterrupted as never before. Commanders would need to give extremely precise orders with exact objectives that suited the specific combat conditions the forces faced. Isserson's emphasis on centralization is especially interesting, reflecting the new spirit of unified control that permeated Stalin's Soviet Union, and contrasting sharply with the decentralization favored by German mission-oriented tactics.

Finally, there was the true purpose behind Isserson's study: to provide the Soviet army with the precise calculations that it would need for the coming war with the imperialists. From the objectives that he used to make the calculations, the opponent would obviously be Poland, seen since the war of 1920 as the natural enemy of the Soviet Union. The emphasis on the breakthrough and the entire sections of the study devoted to the initial period of the war also make it clear that Isserson thought the next war might begin with a preemptive strike by the Soviet Union into the depths of the Polish defensive positions. At the very end of his report, Isserson made precise predictions about the amount of fuel needed for this assault, the length of time that it would take, the conditions of the roads and bridges along the way, and much else. His conclusion was startling: the Soviet army would be unable to carry out deep operations given the current situation on its borders, the state of the army and its logistical supply lines, and the poor command and control of corps, armies, and fronts.

Voroshilov read Isserson's report and some of the ideas it mentioned were incorporated into Soviet war plans. But the problems that Isserson had discovered confirmed that all was not well with the Soviet's new armor forces. The previous year had seen a new confidence in the strength of Soviet manufacturing, in the correctness of deep battle, and in the advanced state of Soviet doctrine compared to that of any foreign army. Now, however, Tukhachevskii, Isserson, and other top leaders were beginning to realize that serious problems remained. On the positive side, Sediakin had created a realistic model for deep battle that should have made it possible for the army to implement at least the tactical doctrine, yet his manual had not produced the results that the army had expected. Industry, too, seemed in something of a muddle, able to produce tanks in close to the numbers of which the army had dreamed, but not yet capable of delivering them. In organization, the Soviets were breaking new ground, spreading tanks more widely than other armies, but they had not answered the question of how the armor units would work together.

Their former military partners, although outwardly in much the same position as in previous years, had more reason for assurance about the future of their armor forces. Although not yet able to build large numbers of tanks, the Germans had decided on models for their future army, had succeeded in producing a few test vehicles, and were planning to manufacture even more. The new ruler of Germany, unlike some in the past, was a supporter of immediate rearmament and had already shown himself to be a proponent of the armor forces as well. The high command also thought that tanks would play an important part in modern combined-arms battle and had a sophisticated tactical doctrine for their tanks. On the downside, agreement on the tactics that the armor forces would use did not mean that there was any consensus about the overall operational or strategic form for future tank warfare, nor did officers agree on an organizational structure for their armor forces. Yet German advocates of the tank could, like Soviet commanders, have some confidence that their problems with armor would sort themselves out over the next few years.

CHAPTER SIX

Trading Places, 1934-1936

T THE BEGINNING of 1934, an outside observer might have thought that Soviet armor affairs were in a far better position than those in Germany. The Soviets had thousands of tanks, a sophisticated armor doctrine, and official support, all of which the Germans apparently lacked. By 1936, the situation in the two countries had changed completely. The Soviet army had tried and, in the opinion of many commanders, failed to implement deep operations. Based on these experiences influential officers decided that the doctrine was unworkable in its current form and suggested substantial modifications. They even argued that the army had been mistaken about its belief in the decisiveness of the tank. It would be best, they concluded, to return to the earlier emphasis on the infantry and artillery and use tanks like mobile shields or artillery to push the foot soldiers forward. The German army during the same period moved in the opposite direction. Hitler's support for Lutz and Guderian, coupled with a growing number of backers within the high command, allowed the implementation of their organizational and doctrinal concept. The adoption of this idea, later called "blitzkrieg," was helped significantly by the fact that Beck, although still unconvinced about organizational questions, supported a very similar doctrine for armor. Finally, industry's ability to produce several hundred tanks, and Hitler's generous funding of rearmament, removed the last obstacle to realizing the new concept. While some opposition still remained within the officer corps, by 1936 the official armor doctrine was very like that suggested by Lutz and his co-workers.

Despite these triumphs, the Germans would never catch up with their Soviet counterparts in one vital area: the mass production of tanks. Hitler had decided to refrain from open rearmament with the forbidden weapons until he had secured his own power and tested the international waters. However in late 1933 he endorsed the army's plans for a twenty-one division army, including armor units, to be created within the next four years.[1] He made clear the reason for this timing at the end of

1. Edward W. Bennett, *German Rearmament and the West, 1932–1933* (Princeton, N.J.: Princeton University Press, 1979), 496–97.

February 1934, when he told the high command that the army had to be ready for a defensive war in four years and an offensive war in eight.[2] Covert production of tanks and other modern technology thus went forward although proceeding at a relatively moderate rate. During the period 1934–36, Krupp and MAN managed to turn out 477 Pz. I tanks, an impressive achievement by German standards, but far short of Soviet manufacturing capabilities.[3] Reports from Krupp showed that tank production in the early part of the period had been especially slow, with only three of ten tanks produced by the end of January 1934.[4] The result was that the first of the Pz. I light tanks only arrived in armor units near the end of 1934.[5] Even as the vehicles came off the production lines, Lutz and others were still not satisfied that they would be able to handle the missions planned for the armor forces. In late February 1934, Lutz met with Krupp representatives and discussed the production of larger six- and ten-ton tanks.[6] After competition with other tank manufacturing firms, the Waffenamt chose MAN to begin work on the ten-ton Pz. II.[7] The chief of the Waffenamt also discussed even larger tanks, including twelve-ton and eighteen-and-a-half-ton mediums, that would add more power to the fledgling German armor forces.[8]

If German tank production was unable to match immediately that of the Soviet Union, the organizational structure of the new Wehrmacht armor forces soon began to resemble that of its former partners. The three choices before the German army were simple: the British, French, or Soviet models. The British had created an independent armor force designed for operational missions that consisted solely of motorized and mechanized elements. The French, in contrast, had distributed their tanks to the infantry to raise the striking power of the foot soldiers. Combining elements from both armies, the Soviets had established independent mechanized corps, but had also given large numbers of tanks to infantry, cavalry, and combined-arms commanders. Lutz and Guderian forcefully argued for a separate organizational structure for the armor forces, like the British, but even tank supporters were not yet agreed on whether this would include large numbers of foot soldiers or should consist mainly of tanks and other vehicles.[9] To complicate mat-

2. Gerhard Weinberg, *The Foreign Policy of Hitler's Germany: Diplomatic Revolution in Europe, 1933–36* (Chicago: University of Chicago Press, 1970), 178.

3. Werner Oswald, *Kraftfahrzeuge und Panzer der Reichswehr, Wehrmacht und Bundeswehr* (Stuttgart: Motorbuch, 1973), 239, 252.

4. "Fertigungsbericht vom 29.1.34," BA-MA, RH 8/v, 2680 (Krupp).

5. Walther Nehring, *Die Geschichte der deutschen Panzerwaffe 1916 bis 1945* (Berlin: Propyläen Verlag, 1969), 80–81.

6. "Niederschrift über Besprechung in Krawa am 24. Feb. 1934," signed Hagelloch (Krupp representative), 24 February 1934, BA-MA, RH 8/v, 2680 (Krupp).

7. Oswald, *Kraftfahrzeuge und Panzer*, 241, 252.

8. Report by Generalmajor Liese, Chef des Heereswaffenamtes, sent to "Herr Stabschef," "Die Rüstungslage Deutschlands, wie sie sich augenblicklich und voraussichtlich in den nächsten Jahren im Falle eines Krieges darstellt," 16 May 1934, BA-MA, RH 8/v, 957.

9. For discussions of these options, see "Gliederung großer motorisierter Einheiten," *Militär-*

ters further, there were also the so-called "light" divisions, motorized and mechanized units that would grant greater mobility to the infantry or cavalry, but which Guderian and others saw as a dissipation of the armor fist.

The final structure decided upon by the high command was very like that of the Soviet Union, with both an independent armor force and light divisions. Without a doubt the reasons for the success of the independent armor concept, and the creation during the following year of armor divisions, were the persistence and persuasiveness of Guderian and Lutz. Guderian's refusal to compromise on combining tanks and other mobile forces into large self-contained units, the famous "panzer divisions," was in fact the most important contribution that he made to German doctrine. Lutz's support for the divisions, and his arguments for a separate command for the mobile forces, were also vital. During the spring of 1934, a large-scale reorganization of the army resulted in the creation of an independent Motorized Forces Command, with Lutz as its head and Guderian as chief of staff.[10] Lutz was subordinated directly to Werner von Fritsch, the new chief of the Army Command, and was charged with creating and training all the motorized forces.[11] Finding the staff, equipment, and men to make up the new armor forces was the next task. As Hermann Geyer pointed out in March, the Wehrmacht's financial resources were still limited and therefore what was given to one area had to be taken from another. This explains some of the hostility that the established forces showed to armor.[12] In April Walter Nehring, who was already one of Guderian's closest collaborators, met with the head of the armed forces offices (Wehrmachtamt), Walther von Reichenau, to discuss how best to organize armor. Reichenau proposed that the armor forces could be structured through the Motorized Forces Inspectorate either by bringing together individual units out of the entire army or by the immediate reorganization of the 3rd Cavalry Division. This second suggestion surprised Nehring, given the rivalry between the Cavalry Inspectorate and the Motor Troops Inspectorate, but it was in fact the path that was chosen.[13]

Attitudes toward mechanization within the cavalry had in fact changed by the beginning of 1934. As the older generation of cavalrymen left the service, the young officers who remained acknowledged that they had to modify their arm to accom-

---

Wochenblatt, no. 4 (1934): 126–29; "Gliederung neuzeitlicher Truppenkörper: Vorschlag der Kriegsgliederung einer 'Kampfwagen-Division' und einer 'Schnellen Division,'" ibid., nos. 11 and 12 (1934): 407–10, 448–50.

10. Nehring, Geschichte der deutschen Panzerwaffe, 79; Heinz Guderian, Erinnerungen eines Soldaten (Heidelberg: Kurt Vowinckel, 1951), 27.

11. Draft memo by Fritsch, "Betr: Inspektion der Kraftfahrtruppen," 8 June 1934, BA-MA, RH 12–6/v, 1.

12. Memo from Geyer to Beck, "Betr.: Umbau der Wehrmacht," 22 March 1934. BA-MA, RH 2/98, p. 61.

13. Walther Nehring, Die Geschichte der deutschen Panzerwaffe 1916 bis 1945 (Berlin: Propyläen Verlag, 1969), 78.

modate the motor vehicle, although a few still hoped to retain the horse.[14] Officers generally recognized that the day of the horse was numbered and that the only way to save the arm was by the gradual replacement of the horse by the motor vehicle.[15] Those who feared that the chivalry of the past would be lost once the horse was gone could take comfort in the thought that "the heroic 'knightly' force of the future is the tank force and the cavalry will form the personnel nucleus of the new force. The tank will not be the 'heir' of the cavalry, as one so often hears, rather it will constitute the new form of the cavalry, filled with the old cavalry spirit."[16] Much of the personnel for the armor forces did come from the cavalry, while the light divisions, designed to fulfill the missions of the old headquarters cavalry, were formed from cavalry regiments combined with motorized elements.[17] In June the redeployed units of the cavalry, meant for the light divisions and tank force, and the staff of the 3rd Cavalry Division, were subordinated to Lutz.[18] Not long afterward the first true tank battalion was formed under the cover name "Motor Instruction Command," a ruse still felt necessary since Hitler had not yet openly defied Versailles.[19] The armor forces and the motorized light divisions were on the way to making the old horse cavalry obsolete.

In a transition that resembles a similar realization within the Soviet army, it was

14. See e.g. Obrstlt. v, Faber du Faur, Kdr. d. 8. (Pr.) R. R., "Die operational Aufklärung im Zukunftskriege," *Militär-Wochenblatt*, nos. 26 and 27 (1934): 849–55, 884–87. Poseck of course wanted to use the motor vehicle to supplement but not replace the horse. General der Kavallerie a.D. M. v, Poseck, "Kavallerie von einst und jetzt," ibid., no. 43 (1934): 1464–68. Faber du Faur expanded his interpretation of the combination of motor vehicle and horse in a later article: "Zusammensetzung schnell beweglicher Verbände: Begründet an den Anforderungen der operationaln Verwendung der Kavalleriekorps der Westfront 1914," ibid., nos. 31 and 32 (1934): 1009–15, 1044–49.

15. See Oberst a.D. Graf Schack and Obrstlt. v, Faber du Faur, "Die Panzerdivision im Kavalleriekorps-Verband," ibid., no. 29 (1934): 952–953; Oberst a.D. Graf Schack, "Kriegserfahrungen mit Kavallerie früherer Prägung," ibid., no. 28 (1934): 922–23; Hansen, Oberstlt. und Chef d. St. d. 3. Kav, Div, "Noch einmal: 'Kriegserfahrungen mit Kavallerie früherer Prägung,'" ibid. no. 33 (1934): 1085–87; Generalleutnant a.D. E. Fleck, "Unsere Kavallerie im Weltkriege und in Zukunft," ibid., no. 37 (1934): 1219–22; Generalleutnant a.D. Erfurth, "Zum Streit um das Kavallerieproblem," ibid., no. 47 (1934): 1625–27.

16. Genlt. a.D. Marx, "Kavallerie und Kraftfahrwaffe in der Zukunft," ibid., no. 46 (1934): 1588–89. At least one writer disagreed, arguing that the German army needed a "mechanical horse" but that the tank was not suited to fulfill this role. "Kavallerie- oder Motorisierungsproblem?" ibid., no. 5 (1934): 164–67.

17. In fact 40 percent of the armor forces officers would be former cavalrymen. Kenneth Macksey, *Guderian: Creator of the Blitzkrieg* (New York: Stein and Day, 1975), 62; Ferdinand von Senger und Etterlin, "Senger," in *Hitler's Generals*, ed. Correlli Barnett (London: Weidenfeld and Nicolson, 1989), 378–79.

18. Draft memo by Fritsch, "Betr: Inspektion der Kraftfahrtruppen," 8 June 1934, BA-MA, RH 12–6/v, 1.

19. B. H. Liddell Hart, *The Other Side of the Hill* (London: Macmillan, 1993), 121. Wilhelm Thoma was the commander of the new tank unit.

only now, as the German army contemplated a wholesale mechanization, that it began to deal with the full implications of this decision. In late March 1934 Geyer, who would shortly be put in charge of an army corps, sent a memorandum to Beck in which he argued that the reconstruction of the army required the high command to fundamentally rethink the tactics, organization, and relationship to each other of the different arms.[20] In his closer examination of these questions, Geyer wrote that while before the world war, the infantry had had over half of the manpower assigned to the land forces, in the future it would have less than 25 percent. This meant that "the infantry will neither in personnel nor in materiel be the true core of the army."[21] This was extremely important because, up to this point, the raison d'être of the other arms had been to help the infantry forward. If the infantry would not be the core of the army, its mission, as well as those of all other branches, had to change. As Geyer put it, the army had now to examine carefully each of the arms and determine how to alter organization, operations, and tactics without allowing "sentiment or thoughts of prestige" to interfere.[22]

Other officers agreed that they needed to rethink official tank tactics to reflect the new relationship between the arms. Official German armor doctrine of 1934 had not changed greatly since the late twenties. In a typical description, tanks would be used in envelopments, against the rear and flanks of the enemy, or against the enemy's reserves. Care had to be taken that the machines did not get too far from the other forces, since close cooperation between all the arms was important. In maneuver warfare, the tank would be decisive as direct support for the infantry, as reinforcement for the artillery, or for creating a breakthrough. Official doctrine continued to endorse mass use, surprise, and deep organization of the attack, while the objectives for the tank attack varied widely, including enemy artillery, infantry, reserves, rear lines of communication, or command posts. The overall stress of doctrine was on the variety of options, dependent on the particular circumstances of the battle, that an officer had at his disposal.[23] What was not settled was the point that Geyer had raised: the exact relationship of armor forces to the other branches on the battlefield. Was the infantry still the center of the effort, or had the pendulum now swung in favor of machine warfare? And, if tanks were to be granted more importance, how would this change future wars?

From 1934 on, the German officer corps spent as much time discussing armor in battle as they did tank organization. Three officers, Geyer, Ludwig Ritter von Eimannsberger, and Nehring, who submitted differing visions for how doctrine could be reformulated, added vital touches to the new discourse. Geyer emphasized

20. Memo from Geyer to Beck, "Umbau der Wehrmacht," 22 March 1934, BA-MA, RH 2/98, p. 62.
    21. Ibid., pp. 66–67.
    22. Ibid., p. 67.
    23. "Kampfwageneinsatz: Offizierlehrgange Berlin, Az. 73/34 geh.," March 1934, BA-MA, RH 12–6/v, 1.

in his memorandum to Beck that armor battle would occur at great speed, but that its high demands for fuel and ammunition would force a rhythm of short blow (ending when supplies were used up) and long pause (to refuel and resupply) on the modern army.[24] Eimannsberger, an Austrian whose major work on the future of tank warfare, *Der Kampfwagenkrieg*, would have a great deal of influence on the Wehrmacht,[25] agreed. Fuller's ideas of war, he wrote, seemed based on inexhaustible supplies of fuel provided at the right moment of battle. This was simply unrealistic.[26] Anyone who wanted to fight a war "must have a river, nay, a torrent of petroleum endlessly flowing to him."[27] Only a nation with secure lines of sea communication, such as Britain, or a country with sure land connections to a friendly producer of oil, could conduct war at all.[28] Critics of the tank would seize on this weakness to prove that armor was not the "panacea" that Guderian, Lutz, and others made it out to be. Eimannsberger also pointed out that tanks would not automatically return movement to warfare and instead foresaw the next war consisting primarily of positional combat.[29] The "Fulleresque" lightening war of machines, rushing through enemy territory to win a quick, bloodless victory, was possible only in completely fluid conditions that would never again occur, a point that, as we shall see, some within the German also agreed with. Meanwhile, Nehring argued that the medium and light tanks should have completely different missions. The heavier machines, the true offensive weapon, would destroy enemy artillery and pave the way for the lighter tanks. The light tanks would remain tied to the infantry, aiding them directly by suppressing enemy machine guns and trench mortars and eventually breaking through to the enemy's field artillery.[30] This idea, already proposed by Heigl, made a great deal of sense to the German high command, and would soon be adopted.

These basically optimistic views of the future of armor forces must be balanced with the two major experiences of tank use during 1934: British maneuvers and the Chaco War in Bolivia. Most officers of the British army considered their large maneuvers, designed to test the idea of mass armor use, a failure. Negative analyses of this experiment were a major factor in their decision not to develop tank forces further.[31] German officers watched the maneuvers closely, still seeing the British as

24. Memo from Geyer to Beck, "Umbau der Wehrmacht," 22 March 1934, BA-MA, RH 2/98, pp. 68–70.

25. See e.g. "Die Verwendung von Kavallerie nach erfolgtem Tankeinbruch," ibid., no. 10 (1934): 374–76.

26. Ludwig Ritter von Eimannsberger, *Der Kampfwagenkrieg* (Munich: Lehmann, 1934), 111.

27. Ibid., 215.

28. Ibid., 216.

29. Ibid., 112.

30. Major Walther Nehring, *Kampfwagen an die Front! Geschichtliche und neuzeitliche Entwicklung des Kampfwagens ("Tanks") im Auslande* (Leipzig: Detke, 1934), 15–19.

31. See Harold R. Winton, *To Change an Army: General Sir John Burnett-Stuart and British Armor Doctrine, 1927–1938* (Lawrence: University Press of Kansas, 1988), 177–83.

the innovators and vanguard of mechanized warfare. The special tank exercises impressed some German observers, who commented in particular on the effective use of the radio, and disputed the British belief that antitank weapons had succeeded beyond anyone's expectations.[32] Another analysis of the maneuvers, made by a cavalry captain, was more critical of the British use of motorized units. He thought that the British had asked too much of their mobile forces, including too long a march and then an advance at night on unknown terrain. He concluded that the reason that these units had not lived up to expectations was not because of some failing in the units themselves, but because their commanders did not have enough experience on which to draw.[33]

In a memorandum that gives some insight into his still developing ideas on armor warfare, Beck agreed that the maneuvers were "a failure" not because the British had dared too much, but because they had not used their armor forces to the fullest. He thought that there had been serious flaws in the conduct and leadership of the exercise, and in the organization of the tank regiments. British commanders had not given the armor units complete freedom of movement, and they had attempted to use the tanks against comparatively small objectives rather than the major ones that the units were designed to attack. He also used British criticisms of the maneuvers to denigrate the effectiveness of independent armor units, comments that were almost certainly directed at Lutz and Guderian.[34] Overall the memorandum showed Beck's wholehearted support for armor, but his continuing caution over the "extravagant" claims of the "extremists."

If Beck thought that the British maneuvers showed that large armor units had their limitations, the Chaco War between Bolivia and Paraguay gave ammunition to those few German officers who believed that the whole idea of decisive tank warfare was wrong. A number of Germans took part in the war and this, combined with the use of a fair number of tanks by the Bolivians, created an interest in the war among German officers. The tanks did not do as well as some had hoped, even when used in ideal tank-fighting conditions, that is against dug-in positions and on the flat pampas. In two battles during July and August 1933, the machines broke down, were shot up by antitank fire, or were unable to exploit breakthroughs.[35] An analysis of the vehicles employed during the war said that the Carden-Loyds "did not prove their worth. In the end they were shoved off to the back as useless for war." This was an important point because the German Pz. I, the only tank available in any numbers for rearming the Reichswehr, and for some the ideal main bat-

32. "Englische Manöver 1934," Militär-Wochenblatt, no. 13 (1934): 489–94.

33. Rittmeister Crisolli, "Kampfweise leicht beweglicher Kräfte," ibid., no. 29 (1935): 1135–38.

34. Remarks by Beck on maneuvers of British armor corps of September 1934, "England: Manöver des Panzerverrbandes 18. bis 21.9.1934," December 1934, BA-MA, H 1/662, Beck-Studien, no. 13, pp. 360–66.

35. "Von einem Mitkämpfer," "Neueste Kriegserfahrungen. Nach Gefechsberichten aus dem Chacokrieg," Militär-Wochenblatt, no. 40 (1934): 1339–44.

tle tank, was a close copy of the Carden-Loyd. The heavier Vickers had done somewhat better, but still suffered frustrating technical failures. The officer who wrote
the report tried to be optimistic about the lessons of the war, saying that tanks had
shown that they could attack decisively, but it was clear to the unbiased observer
that armor forces had not performed as hoped.[36]

As the German army struggled to redefine how war would be fought if the country
ever managed to rearm itself, the Soviet high command began to have serious
doubts about the validity of its own doctrine. In January 1934 Egorov gathered leading members of the Red Army high command, including Sediakin, Konstantin
Ol'shanskii (the chief of the First Directorate of the UMM), and Nikolai Rogovskii
(chief of the Artillery Directorate), to reflect on what could be done about deep battle. Discussion focused on the *Temporary Instructions* and on concerns that those
present had with certain elements of deep battle – concerns provoked by the inability of the Red Army to implement the doctrine during the previous two years.
The principal topics of the meeting were the correct use of motorized infantry and
DD (long-range) tanks and the continued existence of the DPP (long-range infantry
support) echelon.

Rogovskii and Ol'shanskii began by arguing that the doctrine demanded foot
soldiers who could travel everywhere with the tanks. This meant that the Red Army
had to have the armored infantry transporters suggested in previous years, not just
motorized infantry brought to the battlefield in trucks, to penetrate into the enemy
rear or into his tactical reserves.[37] Conversation then turned to the DD echelon,
with Aleksei Fedotov, head of the Leningrad Artillery School, arguing that the main
task of these tanks should be the destruction of the artillery. Rogovskii thought that
the entire question of how the DD tanks ought to fight in battle was a serious problem. If they destroyed the artillery as Fedotov suggested, then they would be unable
to attack the enemy reserves, one of their basic missions. The sequence of actions
demanded of the DD echelon was too complex in his opinion: the standard description of deep battle (according to him) called for the DD group to head for the
enemy's rear, then from the rear attack toward the front of the enemy's positions,
and finally find the reserves. This complicated series of maneuvers would be impossible to carry out in a real battle. He suggested simplifying the DD mission to
immediately seeking the opponent's operational reserves.[38]

Finally the commanders looked at the DPP echelon. Egorov asked whether it was
necessary to have all three tank groups or whether two would do. According to
Ol'shanskii, the experimental studies conducted during 1933 showed that the mis-

36. "Die Waffen des Chacokrieges," ibid., no. 19 (1934): 740–43.
37. Stenogram, "Soveshchanie u nachal'nik shtaba RKKA 19.I.1934g," RGVA, f. 31983, op. 2,
d. 33, ll. 1, 6.
38. Ibid., ll. 2–4.

sions set aside for DPP tanks were already being carried out by the other groups. Rogovskii and Stepan Bogomiakov (who worked in Voroshilov's commissariat) also spoke out against the DPP group. Rogovskii said that if it was supposed to support the infantry, as its name implied, then it should be more closely connected with infantry movements and thus become a sort of NPP (direct infantry support) group. It would be better to have a more powerful NPP group and leave it at that.[39] Bogomiakov agreed that the NPP group could perform the DPP mission while machine gun resistance, one of the primary targets of the DPP attack, would be destroyed during the process of the battle itself.[40] Another officer present dissented, saying that DPP tanks were absolutely necessary to combat machine guns and allow the infantry to approach and attack. As Sediakin pointed out, experience had shown that the greatest threat to infantry came not from the first line of defense, but from the positions that they could not see.[41] Fedotov supported this position, saying that elimination of the DPP tanks would create a rupture between the DD and NPP echelons.[42] Egorov ended the discussion by declaring that the army would need to reexamine the role of DPP tanks. Perhaps the best way to view them was as a tactical weapon. After fulfilling their tasks and with the approach of the infantry, they could immediately be used for other missions.[43] Later in the year he would go further, asserting that the three-echelon system was too complex for implementation. He supported instead the division of tanks into those which would accompany the infantry and those that would attack the artillery, effectively ridding the army of the NPP group.[44]

These concerns about deep battle were given further impetus by the abysmal failure of the 1934 maneuvers. At the annual meeting of the high command, the debacle of the exercises and a debate over the future of deep battle/deep operations dominated speeches and commentary. Tukhachevskii was one of the first to admit that there were serious problems with implementing the doctrine, saying that the Red Army was but at the first stages of learning how to solve problems stemming from it.[45] In his analysis of the Volga district exercises, Voroshilov could only say that "huge tactical mistakes were committed giving a false impression of the character of modern battle."[46] Egorov looked more broadly at the results of maneuvers in the Belorussian, Ukrainian, and Leningrad districts, and flatly concluded that the

39. Ibid., ll. 11–12.

40. Ibid., l. 12.

41. Ibid., ll. 12–13.

42. Ibid., ll. 11–12.

43. Ibid., l. 14.

44. "Stenograficheskii otchet zasedanie Voennogo Soveta pri NKO Soiuza SSR 10–12 dekabria 1934 g.," RGVA, f. 4, op. 18, d. 51, ll. 15–16.

45. Ibid., ll. 253–55.

46. "Sovershennye sekretnye prikazy RVS 1934 No. 0019," 16 September 1934, RGVA, f. 4, op. 15, d. 1, l. 66.

army had not succeeded in working out the basic problems of mobile warfare and especially the use of large mechanized units.[47] In his final report for the year Sediakin, now deputy chief of staff, had to admit that the army had not mastered deep battle or the independent action of mechanized formations in the opponent's operational rear.[48] Khalepskii pointed out that the exercises had shown the need to work on something even more basic, namely driving the tanks. The army had not perfected this, let alone the more difficult tactical elements of deep battle.[49] The large number of accidents suffered by the armor forces, 1,277 during the first nine months of 1934, seemed to prove his contention.[50]

The results of the experimental studies, in conjunction with the failures of previous years, led to calls for a thorough reexamination of deep battle. Some of the criticism directed at the doctrine – from Khalepskii and Sediakin, for instance – required only minor revisions in what they accepted as an essentially correct view of future warfare.[51] Other commanders believed that the exercise had proven that the Soviet army had to rethink deep battle in a more fundamental way. Their proposals touched on four areas: cooperation with other forces; the role of the infantry; organization of mechanized formations; and the need to rely less on set dogma. On cooperation with the other arms, Egorov suggested that artillery could closely support tanks, perhaps even accompany them into battle, although Khalepskii objected that this kind of connection between tanks and artillery might cause the artillery to hit its own infantry.[52] Eideman thought that the parachute troops should not use regular army tactics, but rather act as partisans in the enemy's rear to tie him down.[53] Shaposhnikov made the same proposal as Rogovskii and Ol'shanskii earlier in the year: mounting the infantry on transporters to make cooperation between armor forces and the infantry closer and more effective. Both types of forces had to work together and cooperate completely, so there was no need to argue about which was the core of modern battle.[54]

This last comment was significant because the Soviet army – ironically in view of the direction that German thought was moving – had again opened up the debate over what should be the focus of combat: the infantry or the armor forces. In a surprising shift from his previous convictions on deep battle, Egorov now argued

47. "Stenograficheskii otchet zasedanie Voennogo Soveta pri NKO Soiuza SSR 10–12 dekabria 1934 g.: ob itogakh boevoi podgotovki 1934 i zadachakh na 1935 g.," RGVA, f. 4, op. 18, d. 51, l. 8.

48. "Sekretnye prikazy RVS i NKO 1934, No. 0102: ob itogakh boevoi podgotovki RKKA za 1934 god i zadachakh na 1935 god.," 17 December 1934, RGVA, f. 4, op. 15, d. 3, ll. 417, 427–429.

49. Ibid., ll. 103–4.

50. List of accidents in the RKKA, RGVA, f. 4, op. 14, d. 1449, l. 20.

51. "Stenograficheskii otchet zasedanie Voennogo Soveta pri NKO Soiuza SSR 10–12 dekabria 1934 g.: ob itogakh boevoi podgotovki 1934 i zadachakh na 1935 g.," RGVA, f. 4, op. 18, d. 51, ll. 31, 109–11.

52. Ibid., ll. 16–17, 107–8.

53. Ibid., ll. 195–96.

54. Ibid., ll. 233–34.

that the most important result of the studies was to demonstrate that infantry still had to be preeminent in battle. Infantry, he declared were the decisive force in modern combat and deep operations based all of its armor manual calculations on their movement. All other arms of the service, including tanks, had to direct their efforts toward helping the infantry achieve its basic task; the capture of the opponent's fortified position.[55] Later in the discussion Egorov redoubled his support for the primacy of the infantry, returning to the old formula that living forces were decisive in battle, while technology only strengthened them.[56] Sergei Kamenev, at this point still Voroshilov's deputy, objected to this regression to a view of the infantry as "queen of the field." Before the appearance of aircraft or tanks it was possible to speak this way, but now the three arms in combination were decisive. He added that especially in deep battle, in the far reaches of the battlefield, both aircraft and tanks had decisive roles. Then, in an incident that showed Kamenev's precarious political position despite his rank, he was interrupted by someone who shouted that this was not the problem, the problem lay in where the army's center would be.[57]

Egorov also suggested that the exercises had shown that the mechanized corps were unwieldy and needed reorganization. The studies had not provided conclusive data to decide the organization of these units, but he was convinced that if they were founded on current command and control technology and structuring of the rear, then they would be unable to fulfill their operational missions. The army had to have a very mobile command and rear, otherwise the units themselves lost the necessary mobility.[58] Khalepskii agreed with Egorov: mechanized corps organization was indeed unwieldy. The army had overloaded it with auxiliary units such as chemical, artillery, and engineering detachments, and not enough aircraft for reconnaissance. He suggested that the army reconsider the rifle brigade in the mechanized formation, which was completely inappropriate for its supposed mission, and perhaps combine the mechanized brigade with a parachute brigade. He also pointed out that the army planned to carry operations ninety kilometers deep, but had not calculated fuel use so that tanks could return after the operation. He did not, however, propose any radical changes within the tank units themselves, noting only that a lessening of the number of tanks in each platoon would shorten the rear and cut demand for oil and gas.[59]

The final point of contention was over the dogmatic use of the *Provisional Instructions* and other ideas on deep battle in place of learning to fight on the real, complex battlefield. One commander flatly stated that he was against the "abstract and bare" manual. An exercise that he had attended, based on the *Provisional Instructions*, had gone very badly, demonstrating how wrong was its use of "ready-made cate-

55. Ibid., l. 14.
56. Ibid., l. 16.
57. Ibid., l. 228.
58. Ibid., ll. 23–24.
59. Ibid., ll. 111–13.

gories."[60] Ol'shanskii argued specifically that actual battlefield conditions had to determine the mission of DD tanks rather than fighting solely by the manual, which had stated that this echelon should only suppress the artillery.[61] Eideman had a more sophisticated view of the oversimplified routines that had for some time taken the place of "true" deep battle. Remembering the evolution of his own tactical thought when the army had first encountered the new weapons and the development of technology, he thought that these routines were an inevitable stage of the Red Army's operational-tactical development. Set routines played the same role as a primer did for an illiterate person attempting to learn to read. Only after mastering the new technological culture could commanders begin to really study the tactics of deep battle. Now, he continued, the high command had achieved a certain level of development and was obligated to put an end to dogmatism about how to fight in modern battle.[62]

The growing dissatisfaction with current armor doctrine was expressed as well by two partial revisions of deep battle ideas published in 1934. Nikolai Ernest, who would soon distinguish himself in Spain fighting with the Republican tank forces, sought to redress the disregard of the defensive shown by most theories of armor warfare. In his view the tankette, rather than solely a reconnaissance vehicle, should be the "basic mobile antipersonnel weapon of the defensive." He believed that it could easily attack infantry advancing behind the enemy's tanks.[63] He also saw light tanks, armed with guns, as the army's main antitank weapon. In defensive combat they were to fight independently, although in coordination with the artillery, against tanks breaking through into the battalion area.[64] The other revision came from the assistant chief of the Training Directorate. He placed much more emphasis on encirclements in his delineation of deep offensive battle, and consistently returned to the terms "envelopment" (*okhvat*), "flanking movement" (*obkhod*), and "encirclement" (*okruzhenie*) when describing deep battle.[65] He did not, however, explain how the echeloned DPP, DD, and NPP attacking forces of the standard deep battle description, would carry out these broad movements. Nor did he make clear how commanders confronted with these two interpretations of deep battle, the one an overall principle and the other a detailed, tactically precise description, would resolve their contradictions.[66]

60. Ibid., ll. 227–28.

61. Ibid., l. 217.

62. Ibid., ll. 197–99. The Russian words translated as "dogmatism," "readymade categories," "oversimplification" and "routine" are "skhematizm" and "shablon." They both imply acting by rote and catch phrase rather than dealing with real, complex conditions.

63. N. Ernest, *Sovremennye tanki v oborone i nastuplenie* (Moscow: Gosudarstvennoe Voennoe Izdatel'stvo, 1934), 8–9.

64. Ibid., 9–10.

65. Report by the Assistant Chief of Staff of the BP, "Glubokii nastupatel'nyi boi," 27 January 1934, RGVA, f. 31983, op. 2, d. 33, ll. 32–33.

66. Ibid., l. 63.

By mid-1934, then, the Soviet army had apparently reached an impasse over deep battle. While commanders still thought that the doctrine was valid, there was a great deal of skepticism about the possibility of ever implementing it in actual combat. This may explain why there was greater interest in the progress made by other armies with armor doctrine. In a memorandum from April 1934, the UMM asked Soviet military attachés to seek answers to specific tactical questions from the maneuvers that they attended and from officers with whom they spoke. Ol'shanskii wanted the attachés to find out for instance, foreigners' views on the use of tanks in difficult circumstances such as at night and in forests; the basic principles of tank use in cooperation with other types of forces; the organization of artillery support for tank attacks, and much more. The fact that these were not the kind of questions that one would ask so as to prepare antiarmor defenses supports the view that the UMM was seeking answers to problems that the Red Army itself had encountered.[67] Even German thought, disparaged not long before as inferior to that of the Soviet army, was consulted. Ernest quoted Cochenhausen extensively in his book, as an innovative supporter of the deep battle idea.[68] There were, however, limits beyond which commanders were not permitted to go, and Egorov had to remind them in late 1934 that the army did not have to look at possible opponents and copy everything that they did as better than the Soviet way.[69]

While Soviet doubts increased, German confidence in their new tank units grew stronger during the following year. This confidence was aided by Hitler's decision in March 1935 to renounce openly the restrictions of the Versailles Treaty and call for the immediate creation of an army of thirty-six divisions. Only the size of the expansion came as a surprise to the military, which had always based its war plans on a future twenty-one-division army.[70] Earlier that month Beck in fact had estimated that the army needed at least sixty-three divisions (infantry, armor, and cavalry) and almost a million and a half men for the defense of Germany.[71] The renunciation of Versailles was a calculated gamble by Hitler, who guessed rightly that the Western powers would not risk war to enforce the treaty, and it paved the way for the expansion of the armor and air forces. The armed forces had far to go in both areas,

67. List of questions for which military attaches were to seek answers, signed Ol'shanskii, Chief of the I Directorate UMM, and Miasnikov, Chief of the I Department, 5 April 1934, RGVA, f. 31983, op. 2, d. 146, l. 96.

68. Ernest, *Sovremennye tanki v oborone i nastuplenie*, 13–16.

69. "Stenograficheskii otchet zasedanie Voennogo Soveta pri NKO Soiuza SSR 10–12 dekabria 1934 g.: ob itogakh boevoi podgotovki 1934 i zadachakh na 1935 g.," RGVA, f. 4, op. 18, d. 51, l. 17.

70. Wilhelm Deist, *The Wehrmacht and German Rearmament* (Toronto: University of Toronto Press, 1981), 37–38; Guderian, *Erinnerungen eines Soldaten*, 28.

71. Memo from Beck, "Mindestforderungen für ein Rüstungsabkommen," 6 March 1935, BA-MA, II H 656, Beck-Studien, no. 24, pp. 415–24.

but particularly in regard to armor. In the spring of 1935 the German army had only seven motorized detachments, each with less than five hundred men.[72] In preparation for the planned expansion, the Defense Law of 21 May set up a new military, the Wehrmacht, and created a Motorized Forces Command. By September the latter structure had become the Armor Forces Command with Lutz as its first chief.[73] At the end of June the military produced a detailed plan for creating Hitler's expanded army, which would consist of thirty-three infantry and three armor divisions.[74] In October the armor divisions were established under Lutz's command and Guderian, who was still only a colonel, was named commander of one of the units.[75] That same month Guderian became chief of staff of the Armor Forces Command, while Lutz was made chief of the new "Inspectorate for Army Motorization and the Armor Forces."[76] Guderian's rise to power had begun and would only accelerate in the coming years.

In response to Hitler's call for a modern army, the production and delivery of tanks for the new armor units increased dramatically during 1935. At the same time, the multiplicity of demands placed on available raw materials, added to limited factory capacity, meant that tank production remained well below Soviet levels.[77] Since the Pz. I machine gun tanks were the only vehicles available, units were armed with these.[78] Lutz thought the Pz. I adequate for fighting the majority of Germany's potential enemies, although he added that armor forces would be more effective with tanks armed with guns. To compensate for the lack of firepower over the short term, he suggested following Heigl's (and Nehring's) proposal: giving every armor company a few tanks with small-caliber guns and every battalion one tank with a large-caliber gun.[79] Industry began to turn out the larger machines within the year. Over the next five years Germany would produce about 3,150 of the Pz. II, Lutz's tank with a small-caliber gun, and the more powerful Maybach Pz.

72. Nehring, *Geschichte der deutschen Panzerwaffe*, 80.

73. Wilhelm Deist, "The Rearmament of the Wehrmacht," in Militärgeschichtliches Forschungsamt, *Germany and the Second World War*, vol. 1: *The Build-up of German Aggression* (Oxford: Clarendon Press, 1990.; Nehring, *Geschichte der deutschen Panzerwaffe*, 79; Guderian, *Erinnerungen eines Soldaten*, 29.

74. Deist, "Rearmament of the Wehrmacht," 425–26.

75. Liddell Hart, *The Other Side of the Hill*, 65; Guderian, *Erinnerungen eines Soldaten*, 29; Heinz Guderian, *Achtung – Panzer!* tr. Christopher Duffy (London: Arms and Armour Press, 1992), 163.

76. Nehring, *Geschichte der deutschen Panzerwaffe*, 79.

77. See Erich von Manstein, *Aus einem Soldatenleben 1887–1939* (Bonn: Athenäum Verlag, 1958), 240–43.

78. A typical armor company in 1935 had twenty-one of the machines, although since there were not yet enough of the light vehicles to go around, some exercises still employed dummy tanks. Hanz Voigt, "Tagebuch der 5. Kompanie/Panzer-Regiment 1," by. BA-MA, RH 39/590, pp. 1–2; "IX Armeekorps Schulübung 1935," BA-MA, RH 53–9/22, p. 152.

79. *Erfahrungsbericht über die Versuchsübungen einer Panzerdivision auf dem Truppenübungsplatz Munster im August 1935* (Berlin: Kommando der Panzertruppen. 24 December 1935), BA-MA, RHD 26/2, pp. 8–9.

I-B.[80] The army also began to search for a manufacturer of a fifteen-ton medium with a large-caliber gun, the Pz. III, in 1935.[81]

In direct contrast to the Soviet experience, maneuvers with the new mechanized units only strengthened German confidence in their armor doctrine and organization. In early 1934 Guderian provided a successful demonstration of the armor forces for Hitler at Kümmersdorf.[82] There were also seminal maneuvers under General Erwin von Witzleben, which helped to define the role of the mechanized cavalry unit.[83] The following year did not start off as well, with most exercises employing tanks in a limited way.[84] A larger exercise held during June was also disappointing for armor supporters.[85] These early failures made the success of the summer maneuvers all the more striking. The army had created a practice armor division as soon as Hitler renounced Versailles, and in August 1935 held maneuvers to test the concept of combining tank units with motorized reconnaissance, infantry, and artillery in this large formation. Parts of the exercise had the division fighting independently while others practiced cooperation with the various forces.[86] During the actual exercises, Fritsch planned a small surprise. He thought that the doubters among the spectators would hardly be convinced of the worth of the new units by an ordinary display of their capabilities, and therefore ordered them, after the successful breakthrough with which the exercise should have ended, to turn and suddenly attack the flanks of the advancing enemy.[87] The division performed this maneuver well, to the astonishment of some in the spectators.[88] The result was greater respect for the armor forces in general and the armor division idea in particular.

But doubters still remained within the Wehrmacht. The objections to the new armor forces were the same as those expressed earlier in the decade: that machines could never replace men, that antitank weapons were stronger than armor, that the horse was an integral part of warfare, and so on. The successes won by the tank in organization, production, and maneuvers not only did not convince the doubters, it made their struggle against "excessive" confidence in the tank all the more in-

---

80. Oswald, *Kraftfahrzeuge und Panzer*, 240–41, 252.

81. Ibid., 243, 254.

82. Macksey, *Guderian*, 58.

83. Senger und Etterlin, "Senger," 378.

84. "Übungen des VI Armeekorps: Gedachter Verlauf und Schildrichtersdienst," BA-MA, RH 53–6/28; "IX Armeekorps Schulübung 1935," BA-MA, RH 53–9/22, pp. 132, 144, 160.

85. "Nachträgliche Betrachtungen zu dem Einsatz des Panzerkorps in der Lage der Truppenamtsreise vom 13.6.1935." 25 July 1935, BA-MA, RH 2/v, 134, *Beck-Studien*, no. 35, pp. 460–62.

86. *Erfahrungsbericht über die Versuchsübungen einer Panzerdivision auf dem Truppenübungsplatz Munster im August 1935* (Berlin: Kommando der Panzertruppen, 24 December 1935), BA-MA, RHD 26/2, p. 2.

87. Nehring, *Geschichte der deutschen Panzerwaffe*, 88–89.

88. W. Heinemann, "The Development of German Armoured Forces 1918–40, " in *Armoured Warfare*, ed. J. P. Harris and F. H. Toase (London: Batsford, 1990), 58.

tense.[89] To test the relative strengths of antitank defenses and tanks, a military academy held a war game during the winter of 1935–36 that pitted an armor division against an obstacle construction unit. The armor division was to attack the deep left flank of a well-defended enemy and attempt to break through. The captain who wrote up the conclusions of the war game thought that on a sector with favorable terrain armor divisions could always break through obstacle lines. The defenses could only prevent a breakthrough in the rarest cases (such as in mountains or on rivers), since the tanks were often able to bypass them.[90] The lessons from this significant exercise were, however, not widely publicized and thus did not stop the criticism of the armor division idea.

The one person who did not join in the attacks on the armor forces was the man later identified by Guderian as the main enemy of the tank – the army chief of staff, Ludwig Beck.[91] As we have seen, while Guderian did run into some opposition within the high command, Beck and the staff in general were not completely opposed to the concept of armor divisions fighting for distant independent objectives. The clash between the two men, as many scholars have pointed out, was caused by the fact that Beck had to take into consideration the entire army, and especially the needs of the infantry, while Guderian focused his time and energy on promoting the armor forces.[92] More fundamentally, the underlying factor in the controversy

89. For examples of these objections see Oberst a.D. Immanuel, "Welches ist die Hauptwaffe der Gegenwart?," *Militär-Wochenblatt*, no. 25 (1935) 974–76; General d. Artl. i. R. v. Eimannsberger, "Der Kämpfer und die Maschine," ibid., no. 45 (1935): 1804–6; "Gr.," "Schnelligkeit?" ibid., no. 44 (1935): 1768; "G.," "Für und Wider," ibid., no. 5 (1935): 192–93. One retort to these can be found in "'Für und Wider.' Eine Entgegnung von Major Nedtwig," ibid., no. 8 (1935): 318–20. Nehring also argued strongly for the tank as an antiarmor weapon. Walther Nehring, *Kampfwagen an die Front!* 12–14. The cavalry's arguments can be found in Oberst von Faber du Faur, "Ultra posse nemo obligatur!" *Militär-Wochenblatt*, no. 26 (1935): 1011–13. See also "Kann die Geschwindigkeit moderner Reiterei gesteigert werden?" ibid., no. 37 (1935): 1463–66; "Panzerverbände im Angriff," ibid., no. 48 (1935): 1931–36; General der Kavallerie a.D. M. v. Poseck, "Aus großer Zeit vor zwanzig Jahren: Kriegserfahrungen in der Verwenddung moderner Kavallerie," ibid., nos. 30 and 31 (1935): 1171–75 1211–13. Guderian answered these in Guderian, "Heereskavallerie und motorisierte Verbände," ibid., no. 34 (1935): 1338–39.

90. "Kriegsspiel Panzer-Division gegen Sperrverband: Lehrgang IIb. Winter 1935/36," BA-MA, RH 16/v, 100.

91. See Guderian's bitter criticism of Beck in *Erinnerungen eines Soldaten*, 26–27. Other writers have agreed with Guderian. See Macksey, *Guderian*, 61, 63–64; Nehring, *Geschichte der deutschen Panzerwaffe*, 71, 73–74.

92. See Klaus-Jürgen Müller, *Armee, Politik und Gesellschaft in Deutschland 1933–1945* (Paderborn: Ferdinand Schöningh, 1979), 88–91; Robert O'Neill, "Fritsch, Beck and the Führer," in Barnett, *Hitler's Generals*, 28; Deist, *The Wehrmacht and German Rearmament*, 42–43; Hubertus Senff, *Die Entwicklung der Panzerwaffe im deutschen Heer zwischen den beiden Weltkriegen* (Frankfurt am Main: Mittler, 1969), 20, 29; Manstein, *Aus einem Soldatenleben*, 240–41. See Schottelius and Caspar's special reading of Beck's opposition to Guderian in Herbert Schottelius and Gustav-Adolf Caspar, "Die Organisation des Heeres 1933–1939," in *Handbuch zur deutschen Militärgeschichte 1648–1939*, vol. 8:

between the two men was the relatively weak financial and industrial position of Germany.[93] Unlike the Soviet military, which could call on the entire economic resources of their country to create a technologically advanced army, the Wehrmacht had limited funds on which to draw. Guderian and his supporters argued that these limitations forced the army to choose either to create large mechanized formations; or to give the tanks to the infantry and cavalry; or to give them to the combined arms commanders. It was simply not possible to do all three as the Soviets had.

But this was what Beck hoped to do. By 1935 he was convinced that he had to raise the offensive power of the Wehrmacht and concluded that the saturation of the army, and especially the infantry, with tanks was the best way to accomplish this goal.[94] After the large spring maneuvers, Beck remarked that the army had to distinguish between armor divisions, which would fight independently, and tank units that would support the infantry. For the maneuvers the army had decided not to subordinate the armor formation to the corps, but rather focused on cooperation between both. Beck thought that the best method for coordinating action between infantry and tank units was still an open question. During the first phase of the attack, when only part of the armor division (the tanks and artillery) had fought, he thought that subordination of armor to the corps commander made more sense.[95] The tanks would thus reinforce the combat power of the infantry divisions at the beginning of the attack. He believed that "[o]nly joint work between the tanks and the fighting components of the infantry divisions will succeed in paving the way in and through the enemy, who up to this point is still unshaken; only then can an advance of the rest of the armor division units be considered." The only conclusion that he could draw was that "offensive performance will thus depend on the infantry divisions, and the armor divisions, or at least the units cooperating in the first phase of the attack, being subordinated to them. . . . Only later, if the armor divisions must break away from the slower infantry divisions to exploit a jointly won success, should the subordination relationship be dissolved."[96]

The attack itself had taken place in three waves, as specified by doctrine. The division commanders had led the first attack wave themselves; the second tank wave had followed with the task of suppressing any objectives that managed to recover; and the rifle brigade had then followed the vehicles as soon as the way was open. Beck argued that there were several problems with this offensive style. First, he said, brigade commanders should lead the attack, rather than both divisional chiefs, a direct contrast with a recommendation from Guderian that the comman-

---

Wehrmacht und Nationalsozialismus (1933–1939), ed. Hans Meier-Welcker and Wolfgang von Groote (Munich: Bernard & Graefe, 1978), 343.

93. Senff, *Entwicklung der Panzerwaffe*, 23.

94. Oswald, *Kraftfahrzeuge und Panzer*, 244.

95. "Nachträgliche Betrachtungen zu dem Einsatz des Panzerkorps in der Lage der Truppenamtsreise vom 13.6.1935," 25 July 1935, BA-MA, RH 2/v, 134, *Beck-Studien*, no. 35, p. 462.

96. Ibid., 463.

ders of the assault had to be far forward.[97] Beck also doubted whether it would be possible for the tanks to move beyond the artillery positions in their first assault. Pushing through the enemy infantry and the destruction of the artillery were in themselves a complete engagement. To go farther, the divisions would need to be reassembled and reorganized. The suppression of the enemy's artillery would not break all resistance nor deal with the reserves, and thus the tank brigades had to have artillery and antitank weapons for any further advance. Meanwhile the army had not yet determined the timing for the rifle troops to join the tanks, an extremely important point since the tanks would be unable to achieve much in the enemy's depth without these forces to secure their successes.[98] Beck concluded that infantry divisions had to have the aid of armor forces to attack a strong enemy. "For this, however, it is not independent armor units, but rather strong tank units that are necessary. Therefore tank regiments are urgently required as GHQ reserves, to produce the decision at the battle's point of main effort."[99]

By the end of the year, this central thought by Beck on armor forces had evolved into a comprehensive formula to raise the offensive capabilities of the entire army. The core of his plan was the motorization of all infantry divisions and an expansion of their tank units. He thought, too, that the armor divisions would have their chances for success improved if the army attached fast motorized infantry units to them. Looking more closely at each of these measures, Beck argued that the ideal goal was to have a tank battalion allotted to each active and reserve infantry division of the field army, while the higher command should also have sufficient armor brigades for use at the point of main effort. This would mean a force of sixty-six armor battalions. Unfortunately, financial realities meant that his ideal goal could not be realized, and Beck therefore proposed a more realistic objective, which he defined as one armor brigade (of four battalions) for every peacetime army corps. Along with the armor divisions, his calculations implied a force of forty-eight tank battalions. Like Tukhachevskii so many years before, Beck also questioned whether one tank type could perform the three main missions of the armor forces – support of infantry attacks, armor defense, and independent operations with other motorized forces in armor divisions – or whether there should be a different tank for each task.[100]

Beck, like the rest of the officer corps, recognized that a complete motorization of the army would be impossible within the next several years. He also believed that the "army motorized groups," groups of trucks and cars distributed to each infantry division and meant as a stopgap, would not meet the needs of the field army.

97. Ibid., 464 and n. 8.

98. Ibid., 464–65.

99. Ibid., 465.

100. Memo from Beck, "Erwägungen über die Erhöhung der Angriffskraft des Heeres," to Oberbefehlshaber des Heeres, 30 December 1935, BA-MA, II H 662, *Beck-Studien*, no. 37, pp. 469–72. See also Deist's discussion of the memorandum in "Rearmament of the Wehrmacht," 434–36.

Instead he proposed a partial motorization of selected infantry divisions combined with the use of small army motorized groups that could act as an operational reserve. Finally, he addressed the question of armor divisions. He began by noting the two different demands placed on tanks in future war: frontal assault against an evenly matched opponent and the capture of distant objectives. Like Lutz, Guderian, and the other armor supporters, Beck thought that armor divisions were most suited for the latter mission, but he added that the army had to have infantry associated with the divisions that could travel as quickly as the tanks. This could only mean motorized infantry regiments, and he proposed to test this idea and set up a schedule for the formation of such regiments.[101]

Fritz Fromm, the chief of the General Army Office (AHA) took exception to Beck's support for the armor divisions and used against him many of the same arguments that morale supporters had used in their attack on the tank a decade before.[102] Fromm had written elsewhere that in the final analysis, the infantry were decisive and remained the main force. Tank units, like the artillery, were only support forces. As he saw it, "[t]he main mission of the tank is and remains the support of the infantry attack. . . . Consequently the battle against living objectives stands in the foreground. . . . A deliberate battle . . . of tank against tank seems very unlikely."[103] He therefore demanded that in view of these doctrinal demands, tanks should be made an organic part of infantry divisions.[104] Fromm also thought that for financial reasons the number of armor battalions would have to be held to thirty-six instead of the forty-eight required by Beck's plan.[105]

Beck immediately replied with a note in which he affirmed that Fromm's hostility to an independent role for armor would not change his mind on the proper use of tanks. Support of the infantry attack was but one of the tank's missions, a conclusion he thought buttressed by the experiences of the other great powers. He continued that "*besides* combat with living objectives and antitank defense, the technical shaping and organization of tank units must have as their basis, as first priority, the duel with enemy tanks." Beck argued, therefore, that tanks had to have powerful armor-piercing guns. The weapons would be expensive, but the cost was justified because it was absolutely vital to keep up with developments made by other nations in stronger armor and armaments.[106] He then turned to Fromm's suggestion that tanks be incorporated into infantry divisions, repeating that direct cooperation with the infantry was but one of armor's missions, and therefore sub-

101. Ibid., 472–75.
102. See e.g. Deist, "Rearmament of the Wehrmacht," 436.
103. Memo from Beck to the AHA, 30 January 1936, "Erhöhung der Angriffskraft des Heeres," BA-MA, RH 2/v, 1135, *Beck-Studien*, no. 39, p. 486 n. 2.
104. Ibid., 487 and n. 7.
105. Ibid., 488 n. 11.
106. Ibid., 487.

ordination of the tanks to the infantry in peacetime was wrong.[107] He noted that the army had gone in the opposite direction, placing a number of infantry battalions in armor divisions, and added that "the exercises of the armor force command this summer on the Munster training ground, as well as developments in other states, have produced surer grounds for believing that the guiding principle of creating armor divisions is not wrong."[108]

As for the armor regiments, training requirements and the need to combine these units into armor brigades in wartime argued for their subordination to the corps headquarters and not the infantry. Beck also defended the partial motorization of four divisions as a first step, quickly realized without considerable expense. These units were vital for accelerating strategic concentration, guaranteeing surprise, and avoiding rail transportation which could be threatened from the air, and as a fast mobile reserve under the control of the high command. Fromm had asked for complete motorization of these divisions, using for this purpose the money saved by cutting the number of tank battalions to thirty-six. Beck saw the priorities as exactly the opposite: the armor divisions were more important than a fully motorized infantry.[109] Finally, he agreed that the motorized infantry regiments for the armor division were not the top priority and could be put off for several years, although he fully supported the concept.[110]

In a position paper on the disagreement between Beck and Fromm, Fritsch came down on Beck's side. He decided to create the forty-eight armor battalions for the armor divisions as well as allowing the complete motorization of four infantry divisions.[111] In the end the vision of Lutz and Guderian, of an extremely mobile army with the armor divisions as their iron core, had triumphed, but with one important compromise.

The most comprehensive examination of how these divisions would fight in battle was presented once again by Lutz in two separate reports: his analysis of the 1935 Munster exercises and an official report on the progress made by his command.[112] By the end of 1935 Lutz's concept of armor warfare had evolved into a confident and professional assessment of difficulties and possibilities. The image of war that he now held was one where armor and infantry units created a "community" that guaranteed success through constant cooperation and mutual support. Unlike Soviet

107. Ibid.
108. Ibid., 488.
109. See ibid., 488–89 and nn. 11, 12.
110. Ibid., 489–90.
111. Ibid., 490 n. 15.
112. The following discussion is taken from *Erfahrungsbericht über die Versuchsübungen einer Panzerdivision auf dem Truppenübungsplatz Munster im August 1935* (Berlin: Kommando der Panzertruppen, 24 December 1935), BA-MA, RHD 26/2, pp. 9–22; and *Bemerkungen des Kommandierenden Generals der Panzertruppen im Jahre 1935* (Berlin: Kommando der Panzertruppen, 10. November 1935), BA-MA, RHD 26/3, pp. 26–32.

advocates of armor warfare, he provided general principles while leaving the greatest possible room for decision by individual commanders on the ground. The difference between the two is seen most clearly in his description of the waves of armor that would flow across the battlefield. While the Soviets specified three echelons with completely different tanks and objectives for each, Lutz saw deep echeloning only as a way to prevent resistance from reviving, and never specified a definite number, mission, or kind of tank for the waves.

Three of the principles that Lutz emphasized repeatedly in these reports were soon standard doctrine for the Wehrmacht. First, he viewed rifle units as integral to the armor division because tanks conquered, but the infantry mopped up resistance and secured terrain. However, these infantry had to ride to battle in trucks or transporters – foot soldiers would not be able to keep up with the tanks or support them as they needed. Once in contact with the enemy, the soldiers would dismount to fight, much as the cavalry had done in the last war. Secondly, he agreed with Beck that tanks could fight either in independent operations or in direct cooperation with other units. But like Guderian, he opposed the latter mission, arguing that splitting up the armor forces by giving each infantry division a tank battalion was a fundamental mistake. Decisive success demanded the use of tanks in much larger concentrations. This left independent operational use as the main mission of the armor forces, although they would coordinate their actions at every opportunity with the other branches of the army. His only concession was to suggest that armor divisions could, if necessary, lend tank brigades to support the foot soldiers' attack directly. Finally, he again emphasized the need for heavier tanks to accompany the light Pz. I's into battle. Only tanks with large guns could give the attack the necessary penetration power, battle enemy armor, and protect the light vehicles from antitank defenses and artillery.

While the Germans moved toward a consensus on the organization and use of their new armor forces, the Soviets found themselves facing more problems with their doctrine than ever. The general feeling after the 1934 maneuvers was that Egorov was right: something had to be done about the unwieldy nature of the armor units. On 31 December 1934 the General Staff issued a directive to Khalepskii and all force commanders to reduce the size of the mechanized corps, switching from a four-platoon to a three-platoon system and redistributing the equipment to other forces. They also planned to reduce the number of corps to four.[113] Khalepskii agreed in a report dated 9 January that the fourth tank platoon resulted in great inconvenience when used in battle, as the experimental studies had shown, and added that no other army used such an organization.[114]

113. Nachal'nik Shtaba, "Spravka: Doklad k voprosu ob udarnykh strelkovykh diviziiakh," 9 January 1935, RGVA, f. 31811, op. 2, d. 461, l. 1.

114. Report by Khalepskii, "Soobrazheniia po organizatsii avto-brone-tankovykh chastei v

The decision to reorganize the armor units caused a great deal of confusion over how exactly the army should redistribute the tanks, made all the worse when the army decided simultaneously to create mechanized infantry units known as "shock divisions."[115] Four days after writing his first report, Khalepskii sent a memorandum to Egorov in which he urgently asked the chief of staff to intervene in the chaotic redistribution of materiel that had ensued after district commanders had received the directive to re-form the corps. In the midst of the confusion Levichev, now Egorov's deputy, had informed him that it was also necessary to reconsider the organization and staffing of the newly forming shock divisions. On 7 January the Red Army Staff was given preliminary reference data and two days later Levichev personally handed Uritskii, Khalepskii's deputy and later a head of the GRU, detailed reflections on how to form armor units within shock divisions. Khalepskii thought that the two problems (what to do with the tanks and how to organize shock divisions) had to be considered together, otherwise the army would have to redistribute the machines twice. Yet, in spite of the urgency of the matter, he had been unable to get any instructions from the Red Army Staff and meanwhile the haphazard redistribution of materiel continued. He asked Egorov to telegraph immediately a directive to the district commanders to halt the process until they had received further instructions. Egorov should also summon a meeting of the staff under his own chairmanship, or that of Levichev, to decide all questions connected with the organization of the armor forces.[116]

The following day Khalepskii sent a comprehensive report to Voroshilov in which he outlined his thoughts on this issue. He first listed the studies and maneuvers in which Soviet mechanized brigades had participated over the last five years.[117] The exercises had demonstrated a need for radical organizational changes, yet they had also shown the Soviets that they could use mechanized brigades in a variety of maneuver war conditions. The army as a whole, meanwhile, wanted to increase its mobility, manageability, all-terrain ability, capacity for lengthy military action. In their current composition mechanized brigades – whether as part of mechanized corps or as detached units – were too unwieldy for these demands and needed further reductions as well as organizational and materiel adjustments.[118] He suggested a few specific modifications that would make

sostave udarnykh divizii i ikh material'nomu obespecheniiu," 9 January 1935, RGVA, f. 31811, op. 2, d. 461, l. 4.

115. Khalepskii said that the idea of "shock divisions" was supported by the German officer Faber von Faur [sic], who, as we have seen, wanted the horse and motor vehicle to work together. It is unclear where Khalepskii got his information about Faber du Faur's thought. Report from Khalepskii to Voroshilov, "Ob organizatsii Avto-Bronetankovykh Voisk RKKA," 14 January 1935, RGVA, f. 4, op. 14, d. 1411, ll. 21–23, 26–27.

116. Memo from Khalepskii to Egorov, 13 January 1935, RGVA, f. 31811, op. 2, d. 461.

117. Report from Khalepskii to Voroshilov, "Ob organizatsii Avto-Bronetankovykh Voisk RKKA," 14 January 1935, RGVA, f. 4, op. 14, d. 1411, ll. 17–18.

118. Ibid., l. 18.

the brigades more mobile and manageable: lowering the number of tanks; reducing the number of auxiliary vehicles, and instead having each tank carry supplies on board; replacing part of the heavy reconnaissance tankettes and armored cars with motorcycles; and replacing self-propelled artillery with artillery tanks. Taken together, Khalepskii's suggestions would create brigades that were more nearly pure tank forces than integrated mechanized units. The only other force that he wanted within the brigade was the infantry because, as he put it, tank units could not achieve great successes on their own. To make the infantry more mobile, he suggested reducing personnel somewhat, increasing machine gun equipment, and, in the future, possibly giving infantry in the mechanized units motorcycles or caterpillar vehicles. The important point was that they fulfill those missions that would have them cooperating directly with the tanks.[119]

As for the mechanized corps, he noted that the army had less experience with them since the units had only existed for two years and had participated in only one study. That exercise, held during 1934 in the Ukrainian military district, had exposed the poor state of command and control; shown that the corps was not sufficiently mobile and had few means for holding successes gained; and confirmed that the army had not yet worked out cooperation with cavalry and air forces. Khalepskii therefore concluded that the organization of these units was, like that of the brigades, unwieldy. He proposed stripping mechanized corps down to the bare essentials, shedding their reconnaissance, engineering, chemical, and antiair units, and standardizing vehicle types to one kind of tank, preferably the B-T. The army would take over the discarded units and reduce the corps to three brigades. To give the corps greater mobile striking power, he suggested attaching an assault airplane brigade and replacing the weak rifle brigade with a stronger motorized division.[120]

Khalepskii's proposal directly influenced decision making over armor organization. At the beginning of February, Egorov sent a memorandum to the commanders of the five military districts with the most tank forces, giving Voroshilov's confirmation of a new organization for mechanized corps to come into effect 20 February. The order implemented several of Khalepskii's suggestions, replacing T-26 tanks with B-T's, reducing the number of tanks in each platoon from five to three, and jettisoning many of the units Khalepskii had thought unnecessary.[121] A plan attached to the memorandum showed mechanized corps in wartime with two or three mechanized brigades each consisting of three tank battalions, one rifle battalion, and an additional rifle brigade.[122] Not every commander agreed with the

119. Ibid., ll. 18–20.

120. Ibid., ll. 21–23, 26–27.

121. General memo from Egorov to district commanders, 2 February 1935, RGVA, f. 31811, op. 2, d. 461, ll. 153–54.

122. Outline of organization of mechanized corps in wartime, RGVA, f. 31811, op. 2, d. 461, l. 161.

changes. Uborevich would later protest that armor units had to have five-tank platoons and that there was not enough infantry assigned to each mechanized brigade to fulfill its missions. Nevertheless, the organizational changes were put into effect.[123] The overall impact of the reorganization was to reduce the importance of the mechanized corps and make the infantry once again the absolute center of the army. The fact that the Soviets did not create any mechanized corps after 1935 confirmed the shift in emphasis away from large armor units.[124]

The reorganization, and especially the creation of shock divisions, required the production of even more tanks. Up to this point, industry had been able (more or less) to keep pace with the immense demands placed on it by the army. In January Voroshilov reported that the army had more than ten thousand tanks of all types in the different mechanized and tank formations. His detailed description of the armor forces showed that most units had the tanks specified by their organizational tables, although the tank brigades in the rifle divisions were about a thousand vehicles short. Motorization proceeded more slowly. While the Red Army had 17,875 transport vehicles, it still needed another 6,000.[125] True, by early February a report to Stalin could report that the 1934 program of tank production had been completely fulfilled.[126] This was all well and good, but as Egorov pointed out, the deployment needs for tanks to go into the new shock divisions were far greater than tank orders currently outstanding. The army required 12,770 tanks, the majority top-of-the-line B-T and T-26 tanks, by the beginning of 1936, but orders would fall short by about 4,500 units.[127] He added that the coming war would require no less than thirty shock rifle divisions by early 1938, implying a final total of 14,500 tanks. He also thought that a fully mobilized Soviet industry had to be able to produce an incredible 40,000 tanks in 1935 and 60,000 tanks a year by 1938.[128]

No solution to the problem of production was forthcoming during that year or the next, perhaps because Stalin (and the rest of the Soviet Union) was preoccupied with the beginnings of the purges that would soon sweep the country. In Decem-

123. "Stenograficheskii otchet zasedannie voennogo soveta pri narodnom komissariate oborony SSSR 8–14 dek. 1935," RGVA, f. 4, op. 18, d. 52, l. 41.

124. A. Ryzhakov, "K voprosu o stroitel'stve bronetankovykh voisk krasnoi armii v 30-e gody," VIZh, no. 8 (August 1968): 108.

125. Report from Voroshilov, "Doklad o sostoianii mekhanizatsii i motorizatsii RKKA na 1 ianvaria 1935g.," January 1935, RGVA, f. 31811, op. 2, d. 851, ll. 50–54, 62.

126. Report from Khakhan'ian to Stalin, Molotov, and Voroshilov, 2 February 1935, RGVA, f. 4, op. 14, d. 1272, ll. 10–11. See above, chapter 5, for a description of the new tanks contemplated in 1933.

127. Report from the chief of staff, "Spravka: Doklad k voprosu ob udarnykh strelkovykh diviziiakh," 9 January 1935, RGVA, f. 31811, op. 2, d. 461, ll. 1–3.

128. Ibid. Khalepskii's report showed an even greater discrepancy between the requirement for tanks and the orders placed for the year. Report from Khalepskii, "Soobrazheniia po organizatsii avto-brone-tankovykh chastei v sostave udarnykh divizii i ikh material'nomu obespecheniiu," 9 January 1935, RGVA, f. 31811, op. 2, d. 461, l. 4.

ber 1934 Sergei Kirov was assassinated in the Smolny Institute, one of the most secure places in all of Leningrad. Although the murder has never been solved, Stalin
said he knew who had done it: Trotsky and his "co-conspirators" who remained
within the ranks of the Party, hidden but determined to undermine Stalin's authority. The immediate result of Kirov's death was the secret trial and conviction of
Zinoviev, Kamenev, and seven others, who had already shown themselves to be
against Stalin, for complicity in the murder. Over the next few years the persecu-
tion of supposed Trotskyists involved in the killing and in anti-Stalinist activity
widened.[129] The result was an unprecedented disruption of society and, naturally
enough, the economy as well.

Yet in the short term the Red Army remained untouched, and was in fact re-
warded with the reinstatement of military ranks done away with during the more
egalitarian days of the Bolshevik regime. This may have been because Stalin realized that he needed a strong army at this crucial juncture in international affairs. In
January 1934 Germany and Poland had signed a nonaggression pact, confirming
Soviet fears of a joint attack by the two capitalist nations, now called the "Polish–
Fascist Germany Bloc." The army was given the task of working out how the Soviet
Union, without any allies, would meet an assault by multiple enemies. In February
1935 Uborevich submitted the comprehensive conclusions of the Red Army on this
scenario. He noted that previous war plans had been predicated on conflicts with
either Finland, Estonia, and Latvia, or Poland and Romania. Now the Soviet Union
would have to deal with a combined German-Polish attack, plus the possibility of
another war in the Far East with Japan.[130] Even more ominous was Uborevich's
prediction that Finland would support a German-Polish attack with a strike at
Leningrad, while Estonia and Latvia joined in and England lent its navy to the struggle.[131] The Red Army could only meet the threat with a defense that he hoped would
quickly turn into an overwhelming counteroffensive by mechanized forces. Stalin,
with his own reading of the international situation added to the gloomy predictions
of the staff, decided to radically rethink his opposition to (temporary) alliances with
capitalist nations and even with noncommunist leftist parties. Stalled talks with
France were revived and a bilateral treaty signed between the two nations in May.
And that summer, at its Seventh Congress, the Communist International adopted
a new line of supporting "popular fronts" that would unify all "democratic" forces
against the main danger threatening world peace – and not incidentally the
world's only socialist nation – fascism.

The main army maneuvers held near Kiev that year practiced the scenario pre-

129. Robert C. Tucker, *Stalin in Power: The Revolution from Above, 1928–1941* (New York: Norton,
1990), 288–323.

130. See John Erickson, *The Soviet High Command: A Military-Political History, 1918–1941* (London:
St Martin's Press, 1962), 397–400.

131. Report from Uborevich to Voroshilov, 19 February 1935, "Doklad o novom plane voyny na
Zapade," RGVA, f. 33987, op. 3, d. 279, l. 125.

dicted by Uborevich in his report, with a counteroffensive supported by tanks, bombers, fighter aircraft, and artillery that struck the enemy frontally and in the rear.[132] Over a thousand military machines participated in what was essentially a show of strength for the invited guests – which included German and French military leaders. The mechanized corps and three tank battalions did very well, said the official report on the exercise. The mechanized units had moved at an average speed of 20 kph and some tank units had traveled 600 to 650 kilometers.[133] For the most part other exercises also went well. Voroshilov thought that the army had improved cooperation between the other forces and noted that the speed of battle movement was up to requirements. Khalepskii reported that the army had seen the positive side of mechanized corps, in contrast to 1934.

But not everything was so rosy. In a freewheeling discussion at the annual meeting of the high command, Voroshilov said that command and control were insufficiently mobile and precise, while Shaposhnikov argued that the army still had to integrate the infantry and cavalry with tanks and that the infantry was not consolidating the successes of tanks. An officer interrupted to say that forces should therefore move more slowly to allow time for the rear to adjust, but Shaposhnikov did not agree; the only problem was not to lose any territory seized by tanks and airplanes. He thought the Kiev maneuvers, where infantry had rushed to the attack while cavalry went through the breakthrough created by tanks, a good example for the army to follow.[134] Regardless of the achievements, Voroshilov's official order on the results of the year and tasks for the next year, stressed the negative: the use of armor forces in the depth of the opponent's position was poorly developed and DD tank tactics were still incomplete.[135] As with most everything written by the chief of the Soviet army, the order was nothing more than a slavish imitation of reports sent to him by other commanders, although his conclusion – that the army still had far to go – was entirely his own.

Some of the trouble in the maneuvers may have been caused by the fact that a precise definition of deep battle/deep operations, even with the aid of the *Provisional Instructions*, remained elusive. Commanders assumed, as had Isserson, that the doctrine would be used in a war of positions much like the world war. The battle itself would consist of frontal assaults on the enemy and a breakthrough of a dug-in opponent, assumptions strengthened by the descriptions of deep battle given in all

132. Report from Hagemeier at the German Consulate in Kiev, "Inhalt: Herbstmanöver der Roten Armee bei Kiew," 2 October 1935. PA-AA, R31683K, pp. 134–39. The maneuvers were led by Iakir.

133. Secret NKO order no. 0182, "O rezul'tatakh obshchevoiskovykh manevrov Kievskogo voennogo okruga," 22 Sept. 1935, RGVA, f. 4, op. 15, d. 5, ll. 419–23.

134. "Stenograficheskii otchet zasedannie voennogo soveta pri narkomoborony SSSR 8–14 dek. 1935," RGVA, f. 4, op. 18, d. 52, ll. 1–4, 35.

135. "Sekretnyi prikazy NKO 1935 No. 0103, 'Ob itogakh boevoi podgotovki za 1935 god i zadachakh na 1936 god.,'" 28 December 1935, RGVA, f. 4, op. 15, d. 5, l. 163, 165–66.

the manuals. One commander thought that an equation of deep battle with frontal assaults and breakthroughs was the most basic mistake committed by the Red Army. In the Zabaikal', where the district was supposed to conduct studies on offensive deep battle, there had been a clear case when an flank attack would have destroyed the opponent, but the emphasis had been on frontal assaults.[136] An analysis of the Belorussian maneuvers had to state emphatically that tanks must attack the flanks and rear of the enemy.[137] Shaposhnikov went even further, arguing that deep battle was exclusively a type of encirclement. He suggested that with the new mobile forces at the army's disposal, the air force and mechanized units, encirclements were the only way to defeat and destroy the enemy, yet this was only weakly taught and understood.[138] Kamenev interrupted and argued that there seemed to be a minor "mix-up" between deep battle and encirclement, but Shaposhnikov replied that encirclement "was indeed the most genuine deep battle."[139]

A textbook on tank tactics, designed for use in armor schools and forces, reacted to this confusion and provided as well the most up-to-date summary of official Soviet thought on tank warfare.[140] The focus once again was on deep battle and its practical application in modern warfare, but the book contained some significant innovations. The most important of these, repeated again and again, was that tank assaults would usually be oblique, in other words attacking the flanks and rear rather than the front of the enemy's forces.[141] The textbook emphasized too the need to avoid "schematicism" and the inflexible implementation of principles, a reflection of the previous year's debate. The battle orders for tanks, for instance, were not "rigid, unwavering forms which one needs to stick to no matter what happens. They are only bounds, within the limits of which the commander of each subunit, from the platoon on up, is permitted relative freedom of action and a sweeping demonstration of initiative in conformity with a developing situation."[142] The very nature of tank battle required this kind of flexibility and initiative. The book's other innovation dealt with cooperation between forces and was remarkably close to German ideas current at the time. Tanks would generally cooperate with other forces and when doing so would have to be under the control of a single commander, the chief of combined forces. The textbook added, however, that the commander should link the actions of tanks with the infantry or cavalry in terms of time, but

136. Ibid., l. 86.

137. Report, on maneuvers held in the Belorussian military district during 1935, "Boi tankov s tankami," RGVA, f. 31983, op. 2, d. 188, ll. 122, 129–30.

138. "Stenograficheskii otchet zasedannie voennogo soveta pri narkomoborony SSSR 8–14 dek. 1935," RGVA, f. 4, op. 18, d. 52, ll. 34–35.

139. Ibid., l. 35.

140. A. Gromychenko, Ocherki taktiki tankovykh chastei, ed. K. Stepnii (Moscow: Gosudarstvennoe voennoe izdatel'stvo, 1935), 2.

141. Ibid., 161, 164, 176, 181–82.

142. Ibid., 35.

not space. It was extremely important for tanks to use their great speed and maneuverability to the fullest and not become tied to a "constantly close and physically linked cooperation with infantry (or cavalry)." The vehicles could always come back to help if horse or rifle units became bogged down.[143]

The book's description of mechanized warfare was generally like that in other works on the subject, but differed significantly in tone. Like most studies, the book argued that foot soldiers were absolutely indispensable for mechanized warfare. Battle only ended after the infantry had destroyed the opponent's remaining forces and seized his weaponry. The army therefore had to organize a tank attack to give good support to infantry during the entire battle.[144] The description of how tanks would perform this mission differed, however, in striking ways from other manuals and instructions, in some ways echoing German thought. There was much more emphasis placed on individual initiative, decentralization of command, and continuous movement until the enemy was completely destroyed.[145] The final chapter, on tanks in defensive battle, was also unusual by Soviet standards. Tanks were offensive weapons, according to official doctrine, and most writing on tanks in defense was short and one-sided. Here, though, the emphasis, as in German training manuals, was on defining principles rather than confining tanks to only certain tasks.[146]

The textbook, and other developments during 1934 and 1935, showed in fact that Soviet thought on tank warfare increasingly resembled German practice. There was more emphasis on the infantry and less on the independent mechanized corps, and a move away from the rigid adherence to minute rules of combat that had characterized Soviet tactical thought almost from its inception.

German ideas, in turn, began to look more like those of the Soviet army, most strikingly in a congruence of armor force organization. The German armor divisions formed in 1935 were very like the old Soviet corps, although on a smaller scale. Like the Soviet units, the divisions had tank units, an antitank defense force, motorized infantry, and reconnaissance forces. A serious deficiency in both armies was that although both wanted caterpillar infantry transporters attached to their large mechanized units, neither had such machines in mass production. In Germany a lightly armored transport vehicle was in the process of construction, but few would be available by 1939.[147] Matching the analogous Soviet TRKG units, the Wehrmacht in 1936 created tank brigades for the high command that would support the

---

143. Ibid., 96–98, 225.

144. Ibid., 224–25.

145. Ibid., 237–46.

146. Ibid., 280–316. Later in the decade such a matter-of-fact discussion of retreats or withdrawals would become impossible. For a more typical study see N. Ernest, *Boevye deistviia tankovogo vzvoda* (Moscow: Gosudarstvennoe Voennoe Izdatel'stvo, 1936), 47–48.

147. "Vortrag Oberst Kempfs beim Generals Kurs 1936," BA-MA, RH 12–6/v, 1.

infantry directly. In his memorandum Beck had pushed for the formation of the units, and not long after Guderian and Lutz took up their duties with the new armor command, the first brigade was formed in Stuttgart.[148] The unit consisted of four tank battalions and could be linked closely, when needed, with regular or motorized infantry divisions.[149] Rather than retaining the cavalry and supplementing its horse troops with mechanized elements, as the Soviets had done, the Germans replaced the animals almost entirely with the light divisions.[150] Despite the protests of cavalry supporters, the high command did not see the horse playing a vital role in the next war. The divisions were, however, then subordinated to the infantry to perform long-range reconnaissance, secure gaps in the front, and protect open flanks, and therefore in many ways were like Soviet infantry and cavalry mechanized units.[151]

Tank distribution was also similar to the Soviet model, with the vehicles evenly divided between the three types of armor forces. In accordance with Beck's vision for the army, the mobilization plan from October 1936 showed the army of 1939 with seven tank brigades (more than 1,100 tanks) as headquarters troops.[152] The infantry would have three light divisions each with an armor battalion consisting of four light tank companies (over 800 tanks).[153] The three armor divisions would have approximately 350 tanks in each of their brigades, or about 1,050 in all.[154] Guderian and Lutz were not alone in their distaste for this "splintering" of the tanks. Geyer, now the commanding general of an army corps, wrote to the Army High Command (OKH) in October arguing that the army should organize its armor either for the most difficult combat or for the missions that were earlier allotted to the cavalry divisions, but not for both.[155] Beck and other high-ranking officers concerned with raising the offensive power of the army as a whole disagreed, and it was their concept of saturating the army with tanks that prevailed.

As these arguments worked themselves out, Hitler decided that the restructuring of the army was proceeding too slowly for his war plans. In April 1936 he issued orders to accelerate industry's preparation for total war through what he called the

148. Guderian, *Erinnerungen eines Soldaten*, 30.

149. Schottelius and Caspar, "Organisation des Heeres," 342, 353.

150. One plan showed the cavalry with only one brigade. Deist, "Rearmament of the Wehrmacht," 437.

151. See ibid., 449; Schottelius and Caspar, "Organisation des Heeres," 342, 353. Guderian blames the formation of the light divisions not on Beck, but on the cavalry, who, he says, wanted more influence on motorized units. Guderian, *Erinnerungen eines Soldaten*, 30.

152. "Rechenunterlage für das Kriegsheer nach dem Stande vom 1.10.39 (Gliederung der Verbände nach bes. Anl. 2 zum Mob. Plan Heer vom 6.10.36)," Anlage 1 and Anlage 2: "Rechenunterlagen für das Friedensheer nach dem Stande v, 1.10.39," Beilage 6: "Gliederung eines Korps Kav. Rgts," BA-MA, RH 15/70, p. 15.

153. Ibid., p. 23.

154. Ibid., pp. 21, 27.

155. Memo from Geyer to OKH General Staff "Betr: Organisation," 28 October 1936, BA-MA, N 221/12.

"Four Year Plan." He appointed Hermann Göring commissioner for raw materials and foreign exchange to ensure that Germany would quickly achieve economic self-sufficiency and the arms needed for the coming general conflict.[156] Then in June the General Army Office was ordered to draw up a comprehensive restructuring plan for the army.[157] On 1 August, Fromm reported that the army could have thirty-six infantry divisions (four fully motorized), three armor divisions, and three light divisions, along with thirteen armor brigades, ready by 1940–41. In case of war, it would be possible to create an additional thirty-six infantry divisions, but he did not foresee the formation of any more armor units.[158] A report from the Second Department of the General Staff agreed that the buildup could be completed by 1 October 1941.[159] This was not soon enough for Hitler, who in late summer 1936 wrote a memorandum that stressed the impending danger of war with the Bolsheviks and the need for Germany to be made ready for combat as quickly as possible.[160] On 12 October 1936 the OKH offered its plan to fulfill this objective. The report began by reminding its readers that there were difficulties associated with this task, but that the OKH believed it would be possible to fulfill it, in the main, by Hitler's terminus ad quem, 1 October 1939.[161]

The difficulties mentioned by the OKH were the same as those that the Red Army and the fledgling Soviet industry faced when the Soviet government initiated its push for swift rearmament in the late twenties. German industry had already begun to overheat and raw materials were in short supply, as each branch of the military competed for limited resources. Hitler thought that the problems with industry were primarily a matter of will, that somehow factories could produce what he needed if only they understood how important and necessary rearmament was, but it was soon apparent that the difficulties were very real indeed.[162] Tanks were in worse shape than any of the other motor vehicles (cars and trucks), which Fromm thought would hit their peacetime targets. Even if no unforeseen difficulties arose, by 1 October 1939 the army would still not have received 35 percent of its Pz. III and 80 percent of the new Pz. IV tanks: industry would be able to deliver these

156. R. J. Overy, *War and Economy in the Third Reich* (Oxford: Clarendon Press, 1994), 19, 183–85.

157. Memo to the AHA, 16 June 1936, BA-MA, RH 15/70, p. 10.

158. Report from the AHA (Major General Fromm), "Ausarbeitung über den Aufbau des Friedens- und Kriegsheeres (Befehl des Herrn Ob. d. H. v. 4.6.36)," 1 August 1936, BA-MA, RH 15/70, p. 110.

159. Report from General Staff of the Army II Department to AHA, "Betr: Aufbauplan für das Friedens- und Kriegsheer," with enclosures, 16 June 1936, enclosures 2 and 3, BA-MA, RH 15/70.

160. Wilhelm Treue, "Denkschrift Hitlers über die Aufgaben eines Vierjahresplans," *Viertel-jahrshefte für Zeitgeschichte* 3.Jahrgang (1955): 204–10.

161. Fritsch, report to Blomberg, "Betr: Aufrüstungsplan," with enclosures, 12 October 1936, BA-MA, RH 15/70, p. 189.

162. Treue, "Denkschrift Hitlers," 204–10. For a good discussion of the crisis in industry and Hitler's Four Year Plan, see Michael Salewski, "Die bewaffnete Macht im Dritten Reich 1933–1939," in Meier-Welcker and Groote, *Wehrmacht und Nationalsozialismus*, 141–56.

only by the end of May 1940.[163] If tank development was slow, the production of caterpillar vehicles for the rest of the forces in the armor division was downright glacial. Supporters of the divisions had envisioned lightly armored half-tracks for the rifle troops, engineers, and other support forces, and fully tracked vehicles for the artillery and antiarmor battalion. None of the divisions were fully mechanized in this way before the war began: industry simply could not meet the demands placed upon it by the military.[164] The final report from the OKH to Hitler agreed closely with Fromm's conclusions, and added that, in view of the lack of medium tanks, a dependence on the lighter tanks could not be ruled out.[165]

This was unfortunate because, again as in the Soviet army, officers within the high command now agreed that better-armed and armored tanks were essential for modern warfare. In July, a report put the army's requirement for future warfare at about 700 Pz. I tanks, but close to 2,500 Pz. II, 1,800 Pz. III, and 870 Pz. IV tanks. For the period April 1937–April 1939, however, the last two types would be delivered only as a test series since they would still be in the process of development.[166] When asked why equipping the troops with larger tanks consumed so much time, Colonel Kempf replied that the lengthy period necessary to develop a new type of artillery piece, something with which the German army had decades of experience, was comparable to that necessary to develop a tank, a weapon with which the army had limited experience and which was extraordinarily difficult to build.[167] Even when the larger tanks arrived, the Wehrmacht's armor forces were still not as powerful as Soviet forces, since for each type of tank, light, medium, or heavy, the Soviet machines were larger and better armed than their German counterparts. Thus the Pz. I and II, which many saw as the main weapons of the new armor forces, were more lightly armed and armored than the equivalent T-26 or B-T tanks, while the heavier Pz. III and IV, designed to support the light tanks by combating antitank weapons and field fortifications, were lighter than the Soviet mediums.[168]

---

163. Report from the AHA (Major General Fromm), "Ausarbeitung über den Aufbau des Friedens- und Kriegsheeres (Befehl des Herrn Ob. d. H. v, 4.6.36)," "Anlage 4: Materielle Ausstattung," BA-MA, RH 15/70, p. 126.

164. Heinz Guderian, *Erinnerungen eines Soldaten*, 31.

165. OKH to Blomberg, War Minister and Commander-in-Chief of the Wehrmacht, "Betr: Aufrüstungsplan," with enclosures from Fritsch, 12 October 1936, BA-MA, RH 15/70, p. 192.

166. Report from the Waffenamt to the AHA "Betr: Aufbauplan für das Friedens- und Kriegsheer. Bez. Genstb. 2.Abt. 929.36g. Kdos. II vom 12.6.36, Anlage 5: "Kraftfahrzeug- und Motorisierungsabt. (Wa Prw 6)," 25 July 1936, BA-MA, RH 15/70, pp. 164, 175–177. The main difference between the Pz. III and the Pz. IV was their weaponry: the latter was armed with the much heavier 7.5 cm gun.

167. "Vortrag Oberst Kempfs beim Generals Kurs 1936," BA-MA, RH 12–6/v, 1.

168. Oswald seems to imply that the Germans saw the Pz. III and IV as their main battle tanks even before the outbreak of war. See Oswald, *Kraftfahrzeuge und Panzer*, 244–45. This does not appear plausible in the light of statements made by Guderian and others on the uses of the Pz. II. See Generalmajor Guderian, "Die Panzertruppen und ihr Zusammenwirken mit den anderen Waffen,"

At the same time, a comparison with Soviet tank manufacturing shows that the Germans had more modest and realistic production goals for their smaller tanks. After October 1939 the high command thought that the minimum yearly production of tanks would be about twenty-eight hundred units.[169] By 1940, the army hoped to have twelve brigades (twenty-four regiments) and about four thousand tanks. With the reserve tanks, the total number would be around five thousand.[170] The only movement beyond these limited goals were calls for two more tank types: a vehicle designed specifically to accompany the infantry and one to hunt other tanks (the Panzerjäger).[171] The Soviets, meanwhile, had seven tank and tankette models in production, over ten thousand tanks in hand, and were producing several thousand more every year. Perhaps because they took their own experiences with production as the norm, both the Truppenamt and the Waffenamt wildly underestimated the number of tanks in the Red Army arsenal, stating in 1935 that the Soviets had only three thousand.[172]

The other area where differences remained between the two armies was in doctrine, although as before, the thought of Guderian, Lutz, and their supporters resembled the deep battle idea in the Soviet Union. The most important change in German doctrine was the realization that Beck and others were right: armor divisions would fight differently from tank brigades. An official statement of the Inspectorate of Army Motorization's views, delivered as a lecture by Colonel Kempf, described three different scenarios for war involving armor divisions: either the units could directly support the infantry; or, using their speed, they would push through the infantry and fight in the depth of the battlefield against the enemy's ar-

---

Militär-Wissenschaftliche Rundschau, no. 5 (1936): 607–26. The official doctrinal statement of the Wehrmacht, "D76," gave the Pz. I important battle missions, rather than simply assigning it reconnaissance duties, as Guderian did. See *Panzerangriff im Rahmen einer Infanteriedivision (D76) vom 23.Juni 1936* (Berlin: Reichswehrministerium, 1936)," BA-MA, RHD 8/76, pp. 9–10.

169. Report from the Waffenamt to the AHA, "Betr: Aufbauplan für das Friedens- und Kriegsheer. Bez. Genstb. 2.Abt. 929.36g. Kdos. II vom 12.6.36, Anlage 5:Kraftfahrzeug- und Motorisierungsabt. (Wa Prw 6)," 25 July 1936, BA-MA, RH 15/70, pp. 164, 175–77.

170. "Vortrag Oberst Kempfs beim Generals Kurs 1936," BA-MA, RH 12–6/v, 1.

171. Wim Brandt, SS-Captain in the Verfügungstruppe, "Infanterietanks?" *Militär-Wochenblatt*, no. 3 (1936): 130–31; "Panzerjäger oder Panzerkampfwagen?" ibid., no. 11 (1936): 535–37; "Panzerjäger!" ibid., no. 13 (1936): 636–38.

172. Report prepared by the Truppenamt for Stülpnagel's signature entitled "Potentiel de guerre," 30 January 1935, BA-MA, RH 1/v, 78, pp. 225–71; report, Nr. 659/35 geh. from W.A. (Ausl) to "Herr Minister," 4 March 1935, BA-MA, RW 5/v, 461. In general, however, German intelligence on the Red Army, and vice versa, remained excellent. One example of this can be seen in a report, written by an officer of the German general staff, that Iagoda forwarded (in translation) to Voroshilov. The report described the Soviet army, its weaponry, force distribution, and strength in great detail, and was so accurate that Iagoda, in his cover memorandum to Voroshilov, expressed his doubt that any German officer could have written it without inside help. Report by German staff officer, with cover memo by Iagoda, sent to Voroshilov, 22 February 1936, RGVA, f. 33987, op. 3, d. 861, ll. 259–347.

tillery and his rear; or they could fight as an independent force. Kempf agreed that the first tactical form was faulty. Directly supporting the infantry would prevent exploitation of the tank's speed and mobility and cause it to fall easy prey to the enemy's antitank weapons. The second form, which resembled the "moderate" position, was probably the way that most armor division attacks would occur. Tanks would advance in several waves and, while the individual waves rolled past the infantry, retain a connection with the foot soldiers. As for the third type of tactics, the armor would work with the other arms – but without any direct connection – to attack the deep flanks and rear of the enemy (just like the Soviet DD echelon). Kempf thought that it was extremely difficult to decide whether this would work or not – a conclusion that the Soviets would have more than agreed with. He noted that many officers continued to reject this kind of tank use and they might be to a certain degree correct. But if things continued to develop as they had done so far, then one day the doubters would be regarded as behind the times and people would "shake their heads" over them. The obvious conclusion: the German army had to be as modern as possible, ahead of the times and not behind them, and that therefore armor divisions should be able to fight as an independent force or against the enemy's rear in cooperation with the infantry.[173]

Not long after Kempf delivered this lecture, Guderian made public his views on armor doctrine for the first time in a short article in the *Militär-Wochenblatt* entitled "Motorized Troops." The article had two aims. On the one hand, it was part of Guderian's ongoing dispute with Beck over the armor divisions, and as such sought to prove that – in cooperation with other forces – they would be able to crush the opponent if only the army would allow them the freedom to attack the flanks and rear of the enemy. Just as importantly, Guderian used the article to delineate the shape of future wars and the ways that mechanization would transform combat. The prescience of certain of his predictions is startling. He wrote, for instance, that the next conflict would begin with air strikes against the enemy's government and industrial production centers, while motorized troops moved so quickly over the enemy's borders that they would achieve strategic surprise. Troops in trucks would follow the first waves of airplanes and tanks, unload, and occupy the territory just seized. The empty trucks would race back to pick up more troops while the attacker mobilized the rest of his army. The armor units would not stop once they had reached their first goals, but would use their speed and increased radius of action fully to create a complete breakthrough. Further waves would follow the first to "inexorably" roll up the enemy's front and carry the blow into his deep rear.[174] Cooperation between all of these forces, Guderian concluded, should follow already

173. "Vortrag Oberst Kempfs beim Generals Kurs 1936," BA-MA, RH 12–6/v, 1.

174. Oberst Guderian, "Kraftfahrkampftruppen," *Militär-Wissenschaftliche Rundschau*, no. 1 (1936): 52–77.

established British guidelines. Most significantly, the British believed, as did Guderian, that the entire battle should be built around the tank and its capabilities. All the other units, whether motorized infantry, artillery, or the air force, would reinforce, secure, and complement the armor assault.[175]

The problem was that Guderian did not discuss how cooperation would play out on a battlefield where the enemy was prepared for an attack – a much more likely scenario, in the opinion of the high command. Lutz decided to deal with this difficult puzzle in his official annual report. He stressed, as he had earlier, the need to maintain tight coordination between rifle and tank brigades when assaulting fortified positions. He noted that the most difficult problem was keeping the tanks in tactically correct connection with the rifle units in the depth of the enemy's defenses, something discovered by the Soviets with their DD echelons. His important contribution was the idea that "[t]he *entire armor unit . . . is . . .* committed *as a combined whole to one objective* in the depth of the enemy. . . . To assign the echelons different objectives has not proven worthwhile."[176] After reaching this objective the tanks would create a base, wait for the first elements of the rifle brigade to get a firm grip on the back edge of the enemy's deep position, and then the entire armor division could continue forward.[177] This solution to the problem of cooperation kept the armored fist from splintering or from losing contact with the infantry, two of the major difficulties with coordinating armor and infantry units.

But the armor divisions were only one kind of tank unit within the new Wehrmacht. The German high command also had to find a way for soldiers to cooperate with the tank brigades assigned directly to the infantry and combined arms commanders. Colonel Zuckertort, commander of the 5th Armor Regiment, concluded that the major problem facing these units was whether tanks should attack before, after, or at the same time as the infantry. Since it was extremely important for the infantry to exploit the tanks' success quickly, he suggested that the two forces enter battle at the same time, allowing the foot soldiers to use the cover that the machines provided. As tanks moved faster than attacking infantry, the soldiers would exploit each new tank wave that washed over them to make another jump forward. The infantry were not, however, to wait for the first success of the tanks to advance, nor were they to stop if the tanks sped ahead of them. They should instead continue to conduct battle on their own as in any other attack without armor support. He explained that infantry and tanks might have different missions, so that it was not necessary for the two types of forces to attack from the same direction to achieve the

---

175. Guderian, "Die Panzertruppen und ihr Zusammenwirken mit den anderen Waffen," 607–26.

176. *Bemerkungen des kommandieranden Generals der Panzertruppen im Jahre 1936 und Hinweise für die Ausbildung 1936/37* (Berlin: Kommando der Panzertruppen. 10 November 1936), BA-MA, RHD 26/4, pp. 3–4. Emphasis in original.

177. Ibid., pp. 4, 8–9, 12.

same objective; tanks might even find that part of the battlefield consisted of swamps or minefields, making further advance physically impossible.[178]

In a move which shows that the high command believed armor would be most effective when tied to the infantry in these units, the War Ministry issued a manual to systematize doctrine for the tank brigades – but not for the armor divisions. Entitled *Armor Attack within the Context of an Infantry Division* or D76, the manual described in detail official views on the organization of tank units, general principles for the use of tanks in battle, cooperation with the infantry, possible tank missions, and much else. The armor doctrine in D76 was "moderate," emphasizing in direct contrast to Guderian that tanks were auxiliary to the infantry assault, and that their main purpose was to help the infantry move forward.[179] Yet the manual also emphasized that tanks were to take full advantage of their speed to drive as fast as possible into the enemy's positions.[180] If too closely linked with the slower foot soldiers, tanks would be easy victims of enemy defenses and also would lose the chance of exploiting surprise. How then would the two forces cooperate? First the manual, like Zuckertort, ruled out cooperation in terms of the direction of the attack, since terrain and antitank defenses could easily prevent this; tanks might indeed be used in envelopments or flank attacks without the infantry at all. Instead, the most important rule for cooperation was a coordination of objectives and timing.[181] In the majority of cases, the infantry would simply strive to exploit as quickly as possible any successes gained by the tanks and keep as close to them as possible, since they offered foot soldiers good fire support. In combat with an unprepared enemy, tanks could not wait for their infantry and thus the infantry had to adjust to the tempo of the tank operation, immediately taking advantage of the vehicles' successes and holding any terrain won. In battle against a prepared opponent, the infantry would precede the tank attack so that the foot soldiers would not lose the direct aid of armor too early, while wave after wave of tanks passed them on their way to the enemy's rear.[182] In both types of combat artillery and aircraft would naturally support the infantry and armor forces.[183]

These descriptions of tank warfare showed that the German high command, still divided on the worth of concentrating all armor into huge mechanized formations, had reached agreement on armor doctrine. High speed, loose connection with the infantry, and combined-arms operations were the watchwords of the new doctrine,

178. Oberst Zuckertort, Commander of Panzer Regiment 5, "Einsatz von Panzerverbänden, insbesondere ihre Zusammenarbeit mit anderen Waffen," 17 April 1936, BA-MA, RH 16/124.

179. *Panzerangriff im Rahmen einer Infanteriedivision*, (D76) vom 23.Juni 1936 (Berlin: Reichswehrministerium, 1936), BA-MA, RHD 8/76, pp. 7–8, 12.

180. Ibid., p. 8.

181. Ibid., pp. 13–14.

182. Ibid., pp. 23–25.

183. Ibid., pp. 28–29, 43–45.

whether articulated by Lutz and Guderian or by the high command itself. Skeptics like Fromm, as with Adam earlier, had no influence, although they remained quite vocal in their opposition to "unrealistic" thinking about the tank.

Meanwhile Soviet armor affairs, reflecting the disillusionment of some within the high command, resembled more and more earlier German thought. On the surface, the ideas of Tukhachevskii, Triandafillov, and the other innovators were accepted and firmly entrenched within the high command. Deep battle reigned, and its triumph would be crowned with the publication of PU-36, which presented deep battle as the centerpiece of Red Army doctrine. Behind this seemingly unanimous front, however, was growing dissatisfaction with the concept. The justification for the shift in views of the doctrine was, ostensibly, the failure to implement the idea during maneuvers. As we have seen, however, the 1935 exercises were not complete disasters, while those of 1936 would be even more successful. Nevertheless, Voroshilov and others would describe them in the darkest terms, no longer use the term "deep battle," and even question the value of the tank as a weapon.

The year began normally enough. The plan for studies during 1936 was not very different from that for previous years, as the army practiced battle within the depth of the enemy's position, encirclements, and combat with mechanized units.[184] Khalepskii's more focused instructions on battle training for the armor forces, designed to work with the DD group, were also mundane.[185] The first sign of trouble came in May, when Voroshilov ordered the heavy and medium tank brigades, six in all, taken from the chief of the Armor Forces Directorate (ABTU, which replaced the UMM) and allocated to the TRGK forces. The reason given for the redistribution of forces was to unify "operational-tactical and special-technical training of tank units of general significance."[186] The primary effect of the change was to remove more armor forces from the ABTU's control and further weaken the independent mechanized corps.

After this uncertain start the exercises that year, even those with the mechanized corps, seemed to go well. The large maneuvers in Belorussia featured a huge amount of technology on both sides: the "enemy" had almost 37,000 men with 211 airplanes and 453 combined-arms tanks, in this case T-28s. The "friendly" forces had more than 42,000 men with 240 airplanes, three mechanized brigades, and several rifle and cavalry tank units. With commanders and other personnel, the total number of men participating in the maneuvers was an astounding 85,000 with

184. Enclosure, "Plan takticheskikh i tekhnicheskikh sborov kom. sostava i shtabov, provodimykh v 1936g.," with a memo from Egorov on battle preparation for 1936 to the Red Army high command, 6 January 1936, RGVA, f. 31983, op. 2, d. 178, ll. 208–5.

185. Khalepskii, instructions on battle training for armor forces during 1936 from 6 January 1936, RGVA, f. 31983, op. 2, d. 178, ll. 187.

186. "Sov. sek. prikazov NKO –. 1936 N° 0028," 21 May 1936, RGVA, f. 4, op. 15, d. 8, l. 102.

1,136 tanks.[187] Most of the Soviet high command took part in the maneuvers, including Voroshilov, Tukhachevskii, Egorov, Khalepskii, and Uborevich, who, as commander of the district, led the exercise.[188] Although the idea of a DD group was increasingly under attack, the chief of staff of the district did not hesitate to discuss the DD echelon and the successes of tanks against antitank defenses. He noted that "[t]he leadership thought that a dense defense such as, for instance, the German army has, with seventy antitank weapons to a division, would be able to inflict serious losses on the DD tanks and together with divisional artillery bleed them white."[189] The maneuvers, however, had shown "the vitality of the form of attack if DD tanks, when confronting strong antitank defenses and a second zone of defense, attack simultaneously with the infantry."[190]

In sharp contrast to the favorable picture presented by this officer, reports by Voroshilov and others were extremely pessimistic. The one positive comment Voroshilov made on the use of tanks was that the mechanized brigade had successfully attacked the artillery and reserves of the opponent, allowing an acceleration of the breakthrough by the main infantry forces with their tank battalion. Otherwise he stressed the negative side of maneuvers: for instance, that cooperation between tanks and the infantry, as part of the combined forces troops, was not done properly, and that artillery and tank attacks had been mistimed.[191] Other commanders generally agreed with Voroshilov's gloomy assessment of the tanks' performance. Sediakin thought that cooperation between tanks and other forces was abysmal. Tank units were much better prepared for independent action than for attacks in close coordination with infantry.[192] Tukhachevskii's analysis was more nuanced, differentiating between progress made with tank battalions in mechanized forces and those in rifle divisions. The tanks in rifle units, he said, were better prepared tactically than those in mechanized forces and more or less satisfactorily performed their missions with the infantry. But they were still not doing as well as possible. Infantry commanders did not know how to use tanks to their

187. Plans for the maneuvers to be held in the Belorussian military district, 7–10 September 1936, from Uborevich to Voroshilov and Egorov, RGVA, f. 33987, op. 3, d. 838, ll. 2–5.

188. Order from Voroshilov on maneuvers in the Belorussian military district, September 1936, RGVA, f. 33987, op. 3, d. 838, l. 242.

189. Komdiv Bobrov, chief of staff of the Belorussian military district report on the large-scale maneuvers held in the district, RGVA, f. 31983, op. 2, d. 215, l. 153.

190. Ibid., l. 25.

191. Ibid., ll. 274–78. This should be contrasted with Iakir's view that the maneuvers had shown that the infantry could not prevent breakthroughs. "Stenograficheskii otchet Zasedanie Voennogo sovet pri Narodnom Komissare Oborony SSSR," 13–19 October 1936, RGVA, f. 4, op. 18, d. 53, ll. 316–19.

192. Report on maneuvers held in the Kiev Military District from Sediakin to Voroshilov, 14 September 1936, RGVA, f. 31983, op. 2, d. 213, ll. 61–62; Report on maneuvers held in the Northern Caucusus Military District from Sediakin to Tukhachevskii and Voroshilov, 11 October 1936, RGVA, f. 31983, op. 2, d. 213, l. 32.

fullest extent in battle, nor were tankists accustomed to following behind the commander and doing what he did. The situation with battalions in the mechanized forces was worse because here the army had not even mastered basic cooperation.[193] Egorov pointed out that commanders had ordered armor units into battle without taking care to ensure supplies, that there were difficulties in using armor in independent operations (coordinated with aircraft, cavalry, and artillery), and in cooperation with infantry. Finally, there were serious problems with the command and control of mechanized brigades. When fighting in the enemy's deep positions, motorized infantry were to "prop up" their armor units, allowing them to achieve success and protecting their rear, but instead mechanized brigades were mere attachments to cavalry or rifle corps. While these were supposed to be independent brigades attached directly to armies, most commanders had simply assigned them to infantry or cavalry units rather than taking responsibility for their control.[194]

In his summing up at the annual meeting of the high command, Voroshilov went even further than any of the other officers, harshly criticizing the armor forces. He argued that if the army continued with current tactics, it would end up with only an auxiliary force, not the independent shock units that it wanted. He asked those present to rethink tank tactics and to find some way to improve command and control.[195] His next remarks showed how far his thinking was from that of those who had labored so long to create the army's armor doctrine. The army, he said, could not have tanks acting as they were. "They say that tank action will be facilitated by good artillery preparation. But then why the hell do we need tanks? After good artillery preparation, the infantry will surely move forward. So I doubt whether the existence of such an expensive type of force, like tanks, is justified." Of course, he quickly added, it would be a gross mistake to conclude from this that tanks were unnecessary. Naturally they were necessary, but one had to remember that they were not all-powerful, they had their limits, and their main limitation was that the army had to know how to use them in each individual case.[196] He ended this portion of his remarks by stating that "however many tank units, aircraft, chemical and other weapons we have, the infantry for the present remains the primary and principal arm of the service. Without the infantry neither tanks nor aircraft can perform their military mission fully. No army can manage without modern, well-organized and well-taught infantry."[197] The army, he concluded, needed tanks *to breach the enemy's defenses*, and should create tactics for tank units based upon this principal demand.[198] This conclusion, a direct contradiction of the growing conviction that

193. "Stenograficheskii otchet Zasedanie Voennogo sovet pri Narodnom Komissare Oborony SSSR," 13–19 October 1936, RGVA, f. 4, op. 18, d. 53, ll. 23–25.

194. Ibid., ll. 53, 55–56.

195. Ibid., ll. 716–17.

196. Ibid., l. 718.

197. Ibid., ll. 713–14.

198. Ibid., l. 719. My emphasis.

deep battle was meant for more than just frontal assaults on fortified positions, showed just how far Voroshilov's thinking was from that of Tukhachevskii, Sediakin, and the other deep battle supporters.

Voroshilov's final report for the year reiterated these points, arguing that there were still many unsolved issues with coordination between infantry, artillery, armor, and cavalry units as well as serious problems with command, control, and communication in mechanized and tank units.[199] Unlike previous years he did not mention deep battle and deep tactics or the echelons so often discussed in other orders. This was not unusual for 1936. The directive on operational training and tasks for the coming year also did not discuss deep battle, nor a need to work out the doctrinal idea more clearly, something added to every directive since the adoption of deep battle years before.[200] Even in published textbooks the term "deep battle" disappeared.[201]

Why Voroshilov (and others in the high command) had become so pessimistic about deep battle and the value of the tank is a difficult question. None of the available documents clarify the arguments that must have taken place behind closed doors, and Voroshilov's few comments make it appear that the shift in mood was influenced solely by the failed maneuvers. A comparison with events in Germany, where the armor forces also did less well than expected and yet were still supported, suggests that this is not a sufficient explanation. What is clear is that Voroshilov was more critical of deep battle than most of the high command, and was also the most vocal in expressing his displeasure. Some of this attitude may have been due to the difficult relationship that he (and Stalin) had with Tukhachevskii. There is also the undeniable fact that Voroshilov had stood on the sidelines throughout the long development of the deep battle idea, neither contributing to the concept nor enthusiastically supporting it.

On the surface, all continued as it had before, but there were other signs of dissatisfaction with the deep battle idea. The distinction between DPP and NPP tanks disappeared, as Egorov had suggested, but no replacement for the concept was suggested. The problem of filling the gap between the long-distance DD and the PP tanks, which cooperated closely with the infantry, remained.[202] There was also more emphasis on the use of tanks for breakthroughs, as Voroshilov's speech showed, and less on the possibilities for broad encirclements and flank or rear attacks.[203] Some writers emphasized, like Voroshilov, that above all else,

199. "Sov. sek. prikazov NKO 1936 No. 00105, 'Ob itogakh boevoi podgotovki za 1936 god i zadachakh na 1937 god,'", 3 November 1936, RGVA, f. 4, op. 15, d. 8, ll. 143–45.

200. Booklet entitled "Direktiva Narodnogo Komissariat Oborony Soiuza SSR № 22500ss 10 Noiabria 1936 goda: Ob itogakh operativnoi podgotovki za 1936 god i o zadachakh na 1936 [7] god.," RGVA, f. 31983, op. 2, d. 202, ll. 13–1.

201. See V. Zun, Avtobronetankovye voiska, ed. Sediakin (Moscow: Gosudarstvennoe Voennoe Izdatel'stvo Narkomata Oborony Soiuza SSR, 1936), 63.

202. See e.g. Ernest, Boevye deistviia tankovogo vzvoda, 54, 63.

203. See especially ibid., 53–55.

"tanks must help the infantry and its movement forward." The warning was now that the infantry should not become too dependent on the tank since foot soldiers "ought to know how to fight even without tanks: the infantry uses the aid of tanks, if they are present, only for movement forward that is faster and causes fewer losses."[204]

Yet, in the face of this growing opposition to the use of tanks independently and in the depths of the opponent's defenses, Voroshilov signed a decree putting into effect PU-36, the most important official statement by the Red Army on military doctrine during the thirties.[205] The field manual was written with the close supervision of Isserson and Tukhachevskii and was a resounding affirmation of the interpretation of deep battle developed by them and Triandafillov, Kalinovskii, and Sediakin.[206] Like PU-29, the new manual stated that the infantry decided the outcome of battle, but added that it had to fight "in close cooperation with artillery and tanks." And, where the older manual had argued that all forces worked to support the infantry and help it forward, here the possibility for some units to fight independently from the infantry was left open.[207] War itself could either involve maneuver or be positional in nature, but regardless of these alternatives, the manual restated that modern technology allowed the complete suppression of the enemy's defenses at all depths. With the help of technology, Red Army forces should be able to outflank the enemy, attack him on his rear and flanks, and finally encircle and destroy him completely.[208]

Turning to tanks, the manual showed the influence of Voroshilov's critical attitude, declaring that the basic task of the tank was to suppress the machine guns of the opponent – that is to help the infantry forward. More specifically, there were two basic types of tanks: those that would support the infantry and were organically part of rifle units, and those that, along with self-propelled artillery and infantry in personnel carriers, made up mechanized formations. The main task of the former was to create breakthroughs into the depth of an opponent's position and destroy his reserves, artillery, staffs, and so on in the rear. The mechanized units, on the other hand, were capable of performing independent missions out of contact with other types of forces or in cooperation with them. Their principal type of action in battle was the tank attack, which had to be protected by the artillery, while aircraft would support the maneuver and strike of the mechanized force as a whole.[209] The PP and DD groups were separated organizationally from these mechanized formations. PP tanks, in companies or platoons, were under the con-

204. Zun, *Avtobronetankovye voiska*, 55.

205. *Vremennyi Polevoi Ustav RKKA 1936 (PU-36)* (Moscow: Gosudarstvennoe voennoe izdatel'stvo Narkomata Oborony SSSR, 1937), 3.

206. G. Isserson, "Zapiski sovremennika o M. N. Tukhachevskom," *VIZh*, no. 4 (April 1963): 71.

207. *Vremennyi Polevoi Ustav RKKA 1936*, 11.

208. Ibid., 10, 16.

209. Ibid., 12–14.

trol of the infantry commander in offensive battle, while the DD group was under the command of either corps or divisional commanders.[210]

The most detailed description of offensive battle, and therefore presumably the type that the army most expected to fight, however, was not Voroshilov's attack on a fortified position, but rather an offensive "when approaching from a march." The other types of offensive battle, including the "attack from a line in direct contact" and the "attack on a fortified area," were given much shorter descriptions.[211] This implies that Tukhachevskii at least expected the next war to be extremely fluid and mobile, with more chances for surprise attacks and fewer opportunities for the enemy to fortify his positions. If the enemy was stationary, then as in so many other descriptions, the DD group would fight a deep battle: breaking through to the rear and destroying reserves, staffs, and artillery while cutting off the main paths of retreat.[212] PP tanks would take advantage of the disarray caused by the DD attack and, attacking simultaneously with the infantry on the entire front, would carve a path forward for the infantry, directly supporting them.[213]

The publication of PU-36, with its staunch support for an offensive and mobile war based on deep battle and deep operations, should have been a sign that the concept was firmly entrenched in the Red Army. In fact PU-36 was the last public statement that gave deep battle any recognition. Within a few weeks of its issuance, its main supporter in the high command would be dead and not many months later the Soviet army would publicly repudiate it. The contrast with events inside the German army could not have been more striking. Guderian and Lutz were given the power to begin implementation of their ideas while Beck, unlike some previous chiefs of the staff, was firmly on their side. Although Guderian did not recognize it at the time and would deny it later, the German high command was poised to put "blitzkrieg" into effect long before war broke out with Poland.

210. Ibid., 63–64.
211. Ibid., 124–26.
212. Ibid., 106–7.
213. Ibid., 106–7, 115.

CHAPTER SEVEN

The Evidence of Small Wars

Armor Doctrine in Practice, 1936–1939

URING that summer of 1936, as German and Soviet officers were profoundly rethinking their armor doctrine and organization, war broke out in Spain. The conflict itself was limited to a country that had for many years been on the periphery of the great affairs of Europe, and yet within months three major powers – Italy, Germany, and the Soviet Union – had decided to intervene. By the end of the year, each would send scores of aircraft, thousands of men, and hundreds of tanks to bolster the cause that they supported in the spreading civil war. Attempts by the Western powers and Great Britain in particular, to prohibit the interference of outside parties met with little success. Although the Italian, German, and Soviet leaders publicly stated that they supported a policy of nonintervention, all had good reasons for continuing to ship arms to their clients in Spain.[1]

One of these reasons, at least on the part of German and Soviet officers, was a desire to use Spain to test the ideas on aerial and ground warfare in dispute within both nations' armies. Both the Wehrmacht and the Red Army high commands believed that only actual combat proved or disproved theories about doctrine and organization, and saw Spain as the perfect proving ground to carry out controlled, realistic experiments with live weapons and troops. The lessons that the armies thought that they had learned in Spain would shape the debate over how their armor forces would organize and fight in the next world war.

The Spanish Civil War was not the only conflict to disturb the peace before the outbreak of the Second World War. The Soviet army fought two major battles on its eastern border with the Japanese and would learn as much from their experiences at Lake Khasan and Khalkhin-gol as they did from Spain. Just as important for the Soviet armor forces was the internal war fought by Stalin and his supporters against their supposed enemies within the Red Army's ranks. It was no coincidence that the tank troops were purged more severely than other branches of the service, but rather a direct outgrowth of suspicions already directed at the authors of deep bat-

1. For the complex decision making by the European great powers over intervention, see Dante A. Puzzo, *Spain and the Great Powers, 1936–1941* (New York: Columbia University Press, 1962), 75–148.

tle. The targeting of these men, added to the failures to implement the doctrine, would force a thorough reconsideration of the tank in battle.

Each of these experiences would put its mark on the armor affairs in the Soviet Union and Germany, but the prolonged war in Spain most affected officers' views of doctrine. The first dictator to send aid was Hitler, who decided to supply Franco with aircraft very shortly after the rebellion began.[2] Most German aid would in fact be airplanes and supplies for the air war, but less than three months after the war started both Germany and the Soviet Union had sent tanks to their allies in Spain. A few Pz. I tanks arrived in September and a larger number in October, accompanied by Wilhelm von Thoma, who would lead the German (and Nationalist) armor forces.[3] The ultralight tanks were weakly armed with machine guns and flamethrowers, but they were the only vehicles available to be shipped to Spain.

Meanwhile the Soviets also sent equipment, and by mid-October, fifty T-26 tanks, thirty armored cars, and fifty-one tankists, with fuel and ammunition, had arrived in Cartagena to aid the Republican forces.[4] The T-26s each had a 45mm gun, small by Soviet standards, but making it much more powerful than the lightly armed German tanks.[5] Two days later Ian Berzin left for Spain to take up his post as head of the Soviet military mission.[6] This was only the beginning. At the end of October, Voroshilov passed on a resolution to Stalin that would send 330 tankists and 111 T-26 tanks to the Spanish arena.[7] A more detailed description of material sent to Spain showed that there were four batches of equipment sent by the end of October and a fifth batch planned by early November.[8]

The first battle reports were unanimously disparaging of the small German tank, apparently justifying the most severe criticism leveled at it before the outbreak of the war. One observer wrote that "the machine made a somewhat worn out and by no means modern impression. Its effect is very slight and it can hardly be consid-

2. Hans-Henning Abendroth has a complete description of Hitler's decision making in *Hitler in der spanischen Arena* (Paderborn: Ferdinand Schöningh, 1973), 15–73.

3. B. H. Liddell Hart, *The Other Side of the Hill* (London: Macmillan, 1993), 122–23.

4. "Spravka 17.10.36, Pribylo i razgruzheno v Kartagena," RGVA, f. 33987, op. 3, d. 832, l. 115.

5. Resolution and listing of material to be sent to "X" from Voroshilov to Stalin, 28 October 1936, RGVA, f. 33987, op. 3, d. 832, l. 178. By the end of October, a German agent in Spain had learned that the Soviets had shipped fifty tanks with two hundred men. Report No. 6 from "Guido," 23 October 1936, BA-MA, RM 20/1241, p. 103.

6. "Spravka 'Ob otpravke propovednikov v "X,"'" RGVA, f. 33987, op. 3, d. 832, l. 123.

7. Resolution and listing of material to be sent to "X" from Voroshilov to Stalin, 28 October 1936, RGVA, f. 33987, op. 3, d. 832, l. 178.

8. List of the cost of all armor sent to Spain from the ABTU to Langov, "Sostoiashchemu dlia osobo vazhnykh poruchenii pri narodnom komissare oborony," 1 November 1936, RGVA, f. 33987, op. 3, d. 832, ll. 272–275. A final listing of material actually sent to Spain during 1936 showed 106 T-26 tanks and sixty armored cars. List of all material sent to Spain in 1936 "po osobomu naznacheniiu" from Ol'shanskii to Voroshilov, 2 February 1937, RGVA, f. 31811, op. 2, d. 646, l. 1.

ered a decisive weapon in local combat formations."[9] Later the same officer reported that the tanks had taken part in an attack at the end of October, but had obviously not had a decisive effect since they had even had trouble crossing trenches in the area.[10] Thoma, analyzing several engagements between the German and Soviet tanks, remarked that the superiority of tanks with guns vis-à-vis those armed with machine guns had been well known even in the world war. In the current war Soviet tanks could spot the German vehicles, stop, and shoot from up to a kilometer away, and yet penetrate the thin armor of the smaller tanks. The weaponry on the German tanks was unable to reach this distance, while German antitank guns could not fire with any accuracy beyond a few hundred meters. He urgently requested a shipment of tanks armed with guns or, if this were not possible, to outfit armored cars with guns. As the situation stood at that point in the war, the "Whites" (Nationalists) could not use the German vehicles when Soviet tanks were expected to enter the battle.[11]

Yet, because of the incompetence of their military commanders, the Republicans were not able to exploit their superiority in armor as decisively as they might have. Red tanks took part in several engagements during the first few months of the war, but did not make a significant contribution to any of them. In the course of the desperate defense of Madrid, for instance, the Republicans deployed their tanks on the barricaded streets but the heavy machines, unable to use their speed fully, had little impact on the struggle.[12] By mid-November poor handling in combat and antiarmor weaponry had already cost the Reds thirteen tanks, four of these irrecoverably lost.[13] The Germans handled their smaller number of machines no better. Early in the war Thoma would complain bitterly about the pointless use of armor in combat, which resulted, he said, in bloodying the best troops to no purpose.[14]

The Germans soon found that it was easier to improve their poor tactics than to produce a tank able to effectively combat the T-26. The war in Spain made painfully clear to the German high command that they could not rely on the Pz. I, even as a stopgap: the Wehrmacht had to have better-armed and armored tanks for modern war. Throughout 1937 German industry strove to produce larger tanks, for their own army as well as for the Nationalists, but again ran into trouble with shortages

9. Report No. 6 from "Guido," 23 October 1936, BA-MA, RM 20/1241, p. 108.

10. Ibid., p. 110.

11. Report from Gruppe Thoma, 6.12.36, "Erfahrungen im Kampf zwischen dem deutschen M.G.-Panzer und russischen Kanonen-Panzern," BA-MA, RH 2/288, pp. 34, 36.

12. Report from v, Thoma, "Beurteilung der militärischen Lage vor Madrid," 22 November 1936, BA-MA, RM20/1241, pp. 205–6.

13. List of all men and materiel lost in Spain from Uritskii to Voroshilov, 12 November 1936, RGVA, f. 33987, op. 3, d. 832, ll. 369–70.

14. Report from Gruppe Thoma "Beurteilung der Lage vor Madrid am 22.12.1936," 22 November 1936, BA-MA, RH2/288, p. 49.

of raw materials. As discussed above, Hitler's decision to rebuild the army placed a multiplicity of demands on limited resources. This created a crisis in the factories, interfering not only with tank production, but also with the overall reconstruction of the army. Because of these difficulties Beck reported that the peacetime army would be fully operational only by October 1942 and the wartime army by April 1943. Touching motor vehicles in particular, he noted that orders supposed to be completed for October 1937 would be met only in the summer of 1938. He concluded that the new motorized units would not be available for training purposes until the winter of 1938–39 and not be capable of military action until much later than that.[15] A more specific report on tank production noted that Krupp had sent all of its Pz. I tanks (1,175) while Maybach had delivered slightly more than half of its more powerful Pz. I (220 out of 403). Beyond this the record was very poor. Only seventy-two of the 184 small command tanks and sixty-one of the 844 Pz. II's had been delivered. Meanwhile, the army had yet to receive any Pz. III tanks (161 ordered), large command tanks (thirty ordered) or Pz. IV's (seventy-seven ordered).[16] In fact Daimler-Benz would manage to produce only ninety-five of the Pz. III tanks in the period from 1936 to 1939.[17]

The problems with tank production explained why Germany shipped only the small Pz. I to Spain, and also accounted for the exclusive use of that tank at the crucial fall maneuvers of 1937.[18] Given the vehicles' obvious deficiencies, and their failures to live up to expectations in Spain, it was somewhat of a relief to the armor supporters when they and the unit equipped with them performed well in the exercises.[19] Like the Soviet maneuvers of the year before, the German exercises featured a huge amount of technology and men: an armor division and a tank brigade, 160,000 troops, and 830 tanks participated. Franz Halder, who would soon take over Beck's position and was a supporter of the operational concentration of armor forces, planned and led the maneuvers.[20] The division fought as an independent unit, separated from the infantry and cavalry, and achieved, for the most part, the objectives it was given. Although bad terrain and weather kept the unit from showing any great promise in one assault, in others it successfully attacked with artillery

15. "Entwurf eines Schreibens des Oberbefehlshabers des Heeres an den Reichskriegsminister betr. die Umstellung des Rüstungsprogramms, vom 14. Dezember 1937," BA-MA, RH 15/149, in Klaus-Jürgen Müller, *Armee und Drittes Reich 1933–1939: Darstellung und Dokumentation* (Paderborn: Ferdinand Schöhningh, 1987), no. 141, 305–7.

16. Report "Übersicht der Fertigung," BA-MA, RH 12–6/v, 1.

17. Werner Oswald, *Kraftfahrzeuge und Panzer der Reichswehr, Wehrmacht und Bundeswehr* (Stuttgart: Motorbuch Verlag, 1973), 243, 254. On the other hand, the company would produce over fifteen hundred Pz. III's from 1939 to 1940. Ibid.

18. The significance of the exercises can be seen from the attendance of Hitler and Mussolini. Heinz Guderian, *Erinnerungen eines Soldaten* (Heidelberg: Kurt Vowinckel, 1951), 39.

19. Ibid.

20. Christian Hartmann, *Halder: Generalstabschef Hitlers 1938–1942* (Paderborn: Schöningh, 1991), 49–50.

support, practiced cooperation with an infantry brigade that followed to secure terrain, and aided an infantry attack by pushing through enemy lines far ahead of the foot soldiers. Even so, the tanks suffered significant problems with fuel supply and, more importantly, with command and control.[21]

Some issues concerning armor doctrine were thus still unsettled when Lutz asked Guderian during the winter of 1936–37 to produce a book to propagandize tanks and their prowess in battle. The book, *Achtung – Panzer!* was an effective tool for creating widespread popular interest in tanks.[22] The main purpose of the work was, however, far different. Guderian in fact used the book (as he had tried to use his earlier article) to convince the German army that tanks had to fight together, in one concentrated armor fist, and not spread about in different units to strengthen the infantry, as Beck and others wanted.[23] He argued that the choice was very simple: if one believed that tanks were only suited for positional warfare, then of course they could be used piecemeal. In fact, however, they were designed "to carry out operational envelopments and turning movements in the open field." Tying the tank to the slow-moving infantry or horse-drawn artillery was folly, since the army would be unable to use the vehicle's full potential. In his vision of warfare, the speed of the tank dictated the tempo of warfare and artillery and the infantry had to keep up with the vehicles, not the other way around. There were other problems with incorporating tanks into infantry divisions: this would force the machines to fight on unsuitable terrain, made it impossible to concentrate the vehicles on the decisive spot, and would end in the army forfeiting all hope of surprise and decisive success in battle.[24]

Having made his main point, Guderian then turned to the details of how the pure motorized and mechanized units of the future would fight. The combat style that he described for the armor units was fast and hard-hitting, and depended heavily on a combined-arms approach to battle – as indeed did official descriptions of armor doctrine. To illustrate his views on the new combat, Guderian chose a breakthrough of a fortified defense because, like other German officers, he expected the next war to begin as one of positions.[25] After mobility was returned to the war – through the use of tanks, naturally – motorized infantry and artillery, the air force

21. "Bericht über die Wehrmachtmanöver (Heer) 1937." BA-MA, RH 2/184. Lutz tried to work on the problems with coordinating infantry and tanks later that year. See draft report from Lutz "Betr: Erfahrungen der im Mai 1937 in Döberitz unter Leitung des Gru. Kdo. 1 durchgeführten Versuchsübungen betr. Zusammenwirken von Inf. und Pz. Kampfwagen," 1 August 1937, BA-MA, RH 12–6/v, 20. Also report from the 1. Panzer-Brigade, "Lage für die Brigadeübung am 4.9.37," 1 September 1937, BA-MA, RH 16/v, 16.

22. Guderian, *Erinnerungen eines Soldaten*, 32.

23. Heinz Guderian, *Achtung – Panzer!* tr. Christopher Duffy (London: Arms and Armour Press, 1992), 74–75, 90. See also Wolfgang Paul, *Panzer-General Walther K. Nehring* (Stuttgart: Motorbuch Verlag, 1986), 71.

24. Guderian, *Achtung – Panzer!* 168–70.

25. Ibid., 178.

(including paratroopers), and armor units would cooperate closely with the tanks to successfully break through a strong position. In a direct echo of Soviet thought, he also argued that during this type of combat the army should "strive to bring the entire depth of the enemy defense under simultaneous attack."[26] His more detailed account of the breakthrough battle, like most German descriptions of tactics, gave only broad guidelines for the commander. The most important differences with earlier writers were his emphases on radio communication, on the need to press successful attacks with further deployments, and his stress on the tank's firepower, rather than its simple crushing action.[27]

If Guderian's emphasis on linking operations and on striking the entire depth of the enemy simultaneously sounds eerily familiar, his closer description of modern battle, while obviously following on earlier German and British thought, also held several striking parallels to the Soviet concept. Like all three of these, he agreed that the army should deploy the tanks in echelons, each assigned separate missions. The first echelon, like the Soviet DD (long-range) group, would head for the far rear, attempting to pin down reserves and knock out the headquarters and control centers as well as eliminate antitank weapons. The second echelon would have the task of destroying artillery and any antitank defenses active in its area. The third echelon, similar to the PP (infantry support) tanks, would escort the infantry through the enemy infantry battle zone and in the process suppress opposition so thoroughly that its support forces would be able to follow it. A final echelon could serve as a reserve or for rolling up intact sectors of the front. He ended this short section by adding that "the whole mighty assault must break into the enemy defense simultaneously and on a broad front, and press on to its objective in a series of continuous waves."[28]

Guderian did not see his concept of future warfare as a radical departure, but as a compromise between those who wanted the tank only for infantry support and those who thought that the tank was a cure-all. He stated repeatedly that using the tank solely to support infantry action underestimated its capabilities, but he also warned against those who dreamed that the tank would be able to perform grand operations, raids into the enemy's rear, and so on, without cost or effort.[29] He especially did not think that tanks could achieve success without the close support of all other arms, and the battle outlined above, like most German ideas – as well as deep battle – depended heavily on close cooperation among the forces. Guderian even agreed with other German officers that large numbers of ordinary infantry were absolutely vital for achieving any real success on the battlefield. Unfortunately, he had no new suggestions for how the slow-moving foot soldiers would

26. Ibid., 180.
27. Ibid., 180, 188.
28. Ibid., 190–91.
29. Ibid., 188–90.

keep up with the fast tanks. Motorization of the infantry was the best solution, although he knew that this would take many years to accomplish; the only other recourse was special conditioning and light equipment for those soldiers still on foot.[30]

As we have seen, Guderian was not alone in his inability to find a clear answer to the question of armor-infantry cooperation. This was not the only dilemma over armor doctrine that the Wehrmacht faced. Lutz's remarks for the year showed that German troops, like the Soviet forces, had trouble putting into effect even those ideas on infantry-armor coordination that were generally accepted by the army. In exercises, he noted, the motorized infantry had failed to exploit the effect of the tank attack properly, while foot soldiers had simply jumped to their feet at the appearance of the first tanks and rushed forward "in dense hordes." According to official doctrine, they were supposed to wait until the tanks had already broken through the enemy's lines and then advance by bounds, exploiting fully the tanks' fire.[31]

Critics of the armor division idea pointed to Guderian's weak answers to the problem of infantry-tank cooperation, and the failures that Lutz noted in the same area in exercises, to fault the use of tanks independently in the enemy's depth. The infantry had to accompany armor forces, said the critics, and thus tanks must move slowly on the battlefield. When men such as Eimannsberger, Guderian, and others found an answer in personnel carriers, the critics doubted that infantry would be able to follow directly behind the tanks; unprotected all-terrain vehicles were extremely vulnerable to the enemy's firepower while armored transporters would offer large targets to the enemy's artillery.[32] Another critic argued that since victory consisted of occupying the entire battlefield, and only the infantry could do this, tanks had to closely support the infantry in their fight for terrain, rather than speeding on ahead. His description of the tank battle of the future owed much to old world war images: tanks just ahead of the infantry fighting machine gun nests, while the infantry "cleaned up" behind them.[33]

The compromise solution was that recommended by Lutz, Beck, and other staff officers: different kinds of infantry-armor cooperation depending on the combat situation. As described in one memorandum, "operational" armor units, generally equivalent to the GHQ cavalry, would practice one form of cooperation. These units combined purely armor detachments with other motorized forces to fight only certain types of independent operational missions. The second type of cooperation

---

30. Ibid., 191–97.

31. *Besichtigungsbemerkungen des Kommandierenden Generals des Kommandos der Panzertruppen im Jahre 1937* (Berlin: Kommando der Panzertruppen, 15. November 1937), BA-MA, RHD 26/5, pp. 3–5, 8–9.

32. See Generalmajor a.D. Dihle, "Einsatz von Kampfwagen," *Militär-Wochenblatt*, no. 16 (1937): 974–77.

33. "Panzereinsatz," ibid., no. 19 (1937): 1166–67.

was for the "tactical" armor units, designed for closely coordinated action with an infantry division. Unlike Beck, the author of the memo argued that these units should be bound organizationally to infantry divisions and not to the larger corps. Placing them at the corps level would allow a unified mass attack during a breakthrough battle, but even the high command agreed that these units could not fight en masse since, among other things, their weaponry and armor were insufficient. The alternative, preferred by this officer, was to subordinate one armor detachment to each infantry division. He argued further that the army needed additional infantry tanks for even closer cooperation with foot soldiers. These would act as infantry artillery located in or just behind the foremost infantry lines, or as armor assault detachments, driving ahead of the infantry to clear the way for them. The infantry tanks would not attack as a mass, like the armor detachments, but rather in very small units combined with equally small infantry groups. And naturally these heaviest of infantry weapons would belong to the infantry themselves.[34]

The fighting in Spain did not offer any easy answers to the question of infantry-armor cooperation, primarily because the light Pz. I tanks were almost worthless, while the Germans sent very few of the machines, only ninety-one by November 1937, to Spain.[35] Early in the war the German government and army decided, in fact, to concentrate on aircraft rather than ground forces for Franco, and the Condor Legion had far more airplanes than tanks.[36] By late 1937, the Luftwaffe could request that it be made the "main bearer of action" in the Spanish theater.[37] The situation for the tanks was so bad that Thoma suggested re-forming captured Russian armor into White units, a proposal taken up and used successfully later that year.[38] These factors did not allow a serious test of how the armor divisions would fare in modern warfare and especially prevented a look at the various ideas on coordinating infantry and tank assaults.[39]

For a more complete view of tanks in combat, German officers were forced in-

---

34. "Erfahrungen," BA-MA, RH 12–6/v, 2, pp. 105–111r–v.

35. "Bericht über die zweite Spanienreise," from V-Mann "R" to Chef Abw., 15 November 1937, BA-MA, RM 20/1403, p. 159; intelligence reports on performance of German forces in the Spanish Civil War, 24 February 1937 and April 1937, BA-MA, RH 2/288, pp. 169–70, 240; report from Sonderstab W, 7 July 1937, BA-MA, RM 20/1223, pp. 205–6; report from Sonderstab W, 5 November 1937, BA-MA, RM 20/1223, pp. 209, 212. Out of forty-six German tanks present in October 1936, only twenty-six could be fielded four months later. Sonderstab W, "Lagebericht Nr. 120," 23 February 1937, BA-MA, RM 20/1411, pp. 66–67.

36. Hugh Thomas, The Spanish Civil War (New York: Touchstone, 1986), 469, 798 n. 1.

37. Sonderstab W, "Lagebericht Nr. 117," 19 February 1937, BA-MA, RM 20/1411, pp. 62–63; memo from Blomberg. "Betr: Gestellung für die Übung 'Rügen,'" 9 November 1937, BA-MA, RM 20/1257, pp. 1–2.

38. Sonderstab W, "Lagebericht Nr. 121," 24 February 1937, BA-MA, RM 20/1411, pp. 68–69; Sonderstab W, "Anlage 3 zu Lagebericht Nr. 319," 22 October 1937, BA-MA, RM 20/1421, p. 113.

39. The one exception occurred during the battle of Brunete. Thomas, Spanish Civil War, 710–17.

stead to analyze Republican armor use. Unfortunately, most of the winter and spring assaults by the Reds that were supported by tanks featured only a few machines, and were repulsed with heavy losses for the attackers.[40] During the March campaigns the Soviets employed tanks more intensively than previously, although again usually in small numbers and to support infantry assaults. On 22 March an attack with more Soviet tanks took place and this the Nationalists also beat back with heavy losses for the attackers.[41] One observer's opinion was that the Republican tanks had distinguished themselves by their bold advances, but had moved "without a care in the world" under enemy fire and suffered heavy losses.[42] Only during the counteroffensives around Madrid in July, when the Soviets began to use their tanks in greater numbers, did they achieve any successes.[43] In the end even these larger offensives were stopped and turned back.[44]

German studies of the Soviet tanks in battle noted that they were excellent as strongpoints for the defensive, and had done equally well as mobile artillery. When the infantry had not followed the tanks, however, the Soviets had repeatedly lost positions.[45] The quick tactical penetration at Brunete during the first day of the great Republican offensive around Madrid, and the widening of the break in the following days, was largely due to the mass use of tanks. In this battle the tanks had worked as fast infantry escort artillery, although at times they had also broken away from their own forces and gone beyond the Republican lines.[46] However, when the Loyalists had used fifty tanks to occupy a train station without the aid of infantry, they were quickly driven back by a White counterattack.[47] Other accounts seemed to contradict this assessment. The Condor Legion's tactical operations staff reported in October that two tanks were able to hold a bridge against the determined

40. Sonderstab W, "Lagebericht Nr. 117," 19 February 1937, BA-MA, RM 20/1411, pp. 62–63; "Lagebericht Nr. 165," 19 April 1937, BA-MA, RM 20/1413, pp. 14–15; "Lagebericht Nr. 182," 12 May 1937, BA-MA, RM 20/1414, p. 22; "Lagebericht Nr. 183," 13 May 1937, BA-MA, RM 20/1414, p. 23; "Lagebericht Nr. 198," 1 June 1937, BA-MA, RM 20/1415, p. 25.

41. Sonderstab W, "Anlage zu Lagebericht Nr. 157," 9 April 1937, BA-MA, RM 20/1412, pp. 121–25.

42. Ibid., p. 129.

43. Sonderstab W, "Lagebericht Nr. 229," 7 July 1937, BA-MA, RM 20/1416, p. 39; "Lagebericht Nr. 231," 9 July 1937, BA-MA, RM 20/1416, pp. 46–47.

44. Sonderstab W, "Lagebericht Nr. 232," 10 July 1937, BA-MA, RM 20/1416, p. 51; "Lagebericht Nr. 233," 12 July 1937, BA-MA, RM 20/1416, p. 57.

45. Sonderstab W, "Anlage 1 zu Lagebericht Nr. 254: Rückblick der Legion Condor über die beiderseitige Waffenwirkung beim Angriff auf Brunete," 5 August 1937, BA-MA, RM 20/1417, p. 17; "Anlage zu Lagebericht Nr. 264: Beobachtungen bei den Kämpfen zur Wiederherstellung der Lage bei Brunete," 17 August 1937, BA-MA, RM 20/1417, p. 62.

46. Sonderstab W, "Anlage 2 zu Lagebericht Nr. 265: Querschnitt durch die Berichte über Rote Tanks in der Zeit von 1.3. bis 31.7.37 (Bericht Sorau)," 18 August 1937, BA-MA, RM 20/1417, pp. 69–70.

47. Sonderstab W, "Lagebericht Nr. 312," 14 October 1937. RM 20/1421, p. 56; "Lagebericht Nr. 313," 15 October 1937. BA-MA, RM 20/1421, p. 60.

efforts of cavalry and an entire infantry brigade. Bombing by German airplanes had also failed to dislodge the vehicles and only another attack by aircraft chased the tanks away.[48] The result of this contradictory evidence was that officers concluded that the war had not yet clarified how tanks and infantry should cooperate.[49]

Beyond these unsatisfactory results in infantry-armor cooperation, the German officer corps drew two conclusions about the use of tanks from the first years of the Spanish Civil War. The first was an affirmation of the earliest lesson of the war: the Russian tanks performed better than the lighter Italian and German machines. A corollary was that this superiority was almost entirely due to the fact that the Nationalists' tanks were too lightly armored and armed for the demands of modern warfare. A situation report from August 1937 argued that the Russian tank was excellent as a base for defensive action while a secret service report from about the same time noted that it was also a good offensive weapon. It was greatly feared by the White infantrymen and had proved itself during several breakthroughs in the battle of Brunete and the fight for Madrid.[50] German tanks, on the other hand, were too lightly armored, a secret service report from April 1937 noted. Machine guns could penetrate their armor and a Nationalist decision to use them for close cooperation with the infantry prevented the tanks from exploiting their speed.[51] An official memorandum by the Army Staff on the lessons of the war agreed that the experience of battle had shown that tanks armed with guns were superior to those with machine guns. Machine gun tanks, alone on broken terrain, could not achieve a decisive effect and, since the infantry often did not follow them, were also unable to hold ground.[52]

48. Sonderstab W, "Anlage 1 zu Lagebericht Nr. 331: Kämpfe um Gijon," 5 November 1937, BA-MA, RM 20/1422, pp. 82–84.

49. Intelligence reports on performance of German forces in the Spanish Civil War, 13 November 1936, BA-MA, RH 2/288, p. 166.

50. "Einsatz Lagebericht," 5 August 1937, and Abw. Meldung, August 1937, BA-MA, RH 2/289, p. 123. Thoma had such high regard for the vehicles that he paid rewards for their capture, and by March 1938, two of the six tank companies in the White forces were armed with Red tanks.. Liddell Hart, The Other Side of the Hill, 122–23; Sonderstab W, "Anlage 2 zu Lagebericht Nr. 454: Ausbildung der Spanier durch Gruppe Drohne (1.10.36–März 1938)," 1 April 1938, BA-MA, RM 20/1428, p. 95. In fact, of the 160 tanks in Franco's arsenal, only 91 came from Germany, while another 44 were captured Soviet machines. Generalstab des Heeres, report, "Die beiderseitigen Streitkräfte im spanischen Burgerkrieg 1936/38," 25 May 1938, BA-MA, RH 2/289, p. 183; Oberkommando der Wehrmacht, report on equipment sent to Spain up to 20 April 1938, 20 April 1938, BA-MA, RM 20/1483, pp. 99, 103; OKW, report on equipment sent to Spain up to 1 July 1938, 21 July 1938, BA-MA, RM 20/1483, pp. 109, 113; Sonderstab W, "Anlage 2 zu Lagebericht Nr. 454: Ausbildung der Spanier durch Gruppe Drohne (1.10.36–März 1938)," 1 April 1938, BA-MA, RM 20/1428, p. 95. Some of the White tank units also consisted of Italian or French tanks. Sonderstab W, "Anlage zu Lagebericht Nr. 383: Bemerkungen zur Kriegsgliederung," 8 January 1938, BA-MA, RM 20/1256.

51. Abw. Bericht, April 1937, BA-MA, RH 2/3007, p. 104.

52. Cover memo from the 2nd Department of the Army General Staff, 30.12.1937, for a report,

The second lesson was that it was difficult to make conclusive decisions about the future of tank tactics based on Civil War experiences, because conditions had been so specific to that conflict alone. In the first place, too few of the vehicles had participated in the war and neither side had used the small number of tanks that they possessed en masse.[53] Secondly, the terrain in Spain had been particularly poor for the successful use of tanks, something that was not true of the northern European plains.[54] Finally, the Army General Staff concluded that the belligerents had not used the tanks "in accordance with their offensive purpose." Both German and Soviet armor had been subordinated only to the infantry and had been mostly treated as heavy infantry weapons fit only for close escort duty.[55] For all these reasons, the German high command refused to draw any major conclusions on tank tactics or operational use from its experiences in the Civil War, reserving judgment until it used the machines in a larger conflict.

Soviet officers too drew lessons from the Civil War but, unlike their German counterparts, believed that the conflict presented a valid picture of a future large-scale war. They thus took tactical, strategic, and logistical lessons very seriously, recommending substantial changes in Red Army practice based on what they learned from the war. True, there were some exceptions. In April 1937 Voroshilov wrote on a report discussing the lessons learned from the war that one suggestion needed "further, supplementary testing at our maneuvers, since the experience in 'X' [Spain] cannot be regarded as exhaustive owing to the character of military operations (tank units were excessively burdened, they took the place of infantry, cavalry, and so on) and the nature of terrain in 'X.' On this one needs to think and work a little more."[56] Yet as the war progressed, the command staff became convinced that the conflict was a reliable model of modern war and treated each new experience of

---

"Erfahrungen aus dem bisherigen Verlauf des spanischen Bürgerkrieges," and the report itself, BA-MA, RH 2/289, pp. 64–67v.

53. See Oberst a.D. Rudolf v. Xylander, "Vom spanischen Krieg, XXVIII. Erfahrungen mit neuzeitlichen Waffen, A. Panzer und Panzerabwehr," *Militär-Wochenblatt*, no. 49 (1937, 3134–37; Guderian, *Achtung – Panzer!* 210.

54. Cover memo from the 2nd Department of the Army General Staff, 30.12.1937, for a report, "Erfahrungen aus dem bisherigen Verlauf des spanischen Bürgerkrieges," and the report itself, BA-MA, RH 2/289, pp. 64–67v; and Guderian, *Achtung – Panzer!* 210.

55. Cover memo from the 2nd Department of the Army General Staff, 30.12.1937, for a report, "Erfahrungen aus dem bisherigen Verlauf des spanischen Bürgerkrieges," and the report itself, BA-MA, RH 2/289, pp. 64–67v.

56. Report, "Voprosy boevogo primeneniia tankov," "verno," Secretary Deputy Defense Commissar Levoniuk, 2 April 1937, RGVA, f. 31811, op. 2, d. 640, ll. 259–60. See also report by R. Ia. Malinovskii, "Operativno-takticheskie vyvody i zakliucheniia, sdelannye na osnovanii boevogo opyta voiny v Ispanii za period ot nachala miatezha po mai 1938 goda," RGVA, f. 35082, op. 1, d. 483, ll. 1a, 32.

combat as a valuable lesson for how the Soviet army should fight in the future. Since the Republicans used their tanks to directly support the foot soldiers, much of what the Soviets learned dealt with infantry and tank cooperation. Their conclusions were somewhat contradictory. Sergei Krivoshein, the first head of the Soviet armor forces in Spain, suggested that the infantry had no idea how to work with armor, while another commander argued that only close contact allowed successful cooperation between the two forces.[57]

When Grigorii Bokis, the new head of the ABTU, prepared his first comprehensive analysis of tanks in the war later that year, he too concluded that good cooperation between infantry and tanks was the key to success, but did not have any recommendations for how to achieve it. He began with the battle of Seseña (29 October 1936), the first engagement in which Soviet tanks had participated, and wrote that they had done well, given the circumstances. Fifteen Soviet tanks had fought in the battle, but the infantry not only had not supported the tank attack, they had not even had any communication with them. Yet the infantry and tank attack had stopped the offensive on Madrid and the tanks had fought independently for ten hours.[58] A battle at Fuenlabroda, on 2 November, had ended less successfully. Twelve tanks with infantry took part in an attack, but lack of cooperation meant that objectives were not achieved. While the tanks could fight independently for several hours, they were "unable to definitively mop up an area and hold it by themselves."[59] His general conclusion was that armor could shatter the opponent and seize terrain for some time, but was incapable of holding land, and therefore "a correctly adjusted and systematically executed cooperation with the principal arms and especially with the infantry is an absolutely essential condition for success."[60] The form that this cooperation would take was, however, unclear.

Armor-infantry cooperation was not the only area of concern in Soviet analyses of their experiences of Spain. As Bokis's report shows, command and communications, already recognized as a weakness, were very poor. In contrast to German experience, the Soviets continued to report that radios, because of technological flaws and the inexperience of operators, had not worked well. Two officers suggested that the best means to control a battle remained the personal example of the

---

57. Description of tank battle in Spain from January 1937, RGVA, f. 31811, op. 4, d. 28, l. 78; description of technical and tactical use of tanks in Spain during the period October 1936–January 1937 by Krivoshein, RGVA, f. 31811, op. 4, d. 28, l. 94; "Hero of the Soviet Union t. P.," "Boevaia rabota republikanskikh tankov v Ispanii," in a collection of reports on tanks in Spain from Uritskii to Bokis, 5 June 1937, RGVA, f. 31811, op. 4, d. 28, l. 41.

58. Report by Chief of the ABTU and Chief of the I Department of the ABTU, "Deistviia tankov na frontakh v Ispanii v period oktiabr' 1936 g.-fevral' 1937 g.," 11 May 1937, RGVA, f. 31811, op. 4, d. 28, ll. 186–91.

59. Ibid., ll. 191–95.

60. Ibid., l. 205.

commander.[61] The organization of the rear and logistics was also inadequate.[62] Additional problems pointed out by Soviet observers included lack of reconnaissance before tank attacks, which forced Republicans to attack blind, and the inadequacy of depending on sheer movement to save the tanks. Although the vehicles had traveled at 40 kph, one officer wrote, this had not guaranteed that they would not be hit by artillery and actually increased the chances of falling into antitank traps.[63] Another commander agreed, informing Voroshilov that experience had shown that the assault planned for the DD tank group, a nonstop attack far from other forces, would be unable to achieve its objectives. The visibility from tanks was too poor and the motion of the machines caused inaccurate fire. He proposed instead that only part of the armor unit attack, firing on the move, while the other part would stop and support these tanks with fire from a half-concealed position. He thought too that it might be possible to have all the tanks stop some distance from their objective and direct massed fire on to the area, acting much like the German descriptions of Soviet tanks as mobile artillery.[64]

The result of these combined problems was inordinately high losses of tanks, which led to some interesting conclusions about the future employment of armor. From October 1936 to February 1937, the Reds lost 52 machines, or 25–30 percent of their deployed tanks destroyed for each day of battle.[65] By mid-September 1937, the Republicans had only 170 out of a total of 256 T-26s delivered since the start of the conflict.[66] Kirill Meretskov, a later hero of the Second World War, and another commander named Simonov, used these results to drastically increase the estimate of armor losses in battle. Others argued as follows: the Soviet Union had sent 256 tanks to Spain; in a half-year of combat 63 had been lost; multiplying by two, this meant that 126 would be lost in a year; therefore the normal loss of tanks in a year

61. Report "Voprosy boevogo primeneniia tankov." "verno," Secretary Deputy Defense Commissar Levoniuk, 2 April 1937, RGVA, f. 31811, op. 2, d. 640, ll. 259–61; report from Pavlov, Deputy Chief of the ABTU, to Voroshilov on armor forces in Spanish Civil War, 31 August 1937, RGVA, f. 31811, op. 2, d. 646, l. 145. See also report to Bokis, "Boevoe primenenie," 2 April 1937, RGVA, f. 31811, op. 2, d. 646, l. 26.

62. Report from Pavlov, Deputy Chief of the ABTU, to Voroshilov on armor forces in Spanish Civil War, 31 August 1937, RGVA, f. 31811, op. 2, d. 646, l. 141.

63. "Hero of the Soviet Union t. P.," "Boevaia rabota republikanskikh tankov v Ispanii," in a collection of reports on tanks in Spain from Uritskii to Bokis, 5 June 1937, RGVA, f. 31811, op. 4, d. 28, ll. 42–43; report by Vetrov, Assistant Co. Commander for Technical Units Military Engineer 3rd Class, "Otchet o tekhnicheskom obespechenii deistvii tankov v operatsii pod Fuentes de Edro 13.10.37," 21 October 1937, RGVA, f. 35082, op. 1, d. 78, ll. 869–68.

64. "Voprosy boevogo primeneniia tankov," "verno," Secretary Deputy Defense Commissar Levoniuk, 2 April 1937, RGVA, f. 31811, op. 2, d. 640, ll. 259–61.

65. "Boevoe primenenie" on tanks in Spain to Bokis, 2 April 1937, RGVA, f. 31811, op. 2, d. 646, l. 29.

66. Report on military situation in Spain from Shtern, 4 October 1937, RGVA, f. 33987, op. 3, d. 961, ll. 142, 169.

would be around 50 percent. Meretskov and Simonov noted that because the tanks had arrived in several shipments, rather than all at the same time, and because the fronts where tanks fought were widely separated from each other, the Republicans had never used more than 70 tanks at once. They also stressed that since only T-26 tanks had fought in Spain, the results of their investigation applied only to this vehicle and since tactically the tanks had exclusively provided infantry support, this also narrowed the report's usefulness.[67] With these qualifications in mind, the authors estimated that the norm for yearly permanent tank losses was approximately 300–400 percent, or three to four times the beginning strength of the fighting forces. The losses depended heavily on the kinds of action that the tanks took part in, since attacks on a strongly fortified region would cause casualties of 1100–1500 percent, while maneuver combat caused "only" 140 percent losses.[68] Temporary losses would, however, be even higher, about 500–1000 percent.[69]

The writers then listed the corrections necessary to make their results relevant for a major war. They argued that in a large-scale war the army would use tanks en masse, presenting more targets and therefore causing more losses; that the enemy would have better antitank weaponry in a large war, again raising casualties; that the rebels had not had tanks with guns, but this would not be true in a large-scale war, which would also raise losses. At the same time, there were factors that might decrease losses. In Spain the Republicans had not been able to provide artillery cover for the tanks, which was unlikely to be true in a future war, while most combat in the Civil War had ended with the field of battle not firmly in the hands of the Republicans, adding to the number of irretrievably lost tanks. The authors concluded that these corrections would cancel each other out, leaving permanent losses at 300–400 percent.[70] Significantly, the authors failed to take into account possibilities like better terrain for armor warfare, a short war, or tactical considerations such as surprise, speed, or overwhelming the enemy's command and control centers. In effect they denied that using deep battle tactics would affect tank losses. The only conclusion that a reader could draw from the report was that the next war, regardless of how or where it was fought, would lead to a massive destruction of armor.

The armor doctrine implied by these many "lessons" and proposals was very different from the deep battle concept still supposedly accepted by the Red Army. In place of huge mechanized corps speeding to suppress the entire depth of the enemy's positions, the lessons of Spain suggested a slow, methodical advance by the machines as they worked to perform their older mission of helping the infantry to move forward. The armor assault had to be heavily supported by infantry and ar-

67. Report from Meretskov and Simonov to Voroshilov and Shaposhnikov, 5 August 1937, RGVA, f. 33987, op. 3, d. 1015, ll. 234–35.

68. Ibid., ll. 237–41.

69. Ibid., l. 249.

70. Ibid., ll. 241–42.

tillery, since tanks could not move far without their protecting foot soldiers and certainly should not attempt to fight independently in the enemy's rear or on his far flanks. Even if the machines were fully supported by their accompanying infantry, serious doubts remained about the chances for armor succeeding at all.

Yet not everyone who had seen the tank in action thought that armor had done so poorly. As Dmitrii Pavlov, soon to be named head of the ABTU, put it, despite the "great role of air forces, the infantry's fortitude and perseverance, and the good work of the artillery," if tanks were not present, any offensive would be met with fire from trenches and fortified areas and would bog down after terrible bloodletting. He thought that tanks had fought well in short, independent battles such as at Jarama, and even better when they had cooperated properly with infantry, artillery and aircraft as at Guadalajara.[71] Infantry were helpless against tanks, while artillery and air forces did not present serious problems for an armor attack.[72] Tanks needed their infantry, but the infantry, apparently, needed the tank just as much.

The impact of the Spanish war on Soviet armor doctrine was not fully digested when, in the spring of 1937, Tukhachevskii, Uborevich, Eideman, Kork, Iakir, Vitalii Primakov, and Vitovt Putna were tried, convicted, and executed for high treason. Other sectors of Soviet society had already been touched by Stalin's terror, but the reasons behind his decision to purge the army at this particular point are not yet clear.[73] Its effect on Soviet armor affairs was all too plain. Tukhachevskii was the "ringleader" of the conspiracy, and therefore everyone who supported him in any way, whether personally or professionally, was in danger of imprisonment or execution. This meant that the armor forces in general, and deep battle in particular, of which Tukhachevskii and others of those executed had been firm supporters, were hit disproportionately hard by the purge. This should not be taken to mean that the army as a whole did not suffer terribly between 1937 and 1939.[74] The example of the Kiev military district was typical. Ivan Fed'ko, the replacement for Kork as commander of the district, reported that from the period June through 20 November 1937, 1,894 men had been purged there. Of these 861 had been arrested

---

71. Report from Pavlov to Voroshilov, 31 August 1937, RGVA, f. 31811, op. 2, d. 646, ll. 140–41.

72. Ibid., ll. 143–44.

73. The most complete description of the military purge and its effect are in John Erickson, *The Soviet High Command: A Military-Political History, 1918–1941* (London: St. Martin's Press, 1962), 449–73. For a recent interpretation of Tukhachevskii's execution see Shimon Naveh, "Mikhail Nikolayevich Tukhachevsky," in *Stalin's Generals*, ed. Harold Shukman (New York: Grove Press, 1993), 264–70.

74. Erickson, *The Soviet High Command*, 505–6, has the traditional estimate of the numbers lost during the purges. A contrasting view of the numbers killed and imprisoned during the purge is provided by Reese, who uses the (partial) opening of the post-Soviet archives to argue that far fewer officers were purged than Erickson (and the surviving officer corps) believed. Roger R. Reese, *Stalin's Reluctant Soldiers. A Social History of the Red Army, 1925–1941* (Lawrence: University Press of Kansas, 1996), 132–35.

as spies, wreckers, and participants in conspiracies. The district high command had lost 75 percent of its officers: everywhere from 90 percent of corps commanders and 84 percent of divisional commanders, to 37 percent of the regimental chiefs. As can be seen from these figures, the highest-ranking officers were hit the hardest, and Fed'ko commented on how young the high command was, with three thousand new officers, political workers, and administrators.[75]

The effect of the purges, and of the suspicious, almost paranoid attitudes encouraged by them, was especially pronounced in tank production and troop training. The year had already seen a slowdown in the economy as a whole, traditionally explained by a shift of resources and investment into the arms industry. Yet even with the extra funding the military industry performed no better in 1937 than the rest of the economy. Tank manufacture in 1936 had been entirely normal and industry had apparently had no trouble meeting demands. The following year production hit a wall. In April 1937 Bokis reported to Kuibyshev that industry had not delivered any tanks for the entire first quarter of the year. He added that the saddest part of the situation was that the bureaucracy in charge of tank production had not worked out any concrete steps for eliminating the "confusion and irresponsibility which now exist in tank factories."[76] In another memorandum from early May, Bokis reported that of the five tanks in current production, the B-T, the T-28, and even the latest T-26 tanks were all experiencing problems with defects in manufacturing.[77] Voroshilov informed Molotov in May that industry had still not produced the T-46 and T-29 tanks which the army had decided to develop two years before. Engineers had completed testing in January 1936 and production was organized and supposed to begin that month, but none of the tanks had been actually manufactured. He further noted that there was a real danger that none of the orders for 1937 would be fulfilled, as factories had not produced any tanks in the first four months of the year.[78]

In view of the severe problems that the tank industry had in meeting its targets, even with extra investment, the second traditional explanation for industrial stagnation, the terror, must be given more weight. As one historian pointed out, the purges

> swept away a high proportion not only of leading party cadres, but also of army officers, civil servants, managers, technicians, statisticians, planners, even foremen. Everywhere there were said to be spies, wreckers, diversionists. There was a

75. "Stenograficheskii otchet Zasedanie voennogo Soveta Pri Narodnom Komissare Oborony SSSR," 21–27 November 1937, RGVA, f. 4, op. 18, d. 54, l. 45.

76. Report from Bokis to Kuibyshev (Party Control Military Commission), 10 April 1937, RGVA, f. 31811, op. 2, d. 640, l. 120.

77. Conclusions from Bokis to Voroshilov, 11 May 1937, concerning a lecture delivered by Shaposhnikov, Commander of Forces LVO, on tactical-technical characteristics of tanks, RGVA, f. 31811, op. 2, d. 640, ll. 175–76.

78. Report from Voroshilov to Molotov, May 1937, RGVA, f. 31811, op. 2, d. 640, l. 179.

grave shortage of qualified personnel, so the deportation of many thousands of engineers and technologists to distant concentration camps represented a severe loss. But perhaps equally serious was the psychological effect of this terror on the survivors. With any error or accident likely to be attributed to treasonable activities, the simplest thing to do was to avoid responsibility, to seek approval from one's superiors for any act, to obey mechanically any order received, regardless of local conditions.[79]

Paranoia was soon pervasive, and affected the design and engineering of tanks in particular. In May, for instance, Bokis sent a report to Ezhov (the head of the NKVD) on the politics of a certain engineer Dyrenkov. Everything seemed to go wrong with the tanks that Dyrenkov helped to construct. He had worked on tank armor and "[t]hanks to his suggestion, each year's minimum of experimental work for introducing new types of armor into mass production was delayed." Even more suspiciously, he had built a special tank that had not been accepted by the army, but which had been supported by Tukhachevskii.[80] Another engineer, reporting on the progress made with the modernized version of the BT-5, described in depth the problems that "saboteurs" and "fascists" had caused. The manufacture of the tank had dragged on for three years because "wreckers of every stripe spared no effort to thwart and in every possible way delay the equipping of the army with this machine." Among those listed as enemies who had tried to stop the production of this vital tank was Khalepskii, who by this time had also fallen victim to the purges.[81]

The army and government shortly realized that it was not enough to cleanse the military and industry of "wreckers"; they would have to take practical steps to facilitate tank production. To simplify the manufacturing process, the number of tank types was cut to four in number, each meant for a specific type of armor unit.[82] Bokis also planned a "shopping trip" in America during the summer to buy tank technology, a step, as in the past, to ease the design and production of new vehicles.[83] By September the Council of Peoples' Commissars thought that tank production would soon be back to normal, estimating that Soviet factories would shortly be capable of producing sixty-three hundred T-26 and six thousand T-38 tanks a year.[84] Yet the army did not take advantage of the seeming revival in indus-

---

79. Alec Nove, *An Economic History of the U.S.S.R.* (London: Penguin, 1989), 227–28.

80. Report from Bokis to Davydov, People's Commissar of Internal Affairs (NKVD) SSSR, 25 May 1937, RGVA, f. 31811, op. 2, d. 640, ll. 188–89.

81. Report on progress made with the BT-IS tank from Tsyganov, Military Technician 2nd Class, to Stalin and Voroshilov, 23 October 1937, RGVA, f. 31811, op. 2, d. 640, ll. 421–24.

82. Reports from Bazilevich, Secretary of the Defense Committee SSSR, to Voroshilov and Pavlov, 3 May 1938; one report dated 15 August 1937, RGVA, f. 31811, op. 2, d. 745, l. 18.

83. Report on draft directive STO concerning planned purchase of tank technology in America from Bokis to Voroshilov, 26 June 1937, RGVA, f. 31811, op. 2, d. 657, l. 22.

84. Draft resolution of Council of People's Commissars dated September 1937 from Molotov, RGVA, f. 31811, op. 2, d. 640, l. 410.

trial capabilities, agreeing on 28 November 1937 to a third five-year plan of development that did not foresee the creation of any new tank units.[85]

From reports published at the time, it is clear that Soviet commanders also believed that the "evil" touch of Tukhachevskii and his "co-conspirators" had adversely affected the training and maintenance of the armor forces. The previous year Tukhachevskii had set the amount of time that the tanks would spend actually running at a rather low level, thus, according to Voroshilov, "sharply reducing the military preparedness of the armor forces of the Red Army." He wasted no time in raising the hours.[86] At the annual gathering of the high command, Fed'ko informed commanders that "enemies" had been very active against tank unit preparation, so that, for instance, tank drivers did not know how to overcome obstacles on the battlefield.[87] To combat "wrecking and sabotage activity" within armor units, Voroshilov issued an order that limited crew access to their machines and included detailed instructions designed to keep soldiers from damaging the tanks and stealing parts, fuel, or other supplies.[88]

The attack on Tukhachevskii and other "enemies" was combined with a renewed assault on their tactical and operational ideas, and particularly the deep battle concept. As we have seen, the undermining of the doctrine had begun in late 1936, and by 1937 opposition came from many directions. Some of the criticism was even expressed by Tukhachevskii himself, in a vain attempt before his execution to recant his ideas. He returned to ideas from the old morale argument – that Soviet soldiers had a superior spirit that would overcome any enemy and a "special mobility" because of their proletarian origins.[89] As in the earlier debate, the problems that tanks had with the weather or terrain, and the fact that tanks would only be able to operate for short periods of time, were again raised as serious objections to armor warfare. There were also officers who emphasized that tanks were important only as direct support for in-

85. A. Ryzhakov, "K voprosu o stroitel'stve bronetankovykh voisk krasnoi armii v 30-e gody," VIZh, no. 8 (August 1968): 108–9.

86. Report from Voroshilov to Molotov, June 1937, RGVA, f. 31811, op. 2, d. 640, l. 209.

87. "Stenograficheskii otchet Zasedanie voennogo Soveta pri Narodnom Komissare Oborony SSSR," 21–27 November 1937. RGVA, f. 4, op. 18, d. 54, ll. 51–52.

88. Order no. 0135, "O merakh predotvrashcheniie vreditel'skoi i diversionnoi deiatel'nosti v avtobronetankovykh chastiakh RKKA," 20 August 1937, RGVA,. f. 4, op. 15, d. 13, l. 284. Reprinted in V. A. Zolotarev, ed., Russkii arkhiv: Velikaia Otechestvennaia: Prikazy narodnogo komissara oborony SSSR, vol. 13, 2(1) (Moscow: TERRA, 1994), 22–24.

89. M. N. Tukhachevskii, "O novom polevom ustave RKKA," Krasnaia Zvezda, 6 May 1937, reprinted in M. N. Tukhachevskii, Izbrannyi proizvedienia, vol. 2 (Moscow: Voennoe izdatel'stvo Ministerstva oborony SSSR, 1964), 246–47. Ziemke notes that the theory of "special mobility" also posited that the Red Cavalry was the preeminant element of maneuver, even a kind of secret weapon. Earl F. Ziemke, "The Soviet Armed Forces in the Interwar Period" in Military Effectiveness. vol. 2: The Interwar Period, ed. Allan R. Millett and Williamson Murray (Boston: Allen & Unwin, 1988), 14.

fantry, and that they should not penetrate into the enemy's depth on their own.[90] The term "DD tanks" now meant nothing more than those tanks that would be used during breakthroughs, and the independent use of armor and other elements of the old doctrine could only be discussed as ideas of foreign armies.[91]

The main focuses of criticism of deep battle were, however, the strength of antitank defenses and the need for infantry support, both lessons learned from the Spanish war. Antiarmor weaponry had made a strong impression on those Soviets who faced it in Spain. Nikolai Voronov, a chief of the Artillery Directorate and later hero of the Second World War, returned from the Spanish fighting and informed his colleagues at the annual fall gathering of the high command that the war had proven that antiarmor guns were difficult to find, almost impossible to destroy, and very effective.[92] Even Tukhachevskii, before his death, had acknowledged that the defense had grown stronger in the last few years. Reflecting on the war in Spain, he noted that new antitank artillery in particular would make offenses more difficult in the future. He refused however, to believe that the next war would necessarily be positional, or that offensives were bound to fail. The push forward simply had to be stronger and more concentrated to break through.[93]

The other criticism of deep battle was an extension of the now common judgment that tanks worked best in close conjunction with the infantry. By fall 1937, this conclusion had evolved into a general agreement that the independent use of tanks in the depth of the enemy's positions was a dangerous and erroneous employment of armor. Just weeks before his arrest and execution, Tukhachevskii himself disavowed the concept of completely independent mechanized formations. This idea, he wrote, had arisen from a false concept that the tank's great mobility would not allow it to operate well in conjunction with the infantry. Fully independent tank formations, such as the mechanized corps, were wrong because this separated tanks from the combined-arms army and did not take into account antitank firepower or the fact that tanks could not operate successfully without massive artillery support.[94] Pavlov, who had previously expressed his opinion that tanks worked best as infantry support, become even more adamant at the fall meeting of 1937 that the PP tank group was right while the DD echelon was a flawed concept. The emphasis in Spain, he said, was on infantry following directly behind tanks, supported by artillery and aviation. Experience had taught that tanks thrown into

90. V. Tereshenko, *Sovremennye tanki* (Moscow: Izdanie TsS Soiuza Osoavaikhim SSSR, 1937), 10–11, 39.

91. Ibid., 40; Kombrig Malevskii, *Mekhanizatsiia sovremennykh armii za rubezham* (Moscow: Uchebnyi otdel Akademii General'nogo Shtaba RKKA, 1937).

92. "Stenograficheskii otchet Zasedanie voennogo Soveta pri Narodnom Komissare Oborony SSSR 21–27 noiabra 1937," RGVA, f. 4, op. 18, d. 54, l. 252.

93. Tukhachevskii, "O novom polevom ustave RKKA," 247–48.

94. Ibid., 246.

battle independently, as DD tanks were, would perish.[95] Pavlov, and later that same day Semën Timoshenko, then a district commander, stressed that tankists did not need to learn how to fight independently, they already knew this well. The most important requirement for armor forces was teaching them how to cooperate with the infantry, cavalry, and artillery.[96]

As commanders became convinced that Soviet doctrine had to change, talk turned to a reorganization of the armor units that would reflect the lessons learned in Spain. Earlier that year one participant in the war had reported that the three-tank platoon, designed to make mechanized units more mobile, had shown itself lacking in strength and suggested a return to the five-tank unit.[97] The proposal was in fact adopted, raising the offensive power of tank brigades, but lowering their speed and mobility.[98] With the new emphasis on infantry support, however, this would not be a problem. Voroshilov had something even more drastic in mind. He told the annual gathering of commanders that dispersing tanks in many different kinds of armor units did not suit the demands of modern war. The army was considering a reorganization of its armor, placing more tank units in the hands of general headquarters, in the reserve, and leaving fewer tanks in the divisions.[99] In his listing of the various tank units, he was careful not to mention the mechanized corps – more evidence that years before they were actually disbanded the entire concept of the independent units, like the missions that they were meant to perform, was already under serious attack.

The final orders for the year further undermined an independent role for armor units by specifically emphasizing that the infantry was still the principal arm of the service. The army's basic tasks for 1938 did not include deep battle, concentrating instead on combined-arms combat with the close cooperation of land, air, and sea forces. This could be in maneuver warfare or in fighting for fortified positions "using modern decisive technological weapons (aircraft, artillery, tanks) and taking into consideration the pivotal meaning and role of the infantry in combined-arms cooperation." In a discussion over the wording of this particular sentence, some commanders suggested that there be even more emphasis on the infantry as the main arm, while others asked that the cavalry's central role be mentioned.[100] A still larger step backward was taken by Egorov and Budënnyi, who asked that the army

95. "Stenograficheskii otchet Zasedanie voennogo Soveta pri Narodnom Komissare Oborony SSSR," 21–27 November 1937, RGVA, f. 4, op. 18, d. 54, l. 333.

96. Ibid., ll. 337, 133.

97. Report to Bokis, "Boevoe primenenie," 2 April 1937, RGVA, f. 31811, op. 2, d. 646, l. 26.

98. Ryzhakov, "K voprosu o stroitel'stve bronetankovykh voisk," 108–9.

99. "Stenograficheskii otchet Zasedanie voennogo Soveta pri Narodnom Komissare Oborony SSSR," 21–27 November 1937, RGVA, f. 4, op. 18, d. 54, l. 480.

100. "Stenogramma zasedaniia komissii po rassmotreniiu proekta prikaza NKO 'Ob itogakh boevoi podgotovki RKKA za 1937 g. i zadachakh na 1938 g.,'" 25 Noember 1937, RGVA, f. 4, op. 14, d. 1824, ll. 68–69.

stress the infantry bayonet attack as a necessary part of battle.[101] The change of heart by Egorov in particular is striking and deserves some explanation. As we have seen, Egorov had been at the forefront of the development of deep battle, providing some of the essential theoretical structure for the idea during its early years. It thus seems likely that his complete turnaround was necessitated by his association with the tainted concept, and a need to completely repudiate any point of contact with the "traitor" Tukhachevskii. Egorov in fact took part in the secret tribunal that condemned Tukhachevskii to death, whether willingly or unwillingly, and certainly could not now allow potential accusers an easy way to attack him. Thus at this meeting Egorov took care to support Budënnyi by pointing to Spain, where assaults with the bayonet occurred every day, and to say that "firepower is a decisive element, but after all one needs to seize and secure. In and of itself, fire can not do this. It paves the way but further than that one needs to seize. Class battles are a fight to the death. But the sharp bayonet decides the success of the battle. Fire paves the way, but seizing and holding is the bayonet's affair."[102] Naturally enough, given the dynamics that fueled Stalin's purges, neither participation in the tribunal nor support of Budënnyi and Voroshilov would save Egorov. A year later he too would disappear into the terror.

These developments in the Soviet Union were paralleled, in many ways, by the path that the Wehrmacht chose at about the same time. Like the Soviets in 1937, the Germans too tried to come to definitive conclusions about infantry-armor cooperation and the strength of antitank defenses, and learned conflicting lessons from the Spanish war. Unlike the Soviet Union, however, the German government and army increased their support for mechanization and motorization, while Guderian was placed in a position where he could push for his vision of concentrated armor. The "purge" inflicted on the German officer corps was also far less extensive and devastating than the terror suffered by the Red Army. Hitler did, however, succeed in removing Blomberg and Fritsch in early 1938 and placing men more amenable to his will in positions of power. When Beck retired to protest Hitler's proposed invasion of Czechoslovakia later that year, Hitler was rid of yet another serious critic.[103] The result of the German "purge" was to eliminate three possible opponents of Hitler and replace them with men like Wilhelm Keitel whom he could more

---

101. For Budënnyi's support of the bayonet, see "Stenograficheskii otchet Zasedanie voennogo Soveta pri Narodnom Komissare Oborony SSSR," 21–27 November 1937, RGVA, f. 4, op. 18, d. 54, l. 13.

102. "Stenogramma zasedaniia komissii po rassmotreniiu proekta prikaza NKO 'Ob itogakh boevoi podgotovki RKKA za 1937 g. i zadachakh na 1938 g.,'" 25 November 1937, RGVA, f. 4, op. 14, d. 1824, l. 20.

103. For a discussion of the Fritsch-Blomberg affair and Beck's resignation, see Friedrich Hoßbach, *Zwischen Wehrmacht und Hitler, 1934–1938* (Göttingen: Vandenhoeck & Ruprecht, 1965), 105–40.

easily control. Armor doctrine development was most affected by the loss of Beck who, as we have seen, was an innovative thinker on the issue. Before he left the army, Beck would write several more position papers on tank tactics and coopera-tion with the other forces, continuing to support the need for armor to strengthen the mass of the army (that is, the infantry) as well as to fight independently.[104] His overall influence on the development of the armor forces and German doctrine, contrary to what Guderian and other critics would allege, was thus pro-mecha-nization. After all, as S. J. Lewis has pointed out, when Beck became chief of staff the German army did not even have any motorized units, but by the time he retired the Wehrmacht had five armor divisions, four light divisions, and four motorized infantry divisions.[105]

Hitler effected several major organizational changes at the same time as he dis-missed Fritsch and Blomberg, replacing the old War Ministry with the High Com-mand of the Armed Forces (OKW) and appointing himself supreme commander of the military.[106] In conjunction with ridding himself of independent thinkers like Blomberg and Fritsch, this last move placed total operational control of the army within his grasp. Simultaneously, Guderian was promoted to lieutenant general and made commander of the XVI Army Corps.[107] The advancement was unex-pected, since he had just been elevated to major general and would normally have reached the next rank only after three or more years. The most reasonable expla-nation for his quick rise was the direct intervention of Hitler, who had already shown an interest in the armor forces and who knew that Guderian was the firmest supporter of the armor divisions. Hitler probably also thought that the general, a committed Nazi and something of an outsider, would be an able counterweight to the entrenched interests of the old infantry and cavalry high command.[108] Guder-ian was quickly made commander of the armor forces and later that year named General of the Armor Forces and Chief of the "Rapid Forces," with direct access to Hitler in case he met with "resistance" from the OKH.[109] He was now in a position to push more forcefully for his vision of a further concentration of the tank forces into armor divisions.

Guderian's first task was an urgent one, as Hitler decided in March 1938 to push ahead with the forced union with Austria. The Wehrmacht tried to mobilize quickly

104. See directive from Beck, "Schulung im Begegnungsgefecht," 4 April 1938, BA-MA, RH 53–7/v, 108.

105. S. J. Lewis, *Forgotten Legions: German Army Infantry Policy 1918–1941* (New York: Praeger, 1985), 50–52.

106. Barry Posen, *The Sources of Military Doctrine: France, Britain, and Germany between the World Wars* (Ithaca: Cornell University Press, 1984), 200.

107. Liddell Hart, *The Other Side of the Hill*, 67–68; Guderian, *Erinnerungen eines Soldaten*, 40.

108. Hitler's choice of Wilhelm Keitel as head of the OKW, another outsider and firm Nazi, is further evidence that he was determined not to allow the "Junkers" control of his army.

109. Guderian, *Erinnerungen eines Soldaten*, 53–55.

and efficiently, planning on a defensive posture in the west (in case the French decided to intervene), while marching most of the army into Austria. Armor, motorized, and elite SS units took part in the Anschluss, even though the Germans said that they expected little resistance. The actual course of the maneuver, from Guderian's perspective as head of the 2nd Armor Division, was nearly a farce. His unit had to start its march without its commanders, since they were still at a practice, and then discovered that no one had a map of Austria. The division was forced instead to use a regular Baedeker guidebook to find its way. There were more serious problems, including a lack of fuel. No supply formations were mobilized to accompany the unit and the division had trouble obtaining fuel from the army dump in Passau, where supplies were reserved for forces marching to the western defensive positions only.[110] Guderian's fuel problems had been foreshadowed by the fall exercises of the previous year, which had revealed severe difficulties supplying the many machines that made up the armor divisions.[111]

From a political standpoint the Anschluss was a complete success. Hitler had once again perceived French and British unwillingness to risk war, even to prevent what was quite clearly more than just a minor adjustment of Versailles, and had used this to take over an entire country. The military saw the operation differently. The army as a whole had seemed unfit for combat, mobilizing inefficiently and slowly, while the armor forces were heavily criticized for the high level of breakdowns suffered by the tanks. If the vehicles were incapable of performing this simple maneuver against an unarmed country, how would they be able to fight during a serious war against a well-trained and well-equipped army?[112] The supposedly simple move into Austria had demonstrated that the German army was not yet prepared for a war of machines and especially had not worked out the logistical and engineering techniques necessary to carry out operations of any length.

The course of the Spanish war in 1938 was also discouraging for anyone who thought that tanks were the decisive weapon of the future. Even though more tanks than ever took part in the conflict, they had not made a convincing impact in any battle, nor had they made an overwhelmingly positive impression on any of the observers of the war. Fortunately, as in 1937, German officers generally learned the lessons that they wanted to learn from the conflict. When expectations about how the armor forces would perform were not met, they concluded that the circumstances were so specific to that particular country and war that battles fought there were unlikely to provide general lessons for the rest of Europe. Others, who had their predictions fulfilled, pointed to specific incidents as evidence that the testing ground of war had proven them right.

---

110. Ibid., 42–43.

111. *Besichtigungsbemerkungen des Kommandierenden Generals des Kommandos der Panzertruppen im Jahre 1937* (Berlin: Kommando der Panzertruppen. 15 November 1937), BA-MA, RHD 26/5, pp. 3–5, 8–9.

112. Guderian, *Erinnerungen eines Soldaten*, 46.

Nowhere was this more apparent than in regard to the efficacy of antitank weaponry. Officers who did not like the tank argued that combat in Spain clearly demonstrated the superiority of antitank weapons over armor forces. As one retired officer pointed out, the expected wonders from the combination of armor and speed had not appeared: the war had not ended swiftly, and the tempo of combat had not accelerated. Tanks had shown themselves less than the decisive force that Cambrai and other battles had promised, while antitank weapons now had an advantage in development over tanks.[113] Advocates of the tank repeated the excuses of the previous years – the mountainous terrain in Spain, the fact that this was a civil war, and the piecemeal use of the machines, all of which gave the conflict a special character that favored antiarmor weaponry. The Spaniards, in addition, had not supported their tank attacks with artillery and infantry as they should have done.[114]

Given the ambiguous nature of the "lessons" that the Civil War taught, Wehrmacht officers could also use the experience of Spain to support competing solutions to the dilemma of infantry and armor cooperation. Two articles from the spring of 1938 illustrate the ways that the army looked at the war and then used it for its own ends. The first, by a Major Doege, "proved" that the war in Spain corroborated the views of those who wanted the closest possible connection between armor and infantry. He began his analysis by discounting all the solutions to the problem that differed from his preferred answer. He argued, for instance, that if tanks were allowed to forge ahead of the infantry, they could suppress the first line of defense, but then would fall victim to defensive emplacements further behind enemy lines. If, on the other hand, the infantry closely supported slow-moving tanks, the machines would once again become easy targets for the defenders, while the infantry would suffer heavy loses through their proximity to the tanks. The third possibility, which he called "enticing," was for mass use of large independent armor units without close contact with the infantry. But those who supported these tactics did not take into account actual circumstances on the battlefield, forgetting that the terrain on the other side of the enemy's lines would be completely unknown. There was a real danger that tanks, difficult to see out of and speeding through bomb craters and uncertain terrain, would run over their own infantry rather than help them to advance. The problem of cooperation thus remained without solution. Doege then offered his own answer, arguing that there was nothing to show that modernized infantry, armed with the latest weaponry, would be unable to lead the attack themselves. As he put it, "racial-national superiority and the spiritual and moral superiority which arose from this" allowed the infantry to re-

113. Major a.d. Otto Welsch, "Gedanken über den spanischen Krieg," *Wissen und Wehr*, no. 5 (May 1938): 338, 345–46.

114. Major Sieberg, "Beantwortet der Krieg in Spanien die Frage, ob der moderne Panzerkampfwagen oder das moderne Abwehrgeschütz überlegen ist?" *Militär-Wochenblatt*, no. 33 (1938): 2095–97.

main the main force of an offensive.[115] Yet even "racially superior" infantry had to have some sort of support that was mobile, heavily armed, and strongly armored, to keep advances flowing. The answer was of course the tank, the heaviest infantry weapon, which would keep the tightest possible contact with the infantry while attacking individual enemy positions in advances that were limited and proceeded in bounds.[116]

Two months later, a Major Spannenkrebs presented a rebuttal of Doege's article and a ringing endorsement of the armor division supporters' views of the Spanish war. He thought that Doege, in presenting an argument that basically supported Spanish Republican tank tactics, was making a virtue out of necessity. Beginning with the often repeated truism that dividing tanks among the infantry would dissipate their offensive power, Spannenkrebs presented his objections to Doege's thesis. There were over twenty thousand tanks in Europe, he wrote, and one side might employ two or even ten thousand of them a battle; only by concentrating them to achieve superiority over the enemy could the army use tanks, the best defense against other tanks, most effectively. Beside that, using tanks as Doege suggested, in small, slow-moving groups, would also make tanks most vulnerable to antitank defenses.[117]

Official Wehrmacht doctrine, as expressed in a short manual written by Beck not long before he left the army, was a compromise between the Spannenkrebses and the Doeges in the army.[118] Here Beck argued that the British and French held the same views as those of the German army, that is, himself: that armies would use tanks either in mixed units with armor, rifle, and artillery elements for operational and tactical independent deployment, or as pure armor units for fighting in combined-arms combat. Having established that all the advanced nations of the world agreed with him, Beck then argued that although large offensives had up to this point failed without armor, tanks by themselves could not decide an engagement since battles were won only when the infantry were victorious. Tank attacks would thus first deal with antitank weapons and then enable the quick advance of the infantry by suppressing the enemy's machine guns and artillery. Two great mistakes were to make destruction of the artillery the objective without removing antitank defenses, and to tie tanks to the tempo of the infantry. Infantry needed direct help to advance, but this would be provided by special "weak" tank units that would stay with the foot soldiers.

Beck's description of armor tactics was very familiar. The attack had to have fa-

115. Major Doege, "Infanterie und Panzer: Ein Beitrag über Formen des Zusammenwirkens im Angriff," ibid., no. 44 (1938): 2813.

116. Ibid., 2814.

117. Major Spannenkrebs, "Infanterie und Panzer," ibid., no. 7 (1938): 402–4.

118. The stated purpose of the pamphlet was to establish a unified conception regarding the use of armor units when cooperating with other branches of the army. Introduction to Beck, "Vortrag des O.K.H. über die taktische Verwendung von Panzer-Verbanden," 4 February 1938, BA-MA, RH 37/2378, p. 260.

vorable terrain with no land mines; it should achieve surprise, and use tanks only for decisive battle and in the largest possible number. The vehicles would attack in three echelons, one directed against antitank weapons and artillery, the second against infantry weapons, and the third, subordinated to the infantry, against any left-over resistance. The assault had to be fast and deep and protected by artillery and infantry. Infantry were to fight as usual, exploiting the effect of the tanks, but otherwise unaffected by their presence. They were especially not to cling too tightly to any single tank, but to allow the various waves of tanks to pass them by while advancing in units of shock troops with gaps. The manual ended by noting that there were basically two combat methods: tactical penetration with the infantry, used when the enemy was not well dug-in and had not laid mines; and the "after-thrust," an assault that would catch up with the infantry after it had dealt with tank obstacles. He actually favored the latter method as easier for the armor forces.[119]

This solution to infantry-armor cooperation satisfied neither those who wanted tanks used only in armor divisions, nor those who thought that the tank was an infantry support weapon. Matters were not helped by the fact that the Germans, unlike the year before, were unable to implement any of the competing theories during maneuvers. Exercises held during 1937–38 that worked on the problem of armor-infantry cooperation gave, as one report put it, "little satisfaction."[120] Another memorandum signed by Beck went even further, asserting that "[c]ooperation on the battlefield at present is still completely unsolved."[121] The difficulties with deciding how to use the two forces together were both conceptual and practical. Every officer who proposed a solution enunciated basic principles of battle with which the entire army agreed: the need for combined-arms combat, the efficacy of concentration, and the crucial role of the infantry. But some of these seemed to contradict each other and it was unclear which was most important. On the practical side, the Wehrmacht had trouble approximating wartime conditions in training. The need to prevent accidents played a significant role in hampering the army's attempt to construct realistic maneuvers, in addition to the fact that the army was still using dummy tanks for training as late as April 1938.[122] All these un-

119. General Command VII Army Corps (Wehrkreiskommando VII) Ia-Nr. 59/38 g., "Verwendung von Panzereinheiten im Kampf der verbundenen Waffen," 5 January 1938, BA-MA, RH 53–7/v, 108, pp. 200–207. See also Lieb, Kommandeur, Panzerabwehrtruppen XII, "Merkblatt für Übungen mit Panzerkampfwagen,"13 April 1938, BA-MA, RH 37/2378, pp. 130–28.

120. "Allgemeine Ausbildungsweisungen für das Übungjahr 1939," BA-MA, RH 2/180, p. 285.

121. Beck, introduction to "Vortrag des O.K.H. über die taktische Verwendung von Panzer-Verbanden" 4 February 1938, BA-MA, RH 37/2378, p. 203.

122. Memo from Halder, "Aufbau und Mittel der Ausbildung in der Zusamenarbeit mit Pz.-Kampfwagen," 2 December 1937, BA-MA, RH 53–7/v, 108, pp. 171–72; Lieb, Kommandeur, Panzerabwehrtruppen XII, "Merkblatt für Übungen mit Panzerkampfwagen," 13 April 1938, BA-MA, RH 37/2378, p. 128.

certainties meant that no one was confident that doctrine would meet the demands of a future large conflict.

If this were not a serious enough problem, discussions held during 1938 also showed that officers were even uncertain of the exact form that the next war would take. While Guderian hoped that the army would be able to achieve operational surprise at the outset of war, there were real fears that despite the tank and motorized troops, a conflict could bog down into the positional stalemate of the world war. Even the latest handbook on the use of the armor divisions, published in June, thought that this was the most likely scenario for a future conflict,[123] while the German high command prudently made contingency plans for conducting a war of positions. The emphasis in a manual for this type of warfare was, however, on winning back operational mobility by either breaking through the enemy's front or forcing him to fall back.[124] The task of armor was to facilitate the infantry assault in cooperation with the artillery and aircraft and to help the foot soldiers forward into the enemy's depth.[125]

The picture of the next war that emerged from the discussions within the Wehrmacht was very different from that envisaged by Lutz, Guderian, or their supporters. Rather than a decisive use of tanks concentrated exclusively in armor divisions, which would quickly destroy the enemy's resistance and win back operational mobility, there would instead be a long, difficult struggle for positions made easier, but not guaranteed success, by the employment of armor in both infantry and independent units. If the first half of the decade had seen the German army gradually accept a decisive role for the tank and create powerful armor divisions for operational missions, Beck's more "balanced" view of armor and infantry was still firmly in place during the waning years of the thirties.

While the Wehrmacht decided to retain this compromise view as official doctrine, Soviet commanders were agreeing that Spain and other combat experiences proved the falsity of the ideas of Triandafillov, Tukhachevskii, Sediakin, and the rest of the discredited armor supporters. The result was an ever greater reliance on strong infantry and artillery support for tank forces, even when this could not be correctly implemented.[126] Artillery fire was already recognized as a necessary part of any of-

123. D66+. Richtlinien für die Führung der Panzerdivision vom 1.6.38 (Berlin: Oberkommando der Wehrmacht. 1938), BA-MA, RHD 5/66, pp. 22–35. See also Major Spannenkrebs, "Infanterie und Panzer," *Militär-Wochenblatt*, no. 7 (1938): 402–4.

124. *Der Stellungskrieg* (Entwurf vom 16.6.1938) (Berlin: Oberkommando der Wehrmacht. 1938), BA-MA, RHD 4/91, p. 6.

125. Ibid., pp. 27, 41.

126. Sonderstab W, Anlage 1 zu Lagebericht Nr. 382, "Kurzer Bericht über den augenblicklichen Stand der roten Panzerwaffe," 7 January 1938, BA-MA, RM 20/1256.

fensive, but now such assistance was seen as absolutely vital for armor.[127] On infantry support, a short monograph on tanks in defensive battle during the Spanish conflict stated that although tanks had fought both independently and together with the infantry, independent assaults, regardless of any gains, had only delayed the opponent's attack and not caused it to break off. When the tanks had counterattacked with the infantry, however, the machines had greatly reinforced the striking power of the foot soldiers and when closely cooperating with them, had achieved success.[128] Yet one commander reported that the Reds had not managed to implement cooperation of infantry with tanks in even one operation, a failure he blamed on "inert conservatives," who only reluctantly agreed that lack of cooperation had caused their defeat in offensives.[129]

The Red Army high command also became convinced by the fighting in Spain that their main battle tanks, although better than the German vehicles, were less than ideal for modern warfare. In his report on the war, one commander specifically singled out lack of armor protection as the reason for high losses to defensive weaponry and artillery during the conflict and suggested replacing the T-26 and B-T tanks with machines that had much thicker armor.[130] To deal with weaknesses that the war had revealed in the two tanks, the army suggested a new round of tank design and improvements. This created a serious dilemma, for rather than cutting down on tank types, as had been decided the year before, the new orders would add to an already complicated array of models. The scope of the problem was astounding. By late February 1938 the Soviets had nine different tank and tankette models, yet according to a directive from the Defense Commission, the army would add an-

127. Report by R. Ia. Malinovskii, "Operativno-takticheskie vyvody i zakliucheniia, sdelannye na osnovanii boevogo opyta voiny v Ispanii za period ot nachala miatezha po mai 1938 goda," RGVA, f. 35082, op. 1, d. 483, l. 34.

128. *Voina v Ispanii: Vypusk 10. Tanki v oborone* (Moscow: n.p., 1938), 23.

129. Kombrig Vechnyy P.P., "Upravlenie voiskami i rabota shtabov v armii Republikanskii Ispanii: Po opytu vooruzhennoi bor'by s fashistami i interventami 1936–1938g.g.," May–October 1938, RGVA, f. 31983, op. 2, d. 497, ll. 204–5. German observers, in contrast, thought that the difficulties experienced by Red armor were caused by inadequate training, heavy antitank defenses, unfavorable terrain, and poor weather for tanks. Sonderstab W, Anlage zu Lagebericht Nr. 383, "Bemerkungen zur Kriegsgliederung," 8 January 1938, BA-MA, RM 20/1256; report from Abwehr, "Bericht über die 4. Spanienreise des V-Mannes R.," 15 February 1938, BA-MA, RM 20/1403, pp. 205–7. Another German officer gave a more backhanded compliment, writing that despite poor cooperation with the other forces, Red tanks had attacked decisively several times. Their few successes were not due to any skill, but rather to the absence of unfavorable factors for offensives. Sonderstab W, "Anlage 1 zu Lagebericht Nr. 382, Kurzer Bericht über den augenblicklichen Stand der roten Panzerwaffe," 7 January 1938, BA-MA, RM 20/1256.

130. Report by R. Ia. Malinovskii, "Operativno-takticheskie vyvody i zakliucheniia, sdelannye na osnovanii boevogo opyta voiny v Ispanii za period ot nachala miatezha po mai 1938 goda," RGVA, f. 35082, op. 1, d. 483, l. 35.

other seven beginning in 1939. Four of the vehicles were improved versions of older tanks, but the rest were completely new.[131]

Either because of these ambitious (and confusing) production plans or because the purges had removed so many engineers, industry continued to experience difficulties. In 1938 the Soviet Union was manufacturing "only" 2,271 tanks a year, rather than the 5,000 or even 10,000 expected just a few years before.[132] This was not the sole problem with tank production. As an instructor in the Tank Department at the Stalin Academy reported to Voroshilov, in the last five years the Soviet army had not produced one new tank type. Industry had begun development of the T-46 in 1933, but by the end of 1937 it was taken from production. In the same way, engineers had worked three years on the T-29, meant to replace the T-28, but had only manufactured two or three experimental machines.[133] Tank maintenance, despite the more stringent measures, also remained poor. The NKVD reported in the middle of February that all the materiel in the 8th Mechanized Brigade, located in the Belorussian military district, and taken over from the 3rd Mechanized Brigade, was unfit for action. There were 181 T-26 tanks in the brigade, but only eleven of them were in working condition, and out of 26 T-37 tanks, only five were up and running.[134]

As in previous years armor specialists tried to improve matters by limiting the types of tanks produced by industry. In March 1938 Pavlov argued that the Red Army needed only three tanks: a main battle tank to work with the infantry and cavalry, a heavy "artillery tank" to combat antitank weapons, and an amphibious tank to seize river crossings. The artillery tank was one of his most interesting innovations, resembling in many ways the German concept of a medium tank that would accompany the Pz. I. The new tank would be organizationally part of tank units and closely escort the lighter machines, destroying antiarmor artillery in its path. Significantly, Pavlov no longer placed emphasis on a new machine for independent operational maneuvers, arguing that the main battle tank could perform these duties as well.[135]

The Main Military Council, the body that replaced the RVS, agreed to reduce tank

---

131. Report on tanks in army from Pavlov to Voroshilov, 21 February 1938, RGVA, f. 31811, op. 2, d. 849/850, ll. 1–4.

132. G. K. Zhukov, *Vospominaniia i razmyshleniia*, 10th rev. ed., vol. 1 (Moscow: Avtor [nasledniki] 1990), 215.

133. Report from Gruzdev, Tank Department at Stalin Academy of Motorization and Mechanization, to Chief of ABTU and Voroshilov, 11 February 1938, RGVA, f. 31811, op. 2, d. 745, ll. 8–10.

134. Report from Akseevich, Chief of 3rd Section of 5th Department GUGB NKVD, 13 February 1938, RGVA, f. 33987, op. 3, d. 1003, ll. 14–15.

135. "Tezisy doklada komkora t. Pavlova, Operativnoe i takticheskoe primenenie tankov v budushchey voyne," 20 March 1938, RGVA, f. 31811, op. 2, d. 804, ll. 1–3.

types, although it did not follow Pavlov's proposal. Instead the government financed the design and production of four kinds of tanks. The T-26 and B-T would remain the main battle tanks, although both would be modernized, the T-26 as the STZ and the B-T as the BT-20. In addition, industry was to manufacture a breakthrough tank with extremely thick armor and heavy armaments. While this tank was in the process of development, industry would continue to produce the heavy T-28 and T-35. The final tank was the Amphibia or T-40, a superlight amphibious tank armed only with a high-caliber machine gun, but fast both on land and in the water.[136] Surprisingly, given the state of Soviet design and engineering, by December 1938 experimental models of all the new tanks were ready for testing.[137]

The development of the vehicles may have been aided by a relaxation of terror in industry. From late 1938 through 1939, the purges focused more narrowly on the military, granting the economy a breathing space. The armor forces, however, suffered terribly during this period. Griaznov, who had taken over once Khalepskii was executed in 1937, was himself shot at the end of July 1938.[138] His replacement, Pavlov, reported in November that since the start of the year 62 men had been arrested in his directorate. By July 80 men remained instead of the 196 required by regulations. "Extraordinary" measures had succeeded in finding 63 men to replace those lost, but staffing still was at only 73 percent. In the actual tank units, matters were even worse, with every single commander from the brigades and corps "relieved," with the exception of one brigade commander and the chiefs of some staffs. In addition, no less than 80 percent of the battalion commanders and their chiefs of staff had been removed.[139] It must be remembered that those shot or arrested during 1938 were, like Griaznov, replacements for commanders who had been similarly dealt with during the equally terrible purges of 1937. The armor forces, like the rest of the Red Army, were hit not just once by the terror, but several times, leaving officers in charge of brigades and even divisions who had begun 1937 as the equivalent of lieutenants.

The effect of the purges on armor affairs was a mixture of creation and chaos. On the one hand, accepted ways of thinking about war, doctrine, and the organization of forces were swept away; anything was possible. With no set guidelines,

136. "Protokol No. 4 Zasedaniia Glavogo Voennogo Soveta RKKA, 'O sisteme tankovogo vooruzheniia i plane zakazov narodnogo komissariata oborony 1938 goda,'" 20 April 1938, RGVA, f. 4, op. 18, d. 46, ll. 23–25; report from Pavlov to Kombrig Snegov, Chief of Affairs Directorate NKO, 13 May 1938, RGVA, f. 4, op. 19, d. 55, ll. 28, 45–83. The Amphibia was to have a Dodge motor.

137. "Protokol N° 28 Zasedaniia Glavnogo Voennogo Soveta RKKA," 9–10 December 1938, RGVA, f. 4, op. 18, d. 46, ll. 254–58.

138. Michael Morozow, Die Falken des Kreml: Die sowjetische Militärmacht von 1917 bis heute (Munich: Langen Müller, 1982), 160a photo.

139. Report from Pavlov, "Otchet ob itogakh boevoi podgotovki avto-brontankovykh voisk RKKA za 1938 god," 20 November 1938, RGVA, f. 31811, op. 2, d. 849, l. 31.

commanders were free to propose radical new ideas. Pavlov, for instance, suggested that the army use tanks in a preemptive strike on a threatening country. During the beginning period of war, tank units would form an "invasion group" designed to frustrate the mobilization, concentration, and deployment of the opponent's army; seize and hold important lines; and create the principal transition to the beginning of military action on the enemy's territory. During the war itself, tanks would destroy the opponent's main forces and fight on the flanks and rear of his army groups. In cooperation with aircraft, cavalry, and motorized infantry, tank units would guarantee the destruction of the enemy that as he attacked from the front.[140] The organization of mechanized units was debated by other commanders. One officer proposed that these formations should have thirteen battalions, split into forward and strike groups, a mere three-battalion reserve, and three battalions for defense. There could also be an aviation brigade and a repair depot tied to tank units.[141]

The majority of the high command was, however, intimidated by the purges and did not take advantage of any opportunity for change. Instead, many commanders would spend the purge years trying to stay out of official notice, hide from responsibility for any decisions, and generally do nothing controversial or radical. The absence then of an accepted view of war caused more chaos than renewal within the armor forces. In his yearly report on the state of his command, Pavlov complained that there was not yet a unified view of the battle use of tanks, which greatly hindered the complete "knitting together" of units. He noted that there was a "harmful" theory, supported by PU-36, of the "omnipotence" of tanks and their independent action. The experience of actual tank use in Spain, which said that tanks without infantry and artillery could do very little, spoke against this. This contradiction, he claimed, prevented a unified view in the army and led to great confusion, a confusion strengthened by what he called a refusal on the part of the officer corps and the military academies to reevaluate the tank's capabilities and tactics.[142]

The chaotic state of the armor forces, and the military as a whole, was at least partially responsible for the disaster that the army experienced in July and August at the battle of Lake Khasan. During the summer of 1938 tensions were high on the border between the Soviet Union and Mongolia. The Japanese Empire had stationed tens of thousands of troops in the area as part of an attempt to dominate the state of disorder known as China, and the Soviets had responded with reinforcements and a heightened alert status. In late July, a minor clash between the two forces escalated into a major border incident, and Japanese units seized the heights

140. "Tezisy doklada komkora t. Pavlova, 'Operativnoe i takticheskoe primenenie tankov v budushchey voyne,'" 20 March 1938, RGVA, f. 31811, op. 2, d. 804, l. 1.

141. Report by Komdiv Kolchigin, "Kharakter sovremennogo mekhanizirovannogo soedineniia i upravlenie im," probably June 1938, RGVA, f. 31811, op. 4, d. 28, ll. 22–23.

142. Report from Pavlov, "Otchet ob itogakh boevoi podgotovki avto-brontankovykh voisk RKKA za 1938 god," 20 November 1938, RGVA, f. 31811, op. 2, d. 849, ll. 32–33.

near Lake Khasan, holding them against counterattacks by more numerous Soviet troops. Only after massive reinforcements was the Red Army able to drive out the invaders.[143] Exactly how the incident at Khasan began was, and remains, uncertain. Vasilii Bliukher, the head of the Far Eastern military district, claimed that members of the Soviet border forces provoked the Japanese into the attack by firing across the border and seizing Japanese territory. He even sent a telegram to Stalin, Molotov, and Voroshilov asking them to relieve one officer from his duties and put the engineer most responsible on trial.[144] The Soviet government, meanwhile, blamed Bliukher for failing to attack the Japanese forces after they had seized Soviet territory. The two certainties from the incident were that Soviet forces managed to push back the Japanese, but only after suffering inordinately high losses. Observers also agreed that Soviet tank forces had fought poorly throughout the engagement.[145]

The conflicts at Lake Khasan and later at Khalkhin-gol, small-scale though they were, had as great an impact on the Soviet army as the war in Spain. Unlike that distant conflict, these events occurred on Soviet soil, involved what the Soviet leadership perceived as attempts to invade the homeland, and, in the case of Khasan, led to far greater losses of life and prestige for the Red Army.[146] The protocol of a meeting about the battle with Stalin, Voroshilov, Molotov, Shaposhnikov, and other leaders of the army including Bliukher, noted that all the arms present had "displayed an inability to act on the field of battle." In particular, commanders had used their tank units "unskillfully," which had led to a large loss of materiel. Much of the blame was placed on Bliukher personally: he had not purged his ranks of "enemies of the people," had put into positions of authority men who were not able to fulfill their duties, and, most importantly, although he knew the government's orders to prepare for attack, he had done nothing and questioned the legality of the Soviet border forces' actions.[147]

It was obvious, however, that there had to be deeper explanations for the disaster, and later analyses of Khasan were more balanced in assigning blame. In his yearly report on the state of the armor forces, Pavlov blamed not Bliukher, but the

143. "Protokol Zasedaniia Voennogo Soveta pri Narodnom Komissariate Oborony SSSR," 21–29 November 1938, RGVA, f. 4, op. 18, d. 47, ll. 82–84.

144. Ibid., ll. 82–84, 86, 135.

145. Ibid., l. 89.

146. Ibid., l. 108; At Khasan, the Soviets lost 487 men and suffered 2,761 wounded, while 40 percent of the command and political staff were lost in only a few days of fighting. "Protokol No. 18 Zasedaniia Glavnogo Voennogo Soveta RKKA, 'O sobytiiakh u Ozera Khasan,'" 31 August 1938, RGVA, f. 4, op. 18, d. 46, ll. 183–84. Voroshilov claimed that the Japanese had lost three or four times as many men as the Soviets. An earlier document on the events at Khasan had put the Soviet losses at 408 killed and 2,807 wounded. NKO order No. 0040, 4 September 1938, RGVA, f. 4, op. 11, d. 54, ll. 19–27, printed in Zolotarev, Russkii arkhiv, vol. 13, 2(1) p. 57.

147. "Protokol No. 18 Zasedaniia Glavnogo Voennogo Soveta RKKA, 'O sobytiiakh u Ozera Khasan,'" 31 August 1938, RGVA, f. 4, op. 2 [18], d. 46, ll. 186–88.

fact that the armor knew little about cooperating with foot soldiers.[148] Krivoshein submitted a report two months after the conflict in which he concluded that the tanks had done so poorly because of bad coordination with all the other forces, lack of terrain reconnaissance, and the inability to achieve surprise.[149]

After Khasan, it was painfully obvious that the army could no longer put off a thorough rethinking of its armor affairs. Earlier that summer the military had begun to reorganize its tank forces, changing the names of all armor units from "mechanized" to "tank."[150] The change was more than simply one of nomenclature, as the new units were almost purely tank formations, rather than cohesive groups of different forces. None of the units had more than a company (at brigade level) of motorized rifle division troops, and the auxiliary forces associated with the old mechanized formations were also absent.[151] After Khasan, Pavlov proposed that the engineers and technicians associated with tank forces be transferred to the artillery, and that all motorized brigades be taken out of mechanized corps. He also wanted to further dilute the concentration of tanks by distributing more tanks to the infantry, tying a tank battalion to each company in the rifle divisions.[152] Not everyone thought that ridding the corps of their mobile infantry was the proper course. Shaposhnikov suggested that taking motorized brigades out of the tank corps was a "difficult" problem, since infantry would be unable to manage without transport on automobiles. Voroshilov, on the other hand, agreed with Pavlov.[153]

As for armor tactics after Khasan, commanders urged closer cooperation with the infantry and an end to the independent use of tanks. At a meeting of the new Military Council, Pavlov argued forcefully against allowing tanks, including the DD group, to operate far from their infantry and artillery support.[154] Shaposhnikov concurred with Pavlov that the DD group should confine itself to developing breakthroughs and supporting the infantry.[155] Voroshilov wanted even more done about armor tactics, repeating his statement of the year before that the army had not yet worked out how to use tanks. However, he agreed completely with Pavlov that di-

148. Report from Pavlov, "Otchet ob itogakh boevoi podgotovki avto-brontankovykh voisk RKKA za 1938 god," 20 November 1938, RGVA, f. 31811, op. 2, d. 849, ll. 32–33.

149. Report from Krivoshein on the use of tanks at Khasan, November 1938, RGVA, f. 4, op. 14, d. 2061, ll. 371–72.

150. A. Ryzhakov, "K voprosu o stroitel'stve bronetankovykh voisk," 108.

151. Names of tank units and their locations, 20 August 1938, RGVA, f. 31811, op. 2, d. 826, ll. 5–32.

152. "Protokol Zasedaniia Voennogo Soveta pri Narodnom Komissariate Oborony SSSR," 21–29 November 1938, RGVA, f. 4, op. 18, d. 47, l. 44.

153. Speech by Shaposhnikov at Main Military Council, 21–29 November 1938, RGVA, f. 4, op. 18, d. 47.

154. "Protokol Zasedaniia Voennogo Soveta pri Narodnom Komissariate Oborony SSSR," 21–29 November 1938, RGVA, f. 4, op. 18, d. 47, l. 44.

155. Speech by Shaposhnikov at Main Military Council, 21–29 November 1938, RGVA, f. 4, op. 18, d. 47.

viding tanks between DD and NPP echelons was an "obsolete" and "compromised" idea (that is, one supported by "enemies of the people"). The problem was that no one knew what doctrine would replace it. Voroshilov said that he could not endorse the notion that the army should simply assign tanks to the infantry and have them drive behind the foot soldiers. His reasons for disagreeing with those who urged this course of action were not at all sophisticated – he argued that tanks were simply too "expensive, formidable, and powerful a weapon" to be seen from such a narrow point of view, and the Red Army had a large number of tank units. Apparently having invested so much time, energy, and money in the production of the huge tank armies was incentive enough to find a more decisive way to use them in the next war.[156]

After this comprehensive critique of past doctrinal thought, Voroshilov's December order on training soldiers endorsed the emerging views of the armor forces. In contrast to previous years, the section on mechanized forces came last, after all the main arms, and stated that the primary goal of armor training was to teach complete cooperation with the infantry, artillery, and air force.[157] The second edition of the main textbook on armor forces also revealed the changes taking place within the Soviet command staff. The author now emphasized the need for a close connection between tanks and infantry, beginning with reconnaissance and continuing through the pursuit. Tanks would usually carry out the orders of the infantry commander and act with the same tight connection with artillery as with infantry.[158] The DD tanks were still to work on destroying reserves and artillery and to help surround and destroy the enemy, but the author specifically added that there were many times when these tanks could not go ahead of the foot soldiers.[159]

The further turn away from an independent operational use of armor forces in the Soviet Union coincided with an attempt by certain Wehrmacht officers to reassert the centrality of the infantry. The impulse for this movement was almost certainly the new power and authority granted to Guderian, Lutz, and other armor enthusiasts, which threatened the once secure position of the foot soldier. Like cavalry officers just a few years before, infantry officers tried to prove that their branch of the army was indispensable for future wars; that it could be modernized to meet the demands of technological warfare; and that in any case, the tank was not the all-powerful weapon that men like Guderian claimed it was. As a very last resort, they were willing to concede that the tank was necessary for the infantry, but that it had

156. "Protokol Zasedaniia Voennogo Soveta pri Narodnom Komissariate Oborony SSSR," 21–29 November 1938, RGVA, f. 4, op. 18, d. 47, ll. 119–20.

157. NKO order No. 113, 11 December 1938, RGVA, f. 4, op. 15, d. 17, ll. 198–211, printed in Zolotarev, Russkii arkhiv, 78.

158. V. Zun, Avtobronetankovye voiska, 2d ed. (Moscow: Gosudarstvennoe Voennoe Izdatel'stvo Narkomata Oborony Soiuza SSR, 1938), 62–63.

159. Ibid., 67–69.

to serve the foot soldiers and not the other way around. Thus they were eager supporters of Beck's vision of the tank as an infantry weapon distributed to rifle units and designated for helping foot soldiers forward into the enemy's defenses.[160]

As in the past, the officers who advocated a greater role for the infantry considered themselves "moderates" fighting against too great a reliance on the tank and independent armor divisions. In conjunction with Beck's legacy, they commanded enough respect within the high command to prevent Guderian and his supporters from concentrating all tanks into the armor divisions before the war began. Yet the army also decided not to give any armor units directly to smaller infantry units. Instead the Wehrmacht retained Beck's concept of dividing the machines between tank brigades, armor divisions, and light divisions, while spending the summer of 1939 in exercises that were to test some of the proposed changes in armor organization. One such exercise, held in June 1939, featured an armor regiment subordinated to an infantry division.[161] The regiment's task was to destroy heavy enemy infantry weapons and artillery, thus protecting the infantry attack.[162] The exercise was also to answer the eternal question of how armor and infantry would cooperate in the coming war and, by its structure, suggested how the German army imagined the coming war. The description of the tank attack anticipated a positional war, like the world war, with a well-prepared and dug-in enemy, heavily armed with antiarmor weapons. The Wehrmacht therefore planned to front-load the attack, giving much more power to the first wave, which would take care of antitank defenses and afterward destroy enemy artillery. The problematic part of the attack came when the infantry tried to exploit the break-in of the first wave. They could not count on the tanks destroying all the enemy's defenses, and thus had to use the advance of the vehicles with "short energetic bounds" forward, much like the stormtrooper tactics of the last war. During the advance of the second echelon the infantry could move forward only slowly, since they lacked direct armor protection. This wave then had the task of helping the infantry forward by destroying the enemy's heavy infantry weapons. Its speed would be significantly less than that of the first wave, but once again the infantry had to exploit the effect of the second wave by advancing forward as quickly as possible. Finally, the last tank wave, sub-

160. "2 Jahre Krieg in Spanien," *Militär-Wochenblatt*, no. 37 (1939): 2489–91; Generalleutnant a.D. Adelbert von Taysen, "Probleme des taktischen und operationaln Panzereinsatzes," in *Jahrbuch für Wehrpolitik und Wehrwissenschaften 1939 ed.* Deutsche Gesellschaft für Wehrpolitik und Wehrwissenschaften (Hamburg: Hanseatische Verlagsanstalt, 1939), 46–47; Oberleutnant Hartmann, "Infanteriepanzerkampfwagen?" *Militär-Wochenblatt*, no. 33 (1939): 2197–98; General v. Schobert, Generalkommando VII. Armeekorps, memo "Betr.: Theoretische Ausbildung der Offiziere," 9 January 1939, BA-MA, RH 53–7/v, 108, pp. 60–61.
161. Situation for an exercise of 1. Panzer Brigade, "Zusammenwirken Infanterie u. Panzer," on 12 June 1939, 1 June 1939, BA-MA, RH 39/485.
162. "Divisionsbefehl (9. Inf. Div.) für den Angriff am 12.6.1939 (Auszug)," BA-MA, RH 39/485.

ordinated directly to the infantry regiment, would protect the infantry when needed.[163]

A second exercise, held just six weeks before war began, again looked closely at cooperation between armor and infantry, showing that the high command was still not satisfied with this aspect of its armor doctrine. As foreseen in the earlier exercise, the most serious problem for an attack was the defensive weapons that the first tank echelon would not yet have destroyed before the infantry pushed through the hole in the main battle line. These defenses could continue to threaten the infantry, and the plan for the exercise therefore placed even more emphasis on stormtrooper tactics, recommending that the forward part of the infantry assault not take place in an uninterrupted flow. There would instead be an alteration between "daring assault and firefight," allowing the infantry to exploit the effect of the armor attack and creating a complex interplay between the groups of attacking infantry and the tanks.[164]

Mechanized force organization and infantry-armor cooperation were not the only areas of armor doctrine that concerned German officers on the eve of war. As shown by these exercises, the Wehrmacht was still extraordinarily worried about the strength of antiarmor defenses, and would in fact enter the war uncertain whether tanks could overcome deep defensive areas, such as the Maginot line, that were specifically designed to stop armor. General of the Artillery Dollmann suggested that only close cooperation between tanks and artillery would be able to defeat these kinds of modern defensive structures. He thought that just before an armor attack, enemy antitank defenses would conceal themselves and thus artillery would be unable to destroy or suppress them. It was the task of the stronger tanks, those armed with guns, to take care of the hidden and fortified defensive artillery. As for the artillery that would accompany tank units, he suggested that they should have a "command tank" assigned to them. With the aid of this tank, the battery could use observed fire to assist the armor attack in the deep battlefield, fulfilling a wide variety of support missions. Artillery could suppress antitank groups, deliver concentrated artillery fire on massed defenses, eliminate obstacles, or provide supervision for armor units assembling for a new attack once they had achieved their first goals.[165]

There was no guarantee that Dollmann's solution, or any of these suggestions, would work in actual combat. German armor doctrine was therefore far from settled when the international situation took an ominous turn. The year before, Hitler

163. "Merkblatt für das Zusammenarbeiten von Panzer und Infanterie bei der Übung am 12.6.1939," 7 June 1939, BA-MA, RH 39/485.

164. "Übung im Zusammenwirken mit Panzerverbänden am 12.7.1939: (Ortner, Oberst beim Stabe I.R. 50)," BA-MA, N 447/2, p. 100.

165. Dollmann, General of the Artillery, report, "Vorläufige Anweisung für die Verwendung der Artillerie-Beobachter einer Infanterie-Division bei zugeteilten Panzer-Verbänden," 1939, BA-MA, RH 53-9/20.

had annexed the Sudetenland without serious opposition. The timidity of Britain and France's response to the move convinced Stalin that he could no longer depend on the Western powers for his own security and informed his decision to make overtures to the Führer the next year. In March 1939 Hitler continued his bloodless successes by taking over the rest of Czechoslovakia. Yet unlike the Anschluss and Sudetenland this maneuver was a military triumph, but a foreign policy disaster. The army managed to move into Prague with few of the supply difficulties suffered two years before, and soon had the country under its control. On the other hand, stung by what he saw as Hitler's personal betrayal, Chamberlain resolved to oppose any further annexations and quickly put together a British and French guarantee for Poland.[166] The taking of Czechoslovakia had added more land to the Reich at little cost, but made a peaceful revision of the borders with Poland unlikely.

For the armor forces the most important benefit from the seizure of the Czech lands was the capture of about eight hundred Skoda tanks.[167] These were renamed Pz. 35 and Pz. 38 and were, for the most part, given to the 7th and 8th Armor Divisions which formed during 1940.[168] The incorporation of the Czech vehicles increased the number of tanks in the Wehrmacht by almost one-third, but by September, the German army had only slightly less than three thousand tanks ready for battle. Most of these, about twenty-one hundred of the total, were the relatively light Pz. II and the very light Pz. I.[169] The majority of the Skoda machines, meanwhile, would only be fully integrated and combat-ready in time to fight against Czechoslovakia's old allies in France.[170] Yet the German mechanized army that stood poised to begin the invasion of Poland that late August was a formidable force. Not only were over one-third of all divisions motorized, but the Wehrmacht also had eight armor brigades, four light and five armor divisions, each of the latter consisting of about 350 tanks and 4,000 other vehicles.[171] From nothing more

166. See Williamson Murray, *The Change in the European Balance of Power, 1938–1939: The Path to Ruin* (Princeton, N.J.: Princeton University Press, 1984), 283–309; D. C. Watt, *How War Came: The Immediate Origins of the Second World War, 1938–1939* (London: Heinemann, 1989), 141–87.

167. Murray, *Change in the European Balance of Power*, 292.

168. Werner Oswald, *Kraftfahrzeuge und Panzer der Reichswehr, Wehrmacht und Bundeswehr* (Stuttgart: Motorbuch Verlag, 1973), 242. The Germans wasted no time in taking the Skoda tanks; by late March they already had 469 of the machines. "Vortragsnotiz. Erfassung des Kriegsgeräte in der Tschechei," BA-MA, RW 8/v. 1, p. 43.

169. Walther Nehring, *Die Geschichte der deutschen Panzerwaffe 1916 bis 1945* (Berlin: Propyläen Verlag, 1969), 124. Exactly how many of the larger tanks that the German army had in September 1939 is unclear. Nehring reports 390 Pz. III and IV tanks while Oswald says that there were 600 Pz. IV's. Oswald, *Kraftfahrzeuge und Panzer*, 244–45.

170. Hitler also did not allow the army to keep the tanks in the former Czech lands, and ordered them back to the "old Reich," "since the appearance of these vehicles, known to the Czech people, would always evoke a certain overtone of bitterness." Report from the Führer's Adjutant for the Wehrmacht to the Commander-in-Chief of the Army, 28 March 1939, BA-MA, RW 8/v. 1, p. 65.

171. Herbert Schottelius and Gustav-Adolf Caspar, "Die Organisation des Heeres 1933–1939," in *Handbuch zur deutschen Militärgeschichte 1648–1939*, vol. 8: *Wehrmacht und Nationalsozialismus (1933–*

than dummy tanks just five years before, the German army now possessed one of the largest and best-armed mechanized forces in the world.

When compared to Soviet armor, however, German armor forces were less impressive. Before the beginning of war in Poland, the Red Army included in its arsenal four tank corps, each far larger than the German armor divisions, twenty-one detached tank brigades, three detached armor brigades (not yet re-formed into tank brigades), and eleven tank regiments.[172] The Soviet Union also had so many different types of tanks in development and production that Voroshilov could not keep track of them.[173] Although the sources do not provide hard numbers, based on the quantity of tank units, the Red Army in 1939 had at least four times as many tanks as did the Wehrmacht.

This is not to say that the Soviet army had overcome all its problems with production, nor that its officers had any better answers to the tactical questions faced by both them and the German army. Design and manufacturing of the tanks especially remained a problem, although matters had improved somewhat over the year before. A report on tank order fulfillment during the first quarter 1939 listed five types of tanks currently in production (T-35, T-28, BT-7, T-26, and T-38), and noted that 536 out of 694 of the machines had been delivered on time. The army had, however, received none of the T-38 tanks ordered, while BT-7 and T-26 production was well behind schedule. The list showed, too, that none of the improved versions of tanks decided upon the previous year had been put into actual production.[174] Despite these problems, Voroshilov ordered the design and creation of a new small tank with very heavy armor.[175] The confusion still remaining from the purges was apparent in the follow-up to Voroshilov's order. A week after this directive was issued the director of Factory No. 185 reminded Voroshilov that his plant had already been asked to produce a tank similar to this in September 1936. Designers had finished the blueprints in March 1937, but had met difficulties with obtaining parts, caused, wrote the director, by certain former workers in the armor directorate. He suggested strengthening the armor of this vehicle and making a few other minor adjustments so that it would fit Voroshilov's requirements.[176]

1939), ed. Hans Meier-Welcker and Wolfgang von Groote (Munich: Bernard & Graefe, 1978), 341, 343, 353; Wilhelm Deist, "The Rearmament of the Wehrmacht," in Germany and the Second World War, vol. 1: The Build-up of German Aggression, ed. Militärgeschichtliches Forschungsamt (Oxford: Clarendon Press, 1990), 449; list of personnel for command positions in the Wehrmacht, 1 March 1939, BA-MA, RH 2/226, pp. 181, 197, 200–202, 210, 232–35, 239–41, 243.

172. Ryzhakov, "K voprosu o stroitel'stve bronetankovykh voisk," 108–9.

173. Report on small tank with heavy armor, RGVA, f. 4, op. 19, d. 67, l. 1.

174. Fulfillment of plan of NKO order for tanks during first quarter 1939, 13 May 1939, RGVA, f. 31811, op. 2, d. 856, l. 70.

175. Report on small tank with heavy armor, RGVA, f. 4, op. 19, d. 67, l. 1; characteristics of small tank with heavy armor, RGVA, f. 4, op. 19, d. 67, ll. 16–17.

176. Report on small tank with heavy armor from Barykov, Director of Kirov and Fomin Factory

As for tactics, an updated textbook on armor forces expressed the new orthodoxy on tank usage. The keywords now were cooperation and combined-arms operations; there was no discussion of the DD group, and only a passing mention of attacks on the opponent's rear.[177] The emphasis was instead on the infantry since "only the infantry is capable of beginning, developing, and concluding battle." More than that, the infantry was the pivot of every battle order in combined-arms combat, "around which and for the assistance of which the effort of the other arms is directed."[178] The principal mission of the tank was the same as it had been in manuals immediately after the world war: to pave the way forward for the infantry, in cooperation with the artillery. The only major change from the last war was the speed at which this would take place, although there was no discussion of how the differential in tempo between infantry and armor attacks would be harmonized on the battlefield.[179] The new book discussed quite thoroughly, however, how infantry could help tanks.[180]

In the more detailed description of tank tactics, the book again emphasized that infantry had to play the principal role, and that tanks could achieve success only when cooperating with all other arms. When the armies had violated this "rule" in Spain, throwing tanks into an attack with merely artillery cover, the blow had always ended unsuccessfully, with useless loss of machines. Yet, groups of tanks directly subordinated to the rifle regiment commander might fulfill missions slightly ahead of tanks given to a company or battalion. The latter tanks, however, had to work directly with their infantry, side by side, accompanying them through the antipersonnel defenses of the enemy. The only remnant of the once all-important DD echelon came in a discussion of a tank group that would seek to attack the enemy's depth – but instead of making a quick dash to the rear envisaged earlier for the DD tanks, this group would make its move only under very specific conditions (especially good terrain and lack of enemy defenses). Without these conditions and the support of the air force and artillery, the tanks would certainly perish from antitank and artillery fire.[181]

Not long after the publication of this work, the Soviet army had an opportunity to try out its new thinking on the tank in an encounter that, in a surprising twist, instead showed the validity of the deep battle concept. As the year before at Lake Khasan, the Soviet army again faced a challenge from the Japanese on the eastern borders. At the end of May 1939, the Japanese and Soviets skirmished over bound-

---

No. 185, CC Party Organization, to Voroshilov, 23 February 1939. RGVA, f. 4, op. 19, d. 67, ll. 31–34.

177. V. Tereshenko, *Bronetankovye voiska* (Moscow: Redizdat TsS Osoaviakhima SSSR, 1939), 117, 119. The book was published 27 July 1939.

178. Ibid., 117.

179. Ibid., 118.

180. Ibid., 120–22.

181. Ibid., 130–31.

ary lines at Khalkhin-gol on the border between Mongolia and China. By the beginning of July the Japanese had occupied the west bank of the river that defined the border with 38,000 men, but only 135 tanks. Georgii Zhukov, the commanding officer in the district, attacked these troops with a force that was less than a third their size, but which contained fifty more tanks, and drove the Japanese out. In August the Japanese returned with stronger forces, which Zhukov again attacked with fewer men but greater numbers of tanks and other technology. The tactics that he used in this final attack were very similar to the deep battle concept no longer accepted by the army. Using his armor troops partially as an independent force and partially as support for the infantry, he coordinated the action of the tanks with artillery and motorized infantry, carried out a wide encirclement of the Japanese, pushed toward their rear, and drove them back.[182]

The Soviet high command chose to ignore Zhukov's innovative use of armor and instead drew lessons from the conflict at Khalkhin-gol which reinforced those already learned from the Spanish war and Lake Khasan. In November the inspector of the armor forces sent a report to Pavlov which concluded that the revised Soviet reading of the tank in battle was essentially correct. The report outlined four separate types of actions in which tanks had taken part, each of which showed that they could do nothing without infantry.[183] The Red Army had also used a tank brigade on a marching flank, sometimes independently and sometimes with a small number of infantry. Although they had managed to destroy a few of the opponent's batteries and disorganize his rear, they could not take his defenses apart, and thus were forced to return to their starting position. This, the inspector concluded, taught that tanks without infantry could strike strong blows, but could not hold terrain and would suffer huge losses.[184] Where the tanks had worked closely and in direct contact with their infantry, on the other hand, they had fared much better. One tank brigade had fought as a PP group in late August and, when the infantry had followed directly behind their tanks with artillery support, the assaults had gone well. When commanders had used tanks even slightly ahead of the infantry, machine guns had mown down the attacking men.[185] Tanks acting as fire support for the infantry in defense or fighting in front of forward lines had also proven successful. In the second type of action, the tanks had fought directly as part of an in-

---

182. Morozow, *Falken des Kreml*, 194–95; Erickson, *Soviet High Command*, 532–37. For a description of the events at Khalkhin-gol from the Soviet perspective, see Zhukov, *Vospominaniia i razmyshleniia*, 1:255–58, 272.

183. In one case a brigade of tanks had attacked without artillery or infantry support a group of Japanese soldiers who had had only a short time to prepare for the assault. The enemy had been pushed back, but only after inflicting great losses on the Soviets. Report, "Opyt ispol'zovaniia brone-tankovykh voisk na r. Khalkhin-gol mai-sentiabr' 1939 goda," from Drugov, Inspector of the Front Group ABTV, to Pavlov, 16 November 1939, RGVA, f. 31811, op. 4, d. 22, l. 48.

184. Ibid., ll. 50–51.

185. Ibid., l. 49.

fantry regiment's defensive position. Some had fired from fixed positions while other tank battalions had moved around to the enemy's flanks and, firing together with the unmoving group, had caused great losses among the attacking Japanese.[186]

The inspector ended his report on Khalkhin-gol by outlining his views of the correct battle order for tanks. Most should fight as part of the PP group, divided into two echelons. The first would follow the reconnaissance troops, destroying the opponent's fire centers and leading the infantry who would follow directly behind them. The second echelon either received a mission that fit the circumstances, or followed the first echelon, suppressing antitank weapons. This latter use of the second echelon made sense when the opponent had strong antitank defenses. If defenses were weaker, the echelon could simply reinforce the first wave or even take its place when those tanks had used up their fuel. He added that the speed of an attack on the terrain encountered during Khalkhin-gol had not been much greater than in the world war, 5–8 kph.[187]

To study the lessons of the events of 1938–1939, the army set up a special commission under the leadership of Kulik, now Deputy Defense Commissar. The group worked for three weeks in August and soon faced a direct challenge from Pavlov, who thought that the continued existence of the tank corps was pointless. As we have seen, Pavlov had decided from his experience in Spain that using a corps for attacks on the enemy's rear did not work. The organization of the units was too unwieldy for developing breakthroughs and in addition tanks had to be reinforced with infantry, artillery, and aircraft for successful operations. A tank corps commander was, however, incapable of directing the action of all these different units. The final decision of the commission disagreed with Pavlov's reading of the situation. Instead the commanders suggested that "(1) The tank corps be retained, but without its rifle–machine gun brigade. Likewise the rifle–machine gun battalions should be excluded from the tank brigades. (2) In an offensive developing a breakthrough, the tank corps ought to work with infantry and cavalry. Under these conditions tank brigades should work in tight connection with infantry and artillery. A tank corps may also act independently when the opponent is in disorder and not capable of defensive action."

Like the Wehrmacht, the commission recommended two types of tank brigades, one meant for independent action and a second designed for reinforcing infantry forces. In November the Main Military Council examined this recommendation and nevertheless decided to disband the tank corps.[188] With this decision, the new Soviet army finished off the last remainder of the brilliant work done by Tukhachevskii, Triandafillov, Sediakin, and the other innovators.

---

186. Ibid., ll. 51–52.
187. Ibid., ll. 53–54.
188. Ryzhakov, "K voprosu o stroitel'stve bronetankovykh voisk," 109–10.

Epilogue

Armor Doctrine and Large Wars, 1939–1941

ITH THE DUAL invasion of Poland in September 1939, the German and Soviet armies finally tested in battle the armor doctrines that they had spent the past twenty years developing. For the Germans, the attack resulted in two triumphs: one of the Wehrmacht over the ill-prepared Polish army and the other of the concept of warfare developed by Lutz, Guderian, and other supporters of the armor division over competing ideas of combat. The initial period of the conflict followed the ideas of some officers (including Guderian) on how future warfare would begin: not with a prior declaration of war and time spent on mobilization and deployment, but rather with immediate, surprise assaults by land, sea, and air to seize vital zones and disrupt the mobilization of the opponent.[1] With the advantage of surprise, the armor divisions more than proved their worth. The army exploited the speed of the tanks to their fullest, but in close combination with aircraft, motorized infantry, and mobile artillery, to push past strongpoints, attack the enemy's rear and flanks, and encircle whole armies.[2] The light divisions also performed well, but not as brilliantly as the armor divisions, and were soon disbanded.[3]

The Soviets too had an opportunity to try out their tank units in battle, but they did not learn the same lessons from their Polish campaign. In the first place, they paid little attention to the German victory, instead choosing to concentrate on their own experiences, which were not particularly successful.[4] An official report on the action optimistically stated that tank units had been ready to fulfill their missions

---

1. Beck, memo on "Grenzschutz," 11 December 1933, BA-MA, RH 2/25, pp. 52–53.

2. For the story of the Polish campaign, see Horst Rohde, "Hitler's First Blitzkrieg and Its Consequences for North-eastern Europe," in *Germany and the Second World War*, vol. 2: *Germany's Initial Conquests in Europe*, ed. Militärgeschichtliches Forschungsamt (Oxford: Clarendon Press, 1991), 101–26.

3. Erich von Manstein, *Aus einem Soldatenleben 1887–1939* (Bonn: Athenäum Verlag, 1958), 240–43.

4. Isserson thought that there were specific conditions that made this campaign especially unsuitable for deep operations, which explained the Soviet inability to see these operations in the same way as the German army. G. Isserson, "Razvitie teorii sovetskogo operativnogo iskusstva v 30-e gody," *VIZh*, no. 1 (January 1965): 54–55.

and had done well, but there were clear signs that many formations had in fact performed poorly. The tank corps that participated in the fighting had been difficult to command and control, even lagging behind the cavalry units to which they were assigned, while the tank battalions in rifle divisions had not shown themselves to best advantage.[5] In addition the armor units had suffered inordinately high losses, especially if one considers that they attacked an army beset from two directions and ill equipped for modern warfare. When the Red Army entered Poland on 17 September, it had six tank brigades and one tank corps with 1,726 tanks in all, subordinated to cavalry or infantry corps.[6] Despite reinforcements, by the time fighting had stopped on 15 October there were only 1,395 tanks still in the field.[7]

As a result of the war in Poland, the Soviets proceeded to take two steps of far-reaching significance. Most importantly, the poor showing by the tank corps informed the decision by the army to disband the units and distribute the machines among the infantry. At the November meeting of the Main Military Council, Voroshilov, Stalin, Molotov, and the other members ordered the tanks distributed to twenty-nine tank brigades and ten tank companies. Later the army would form fifteen "mechanized" divisions, that is, rifle divisions with weak tank elements. In view of subsequent events, the one positive consequence of the Polish campaign for the armor forces was a decision to rearm the brigades with a new, more powerful tank, the T-34.[8] A week later, Voroshilov reported to Stalin that by 1941 industry would be able to produce thirty-six hundred of these tanks annually.[9]

The Soviets tested their new organizational structures in battle not long after the partition of Poland. On 30 November 1939, the Red Army attacked Finland after negotiations failed to convince the Finns to cede certain strategic islands near Leningrad. Although badly outnumbered in both manpower and weaponry, the Finnish army had trained well for a defensive winter war and had prepared effective deep defenses in the form of the Mannerheim Line. A month of frontal assaults by massed Soviet infantry supported by small groups of tanks did not break the line and the Red Army high command was forced to call a halt to rethink its options. A

5. Report on action in "Western Ukraine," September–October 1939, from Kombrig Fedorenko, Chief of Ukraine Front ABTV, to Pavlov, 26 October 1939, RGVA, f. 31811, op. 4, d. 20, ll. 244–45; A. Ryzhakov, "K voprosu o stroitel'stve bronetankovykh voisk krasnoi armii v 30-e gody," *VIZh*, no. 8 (August 1968): 110.

6. Report on action in "Western Ukraine," September–October 1939, from Kombrig Fedorenko, Chief of Ukraine Front ABTV, to Pavlov, 26 October 1939, RGVA, f. 31811, op. 4, d. 20, ll. 234, 236, 250.

7. Ibid., l. 252.

8. "Protokol No. 6 Zasedaniia Glavnogo Voennogo Soveta RKKA," 21 November 1939, RGVA, f. 4, op. 18, d. 49, ll. 8–2. For the full story of the development of this remarkable tank from the BT-7 and other earlier vehicles, see K. M. Slobodin and V. D. Listrovoi, eds., *T-34, Put' k pobede: Vospominaniia tankostroitelei i tankistov* (Kharkov: Prapor, 1985).

9. Draft directive on new tanks to take into arsenal from Voroshilov to Stalin and Molotov, 27 November 1939. RGVA, f. 4, op. 14, d. 2222, ll. 71–73.

second offensive in February–March succeeded in breaking through and encircling the Finnish defenders, but only with massive use and losses of men, armor, and artillery.[10]

The army's official report on tanks in this war stressed the enemy's effective defenses, as well as poor terrain and bad climatic conditions that had worked together to make armor warfare extremely difficult.[11] In the first offensive of the war, armor had been almost useless. Tank brigades that had attempted to fight independently or far from their infantry had not fared well. Even when armor had fought together with rifle units, however, cooperation between the two and with the artillery had been weak and the infantry had failed to exploit any successes that the tanks had managed to win. Commanders had also not taken into consideration the capabilities of the tanks, nor the specific conditions of the situations in which they found themselves, and the result was an "uneconomical, wasteful use of tanks that was frequently without any benefit, and [led to] huge losses of materiel." In addition, attempts to use the tanks as a moving screen for the infantry, to protect communications or staffs, and so on were "an example of the wasteful and crude use of tanks."[12]

In contrast, many more tanks, about 1,330 altogether, took part in the second offensive and they had fought almost exclusively in very close cooperation with the infantry. Their main mission had been to break through the Finnish line, paving the way for the infantry while destroying fortified fire zones. In actual combat, one of the major roles for the vehicles had been transportation of the infantry and their supplies when deep snow had prevented easy movement. Many infantry had in fact ridden to battle on the tanks.[13] Yet the report concluded that even though the infantry had been instructed to stay close to and coordinate their actions with the tanks, cooperation between them had been extremely poor. Without this help, tank elements had been able to carry out their assignments with some success, but had then been forced to abandon any seized areas, all the while suffering heavy losses.[14]

By April a commission headed by Pavlov, who had participated in the fighting while chief of the ABTU, had put together a complete analysis of armor in the war. The group concluded first that "the past war showed that the combat and special preparation of armor forces of the Red Army was correct." Yet it also recognized that the small tank units that had been distributed to the infantry were "completely impractical. These kinds of organizational forms lead only to a scattering of combat vehicles, incorrect usage (they were even used to guard the headquarters and

10. For a complete description of the "Winter War," see Carl van Dyke, *The Soviet Invasion of Finland, 1939–40* (London: Frank Cass, 1997).

11. "Otchet o boevykh deystviiakh tankovykh voisk protiv belofinnov s 30.11.39 po 13.3.40 g.," RGVA, f. 31811, op. 4, d. 36, ll. 3–17.

12. Ibid., ll. 18–20.

13. Ibid., ll. 30–31.

14. Ibid., l. 43.

rears), the impossibility of refitting them in a timely fashion, and at times the impossibility of using them at all." The commission therefore recommended that the army combine the small units into tank brigades consisting of four tank battalions each.[15] The officers also suggested that it was possible to use tanks independently in positional warfare to develop successes when the army had broken through the main area of defense. Armor might even be capable of independent action during maneuver warfare in the enemy's depth, although this depended on the strength of antitank defenses.[16]

While the Soviet army considered these proposals, which would together constitute a partial rehabilitation of its old armor organization and doctrine, the Wehrmacht once again exploited the ideas of its tank innovators to win a stunning victory, this time over the Allies in the West. Following a plan first suggested by Erich von Manstein, the bulk of the infantry (and some tank units) attacked British and French positions through the Low Countries while the armor divisions, supported by motorized infantry and aircraft, spearheaded a surprise assault on the Allied right flank. As in Poland, German armor did not attempt to take the entire front, but instead pushed as quickly as possible through any breaches in the line, attacking the flanks and rear of the enemy while completing huge encirclements of bewildered and demoralized troops. Within ten days it was obvious that Allied forces were in serious trouble and six weeks after the fighting began, the war on the Continent was over.[17]

The almost effortless victory in the West had important consequences for German strategy and doctrine. In the first place, the Wehrmacht invested even more heavily in tanks and other vehicles so that by June 1941 the army had twenty armor divisions and ten motorized infantry divisions.[18] Yet the course of the Western campaign, combined with the earlier easy victory over Poland, created a disastrous overconfidence within the high command. This, together with an underestimation of the Red Army's strength, encouraged the Wehrmacht to agree to Hitler's decision

15. Results of the study on the experience of using tanks in Finland, written 22 April 1940; part of a complete study finished 2 July 1940 with Pavlov as head of commission, RGVA, f. 4, op. 14, d. 2737, ll. 91–92.

16. Ibid., l. 26.

17. Hans Umbreit has a complete description of the campaign in the West in "The Battle for Hegemony in Western Europe," in Militärgeschichtliches Forschungsamt, *Germany and the Second World War*, 2:281–304.

18. "Stellenbesetzung der Panzergruppen, 22.6.1941," BA-MA, RH 2/49, pp. 47–49. It should be pointed out that not every German officer was convinced by the fighting in Poland and France that the armor forces were indispensable for modern warfare. Rundstedt told Liddell Hart after the war that he supported motorization but saw tanks as "useful servants" rather than future masters of the battlefield. The infantry were still the most important arm and he devoted most of his efforts to raising their morale and modernizing their equipment, supporting the armor divisions only in so far as this did not interfere with the rearmament of the infantry. B. H. Liddell Hart, *The Other Side of the Hill* (London: Macmillan, 1993), 104–5.

to attack the Soviet Union.[19] The particular form of the war in the West also allowed the Germans to overlook a serious flaw in their armor doctrine. The fighting in France had covered a (relatively) small area, and therefore the high command did not recognize that it had not yet solved the seminal problem of infantry-armor co-operation. Following doctrine, the armor divisions had fought ahead of the slower infantry, pushing directly into the enemy's rear while men in trucks or even on foot had secured the territory seized. Pockets of Allied forces had been entirely encircled and eliminated, primarily because the distances involved in these movements, while large by the standards of any previous war in Western Europe, were still reasonable. In contrast, while massive encirclements of Red Army troops did take place, the huge stretches of land that the army had to traverse in the Soviet Union, combined with the slowness of the infantry, would allow many to escape to the rear.[20] The situation was not helped by the fact that German artillery was still mostly horse-drawn and therefore also unable to keep pace with the faster armor.[21] Added to problems with logistics, bad roads, and terrain, an abnormally cold winter and staunch Soviet resistance, lack of good cooperation helped to stall the German drive on Moscow.

If the successes in Poland and France induced the German army to ignore problems with doctrine, the quick defeat of the Allied forces acted on officers of the Soviet army as a catalyst for reform. Immediately after the success of blitzkrieg in the West, the Soviets began to re-create the old mechanized corps along with smaller armor divisions.[22] How the new units would fight in battle remained problematic, however. At the end of December 1940 when the Soviet high command gathered to discuss this question, the leading voice for change came from Zhukov, now commander of the Kiev military district. He argued forcefully that the experience of combat over the last five years showed the decisiveness of technology and surprise in modern warfare.[23] Just as importantly, Germany's attack on the Allies had shown that the basic idea of deep operations, delivering a blow that would strike the entire operational depth of the enemy, was possible, and that one could organize continuous operations as well. The campaign in the West demonstrated, too,

19. Rudolf Steiger, Armour Tactics in the Second World War: Panzer Army Campaigns of 1939–41 in German War Diaries (New York: Berg, 1991), 8–12; Bryan A. Fugate, Operation Barbarossa: Strategy and Tactics on the Eastern Front, 1941 (Novato, Calif.: Presidio, 1984), 73–75; Barry A. Leach, German Strategy against Russia, 1939–1941 (Oxford: Clarendon Press, 1973), 91–94.

20. Although it should be pointed out that approximately two million Soviet soldiers were captured during the first four months of the war. John A. English and Bruce I. Gudmundsson, On Infantry, rev. ed. (Westport: Praeger, 1994), 82.

21. Steiger, Armour Tactics in the Second World War, 39–52.

22. David M. Glantz, "The Soviet Army in 1941," in The Initial Period of War on the Eastern Front, 22 June-August 1941, ed. David M. Glantz (London: Frank Cass, 1993), 16–20.

23. "Stenogramm vystuplenii na Voennom soveshchanii 25-go dekabria 1940 goda po dokladu Generala Armii t. ZHUKOVA, 'Kharakter sovremennoi nastupatel'noi operatsii,'" RGVA, f. 4, op. 18, d. 56, ll. 1–2, 6.

the need for "decisive blows by mechanized corps in encounter battles and courageous and independent efforts on their part to break through into the rear of the opponent's operational groups."[24] The best form for these operations was either a breakthrough of a front on several sectors, which would set up the encirclement and destruction of the enemy, or simultaneous strong blows on both of the opponent's flanks.[25] More precisely, Zhukov argued, a modern operation would closely resemble the older ideas of armor tactics. Three echelons of tanks, closely supported by artillery, would destroy various sectors of the enemy's defenses, with the last wave helping the infantry forward for the "destructive bayonet blow."[26]

Some participants in the meeting agreed with Zhukov's reading of modern war, while others thought that he went too far in his support for the tank. Prokofii Romanenko, head of the Leningrad district, stressed that it was tanks, collected into massive mechanized armies and acting independently (although in cooperation with the air forces), which had finished off France and had the decisive role. The Soviet army, he concluded, must do the same with its armor.[27] Shtern disagreed. Tanks, aircraft, and artillery were fine, but the initial stage of modern operations, as a rule, demanded a huge breakthrough in which the infantry was the main force. Rather than look solely at the example of Germany, he suggested that the Red Army study the Brussels breakthrough of 1916, Catalonia in 1938, and the end of the war in Spain in 1939.[28] He could not agree with Zhukov that tank corps would be able to break through into the depth of the defense. He knew well how hard it was to achieve this and suggested that the army had to use more infantry. Of course, he added, everyone wanted to throw their tanks forward, but such tactics were not always effective against a well-defended opponent. Even the Germans had failed against parts of the Maginot Line.[29]

As a result of these debates the Soviets began to re-create their mechanized corps in 1940, but Red Army troops were not fully trained for the new (old) ideas on warfare when the Germans attacked the Soviet Union in June 1941. The Soviets had approximately seventeen thousand tanks overall, compared to only thirty-two hundred in the attacking Wehrmacht forces, but they chose to use them poorly.[30] Descriptions by German officers who observed Soviet armor forces in action after June emphasized their tendency to fight in small groups and as direct support for the infantry.[31] Throughout the year increasing numbers of tanks were thrown into battle, but commanders did not use the combined-arms tactics supported by Zhukov,

24. Ibid., ll. 10–11.
25. Ibid., ll. 18–21.
26. Ibid., ll. 42–43.
27. Ibid., ll. 59–61.
28. Ibid., ll. 63, 66.
29. Ibid., l. 68.
30. Glantz, "The Soviet Army in 1941," 16–20; Fugate, *Operation Barbarossa*, 101.
31. Steiger, *Armour Tactics in the Second World War*, 82–86.

nor were the tanks gathered into large enough formations to make a decisive impact.[32] The price for these tactics was the piecemeal destruction of enormous numbers of the vehicles, with very little to show for their sacrifice. Not until Zhukov gathered 744 tanks together for the final defense of Moscow, and used them as he had outlined in his speech the year before, did the Red Army stop the invaders and begin to roll them back.[33]

The first two years of war in Europe suggested that only the Wehrmacht had learned how to use armor forces, although as the preceding discussion shows, neither the German nor the Soviet army had been able to solve certain intractable problems associated with modern technological warfare. In fact these two very different militaries, after twenty years of imagining future wars, had decided upon doctrines that shared many of the same specific weaknesses – as well as many specific strengths. Why the two doctrines should have been so alike is a question that is central to the story of the development of armor doctrine in both nations. This study indicates that four key factors encouraged German and Soviet high commands to adopt similar views of the tank. Of special importance were British experiences and ideas, which both militaries respected and followed closely. The Reichswehr and Red Army also had a common reading of how tanks had been used in the world war and how technical innovations affected these tactics. They had, too, a commitment to a mobile, offensive, combined-arms style of combat, which centered on the infantry and yet was open to technical innovation. Finally, both militaries produced outspoken innovators who were supported at key moments by their respective high commands and political rulers. Taken together these elements persuaded the Red Army and the Reichswehr to find similar ways to integrate the new technology into their overall views of warfare.

   This is not to say that German and Soviet doctrines were carbon copies of each other. The restrictions of Versailles, specific political situations within each country, shifting relations with the other nations of Europe, and Soviet industrial development affected their militaries in very different ways. There were also cultural differences that distinguished the two doctrinal styles. The German military was convinced that only a loose-order advance, like the stormtroop tactics of the world war, answered the demands of modern warfare, and they supported a decentralized command structure that gave great latitude to junior officers. The Soviet high command, in contrast, planned to push straight through an enemy's strongest point, to use a more centralized command and control of their forces, and to fight in operations that were far deeper than those of the Germans. In balance, however, these differences were relatively minor compared to the many details that the two doctrines held in common.

32. Fugate, *Operation Barbarossa*, 299–300.
33. Ibid., 294–96.

The interaction between these factors created three periods in the development of German and Soviet armor doctrine. The first, which lasted from the end of the world war until the introduction of the Vickers fast tank in 1926, saw both armies decide that the tank would not radically alter war. As Posen has argued, the new technology, rather than pushing militaries toward innovative ideas, was simply grafted on to old tactics. At the same time, contra Posen, the defeats of the world war did not "teach" either army anything about war in general. Although more than willing to learn from world war tank tactics, the Red Army and the Reichswehr believed that the conditions of the Western Front (where the tank had been deployed), would never again occur. Soviet officers argued that a mobile and fast-moving "proletarian" military would not be trapped into a stalemate as imperialist armies had been, while German officers believed that only exceptional circumstances had allowed trench warfare in the first place. The entire "materiel and morale" debate also ended speculation that machines might replace men entirely on the battlefield of the future: tanks were fine as long as they knew their place – as a tool for the soldier and not as his master. The result was a reaffirmation by both militaries that the specific conditions and technology of war might change, but that its eternal principles – that it had to be mobile, offensive, and fought in a combined-arms way with the infantry as the principal arm – would never alter.

There was no serious rethinking of doctrine until the next period (1926–34), when specific events – including the new Vickers tank, military collaboration, the Soviet industrialization drive, and the rise of innovative thinkers – convinced the Red Army and the Reichswehr to reconsider their views of warfare. The most significant development was the Vickers tank, which unlike its predecessors was fast, mobile, and reliable. Inspired by the new machine, the number of officers in Germany and the Soviet Union who believed that armor would revolutionize war grew exponentially. This did not mean that they rethought basic preconceptions about warfare. Rather, they argued that the new tank would simply confirm already accepted views, restoring the offensive, speed, and mobility that the last war had stolen. Meanwhile, the Versailles Treaty and economic underdevelopment in the Soviet Union encouraged the two militaries to consider working together to solve their problems. The result, the collaboration at Kazan and elsewhere, provided a safe haven for German industry and army to experiment with the production and development of suitable tanks. It also allowed the Soviet Union to receive free of charge the latest designs and technology from the West. It would be a mistake, however, to believe – as the Seatons do – that the two nations simply copied each other's ideas while working together.[34] Stalin's forced industrialization drive persuaded the Soviets that they had the best military technology in the world and did not need to look to their partners, still hampered by Versailles. The vistas of limit-

34. Albert Seaton and Joan Seaton, *The Soviet Army. 1918 to the Present* (New York: New American Library, 1986), 82–88, 90–92.

less technology opened up by the first Five Year Plan also inspired high-ranking commanders like Tukhachevskii, Triandafillov, and Egorov to integrate armor with other technology and their own innovative thinking to create the comprehensive military doctrine known as "deep battle." This process supports the argument made by Bayer that industrialization had a crucial role in shaping doctrine.[35] It supports as well Rosen's contention that doctrinal innovation comes from ideological struggles within the high commands and not from "mavericks" who fight the establishment.

The Germans, in their turn, had only contempt for the Soviets' poor implementation of tactics and did not consider copying their ideas. Reichswehr leaders such as Seeckt, Heye, Bockelberg, and Stülpnagel were more impressed by the new fast tank, and only with its appearance did they reimagine a doctrine that was essentially unchanged since the world war. They were also much taken with the British use of the tank in maneuvers, and followed these closely. Yet as we have seen, scholars have surely overstated the case when they argue that the Germans simply took over the ideas of Fuller or Liddell Hart wholesale. Reichswehr military thinkers like Volckheim, Bockelberg, and Lutz instead borrowed some of what the British had to offer (the concept of echelons and dividing tank waves by weight, for instance) and then integrated this with their own concepts of warfare. In one of the coincidences that gave deep battle and blitzkrieg their eerie similarity, the Soviets decided that these same principles were also worth adopting. Significantly, both the Soviets and the German army resisted the Fulleresque concentration of all tanks in huge armor units. Instead both militaries would stay true to their concept of the infantry (or "proletariat") as the principal arm, and would choose to raise the offensive power of the army as a whole by spreading their tanks in many different types of units.

The final period in the development of armor doctrine (1933–39) began with Hitler's seizure of power and the almost simultaneous adoption of deep battle as the official doctrine of the Soviet army. Strangely enough, given the high regard with which the concept was supposedly held, this official recognition spelled the beginning of the end for deep battle. During this final period, which would produce the doctrines followed by the Wehrmacht and the Red Army at the start of the Second World War, three factors dominated. First was the influence of Hitler and Stalin, which shows that the support of the political leadership – particularly in authoritarian countries – can be essential for the development of doctrine. Stalin had always shown a great deal of interest in military hardware, while his Five Year Plans provided the economic underpinnings to produce the technology that so affected deep battle. Thus, while it is true that he did not determine the particulars of his country's doctrine, Stalin did provide the overall framework within which it could

35. Philip A. Bayer, *The Evolution of the Soviet General Staff, 1917–1941* (New York: Garland, 1987), 182.

develop. After he became convinced that Tukhachevskii was a real threat to his power, Stalin again intervened, and by executing the marshal and his associates, made certain that deep battle was doomed. Meanwhile, Hitler's defiance of Versailles, combined with his support for Guderian, meant that the Wehrmacht was simultaneously able to obtain the tanks necessary for its doctrine and to create the armor divisions that Lutz and Guderian championed.

Just as important were decisions by the German and Soviet high commands. Despite what Guderian would later say, Beck and other high-ranking officers sided with him in the face of persistent resistance from older infantry and cavalry officers. It was, in fact, Beck's direct intervention at critical moments that ensured that the Wehrmacht accepted armor as the offensive core of the army. Voroshilov had a more contentious relationship with Tukhachevskii. As comments at high command meetings show, Voroshilov attacked Tukhachevskii and the doctrine associated with him even before the purges, and afterwards became even more vociferous in criticizing deep battle. The fact that Voroshilov and Budënnyi, the two commanders who hated armor and Tukhachevskii the most, were also close friends of Stalin, ensured that their views about the doctrine were taken very seriously indeed by the Soviet ruler. Just as important for later events was the fact that neither these men, nor those who replaced Tukhachevskii, had the intellectual capabilities necessary to create a new armor doctrine to replace the one that they had destroyed.

The final factor was the "lessons" of the small wars fought by both nations in the late thirties. Whether in Spain, Finland, or the near eastern borderlands, the Soviet and the German armies tried out their ideas about warfare for the first time on far-flung battlefields. The results were mixed. The Soviets believed that they could learn a great deal from their experiences and used the wars to justify significant changes in doctrine. The Germans, on balance, were more wary about trusting the war in Spain to provide an accurate picture of a future great conflict, and therefore did not alter doctrine on the basis of that war. The reaction of the two armies suggests in fact that militaries learn what they want to from combat, and can justify almost any tactical or operational changes that they wish. The quite different reactions of the Wehrmacht and Red Army to failures in their maneuvers supports this conclusion as well.

On balance, then, there is no one factor which definitively explains the development of armor doctrine in Germany and the Soviet Union. Rather, the complex story told here shows that a multitude of elements interacted over the course of the entire interwar period to produce the concepts of warfare that determined how the Second World War would be fought. It also shows that neither nation had gotten it right when that conflict began. The Germans had spread armor between light and armor divisions and were still dependent on the horse when fighting started in Poland. More importantly, the Wehrmacht had not solved two crucial problems: how to keep armor and the other forces together on the modern battlefield and how to supply tanks and other vehicles with the "ocean" of fuel that they would need.

The Soviets had done little better. Although the concept of deep battle seemed brilliant on paper, the Red Army was not able to implement it in practice. Disappointments in maneuvers and internal political maneuvering eventually led the Soviets to discard the concept and retreat to a more simplified and less modern vision of future warfare. Perhaps, then, the most important lesson of this story is that no amount of theorizing and work before the conflict could prepare an army completely for the revolutionary changes that the motor vehicle would bring. Only the actual experience of war could show the way.

Abbreviations

ABTU	Avto-Bronetankovoe Upravlenie (Armor Directorate)
AU	Artilleriiskoe Upravlenie (Artillery Directorate)
BA-MA	Bundesarchiv-Militärarchiv (Federal Military Archive)
Beck-Studien	Klaus-Jürgen Müller, *General Ludwig Beck. Studien und Dokumente zur politisch-militärischen Vorstellungswelt und Tätigkeit des Generalstabschefs des deutschen Heeres 1933-1938* (Boppard am Rhein: Harald Boldt, 1980)
B-T	*bystrokhodnyi tank* (fast tank)
d.	*delo* (file)
DD	*dal'noe deistvie* (long-range [tanks])
DPP	*dal'naia podderzhka pekhoty* (distant infantry support [tanks])
f.	*fond* (record group)
FPU	Finansovoe-Planirovanoe Upravlenie (Financial Planning Directorate)
F.u.G.	*Führung und Gefecht der verbundenen Waffen vom 1. September 1921.* (d.V.Pl.Nr.487) (Berlin: Verlag Offene Worte, 1921)
GARF	Gosudarstvennyi Arkhiv Rossiskoi Federatsii (State Archive of the Russian Federation)
GRU	Glavnoe Razvedyvatel'noe Upravlenie (Main Intelligence Directorate; Soviet military intelligence)
GVIU	Glavnoe Voenno-Inzhenernoe Upravlenie (Main Military Engineering Directorate)
KVR	Leon Trotskii, *Kak vooruzhalas' revoliutsiia*, 3 vols. (Moscow: Vysshii voennyi redaktsionnyi sovet, 1923-1924)
l./ll.	*list(y)* (page or folio)
LaS	*Landwirtschaftlicher Traktor* ("agricultural tractor")

Leplevskii documents	Collection of documents by Germans taken from agent material; sent by Leplevskii, Chief of the Special Department of the OGPU to Voroshilov, 21 December 1931. RGVA, f. 33987, op. 3, d. 70
NARA	National Archives and Records Administration
NEP	Novaia Ekonomicheskaia Politika (New Economic Policy)
NKVD	Narodnyi Komissariat Vneshnykh Del (People's Commissariate of Internal Affairs; a precursor to the KGB)
NPP	*neposredstvennaia podderzhka pekhoty* (direct infantry support [tanks])
OGPU	Osoboe Gosudarstvennoe Politicheskoe Upravlenie (Special State Political Directorate; a precursor to the KGB)
OKH	Oberkommando des Heeres (Army High Command)
OKW	Oberkommando der Wehrmacht (High Command of the Armed Forces)
op.	*opis* (finding aid)
PA-AA	Politisches Archiv des Auswärtigen Amts (Political Archive of the Foreign Office)
PP	*podderzhka pekhoty* (infantry support [tanks])
RGVA	Rossiskii Gosudarstvennyi Voennyi Arkhiv (Russian State Military Archive)
RKKA	Raboche-Krest'ianskaia Krasnaia Armiia (Red Army)
RVS	Revolutsionnyi Voennyi Sovet (Revolutionary Military Council)
RZ-STO	Rukovodiashchee Zasedanie Soveta Trudy i Oborony (Executive Session of the Council of Labor and Defense)
STO	Sovet Trudy i Oborony (Council of Labor and Defense)
TRGK	Tankovyi Rezerv Glavnogo Komandovaniia (Tank Reserve for the High Command)
UMM	Upravlenie Motorizatsii i Mekhanizatsii (Directorate of Motorization and Mechanization)
ViZh	*Voenno-istoricheskii zhurnal*
VPU	Voenno-Promyshlennoe Upravlenie (Military-Industrial Directorate)
VSNKh	Verkhovnyi Sovet Narodnogo Khoziaistva (Supreme Council of the National Economy)
WO	Public Record Office, London, War Office Records

Index

MAN factories, 207

Mannerheim Line, 289–90

Manstein, Erich von, xii–xv, 146, 291

Materiel or morale debate, 36–70, 139, 295

   German view of, 39–40, 49–70, 186,
     270–71

   Soviet view of, 41–49, 54–55, 68–69,
     172–74, 264

   Taysen on, 52–55

   Trotsky on, 12, 39, 41

Maybach industries, 250

Meretskov, Kirill, 259–60

Mikoian, Anastas, 130

Model, Walter, 146

Molotov, Vyacheslav, 149–50

Morale. See Materiel or morale debate

Motorized Forces Command, 208, 219

Motor-Transport Battalions, 21

MS-1 tank, 77, 90–92

   maneuvers with, 133–34

   modifications of, 93, 105

   production of, 112–14

   speed of, 135

Muff, Lieutenant Colonel, 50–51

Napoleonic Wars, 50

Nature of Operations of Modern Armies, 108–9

Nazi Party

   rise to power of, 125, 160

   as Soviet threat, 230

Nehring, Walter, xiii, 208, 210–11

New Economic Policy (NEP), 32, 45

Neznamov, A. A., 41–42

Niedermayer, Oskar Ritter von, 82, 147

NPP ("direct infantry support") tanks, 155–
   57, 168–69, 198–99, 201

   revised plans for, 214, 217, 244, 280

Ol'shanskii, Konstantin, 213–15, 217–18

Ordzhonikidze, Sergo, 114

Organization and Mobilization Directorate,
   90–91

Panzer divisions, 208

Panzerjäger, 237

Panzer I tank, 122, 162, 190, 207, 236

   deployment of, 219, 283

manufacturing of, 250

protection for, 226

Spanish Civil War and, 248–49, 250

See also LaS tank

Panzer I-B tank, 219–20

Panzer II tank, 123, 236, 283

   manufacturing of, 207, 219, 250

Panzer III tank, 123, 220, 235–36, 250

Panzer IV tank, 124, 235–36, 250

Panzer 35 tank, 283

Panzer 38 tank, 283

Papen, Franz von, 181

Parachute troops

   German, 252

   Soviet, 169–70, 177, 180, 200, 215–16

Paraguay, 211–13

Pavlov, Dmitrii, 261, 265–66, 275–79

   Finnish War and, 290–91

   Spanish Civil War and, 287

Pilsudski, Jozef, 13, 27

Poison gas. See Chemical weapons

Poland, 146, 283–84

   German blitzkrieg of, ix, xvii, 288–89

   Soviet nonaggression pact with, 149, 230

   as Soviet threat, 78–79, 89–90, 138,
     204–5

   Soviet treaties with, 166

   Soviet war with, 13–16, 27

Poseck, Max von, 6–7, 64–68, 70 n.137

PP ("infantry support") tanks, 111, 244–46,
   265, 286–87

   German view of, 252

*Preliminary Instructions for the Battle Use of
   Tanks*, 95–98

Primakov, Vitalii, 261

Proletarian military, 36, 38–39, 41–43

*Provisional Instructions for Organizing Deep
   Battle*, 179–80, 201, 213–17, 232

PU-28, 95–98

PU-29, 95, 111, 133, 135, 178, 180, 245

PU-36, 95, 241, 245–46, 277

Pugachev, S., 78–79

Putna, Vitovt, 261

Pyrrhus, 1, 21, 100

Rabenau, Friedrich von, 73

Racism, 55, 270–71

Crucible of Beliefs: Learning, Alliances, and World Wars
   by Dan Reiter

Eisenhower and the Missile Gap
   by Peter J. Roman

The Domestic Bases of Grand Strategy
   edited by Richard Rosecrance and Arthur Stein

Societies and Military Power: India and Its Armies
   by Stephen Peter Rosen

Winning the Next War: Innovation and the Modern Military
   by Stephen Peter Rosen

Vital Crossroads: Mediterranean Origins of the Second World War, 1935–1940
   by Reynolds Salerno

Fighting to a Finish: The Politics of War Termination in the United States and Japan, 1945
   by Leon V. Sigal

Alliance Politics
   by Glenn H. Snyder

The Ideology of the Offensive: Military Decision Making and the Disasters of 1914
   by Jack Snyder

Myths of Empire: Domestic Politics and International Ambition
   by Jack Snyder

The Militarization of Space: U.S. Policy, 1945–1984
   by Paul B. Stares

The Nixon Administration and the Making of U.S. Nuclear Strategy
   by Terry Terriff

The Ethics of Destruction: Norms and Force in International Relations
   by Ward Thomas

Causes of War: Power and the Roots of Conflict
   by Stephen Van Evera

Mortal Friends, Best Enemies: German-Russian Cooperation after the Cold War
   by Celeste A. Wallander

The Origins of Alliances
   by Stephen M. Walt

Revolution and War
   by Stephen M. Walt

The Tet Offensive: Intelligence Failure in War
   by James J. Wirtz

The Elusive Balance: Power and Perceptions during the Cold War
   by William Curti Wohlforth

Deterrence and Strategic Culture: Chinese-American Confrontations, 1949–1958
   by Shu Guang Zhang